TAKING DOWN THE LION

TAKING DOWN THE LION

THE TRIUMPHANT RISE AND TRAGIC FALL
OF TYCO'S DENNIS KOZLOWSKI

CATHERINE S. NEAL

palgrave
macmillan

This book is dedicated to my parents

Joyce Honaker Neal and Creston Neal—
the best people I know.

And to Kora Jane.

TAKING DOWN THE LION
Copyright © Catherine S. Neal, 2014
All rights reserved.

First published in 2014 by PALGRAVE MACMILLAN® in the U.S.—a division of St. Martin's Press LLC, 175 Fifth Avenue, New York, NY 10010.

Where this book is distributed in the UK, Europe and the rest of the world, this is by Palgrave Macmillan, a division of Macmillan Publishers Limited, registered in England, company number 785998, of Houndmills, Basingstoke, Hampshire RG21 6XS.

Palgrave Macmillan is the global academic imprint of the above companies and has companies and representatives throughout the world.

Palgrave® and Macmillan® are registered trademarks in the United States, the United Kingdom, Europe and other countries.

ISBN: 978-1-137-27891-3

Library of Congress Cataloging-in-Publication Data
Neal, Catherine S.
   Taking down the lion: the triumphant rise and tragic fall of Tyco's Dennis Kozlowski / Catherine S. Neal.
      pages   cm
   ISBN 978-1-137-27891-3 (hardback)
   1. Kozlowski, Dennis. 2. Chief executive officers—United States—Biography. 3. Tyco International Ltd. 4. Business ethics—United States. 5. Corporations—Corrupt practices—United States. I. Title.
HC102.5.K69N43   2014
338.7'681092—dc23

2013032153

A catalogue record of the book is available from the British Library.

Design by Letra Libre, Inc.

First edition: January 2014

10 9 8 7 6 5 4 3 2 1

Printed in the United States of America.

CONTENTS

PART FOUR
INGLORIOUS ENDING

PREFACE

I first became aware of Tyco International Ltd. and its then CEO Dennis Kozlowski when both appeared on the radar during the 1990s as the company achieved impressive results for its shareholders quarter after quarter, year after year. My interest grew during the early 2000s when Tyco and Kozlowski became involved in a highly publicized scandal. I left the private practice of law for academia in 2002, the same year that Kozlowski's tenure as the remarkably successful CEO of Tyco came to a sudden end. The textbooks I used in my business ethics and business law courses began including case studies about the Tyco corporate scandal soon after I began teaching.

I began this project with a clear objective, but with no plans to write a book. I simply wanted to understand a situation that on its face didn't make sense to me. How did a successful, high-profile executive end up in a New York State prison? Why was he prosecuted by a local district attorney, and not a U.S. attorney? It was a very unusual circumstance that set the case apart from others. In the other major corporate scandals that occurred during the same time period, only federal crimes were alleged and charged. But federal prosecutors declined to charge anyone connected to Tyco. Instead, Tyco executives, including Dennis Kozlowski, were indicted and tried by the Manhattan District Attorney under the state laws of New York.

In addition to being intrigued by his unusual prosecution, I was confused by how Kozlowski's crimes were described. Why did prosecutors and the media say that he received "undisclosed" compensation and took "secret" loans through the company's employee loan programs? How could his compensation and loans be considered secret when so many people knew about them? The transactions were processed and recorded in the normal course of business and were audited by one of the most respected accounting firms in the world. During Kozlowski's criminal trials, not a single Tyco employee testified that he or she concealed information, and not one believed anything was wrong inside the company. Plus, Tyco's accounting methods were examined and investigated numerous times, yet no material errors were ever identified. It didn't add up. The more I knew, the less I understood.

I first contacted former CEO Dennis Kozlowski in January of 2011. Spurred by my curiosity about the scandal, I wrote a letter to him at the Mid-State Correctional Facility, what he often referred to as the "gated community," in upstate New York. I simply asked if he would discuss his case with me.

Kozlowski responded with a one-page, handwritten letter in which he indicated his willingness to address my questions. We exchanged several letters and in May of 2011, I met Kozlowski face-to-face at the prison. I visited Kozlowski several times and maintained regular contact with him for two and a half years. I asked and he answered hundreds of questions about his life, his career, and the twenty-seven years he spent at Tyco. Kozlowski gave me access to his attorneys, former colleagues, family members, and friends. Our ongoing conversation and thousands of hours of research evolved into this book.

In addition to interviewing Kozlowski, I spoke with another former Tyco CEO, and with former Directors, executives, and other Tyco employees. I talked with Kozlowski's family members, his friends, the man who served as foreperson of the jury that convicted Kozlowski, and I met with legendary former Manhattan District Attorney Robert Morgenthau, who prosecuted the Tyco executives. The information in this book was found in tens of thousands of documents, hundreds of articles, Securities and Exchange Commission filings, the applicable laws and regulations, and numerous court opinions. I also relied on the evidence presented during two criminal trials that, in total, stretched over eleven months and spawned transcripts that contain 28,338 pages of sworn testimony, legal arguments, judicial decisions, a mistrial, and shocking verdicts. I sought the counsel of experts when I needed help interpreting and understanding what I found.

It's fair to say that I am biased. I'm a business ethics professor. I spend my life studying and teaching the importance of thoughtful, legal, and ethical behavior in business. I'm probably more critical than most people about right and wrong. I have strong opinions about what is acceptable and what is unacceptable behavior, with particularly high expectations of those in positions of leadership. I'm not a likely advocate for a man who is widely considered one of the most notorious of all the corporate executives tried and convicted as a result of Enron-era scandals.

But here is what I know (and I've heard myself say it dozens, maybe hundreds of times in classrooms full of business students): It's important to do what's right, even when it's unpopular, even when it's criticized, even when it's difficult. Especially when it's unpopular, criticized, and difficult. As I looked into Dennis Kozlowski's life and explored the Tyco scandal, I didn't find what I expected to find. As I studied, read, researched, asked hundreds of questions, dug through thousands of documents, and immersed myself in the scandal and criminal prosecutions, I found far more than, and not at all what I expected.

It would have been easy for me to write the same story about Kozlowski that has been written hundreds of times. I could have focused on the $6,000 shower curtain and his Roman orgy-themed birthday party on the Italian island of Sardinia. I could have skimmed the surface of the facts (saved myself thousands of hours of work) and written a book consistent with the public's perception of the former CEO of Tyco International. Instead, I decided to write *exactly* what I found, what I read, what I heard, and what, after more than thirty months of reasoned thought, I believe to be the truth.

This account of the Tyco scandal is accurate. My research was copious and meticulous and because I know Kozlowski is controversial, I checked and rechecked thousands of facts. I was able to verify about 80 percent of the information I received directly from Dennis Kozlowski and to his credit, there was not a single discrepancy between what he told me and what I found in reliable, independent, objective sources. Nothing he said or wrote was changed, twisted, fabricated, or misrepresented. From our first meeting, Kozlowski challenged me to look at everything, to talk to anyone and everyone involved, and to reach my own conclusions.

So that's what I did. I spent two and a half years going through Dennis Kozlowski's life and career with a fine-tooth comb. I worked until I was comfortable with my understanding of the facts and the law.

This book is the culmination of what I learned.

ACKNOWLEDGMENTS

Writing an accurate, thoroughly researched nonfiction book is a colossal undertaking; it is interesting and arduous work. It was far more of both than I anticipated. This project was time, thought, and energy consuming—it was the most all-consuming project I've ever undertaken. It was by far the most enriching and rewarding professional challenge of my career, and it took many people to make it happen.

Many thanks to my agent Coleen O'Shea of the Allen O'Shea Literary Agency, who believed in this project when it was still an overwhelming, underdeveloped idea. Coleen provided candid guidance and prudent advice, which as a first-time author was invaluable. I had a lot to learn about the world of publishing.

I am also grateful to my editor Karen Wolny, Editorial Director at Palgrave Macmillan, whose positive encouragement was very much appreciated.

I appreciate the insights shared by Eric Rayman, Esq. of the New York law firm Miller Korzenik Sommers LLP. Eric's objective and discerning point of view was of great value.

Many people contributed to the content of the book. I consulted with several experts who helped untangle complexities and technical issues. In addition, several individuals shared with me their experiences at and with Tyco International Ltd. This book would not have been possible without them.

I am deeply indebted to attorney Alan Lewis of the Wall Street law firm Carter Ledyard & Milburn. Alan was a rich source of information, counsel, and perspective from the early stages of this project until it was completed. Thank you, Alan, for everything you contributed to this book. Alan also strongly encouraged (i.e., forced) me to take my first solo subway ride in Manhattan, for which this small-town girl from the Midwest is also grateful.

I am indebted to Mark Belnick, who allowed me to stir up memories of a very difficult period in his life. Mark's unfiltered honestly was unexpected and more valuable than he knows. His still-raw pain crystallized my understanding of what it felt like to be wrongfully accused of serious felonies and to have a reputation damaged by unproven allegations.

I owe a debt of gratitude to Joyce, Dennis Kozlowski's younger sister, who provided research of Kozlowski family history, arranged for me to visit her brother at the Mid-State Correctional Facility, gave me detailed and helpful instructions for how to visit an inmate, and provided valuable insight into her brother's life.

I am more grateful than I can express to Robert A. G. Monks for graciously sharing with me his knowledge of corporations generally and of Tyco International specifically. Mr. Monks allowed me to contact him over and over again, and he told me about his experiences as a longtime Tyco Director. I am especially appreciative to him for pushing me to ask the right questions of the right people and for illuminating some of the most important issues discussed in this book.

I am thankful to former Manhattan District Attorney Robert Morgenthau who at the age of ninety-three sat down with me and discussed Dennis Kozlowski's prosecution and conviction. Our meeting was one of the most unexpected and enlightening experiences of this project and is something I will always remember and value.

I am also indebted to Ida Van Lindt, Mr. Morgenthau's longtime personal assistant. Thank you, Ida, for so efficiently and graciously coordinating my visit to your offices.

I am grateful to Robert Pastore, who has known Dennis Kozlowski since the two were boys growing up on South 10th Street in Newark, New Jersey. Thank you, Robert, or as Kozlowski would call you, Bobby, for sharing your memories with me.

I owe a thank you to Isaac Rosenthal, who shared with me his experiences as the foreperson of the jury that convicted Dennis Kozlowski in 2005.

I am very grateful for the time and insights of Christo Lassiter, Professor of Law in the College of Law at the University of Cincinnati. I had not spoken with Professor Lassiter since I was a student in his criminal law class many years ago, but when I contacted him about my research, he graciously granted me access to his expertise in the areas of criminal law and white-collar crime. Thank you, Professor Lassiter.

I also owe a big thank you to Robin Engel, Associate Professor of Criminal Justice and Director of the Policing Institute in the College of Education, Criminal Justice, and Human Services at the University of Cincinnati. Professor Engel very quickly responded to my unexpected request and provided data I needed from the Bureau of Justice Statistics. Thank you so much, Robin.

I am grateful to Brad McGee, whose knowledge of Tyco and insightful observations allowed me to better understand what it was like to be part of Tyco corporate operations during the years Dennis Kozlowski served as the company's CEO. Thank you, Brad. This book would not be as accurate or complete without your contributions.

I am indebted to Joshua Berman, former CEO and longtime Director of Tyco International, for generously and candidly sharing his experiences with me. Mr.

Berman has more history with and knowledge of Tyco than anyone—ever. Thank you, Mr. Berman.

Thank you to attorneys Nathaniel Z. Marmur and Michael J. Grudberg of Ballard Spahr Stillman & Friedman for your time and consideration.

I am very fortunate to be a faculty member at a university that values, supports, and encourages research and creative activities. I am forever grateful to Northern Kentucky University (NKU) for my sabbatical leave, which allowed me to undertake a project that enhanced my research skills and added to my substantive knowledge more than I thought possible.

For his ongoing support, encouragement, and enthusiasm, I'm grateful to Richard Kolbe, Dean of the Haile/US Bank College of Business at NKU.

I want to thank the members of the Department of Accounting, Finance, and Business Law (AFBL) in the Haile/US Bank College of Business at NKU—my valued colleagues and friends. I very much appreciate the support provided by Dr. Peter Theuri, Chair of AFBL. A special thank you to Professor Teressa Elliott and Dr. Linda Marquis who submitted our research papers while I was consumed with writing this book, and to Dr. J. C. Kim who provided analysis of fluctuations in the price of Tyco stock. I am especially grateful to my colleagues and friends Dr. Darius Fatemi and Dr. Duke Thompson whose enthusiastic encouragement was frequently needed and very much appreciated.

I am also appreciative of the assistance of Ann Peelman, former AFBL Academic Coordinator. Thank you, Ann.

I tip my hat to my students of the past eleven years. They have been my sources of inspiration. My students (at the University of Cincinnati-Clermont from 2002 to 2005 and at NKU from 2005 to present) pique my curiosity and make my job challenging, rewarding, and always enjoyable. This book would not have happened without our classroom discussions about Tyco and Dennis Kozlowski.

I am grateful to my friend and formal mentor Dr. Fred Beasley, and to his brilliant and beautiful wife Paula Beasley, for their interest, support, and enthusiasm when I decided to undertake this project.

I would not be a faculty member at NKU without the encouragement and guidance of my friend Dr. Matthew Shank, now President of Marymount University. Thank you, Matt, for inspiring me to be as good at my job as you are at yours.

I was blessed during the writing of this book with the input and contributions of my family members, who were my advisors, focus group, readers, and enthusiasts.

I am forever indebted to Dr. Douglas Havelka, my husband, my best friend, my love, and my most trusted advisor. I could not have started or completed this project without you. Thank you for your love, support, unlimited understanding and patience, and for your valuable technical and professional advice.

I am the very lucky mother of two adult children who are exceedingly kind and thoughtful individuals.

I am grateful to my strikingly beautiful, brilliant, and kind-hearted daughter Alex Womacks Klingensmith who cooked for me, checked on me, and encouraged me during the many months I worked on this project. Thank you for being so thoughtful and understanding while you were pregnant and doing nice things for me when I should have been taking care of you. Thank you for allowing me to be with you when you delivered our beautiful Kora Jane. It was miraculous and one of the best moments in my life (and the best excuse *ever* for taking a break from work). Thank you to my smart and ambitious son-in-law Kyle Klingensmith for your support and your interest in the book.

I am indebted to Adam Womacks, my talented, intelligent, and handsome son who made sure I was alive, fed, and ensured that I had a good chair to sit in while I wrote this book. Thank you for your patience and for taking care of *everything* while I was focused on writing. I know you don't want anyone to know what a kind and thoughtful man you are, so it will remain our secret.

I am fortunate to have wonderful parents whose unwavering support has allowed me to try whatever I want in life. Thank you for expecting me to excel in school, making the long drive to the orthodontist many, many, many times, paying for my college education, bringing me fresh Mt. Orab vegetables every summer, repairing my vehicles, and for the tens of thousands of other things you do for me and my family, including your encouragement while I was working on this book.

Thank you to my beautiful and brilliant sister Dr. Denise Neal White, my smart, hardworking brother-in-law Mike White, and to my wildly talented and handsome nephews Tyler White, Justin White, Matt White, and Blake White, who were always just a text message away when I needed help.

Thank you to my friend Ethan Arnold, a talented writer who helped me during the initial phases of this project.

I'm appreciative of all of my friends who encouraged me, and who forgave me (or will forgive me, I hope) for being a bad friend during the months that I was consumed with writing this book.

Finally, I am eternally grateful to Dennis Kozlowski, who gave me unfiltered access to everyone and everything in his life. I could not have written this book without his cooperation, honesty, countless hours of interviews, and his challenge to me to examine all of the facts and to reach my own conclusions. Thank you, Kozlowski. I hope I adequately captured your experiences. I tried to portray you accurately. I hope you read this book and find it to be the truth.

PART ONE
MOGUL STYLE

ONE

SIX WOMEN AND SIX MEN

Supreme Court, New York County
Manhattan Criminal Courthouse, 13th Floor
100 Centre Street
New York City, New York
June 17, 2005

THE PEOPLE OF THE STATE OF NEW YORK
AGAINST
L. DENNIS KOZLOWSKI & MARK H. SWARTZ, DEFENDANTS

COURT OFFICER: Come to order, part 51 is now in session.

THE COURT: As the parties are aware we have a note from the jury which states we have reached a verdict, so in a moment we will have the panel come out and take their verdict. I will just ask that everybody not react to whatever the verdicts may be and remain in the courtroom until we are finished taking the verdicts. If you have a Blackberry or something like that and you want to operate it that is fine, but nothing that is going to make noise and I don't want people running in and out while the verdicts are being taken, so whoever is here can remain but should remain until the verdict is taken. If anybody wants to leave now you are welcome to do that.

(Jury enters courtroom).

THE COURT: Good afternoon ladies and gentlemen, we have received your note which indicates you have reached a verdict.

THE CLERK: Will the foreperson please rise. Mr. Foreperson, have you agreed upon a verdict?

THE FOREPERSON: Say again.

THE CLERK: Have you agreed upon a verdict?

THE FOREPERSON: Yes, we have.

THE CLERK: I'm going to take the verdicts as to defendant L. Dennis Kozlowski first and then the verdicts of the second defendant, Mark Swartz.[1]

* * *

At one point in his life, Dennis Kozlowski could get just about anyone on the phone. "Except maybe the Pope," he conceded.[2] He was successful, wealthy, well-known, and well-connected with a lifestyle that reflected his status. Kozlowski enjoyed expensive hobbies, homes, and habits, and he regularly rubbed elbows with celebrities, politicians, business moguls, and world leaders. He seemed to be blessed with the Midas touch; he was admired for his business acumen and frequently recognized for his achievements. After working hard almost his entire life, L. Dennis Kozlowski relished the rewards of twenty-seven extraordinarily successful years at Tyco International Ltd., the last ten of which were spent as the multi-national conglomerate's Chief Executive Officer (CEO) and Chairman of the Board of Directors.

During Kozlowski's decade of leadership, Tyco successfully acquired hundreds of companies; many were small and others were multi-billion dollar deals. Through both acquisitive and organic growth, Tyco expanded exponentially from a little known New Hampshire company with around $20 million in annual revenue when Kozlowski joined the organization in 1975 to a global giant with a quarter million employees in more than a hundred countries and annual revenue of close to $40 billion in fiscal year 2001—Kozlowski's final year with the company.[3]

In his letter to shareholders published in Tyco's 2001 Annual Report, which was Kozlowski's ninth opportunity to address his constituents at the conclusion of a fiscal year, the CEO described a year of outstanding performance. It wasn't the first time he shared good news with shareholders. Tyco experienced forty consecutive quarters of increasing profits when Kozlowski was the company's CEO.[4]

At the close of the 2001 fiscal year, Kozlowski bolstered shareholder confidence by pointing to Tyco's consistently strong results—double-digit percentage increases in revenue and earnings that were especially meaningful in 2001, a year in which a global economic downturn was exacerbated by terrorist attacks on September 11, 2001.[5] Kozlowski reminded shareholders that "[m]any outstanding companies found it impossible to meet their financial targets last year; and some couldn't make any money at all. Yet in the worst economic environment we have seen in a decade, Tyco managed to exceed its profit goals. All of us at Tyco are very proud of that achievement."[6] Kozlowski backed his rhetoric with results and took great satisfaction in informing Tyco shareholders that "[f]or the ninth consecutive year, we increased revenues and earnings substantially. Revenues rose 25 percent to $36.3 billion and earnings grew $1.4 billion to $5.1 billion, a 38 percent increase over the prior year."[7]

Kozlowski was correct. It was tough to flourish when the recession hit. Of course, he and Tyco had benefited from the booming economy of the prior decade. The longest economic expansion in history began in 1991 and stretched until early 2001,[8] overlapping almost entirely Kozlowski's tenure as Tyco's CEO (July 1992–June 2002). But the bull market ended; for the first time since he was named CEO, Kozlowski had to steer the company in a faltering economy.

And he did. Tyco weathered the recession of 2001 and Kozlowski felt certain the company was solid. He had spent ten years reducing Tyco's dependence on cyclical industries and establishing steady, predictable earnings growth, thus making the conglomerate less vulnerable to fluctuations in the economy. His vision for the company had become a reality and the results were convincing. To shareholders in 2001, Kozlowski stated with conviction that Tyco could grow its business in virtually any environment. He also expressed confidence in the state of the company, unconditionally declaring that Tyco was "poised to deliver many years of exciting returns." Even though Tyco was facing some atypical difficulties near the end of 2001, Kozlowski made it clear that he was "optimistic about Tyco's future."[9]

The CEO's buoyant letter to shareholders in the 2001 Annual Report would be his last, and his optimism about a bright future proved erroneous. When he penned the letter to Tyco shareholders in December of 2001, Kozlowski did not predict that less than six months later, he would be fired. He didn't anticipate that three months after being fired, he would be indicted by the Manhattan District Attorney along with then Chief Financial Officer (CFO) Mark Swartz, Chief Corporate Counsel Mark Belnick, and Frank Walsh, a former member of the Board of Directors—the four accused of malfeasance in Tyco's C-suite and boardroom. As he approached the ten-year mark and looked back at a wildly successful decade as Tyco's Chairman and CEO, Kozlowski must have felt invincible. Nearly everything had gone his way. He could not have imagined his career ending the way it did, with him and the company to which he devoted most of his adult life entangled in a very public scandal.[10]

* * *

Several extraordinary events happened around the time Dennis Kozlowski addressed Tyco shareholders at the end of 2001. Enron Corp., a global energy corporation based in Houston, Texas, a company with nearly 21,000 employees in over thirty countries and with stated annual revenue of more than $100 billion, on December 2, 2001 filed for bankruptcy protection under Chapter 11 of the United States Code. The $65 billion bankruptcy was, at the time, the largest corporate bankruptcy in U.S. history. The New York Stock Exchange de-listed Enron stock on January 15, 2002 after the price plummeted from a high of $90 a share in August of 2000 to $.40 a share on December 3, 2001, the first day of trading after Enron sought bankruptcy protection. The massive bankruptcy forced an autopsy of the corporate corpse and the pathology revealed a litany of diseases; accounting irregularities, conflicts of interest, shredded documents, securities violations, and unprecedented fraud were among the allegations that created a line of Enron executives invoking their Fifth Amendment right against self-incrimination when they were questioned before the United States Congress in February of 2002. Some of those who testified were later charged with and convicted of crimes related to their leadership of the defunct energy giant.[11]

The wake of Enron's failure was wide and powerful. One of the direct casualties was Arthur Andersen, an enterprise that for decades set the standard for excellence and integrity in the accounting profession.[12] Arthur Andersen suffered irreparable damage when the firm was implicated in some of the wrongdoing at Enron. The accounting firm was one of many organizations directly affected by the Enron scandal, in addition to the impact felt by tens of thousands of employees, retirees, creditors, and shareholders. The unparalleled direct costs of Enron's bankruptcy were compounded when the magnitude of the failure shook the entire market and caused both immediate and long-term changes in American business and legal environments. The lasting effects of Enron's collapse are significant; the ultimate costs, incalculable.

Enron was undoubtedly the linchpin of the scandals exposed during the early 2000s, but many others came to light during the same brief yet critical time period. Enron's bankruptcy was the "largest in U.S. history" for fewer than eight months before telecommunications giant WorldCom filed a $107 billion bankruptcy in July 2002.[13]

The same summer that WorldCom collapsed, Sam Waksal, the founder and then CEO of ImClone Systems, Inc., was charged with illegal insider trading for tipping off family members and friends when he learned that the Food and Drug Administration (FDA) would soon deny approval of the biopharmaceutical company's anti-cancer drug Erbitux. In addition to alerting those close to him of the imminent drop in ImClone's stock price, Waksal attempted to sell millions of dollars worth of stock he owned before the company's bad news from the FDA reached the market.[14]

One of the shareholders allegedly tipped off was domestic guru, media mogul, corporate executive, and Sam Waksal's friend Martha Stewart, who was convicted of lying to federal investigators about the timing of her sale of ImClone stock. Alleged tippee Stewart, who was a very wealthy and successful CEO at the time, avoided a loss of only $45,673 by selling a relatively small number of ImClone shares a day before news of the FDA's decision on Erbitux was made public. Had she waited twenty-four hours to sell her ImClone stock, after the bad news was made public, the transaction would not have been tied to Sam Waksal's inside information and would not have caught the attention of federal investigators. Interestingly, Stewart was never convicted of illegal insider trading, only of obstructing justice and lying to investigators. She was sentenced to and served five months in a federal prison.[15]

Joining Enron, Arthur Andersen, WorldCom, ImClone, Waksal, and Stewart in this very ugly episode of U.S. business history were Adelphia and the Rigas family,[16] Global Crossing,[17] Fannie Mae and Freddie Mac,[18] HealthSouth and its CEO Richard M. Scrushy,[19] and with timing and allegations that forever placed them in this undesirable group, Tyco International, CEO Dennis Kozlowski, and CFO Mark Swartz.

In addition to rousing the interest of the U.S. Congress, federal and state regulators, and law enforcement agencies, the Enron-era scandals grabbed the attention of the media. When similar scandals happened in decades past, the news cycle and the number of outlets were limited. For example, during the savings and loan crisis of the 1980s, business news was primarily found once a day in the *Wall Street Journal*. But by the early 2000s, the news cycle was never ending. Coverage of the scandals was 24/7 and appeared in almost limitless outlets: newspapers, tabloids, periodicals, on the Internet, and on network and cable television. The public was deluged with stories about massive corporate bankruptcies, lost jobs and pensions, greedy CEOs, and a shocking list of legal and ethical lapses. Scrutiny of corporations, their boards of directors, and corporate executives was at its peak when Dennis Kozlowski and Tyco made headlines in 2002.

For several years, the media lauded Kozlowski's success as a CEO. He appeared on covers of magazines, was described as "impressive," "ambitious," a "deal-maker," a "top manager," and some even said there wasn't a better CEO in America than Dennis Kozlowski.[20] That was before the summer of 2002.

Once scandal was suggested, the media immediately portrayed Kozlowski very differently. There was no more praise and admiration; instead, his career and his character were mercilessly attacked. He was called "greedy," "Dennis the Menace," a "pig," and a "thief."[21] Kozlowski's legacy was forever changed. He would no longer be remembered as the successful and respected CEO who helped build one of the largest companies in the world; instead, he would be identified as one of the loathed executives who made headlines for all the wrong reasons. Seemingly overnight, and well before he was tried and convicted, Kozlowski's accomplishments were reduced to a mere footnote.

Dennis Kozlowski's story should not have taken a tragic turn. He was on a hard-earned and enviable trajectory. He was supposed to enjoy the security of lucrative retirement benefits, a golden parachute, and the wealth he earned and amassed during decades of hard work. He likely would have become an angel investor and dabbled in private equity. He could have been mentoring young entrepreneurs and perhaps teaching in a business school. He was supposed to spend time with his family and friends—the people he loved and neglected during the decades he was a busy executive. Dennis Kozlowski planned to travel for pleasure, to cook, and to play with his dogs. He wanted to teach his grandchildren to sail. For the first time since he started delivering newspapers as a kid, he would have been able to unchain himself from work and kick back. His life should have been filled with handshakes and hugs, not handcuffs and strip searches. His career should not have come to an inglorious end; he should be known as the architect of a giant global conglomerate, not as the "laundry czar" (his self-appointed title) in a New York State prison.[22]

Not once during his twenty-seven years with Tyco, and most certainly not when he expressed optimism about the future to Tyco shareholders in December of 2001, did Dennis Kozlowski imagine he'd be in a courtroom charged with nearly two dozen felonies—accused of wrongfully taking millions of dollars from the company he loved. But that's where he found himself in June of 2005. He was standing with his defense team in front of the Supreme Court of the State of New York at the conclusion of a lengthy criminal trial, facing a jury of six women and six men who held his fate in their hands.

TWO

BA 0.043

In baseball, one measure of performance is a player's batting average (BA) which is calculated by dividing the number of base hits by the number of official times at bat. For example, if a player has 25 hits in 100 times at bat, the player's BA is 0.250. Going 1 for 23 (BA 0.043) is crushing.

*   *   *

Supreme Court, New York County
Manhattan Criminal Courthouse, 13th Floor
100 Centre Street
New York City, New York
June 17, 2005

THE CLERK: How say you to count number one against the defendant L Dennis Kozlowski, grand larceny in the first degree?

THE FOREPERSON: Guilty.

THE CLERK: How say you to the second count of the indictment charging defendant L Dennis Kozlowski with the crime of grand larceny in the first degree?

THE FOREPERSON: Guilty.

THE CLERK: How say you to the third count of the indictment charging defendant with grand larceny in the first degree?

THE FOREPERSON: Guilty.

THE CLERK: How say you to the fourth count of the indictment charging defendant with the crime of grand larceny in the first degree?

THE FOREPERSON: Guilty.

THE CLERK: How say you to the fifth count of the indictment charging defendant with the crime of grand larceny in the first degree?

THE FOREPERSON: Guilty.

THE CLERK: How say you to the sixth count of the indictment charging defendant with the crime of grand larceny in the first degree?

THE FOREPERSON: Guilty.

THE CLERK: How say you to the eighth count of the indictment charging defendant with grand larceny in the first degree?

THE FOREPERSON: Guilty.

THE CLERK: How say you to the ninth count of the indictment charging defendant with grand larceny in the first degree?

THE FOREPERSON: Guilty.

THE CLERK: How say you to the 10th count of the indictment charging defendant with the crime of grand larceny in the first degree?

THE FOREPERSON: Guilty.

THE CLERK: How say you to the 11th count charging the defendant with grand larceny in the first degree?

THE FOREPERSON: Guilty.

THE CLERK: How say you to the 12th count charging defendant with grand larceny in the first degree?

THE FOREPERSON: Guilty.

THE CLERK: How say you to the 13th count charging defendant with grand larceny in the first degree?

THE FOREPERSON: Guilty.

THE CLERK: How say you to the 14th count charging defendant with conspiracy in the fourth degree?

THE FOREPERSON: Guilty.

THE CLERK: How say you to the 15th count of the indictment charging defendant with violation of General Business Law 352 C subsection five?

THE FOREPERSON: Guilty.

THE CLERK: How say you to the 16th count of the indictment charging defendant with falsifying business records in the first degree?

THE FOREPERSON: Guilty.

THE CLERK: How say you to the 17th count charging defendant with falsifying business records in the first degree?

THE FOREPERSON: Not guilty.

THE CLERK: How say you to the 18th count of the indictment charging defendant with falsifying business records in the first degree?

THE FOREPERSON: Guilty.

THE CLERK: How say you to the 19th count charging defendant with falsifying business records in the first degree?

THE FOREPERSON: Guilty.

THE CLERK: How say you to the 20th count charging defendant with falsifying business records in the first degree?

THE FOREPERSON: Guilty.

THE CLERK: How say you to the 21st count charging defendant with falsifying business records in the first degree?

THE FOREPERSON: Guilty.

THE CLERK: How say you to the 22nd count charging defendant with falsifying business records in the first degree?

THE FOREPERSON: Guilty.

THE CLERK: How say you to the 23rd count charging defendant with falsifying business records in the first degree?

THE FOREPERSON: Guilty.

THE CLERK: How say you to the 24th count of the indictment charging defendant with falsifying business records in the first degree?

THE FOREPERSON: Guilty.[1]

* * *

By the following day, news of the verdicts was everywhere; the high-profile legal drama had finally reached a conclusion after three *crazy* years. There was an earlier trial of the same Defendants—it ended without a verdict after an exhausting six months that stretched from the fall of 2003 into the first half of 2004. The prosecution and defense teams learned their efforts were for naught and the Defendants remained in legal limbo when the court declared a mistrial during jury deliberations at the end of the first trial. Then in January of 2005, there was a courtroom reunion. Everyone was back for a second trial, this one five months in duration. So when the jury reached verdicts in June of 2005, the decisions were much anticipated and long awaited. It was the end of a prolonged and painful journey. At least Dennis Kozlowski thought it was the end.

He was wrong.

Kozlowski envisioned a different outcome during the eleven days the second jury deliberated. In fact, he anticipated a different outcome since the moment he was indicted nearly three years earlier. "Nothing prepares you for that moment," Kozlowski said as he remembered the jury's verdicts and the words that transformed him into a convicted felon.[2] He was guilty of the largest larceny ever prosecuted by the State of New York.[3] In a dark suit and tie, looking every bit the corporate executive he had been for most of his adult life,[4] a stoic Dennis Kozlowski stood and received the verdicts: guilty of twelve counts of grand larceny in the first degree, guilty of one count of conspiracy in the fourth degree, guilty of one count of violating New York General Business Law Section 352-c(5), and guilty of eight counts of falsifying business records in the first degree. Guilty of twenty-two of the twenty-three felony counts for which he was tried.

Guilty.

*   *   *

Mid-State Correctional Facility
Marcy, New York
March 17, 2011

Dear Cathy,

You asked about my worst moments since January 2002. There were a few. The jury in my second trial returning with a guilty verdict was a horrible moment. The words guilty were repeated over and over. My daughter's accident in Bali last July 31 was incredibly stressful for me and horrible for her. Not being at her side at such a difficult time was devastating. Sandy continues to recover.

I had a heart problem in January 2007. I was taken to an outside hospital emergency room and spent a week there. I was chained and cuffed. I was scared and my family had no access to me. All is well now. It was the first time I was ever admitted to a hospital. At one point I thought I might die chained to a gurney in a strange emergency room.

Missing happy, joyful events also hurts. I could not attend Cheryl's wedding some three years ago and missed the births of two grandchildren. The last nine years of my life have been dedicated to two trials and almost 6 years in jail. That's about 20% of my adult life. It's difficult seeing violent criminals and child molesters come and go here (serving 2 to 3 years) while my life passes me by. Many investors, employees, vendors, and communities benefited from the 27 years I spent growing Tyco and they continue to benefit today. I feel I deserve better than the rough justice of New York State.

Regards,
Dennis[5]

THREE

950 FIFTH AVENUE

In a supposed conversation between F. Scott Fitzgerald and Ernest Hemingway, Fitzgerald said, "The rich are different from us," to which Hemingway replied, "Yes, they have more money."[1] If Hemingway had known Dennis Kozlowski, he may have added, "and very expensive shower curtains."

* * *

In the history of civilization, there have been only two famous shower curtains. The first hung between Anthony Perkins and an unsuspecting Janet Leigh in Alfred Hitchcock's *Psycho*.[2] Since 1960, Hitchcock's shower curtain has been a widely recognized symbol of suspense and horror; it is an American pop culture icon. More than forty years after Hitchcock's gruesome shower scene, another shower curtain also reached icon status. The second, with its extraordinary price tag, is not part of pop culture but instead is a damning icon of American corporate culture.

A $6,000 shower curtain came to symbolize the greed and excesses exposed during Enron-era corporate scandals. It was held up as the epitome of failed governance, lax regulatory oversight, and questionable judgment of highly compensated leaders in some of the largest corporations in the world. The garish, overpriced burgundy and gold shower curtain was mentioned in tens of thousands of articles, became a media darling during an appearance on *60 Minutes,* and had a cameo role in an episode of CNBC's *American Greed*.[3] It was photographed, filmed, and the butt of jokes. At the peak of its notoriety, the shower curtain was confiscated by the New York City Police Department and used as evidence in criminal trials. The cloudy plastic curtain through which Hitchcock revealed the blurred silhouette of a knife-wielding Anthony Perkins and vulnerably nude Janet Leigh pales in comparison to the one that draped the shower in a Tyco corporate apartment when Dennis Kozlowski served as the company's CEO.

After reaching the pinnacle of business success, then being publicly castigated and labeled the "poster child for corporate greed,"[4] despite magazine covers that heralded his talent followed by a very public fall from grace, irrespective of a shocking indictment and two criminal trials that were covered by the media almost every day for three years, it seems Dennis Kozlowski will forever be *best* known as the guy who bought the $6,000 shower curtain. Of all of the wonderful, terrible, fascinating, scandalous, and tragic things that happened in Dennis Kozlowski's life, it's the shower curtain that people remember.

* * *

Upper East Side, Borough of Manhattan
New York City, New York
June 23, 2012

I walked with Dennis Kozlowski along the eastern edge of Central Park in Manhattan's Upper East Side on a sunny Saturday morning during the summer of 2012. As we walked, I talked with the former CEO about his career, his crimes, and his punishment. After six years and nine months in prison and more than four months in the State of New York's temporary work release program, Dennis Kozlowski received his first full day of furlough time on a Saturday in June of 2012. Kozlowski was, at the time, housed at the Lincoln Correctional Facility on 110th Street in Manhattan. After being approved for the work release program at the end of 2011, he was moved from the Mid-State Correctional Facility in Marcy, New York, to Lincoln in Harlem, and he began working at his approved job in February of 2012.[5] Like the other participants in the program, Kozlowski was permitted to leave Lincoln to go to work during specified weekday hours.[6] Most were eventually granted furlough time in the evenings and on weekends, when they could leave the facility to spend time with friends and family.[7] The program helped inmates transition back into society after years in prison; those adjustments occurred in large part during hours like those Kozlowski enjoyed outside of prison on the day in June when I had the opportunity to speak with him.

As we walked, my objectives for the day were different than Kozlowski's. He wanted to enjoy his first few hours of quasi-freedom in nearly seven years, to walk the streets without handcuffs and shackles, and to remember how it felt to be without constant supervision. As he acclimated to the world outside of prison walls, I tried to better understand Dennis Kozlowski: a man who once ran a huge multinational conglomerate, a man who spearheaded the acquisitions of hundreds of companies for billions of dollars, and a man who earned more than $100 million a year during some of the years he was a CEO. He had brains, power, and money and achieved extraordinary success in business and in life. Why was this man charged with a long list of felonies, convicted of twenty-two, and how did he end up in a

New York State prison? And there was one other question, the response to which would probably help answer all of the other questions. How did Dennis Kozlowski come to own a $6,000 shower curtain?

* * *

We made our way south along Fifth Avenue on the shady sidewalk bordering Central Park. As we walked the entirety of Museum Mile, Kozlowski spoke knowledgeably about the park, the buildings, the museums, and the history of the city. He specifically pointed out The Frick Collection on East 70th, a museum he mentioned in a letter he sent to me a year earlier. About the museum, Kozlowski wrote, "it was my favorite destination from my college days until 6 years ago."[8] Kozlowski first viewed the work of J. M. W. Turner at The Frick house. Turner was a British artist known for his landscape paintings. A significant number of Turner's paintings are maritime scenes—ships, sails, and the sea—and it was those pieces that attracted Kozlowski to The Frick Collection again and again.[9]

In addition to telling me about specific Manhattan landmarks, Kozlowski identified properties where he lived at various times during his adult life. He explained the peculiarities of buying shares of a co-op in New York City, and he shared frustrating experiences of being rejected by two co-op boards in the early 1990s, after which he opted for many years to rent instead of buying apartments in New York City.

Kozlowski stopped at the intersection of Fifth Avenue and East 76th Street and pointed across the street to the property on the northeast corner. He identified the high-rise apartment building as 950 Fifth Avenue. "That's it," he said. "That's where the $6,000 shower curtain once hung."[10] The beautiful thirteen-story building was located in the affluent Lenox Hill neighborhood of the Upper East Side and the exclusive address came with coveted Central Park views. It was exactly 1.8 miles from the Lincoln Correctional Facility on 110th Street—where Kozlowski would return later that day—to the 950 Fifth Avenue apartment. It was less than a thirty-minute walk and yet a world away.

Standing outside the building that summer morning, Kozlowski recalled that "the shower curtain hung in the bathroom on the first floor of the apartment, near a bedroom at the back of the kitchen that was probably once used as staff quarters. When we remodeled, that bathroom wasn't renovated." He also said, "I think the decorator hung the shower curtain there because it was less expensive than restoring the bath."[11] Kozlowski explained that he stayed in the apartment generally one or two nights a month; he didn't spend many nights in the city during those years. When he was CEO, Kozlowski lived in New Hampshire, then Nantucket, and then Boca Raton. He never considered New York his home.[12] The transcript of his first criminal trial confirms his recollection of the frequency with which he used the apartment; the housekeeper for the apartment testified that Kozlowski didn't live there but he sometimes stayed one or two nights a week, sometimes he stopped by just to change his shirt, and at other times he wasn't in the apartment for months at a time.[13] As we stood on the sidewalk outside the building, Kozlowski said, "When I stayed here, I slept in an upstairs bedroom. There were three bedrooms upstairs, and I only stayed upstairs, never downstairs."[14] He distinctly remembered that the shower he used in the upstairs bathroom didn't have a shower curtain but instead had glass doors. Ironically, Dennis Kozlowski had never seen the $6,000 shower curtain, even though it was irrevocably linked to him.[15]

Kozlowski gave the CEO stamp of approval for the purchase of the Fifth Avenue apartment in March of 2000. Dolly Lenz, a Manhattan super-broker with whom he had worked previously, knew that Kozlowski might be looking for an apartment and alerted him when the property became available. Years later when Lenz testified in Kozlowski's criminal trial, she said she called him about the apartment before it was even on the market. Lenz described the Fifth Avenue property as " . . . a duplex, probably 6,000 square feet, the 10th and 11th floors overlooking Central Park," and with an asking price of $18 million.[16]

In order to facilitate the sale of the property, Lenz arranged for Kozlowski to be pre-approved by the building's co-op board to avoid issues he faced with similar boards in the past. In her trial testimony, Lenz explained that in the mid-1990s, she worked with Kozlowski on the purchase of another Fifth Avenue property. That sale was never consummated because, for reasons unknown to Lenz, the co-op board did not grant an interview. Kozlowski said he wasn't concerned about approval by the 950 Fifth Avenue co-op board because he knew some of the building's residents who sat on the board including Mort Zuckerman, owner of the *New York Daily News* and perennial presence on the *Forbes* list of richest Americans, Jonathan Tisch, co-chairman of the board of Loews Corporation and co-owner of the New York Giants, former Goldman Sachs executive Bob Hurst, and Steve Schwarzman, chairman and CEO of the Blackstone Group, who was selling the apartment Kozlowski wanted to buy. In addition to the 950 Fifth Avenue apartment, Schwarzman and Kozlowski shared another interesting commonality. Both made headlines for throwing extravagant birthday parties—Schwarzman for himself and Kozlowski for his wife. When Lenz persuaded Kozlowski to purchase the apartment, she used as a selling point the fact that "Schwartzman [*sic*] had just purchased 740 Park, a duplex triplex, the most expensive apartment to date ever sold in New York, so it had a lot of buzz." The building at 950 Fifth Avenue had only seven units with an elite list of owners who, like Dennis Kozlowski, were well-known, successful, and wealthy men. It's no surprise he felt comfortable there.[17]

Kozlowski made several ill-advised decisions when approving the purchase of the apartment. The co-op board at 950 Fifth Avenue would not allow a corporate owner, which was typical of New York City co-ops, according to Lenz.[18] So Kozlowski allowed the apartment to be titled in his name, even though Tyco funds were used to purchase the property. He submitted the application to the co-op board in his name, personally.[19]

Joshua Berman, a former CEO of Tyco and a member of the Tyco Board of Directors at the time of the purchase, wrote a letter of reference on Kozlowski's behalf to the building's co-op board. In the letter, Berman stated that he had known Kozlowski for twenty-five years and the two were good friends; of Kozlowski he said, "Without qualification I know of no finer human being." Berman described Kozlowski as "a man of his word, thoroughly responsible, exceedingly consider-ate of others, very giving of himself, scrupulously honest, a devoted family man and a wonderful friend." The glowing description continued when in the letter Berman noted that "Dennis will always do the right thing." Berman informed the co-op board that Kozlowski's success had not changed him one iota, that Dennis Kozlowski did not impose his will on others, and that Kozlowski went to great lengths to avoid controversy.[20] Kozlowski's habit of avoiding controversy quickly and involuntarily ended very soon after he completed the purchase of the Fifth Avenue apartment.

When the transaction closed in August of 2000 and ownership transferred, the 1,250 co-op shares were titled in Dennis Kozlowski's name. The purchase price paid by Tyco: $18 million plus $600,000 in transfer taxes.[21] According to Kozlowski, an agreement was drafted and recorded at Tyco that documented the company's own-ership interest in the apartment. The apartment belonged to Tyco, not to Dennis Kozlowski.[22] During the second criminal trial, five years after the real estate clos-ing, Kathy McRae, formerly of the Executive Treasury Department at Tyco, testified that the company entered into a nominee agreement with Kozlowski, which she explained as " . . . an agreement between Tyco and Dennis Kozlowski to acquire title to 950 Fifth Avenue asking him to acquire title to apartments ten and eleven." McRae explained that the Tyco legal department requested the nominee agreement and she believed the request was prompted by PricewaterhouseCoopers, Tyco's independent auditor.[23] The nominee agreement with Kozlowski was just one of several that Tyco executed with its employees. Brian Moroze, a Tyco in-house attorney, drafted nomi-nee agreements for Kozlowski and at least four other Tyco employees.[24]

When Kozlowski took the stand in his own defense during his second criminal trial, attorney Steven Kaufman questioned him about the nominee agreement. It read: "Employee and Tyco agree that employee shall hold title to the apartment solely in the capacity as nominee, agent and non-title holder for Tyco. Employee agrees and understands that he will have no discretion or authority to act with respect to the apartment, but may act only upon discretion from Tyco." Kozlowski assured the jury that it was not his apartment and that the books and records of the company reflected Tyco's ownership, a fact verified by several witnesses during Kozlowski's trials.[25] There was no factual dispute; the evidence was uncontroverted. The property at 950 Fifth Avenue belonged to Tyco, not to Dennis Kozlowski.

Even though McRae was clear about Tyco's ownership of the property and despite the fact that she personally stamped Kozlowski's signature on the nominee agreement, when during the trial the Assistant District Attorney asked her about 950 Fifth Avenue, her first damning response was "[t]hat was Dennis' apartment." Dolly Lenz referred to the property in the same way, and she testified that Kozlowski didn't tell her that the apartment was for Tyco.[26] Kozlowski was certain Lenz knew it was a corporate apartment. Or perhaps he didn't disclose Tyco as the buyer because of the co-op's restriction on corporate owners. Maybe he didn't feel the need to differentiate to a real estate broker his ownership versus the company's ownership. It's possible that Lenz was informed but the information was irrelevant to her because the property had to be titled in the name of an individual. Whatever the reason, it was an unnecessarily complicated arrangement that no doubt confused and biased the jury during Kozlowski's trials.

Less than two years after Kozlowski approved the purchase of the Tyco apartment on Fifth Avenue, questions arose about whether the CEO misappropriated corporate assets to purchase and furnish a luxury apartment for himself. The appearance of impropriety is sometimes just as damaging as actual wrongdoing. Unfortunately, Kozlowski and other individuals at Tyco, including the CFO, the employees in Executive Treasury, corporate counsel, and the Tyco Board of Directors did not protect the company or Kozlowski from the potential problems created by using corporate funds to purchase an apartment titled in the CEO's name. The confusion and controversy were completely avoidable had the company and Kozlowski made better decisions—had they done what was simple and obvious. If he wanted the apartment, Dennis Kozlowski could and should have purchased the 950 Fifth Avenue property personally, with no connection or ties to Tyco. If the corporation needed an apartment, Tyco could and should have purchased other property that could have been titled in the corporation's name. Unfortunately, simplicity, oversight, and common sense seemed in short supply at Tyco. The purchase of the 950 Fifth Avenue apartment was one of many incidents of sloppy, careless decision-making, needless complications, and shoddy record keeping that, at least for the sake of appearances, unnecessarily blurred the line between personal and company assets.

When Dolly Lenz told Kozlowski about the Fifth Avenue property, he believed the building's location and the apartment inside would work well for Tyco; it would be a private meeting place where deals could be negotiated outside corporate offices and away from prying eyes.[27] Tyco's Manhattan offices were in a high-profile building on West 57th Street where visitors' comings and goings were sometimes noted by analysts and reported by the press. Dennis Kozlowski was well known at the time for his aggressive acquisition strategy. During the years he served as CEO, Tyco acquired hundreds of companies. So when the CEO of a potential target company or an investment banker was spotted visiting Tyco's corporate offices, it raised eyebrows and sometimes became public knowledge. Kozlowski believed the lack of privacy jeopardized or even ruined deals. He also feared speculation about certain meetings generated inaccurate information that had the potential to affect the market and the price of Tyco stock, positively or negatively, but in either case, erroneously. "We did the CIT acquisition in the apartment," he said. "Those talks started in the Tyco offices and that resulted in a *Wall Street Journal* article. We needed privacy." Kozlowski said other acquisitions were negotiated in the Tyco apartment as well, and he cited privacy as the primary reason he approved the purchase of the luxury apartment.[28]

Shelling out more than $18 million for a luxury apartment seems an unnecessary extravagance for a publicly traded corporation. Certainly there were far less costly ways to conduct private business meetings. However, the purchase was well within Kozlowski's Board-approved spending authority. During Kozlowski's second criminal trial, Mark Foley, Senior Vice President of Finance at Tyco, testified that during the October 3, 2000 meeting of the Board of Directors, the Board granted Kozlowski spending authority of $200 million for corporate acquisitions and capital expenditures.[29] The increased spending authority was reflected in the minutes of the October 3, 2000 Tyco Board meeting and was just one in a string of Board resolutions that increased the CEO's spending limit. Kozlowski said that, at the time, it felt as if the Board wanted to push all responsibility, decision-making, and oversight to him; it seemed as if Board members wanted to be bothered with Tyco business as infrequently as possible.[30] On July 7, 1998, the Board granted Kozlowski spending authority of $50 million. Less than a year later, on May 12, 1999, the Board doubled the authority to $100 million and then doubled it again in October of 2000.[31] The purchase price of the Fifth Avenue apartment didn't come close to Kozlowski's Board-established spending cap.

In addition to satisfying the company's privacy needs, Kozlowski also believed the real estate was a sound investment and would appreciate over time.[32] He explained that "at the time, 950 Fifth Avenue was not an 'A' building in that area, but more of a 'C' building, primarily because it was narrow, making the rooms in the apartment very narrow." He felt confident the property would appreciate because of the prime location. "It was a good investment," Kozlowski said in justification of the purchase.[33]

New York City (NYC) Department of Finance records show that units 10 and 11 of 950 Fifth Avenue were sold on December 14, 2004 for $20,200,000 and technically confirm Kozlowski's assertion that the property appreciated.[34] The apartment did in fact sell in the tough post-9/11 Manhattan real estate market for more than Tyco paid for the property in 2000. However, Kozlowski approved additional expenditures related to the apartment over and above the purchase price. During Kozlowski's second criminal trial, former Tyco employee Linda Auger testified that between June of 2000 and June of 2002, Tyco spent a total of $31.5 million, which included the purchase price, taxes, as well as furniture and fixtures for the 950 Fifth Avenue duplex.[35] No available records indicate how much, if any, of those additional expenditures were recouped by Tyco when the apartment was sold in 2004. NYC Department of Finance records name "L. Dennis Kozlowski as Nominee" as the seller of the property in 2004 and the seller's address is recorded as Tyco International (US), Inc., 9 Roszel Road, Princeton, New Jersey. The records include no information about Schwarzman's sale and Kozlowski's purchase of the property in 2000.[36]

FOUR

EXECUTIVE PERQUISITES

In 1966, the Beatles recorded "Strawberry Fields Forever," with lyrics written by John Lennon although attributed to both Lennon and Paul McCartney.[1] In the fall of 1980, Lennon gave an interview that appeared in *Playboy* magazine in January of 1981. Lennon and his wife Yoko Ono sat down with freelance writer David Sheff in their home at the Dakota on Central Park West in Manhattan. When during the interview Sheff asked Lennon about the meaning of "Strawberry Fields Forever," Lennon responded with an explanation of the lines *Living is easy with eyes closed. Misunderstanding all you see.* Lennon said, "I was different from the others. I was different all my life. The second verse goes, 'No one I think is in my tree.' . . . Nobody seems to be as hip as me is what I was saying. Therefore, I must be crazy or a genius." In sum, Lennon said reality was whatever he wanted it to be; that to him, surrealism was reality.[2] Before the interview appeared in *Playboy,* John Lennon was shot and killed outside the Dakota on December 8, 1980.[3] With the shots fired by Mark David Chapman, the building across the street from Central Park where the rich and famous lived was transformed from the luxurious New York home John Lennon shared with his wife into the place where his life came to a tragic and premature end.

*   *   *

For many people, it would have been easy to see the potential problems created by a publicly traded corporation's purchase of a luxury apartment that would be used by its CEO, a purchase that was authorized using less than one-tenth of the CEO's Board-granted $200 million spending authority, that required only the CEO's approval, and was structured to title the property in the CEO's name personally. Why did a company the size of Tyco lack internal controls and Board oversight that would have prevented the purchase? Or at least would have required the CEO to seek advice and approval? In this case, the only involvement of Directors was Josh Berman's letter of reference. The potential problems should have been obvious. But in 2000, Tyco and Kozlowski were on top of the world and Kozlowski didn't foresee any problems with the decisions he made about the $18 million duplex.

Charles Lindbergh, one of Kozlowski's heroes, once said that "[l]ife is like a landscape. You live in the midst of it but can describe it only from the vantage point of distance."[4] More than a decade after he approved the purchase of the 950 Fifth Avenue residence, a self-reflective Kozlowski wondered why he didn't anticipate the trouble and questioned how he failed to better protect Tyco shareholders and himself. Kozlowski said, "We didn't need that apartment. I don't know why at the time I thought it was necessary."[5]

Living is easy with eyes closed.

*   *   *

Dennis Kozlowski and Tyco were not alone in the world of extravagant executive perquisites—like having access to a luxury corporate apartment. In the late 1990s and early 2000s, Tyco's purchase of the 950 Fifth Avenue apartment was not beyond the pale or even unusual for a company of its size.

During the ugly and very public 2002 divorce of Jack F. Welch, Jr., the former CEO and Chairman of the Board of General Electric (GE), court filings disclosed a long list of executive perquisites GE provided to Welch. Included among the profligacy was a company-owned $11 million luxury apartment at the Trump International Hotel and Towers on Central Park West. In addition to providing Welch an expense-free home in Manhattan, GE also provided fresh flowers for the apartment, regular shipments of wine, a kitchen staff, a housekeeper, and dry cleaning and laundry services. The company even paid for part of Welch's tab at Jean Georges, a pricy restaurant in the building.[6]

When Welch's perks were made public by his soon-to-be ex-wife, neither he nor GE disputed the expenditures. GE gave undivided, vocal support to its CEO and insisted that the company complied fully with disclosure requirements. Jack Welch, in his own and the company's defense, stated that his generous compensation and perquisites "worked to the benefit of all constituencies." Of note is the vast difference in support Welch received from GE when he was attacked for receiving lavish company benefits compared to the absolute lack of support offered by Tyco to its CEO. Instead of acknowledging the generous compensation and perks, or justifying them by pointing to the company's performance under Kozlowski's leadership, or even admitting that the company had paid its executives too much, Tyco Directors cut Kozlowski loose. GE had Welch's back. Tyco fed Kozlowski to the sharks.

During the barrage of media coverage at the time of Welch's divorce, experts and commentators weighed in on the extravagant executive benefits GE bestowed on Welch. For example, corporate governance expert Nell Minnow called Welch's compensation too generous and stated that "[t]here is really no justification to pay for any living or traveling expenses at that level. . . ." Rakesh Khurana, then Assistant

Professor at the Harvard Business School, explained during a 2002 *PBS NewsHour* interview that "it's an extension of the sort of super-star CEO mentality that had been created over the last 15–20 years in which a CEO was sort of thought to deserve everything he got because he created all this value for the corporation."

With a legitimate, purely capitalistic counter argument, Welch pointed out that " . . . [i]t was an employment contract. I fulfilled my obligations. GE did fantastically. It increased market cap \$250 billion over the time frame, and became number one market cap in the world, most admired global company for five years in a row." Despite the logic of his argument, Welch took a beating in the press. Shortly after news of his company-supported lifestyle became public, the embattled CEO gave up many of his perks.

In stark contrast to the detractors, there were commentators who disagreed with the criticism of Welch and GE. Edwin A. Locke, then Professor Emeritus at the University of Maryland at College Park, said in Welch's defense that he should have answered critics by saying "I earned the benefits through decades of hard and successful work. I am proud of what I earned, and I intend to keep it."

Nearly a decade after former CEOs Kozlowski and Welch were harshly criticized for their executive perks, Kozlowski addressed the Welch controversy. In a letter written from his prison cell in upstate New York, Kozlowski said he knew Jack Welch. "He's a great business leader who was very lucky to have G.E. Capital during the booming days. Jack got away with less disclosure because he was Jack." Kozlowski added, "We modeled my compensation system and retention agreement after Jack's. It did not work out very well for me." Kozlowski compared their relative consequences and noted that "Jack said he was sorry he got piggy and all was forgiven. It must be good to be Jack Welch."[7]

Lavish executive perquisites did not end with Welch-era CEOs. Chief executives and other Named Executive Officers (NEOs) continue to receive perks and the goodies get bigger and better with time.[8] Publicly traded corporations are required to disclose to the U.S. Securities and Exchange Commission (SEC) and to shareholders the compensation paid to CEOs, CFOs, and other NEOs. A publicly traded corporation is a business organization that issues securities to the public. The securities are typically bonds, debt the company owes to investors, or shares of stock that give investors ownership interests in the corporation. A publicly traded corporation's stock is made available to the public through a stock exchange or in the over-the-counter market. Both GE and Tyco International were (and continue to be) publicly traded corporations—the stock of both trade on the New York Stock Exchange using ticker symbols GE and TYC respectively.[9]

The obvious advantage of being publicly traded is access to capital in amounts that are almost infinite so long as the investing public is willing to take a risk on the business. Along with the advantages come vastly increased reporting requirements and the burden of complying with thousands of state and federal securities regulations. A large number of these regulations require corporations to disclose financial and other significant information to the public so that investors can make educated judgments about buying securities.

Executive compensation is one of the many required disclosures and must be included in proxy statements corporations file annually with the SEC. In addition to salaries, bonuses, stock options, and performance-based payments, a corporation must disclose perquisites provided to its executives.[10] Even though the SEC requires disclosure of executive perquisites, the agency does not specifically define "perquisite." During its most recent update of the regulation, the SEC confirmed a continuing belief "that it is not appropriate . . . to define perquisites or personal benefits, given that different forms of these items continue to develop, and thus a definition would become outdated."[11] The SEC offers only that "perquisites" should be interpreted broadly and that the following guidelines be used in the determination of what should be disclosed:

> An item is not a perquisite or personal benefit if it is integrally and directly related to the performance of the executive's duties.
>
> An item is a perquisite or personal benefit if it confers a direct or indirect benefit that has a personal aspect, without regard to whether it may be provided for some business reason or for the convenience of the company, unless it is generally available on a non-discriminatory basis to all employees.[12]

Among the examples provided by the SEC of items considered perquisites and therefore must be disclosed are club memberships not used solely for business purposes, personal financial or tax advice, housing and relocation expenses, personal travel using company vehicles, and security provided at a personal residence.[13]

After being disclosed to the SEC and shareholders, executive perks are frequently examined by analysts, watchdog organizations, journalists, and others who trudge through proxy statements to ferret out "All Other Compensation,"[14] which is the category under which perks are disclosed.[15] Although these watchdogs, through the media, occasionally criticize elaborate perks granted to executives,[16] the attention hasn't shamed boards of directors into reducing the lavish benefits offered to C-level executives.

Perhaps corporations that provide generous perks to their executives are doing the right thing. Perquisites are arguably good investments and in shareholders' best interests. The most common justification voiced in favor of offering executive perquisites is the same core reason employers offer any type of employee benefit; executive perquisites allow a board of directors to recruit and retain the best talent, to attract and keep a CEO capable of growing a company as successfully as Jack Welch grew GE or as effectively as Dennis Kozlowski grew Tyco.[17] In addition to helping with recruitment and retention, perks like company cars, use of corporate jets, and administrative and personal assistants allow executives to use their valuable time more productively. Other perks, like an annual physical exam, the services of a physician, and security services are provided to protect the health and safety of executives, and benefits like financial planning and tax gross-ups ensure compliance by executives with state and federal regulatory requirements.[18]

In response to the financial crisis of 2008, the U.S. Congress passed in 2010 the Dodd-Frank Wall Street Reform and Consumer Protection Act (Dodd-Frank or the Act). Under Dodd-Frank, publicly traded corporations became subject to more rigorous disclosure mandates, including a requirement that executive pay be directly compared to the performance of the company. Another Dodd-Frank provision requires disclosure of executive compensation in comparison to the median salary of all other employees in the company. The Act also created a "say-for-pay" requirement under which corporations must allow their shareholders to vote at least once every three years on executive compensation. Although the results of shareholder voting are technically non-binding, boards of directors at even the largest organizations recognize it is patently unwise to award executive pay packages that shareholders do not support.[19]

Dodd-Frank was enacted to regulate the financial services sector, however the provisions related to executive compensation reach far beyond Wall Street. The desired effect of the enhanced disclosures required by Dodd-Frank is to provide additional information to shareholders and to promote shareholder engagement—to bolster basic corporate governance mechanisms. Even though sweeping legislation like Dodd-Frank creates expensive and burdensome compliance issues for publicly traded companies, perhaps the additional regulations will prevent another instance like Jack Welch and GE having to defend executive perquisites disclosed during a messy divorce and reduce the possibility of an executive like Dennis Kozlowski and a company like Tyco having to explain the CEO's luxury apartment during criminal trials. Compliance is expensive, but it is not nearly as costly as scandal, litigation, indictments, and loss of investor confidence.

*   *   *

Criticism of Kozlowski's purchase of the units at 950 Fifth Avenue grew exponentially when the media found out that, in addition to the multi-million dollar apartment, Kozlowski authorized the services of an interior designer to redecorate it. In more damning testimony during Kozlowski's second criminal trial, Kathy McRae testified that "Mr. Kozlowski had told me that there was going to be a cap of ... six million dollars for renovations and furniture for the apartment, and I kept a running total of what invoices were paid and what was left for a balance; and I got the invoices in the Executive Treasury and asked they be paid from a Tyco account."[20]

Kozlowski hired Seldom Scene Interiors of Nantucket to decorate the apartment.[21] The firm was owned by Wendy Valliere, a friend of Kozlowski's second wife

Karen. According to the testimony of several witnesses during Kozlowski's trials, Kozlowski and his wife were very friendly with Valliere, and the witnesses noted that Kozlowski used Valliere's firm for many decorating and renovation projects in several states over a number of years. When questioned about the expensive redecorating project during his second trial, Kozlowski insisted that renovations were necessary before he was able to use the apartment.[22] About hiring Valliere, Kozlowski said, "I hired someone I knew—someone from Nantucket," and he emphasized (about someone he once considered a friend), "I have not spoken to [Valliere] since."[23]

Cognitive psychologists have studied how a seemingly intelligent person like Dennis Kozlowski could misjudge the potential problems of hiring his wife's friend for a multi-million dollar project. Research has shown that risk-perception systems are affected by trust, and even intelligent people tend to minimize the assessed risk when dealing with those they trust. When the same people deal with individuals with whom no level of trust has been established, they tend to assess the risk as greater than it is in reality—they exaggerate the risk.[24] If Dennis Kozlowski had insisted on a more arm's-length relationship, if he had hired an unknown decorator, a decorator he didn't trust, perhaps he would have been more diligent in overseeing the project. Kozlowski's ability to accurately assess and manage the risks was clouded because he hired his wife's friend, because he hired someone he trusted. His use of Valliere in the Fifth Avenue redecorating project was one of many relationships of trust that became problematic for Kozlowski.

In retrospect, Kozlowski admitted that he made mistakes with the renovation. He said, "There were purchases that I would never have made, one of which was that damn shower curtain. No one in their right mind would pay $6,000 for a shower curtain." Kozlowski said he wanted a "corporate looking" apartment suitable for business meetings. "The apartment was off the beaten path. We were going to use it for meetings. We were going to buy companies there," he insisted.[25]

During his second trial, Kozlowski recounted the instructions he gave Valliere about the apartment. He said, "My instructions were to work with Tyco's facilities manager, a fellow by the name of John [Taylor], to coordinate with him and to call me when the apartment was habitable, when I could move in and use the apartment when I was in New York."[26] Neither Kozlowski nor his then wife Karen selected anything for the apartment during the renovation—not one piece of furniture, not one fixture. He left all of the decision-making to the decorator. In one of the hundreds of articles written in criticism of the adornment of the Tyco corporate apartment, a journalist coined as "Mogul style" the practice of providing CEOs with extravagant homes. In the same article, a New York interior designer who worked with high-end clients like Kozlowski said it was not unusual and in fact quite feasible for the rich to spend the kind of money that Tyco, at Kozlowski's direction, spent on the 950 Fifth Avenue apartment.[27]

Among the Mogul style design choices for the duplex were a $15,000 dog-shaped umbrella stand, a $6,300 sewing basket, a $17,000 traveling toilette box, a $2,200 gold-plated wastebasket, $2,900 worth of coat hangers, a $1,650 appointment book, a set of sheets that cost $5,900, a $445 pincushion, and the $6,000 shower curtain.[28] In the end, Tyco spent $11 million to redecorate the Fifth Avenue apartment—a budget-blowing expenditure approved by CEO Dennis Kozlowski.[29] He expressed strong feelings about the lavishly decorated duplex. "I could live comfortably on a 30-foot sailboat. That's how I'd like to live," Kozlowski explained. "I couldn't give a shit about the redecorating. I had no interest. I was busy running the company."[30]

He should have given a shit about the redecorating. His failure to oversee the project proved a costly mistake, ultimately far more detrimental to him than the $11,173,927 price tag.[31] The extravagant purchases for the Fifth Avenue apartment became public knowledge when unnamed sources revealed the list to *Wall Street Journal* reporters in August of 2002. In the resultant article, reporters Mark Maremont and Laurie P. Cohen cited as their sources "people investigating the company" and revealed the list of expensive furnishings purchased for the corporate apartment. In the same article, interior designer Wendy Valliere described the furnishings as "so mid-range compared to what a lot of people do."[32]

More than a month later, on September 10, 2002, Tyco filed a Form 8-K with the SEC in which the company chose to officially disclose the list of furnishings for the Fifth Avenue apartment.[33] Publicly traded corporations like Tyco use a Form 8-K to report to the SEC unscheduled or unexpected material events. Tyco's September 2002 8-K disclosed to the SEC, to shareholders, and to the public details of a corporate scandal unfolding inside the company—events that resulted in indictments that month of the company's former CEO Dennis Kozlowski, its then CFO Mark Swartz, and former Chief Corporate Counsel Mark Belnick. Tyco disclosed that "[t]he improper and unlawful conduct of Tyco's former CEO, CFO and Chief Corporate Counsel in enriching themselves at the expense of the Company with no colorable benefit to the Company has damaged Tyco. The amount of money improperly diverted by Tyco's former executives from the Company to themselves is very small in comparison with Tyco's total revenues and profits, but it is very large by any other relevant comparison; and the extent of the former executives' misconduct has harmed Tyco's reputation and credibility with investors, lenders, and others."[34]

The Board opted to disclose the list of purchases, noting that "in the interest of restoring confidence in the Company, the extent of the Company's disclosures in this filing will go beyond what the law requires, or what might ordinarily be disclosed in other circumstances."[35] The disclosures of what were non-material amounts—a $6,000 expenditure by a company with nearly $40 billion in annual revenue, an expenditure that was .00000015 percent of the company's income—was

questionable. Perhaps the extraordinary transparency, the disclosure of information not required of Tyco, caused an avoidable negative reaction. It may have
caused a damaging and intentionally induced overreaction in the market, which is
one of the reasons the SEC does not require disclosure of such items. Would Tyco
shareholders have been better served if the company didn't disclose those sensational but non-material expenditures in the September 2002 8-K? Or was absolute
transparency the right decision, especially after the information had been leaked to
the media a month earlier? Were Tyco shareholders entitled to know the types of
expenses CEO Dennis Kozlowski approved with the authority he was given by the
Tyco Board of Directors? Why didn't the 8-K disclose the $200 million spending
authority the Board had granted the CEO? Weren't Tyco shareholders entitled to
that information as well? Surely the Board, "in the interest of restoring confidence
in the Company," would not have *selectively* disclosed information in the 8-K.

Although the outrageous details disclosed in the 8-K temporarily affected the
value of Tyco stock, were embraced by the media, and used by Tyco, the Board of
Directors, and the Manhattan District Attorney to initiate assaults on Kozlowski,
Swartz, and Belnick, the opulent furnishings in the Fifth Avenue apartment were of
little concern in comparison to the other problems that snowballed out of control
after the 8-K was filed with the SEC.

FIVE

BEHIND THE ELEPHANT

Dennis Kozlowski began his business career in 1969 as an internal auditor with the SCM Corporation, first in New York City and then in Syracuse, New York. With more than three years of internal audit experience under his belt, Kozlowski left SCM and moved to Boston and into a second audit position with the Cabot Corporation. He spent the entirety of his career in what would be considered unglamorous businesses: SCM, Cabot, Nashua Corporation, and Tyco—no dot-coms, no sexy consumer goods, no Apples or Microsofts or hedge funds or investment banks.

The years Dennis Kozlowski worked for the Cabot Corporation were also the years he and first wife Angie became a family. They had two daughters; Cheryl was born in 1974 and Sandy in 1977. When Cheryl was born, the couple was living in Atkinson, a small town in New Hampshire near the Massachusetts state line. Kozlowski said he was traveling frequently, including several trips to Europe, which at the time were rare and very expensive. When he wasn't traveling, Kozlowski made the ninety-minute commute from Atkinson to Boston in a yellow 1973 Volkswagen Beetle. "A Super Beetle," he clarified. "This was during the years of the oil crisis," he said, explaining his rationale for purchasing the tiny vehicle, "when Ford and Carter were in the White House." Before he traded it, Kozlowski folded his six-foot two-inch frame into the yellow Super Beetle for more than 100,000 miles.[1]

On top of the three years he spent honing his auditing skills at SCM, Kozlowski earned another three years of internal audit experience at Cabot Corporation before he left the company in 1975.[2] Feeling the relatively new responsibility of supporting his young family, Kozlowski decided to make a move when he had the opportunity to become the Director of Internal Audit at Nashua Corporation in Nashua, New Hampshire.[3] He stayed with Nashua Corporation for less than a year and said, "I knew the day I started that it was a mistake." Kozlowski was manager of administration, which in reality was the job of cost-cutter; he was the ax man. "It was a financially difficult time for the company," he said, "and nobody liked to see me coming."[4] Kozlowski was dissatisfied with his role at Nashua Corporation so when a Massachusetts headhunting firm contacted him about an opportunity with a company called Tyco, he was more than willing to take a look.

In 1975, Tyco was a small company in Exeter, New Hampshire with between $15 and $20 million in annual revenue; it was smaller than any of the other organizations for which Kozlowski had worked since he graduated from Seton Hall University with a Bachelor's degree in accounting in 1968.[5] When during his second trial he was asked to describe the type of company Tyco was in 1975, Kozlowski said, "Tyco was a smaller company than Nashua, but had a far greater potential from what I saw."[6] Tyco was in search of an Assistant Comptroller, a position that, if offered and accepted, would have the internal audit function at Tyco reporting to Dennis Kozlowski. It was a position similar to the one he held at Nashua Corporation. During his Tyco interviews, Kozlowski met with Howard Hull, who was Vice President and Comptroller, with the Vice President of Finance, and Kozlowski met with Tyco's CEO Joe Gaziano. "In fact, we had a few meetings," Kozlowski recalled, "and subsequently they offered me a job as Assistant Comptroller and Director of Internal Audit at Tyco."[7] Dennis Kozlowski became a Tyco employee when he was twenty-eight years old. He noted that "[m]y starting salary because of my age was $28,000 a year."[8]

Kozlowski's career at Tyco began under the leadership of Joseph Gaziano, who was the company's third CEO. The company was founded in 1960 by Harvard PhD Arthur J. Rosenburg. In the beginning, the company operated as a research laboratory in Waltham, Massachusetts where Rosenburg did experimental work primarily in fulfillment of government contracts.[9] In 1962, two years after Rosenburg opened shop, Tyco was incorporated as Tyco, Inc. and two years later, in 1964, became a publicly traded corporation. The progress continued in 1965 when the company's name was changed to Tyco Laboratories, Inc. and in the same year, it acquired Mule Battery Manufacturing Company, the first of hundreds of companies it would acquire over the next several decades.[10] Seemingly setting the tone for his successors, Rosenburg began to aggressively grow the company through numerous acquisitions during the 1960s. By 1970, the company had grown significantly and was in need of restructuring, which is why the Tyco Board of Directors made a change in management, replacing the company's founder with Joshua M. Berman.[11]

At the time, Josh Berman was a member of the Tyco Board. He was also a practicing attorney; Berman was a partner in the Boston law firm Goodwin, Proctor & Hoar. Berman headed Tyco as both Chairman and CEO until April 1973, when Joseph P. Gaziano was named Tyco's President, CEO, and Chairman of the Board.[12]

Gaziano was a Massachusetts Institute of Technology graduate—a member of the class of 1956. Before heading Tyco, Gaziano was a Vice President at the Raytheon Company. He left Raytheon in 1967 to run Prelude Corporation, a Westport Point, Massachusetts company that operated deep-sea lobster boats. Gaziano became a legend in the commercial fishing industry when in 1971, he almost started a war with Russia over the destruction of equipment caused by Russian trawlers

fishing in the same waters on the continental shelf where large Prelude ships operated. Gaziano was beyond frustrated with the ongoing damage to the company's
gear, so he instructed captains of Prelude ships to keep logs of the Russians' de-
structive actions. Once he collected the captains' logs along with Coast Guard sur-
veillance of the Russian ships, Prelude filed an action in a United States District
Court in which the company sued the Russian government to recover damages to
Prelude equipment. According to Carlton "Cukie" Macomber, a company insider
in 1971, once the legal action was filed, the U.S. State Department immediately told
Gaziano, "We are in the middle of a Cold War and you are going to start a real one."
The Russian government did not respond immediately to Prelude's legal action,
so with an aggressive move that exemplified Gaziano's style, the company took a
second jab by placing a lien on the *Suleyman Stalskiy*, a Russian freighter that had
entered San Francisco Harbor. On June 9, 1971, U.S. Marshals seized the vessel and
held it in the harbor for six days—days during which, Macomber reported, "the
State Department became very frustrated with us."[13]

The seizure had the desired effect. Within days, limousines carrying Russian
delegates arrived in Westport Point; the Russian government came knocking at Joe
Gaziano's door. In its lawsuit, Prelude asked for $300,000 in damages. After days of
negotiations, the parties reached a settlement under which the Russian government
paid Prelude in excess of $80,000 for the damage caused to the company's equipment.
After the international incident was peaceably concluded, Gaziano contacted President Richard Nixon and began an effort that would become his legacy to the fishing
industry: work that resulted in a 200-mile zone around domestic shores that protects
U.S. commercial fishing vessels from encroachment by foreign fishing operations.[14]

Of his predecessor's face-off with the Russians, Dennis Kozlowski said, "That's
classic Joe."[15]

Gaziano's arrival at Tyco in 1973 triggered a decade of significant growth and
change for the company. Soon after Gaziano became CEO, Tyco stock was listed on
the New York Stock Exchange in early 1974 under the ticker symbol TYC.[16] Later
that same year, Gaziano followed Rosenburg's lead by growing Tyco through mergers and acquisitions, but he upped the stakes. Gaziano became known as one of the
first corporate raiders as he pursued hostile takeovers of several companies during
his tenure as Tyco's CEO.

Kozlowski said he accepted the position offered by Tyco in 1975 because of
the company's dynamic CEO.[17] He was impressed with Gaziano—his background
heading the missile program at Raytheon, his commanding presence, and his plans
to grow Tyco. "Joe Gaziano was a ballsy guy," he said, "and I liked him. I don't know
how well he could read a financial statement, but he was smart and he had great
instincts."[18] Gaziano's plan to grow Tyco to a $1 billion company primarily through
acquisitions also drew Kozlowski to the company. During his criminal trial in 2005,
Kozlowski was asked to describe Tyco at the time he joined the company. He provided a vivid picture:

Well, way back then Tyco was a very small company. It did about 20 million dollars in sales and had about ten or 15 different businesses. And the businesses did anything from using nuclear technology to measure stress on helicopter rotor blades to making [quartz] chips for old time radios before you had transfusers [sic] and other products. It made honing [sic] devices for submarine torpedoes. It was a solar energy company. It was really the spin-off of some really bright people that had more of a scientific background and they would start-up some of these businesses and try to create them into commercial businesses. Joe Gaziano, who was the new CEO at the time, had a focus to develop some of these businesses into good long-term businesses which would be able to sustain worldwide competition. So he had a big time vision. It was an exciting time and he asked me to sign up and be part of that team.[19]

Kozlowski described an organization of approximately 2,000 employees that operated almost exclusively in the United States. He noted that the company's name was Tyco Laboratories, even though the company neither owned nor operated any laboratories at that time.[20]

Not long after he joined Tyco, Kozlowski was moved from internal audit to operations, a path that one former Director said placed Kozlowski "in the bowels of the operating businesses for many years" as he worked his way up the corporate ladder.[21] Kozlowski became a Tyco loyalist and by all accounts, he knew every business the company operated. The depth and breadth of his knowledge of Tyco operations was one of the reasons Dennis Kozlowski was widely respected by customers, suppliers, and the management of companies he acquired.[22] Kozlowski said it would have been impossible for him to lead Tyco and successfully acquire hundreds of companies had he not understood the businesses.[23]

During his second trial, Kozlowski described the twenty-seven years he spent with Tyco and the path that ultimately led to the chief executive's position. He spent four years at Grinnell in Tyco's fire protection and prevention division, beginning in 1977. He was first an Assistant Comptroller, after which he was promoted to Comptroller, and then Kozlowski was named CFO of Grinnell.[24] From there, Kozlowski was moved to Ludlow, a $27 million acquisition Joe Gaziano closed in 1981. Ludlow Corporation manufactured packaging materials and was not operating efficiently when Tyco added it to the growing conglomerate. Ludlow was the second acquisition that moved Tyco into the packaging business. Two years earlier, Gaziano arranged the acquisition of Armin Corporation, a company that manufactured polyethylene films used in packaging. Armin was immediately accretive to earnings, but Ludlow needed help. So Gaziano moved Kozlowski from Grinnell and named him CFO of Ludlow in 1981, where and when Kozlowski inherited the job of managing the messy integration of Gaziano's hostile takeover.[25]

The year after Kozlowski began his work at Ludlow, Tyco suffered a significant loss. After a decade of bold, aggressive leadership as the company's CEO, Joseph

Gaziano died suddenly on December 17, 1982 after being diagnosed with a rare cancer of the heart. He was only forty-seven years old at the time of his death. In response to the unexpected circumstances, the Tyco Board of Directors chose Gaziano's successor; the Board tapped John Fort III to serve as Tyco's fourth CEO. Fort had been with Tyco since 1974. At the time of Gaziano's death in 1982, Fort was Senior Vice President of Operations, a position Gaziano had placed him in two years earlier.[26]

By all accounts, Joe Gaziano was a big personality. He was a manager known for engaging in hostile takeovers, he was outspoken and aggressive, and in a move that typified his bravado, Gaziano sued the Russian government during the Cold War. He was bold, fearless, and as Kozlowski described him, "ballsy." As part of his total compensation as CEO, Gaziano reportedly enjoyed a number of lavish executive perquisites; he had access to company cars and planes, and he lived in expensive corporate homes and apartments.[27] He was said to have an extravagant and luxurious lifestyle. That's how Tyco's Board of Directors compensated the Chief Executive Officer when Dennis Kozlowski joined the company.

As compared to Gaziano's swing-for-the-fences style, John Fort was staid. Fort was known as a cost cutter and he did not insist on or negotiate as part of his compensation package the executive perks his predecessor enjoyed. Soon after he was named CEO, Fort reportedly disposed of Joe Gaziano's perks; he sold the corporate planes, houses, and apartments, and reduced the size of corporate operations.[28] Under Fort's leadership, Tyco made more deliberate and often smaller acquisitions. However, not all of the acquisitive growth during the decade John Fort was CEO was accomplished via small deals. In 1987, Tyco acquired Allied Pipe & Tube Corporation, and the following year, the company acquired for the sizeable cost of $350 million the Mueller Company, a well-established water and gas pipe manufacturing company.[29]

Kozlowski said that during the 1980s, Tyco was buying a lot of pipe and he believed the company would profit from vertical integration of the supply chain.[30] For that reason, he spearheaded the acquisitions of Allied Pipe & Tube and Mueller during Fort's tenure as CEO. In 1987, after Kozlowski became a member of the Board of Directors, he became even more involved in the company's corporate operations and strategic decision-making.

When Fort was CEO, he named thirty-six year old Dennis Kozlowski President of Ludlow—in 1982.[31] Kozlowski described his effectiveness at Ludlow during his second criminal trial. He said:

> When I first got to Ludlow we were break even or maybe earning a little bit of money. It was—we had a lot of work to do. We had a number of divisions that were losing money. A number of operations that were not functioning very well. People there, the morale was pretty low in the organization. They went through this lengthy takeover, but by the end of my stay at Ludlow, by putting in pay for

performance systems, good incentive systems, motivating the management with these types of systems, which I thought were key—one of the key things to running a business, Ludlow became quite profitable."[32]

Because of his success at Ludlow, Fort placed Kozlowski at the head of other Tyco divisions. As President of Grinnell, for example, Kozlowski transformed in a very short time frame a company that was barely breaking even into a profitable one, with annual revenue of over $100 million.[33] Kozlowski's skill as a manager took him to the head of three of the four operating businesses[34] before he was named President and Chief Operating Officer of Tyco in 1989 at the age of forty-three.[35] By the end of the 1980s, John Fort was leading the company with Kozlowski pushing him from behind. Robert A. G. Monks, a Director at the time, said that Fort was CEO but that "Dennis was doing all the hard work."[36]

The somewhat frenetic collection of businesses under the Tyco corporate umbrella at the time of Joe Gaziano's death had transformed into four cohesive operating divisions: electrical and electronic components, healthcare and specialty products, fire and security services, and flow control products.[37]

* * *

During the 1970s and 1980s, Dennis Kozlowski became a manager by running businesses in all of Tyco's operating divisions.[38] During his years in the trenches, he honed his management skills and his successes solidified his belief in a few strongly held strategies for achieving organizational goals: hire the right people, motivate them with pay-for-performance compensation programs, decentralize control, allow only minimal bureaucracy, engage in no hostile takeovers, and always look for ways to "make more for less."

Kozlowski admittedly worked almost nonstop for most of his life. His increasingly busy schedule and the demanding positions he held as he built his career at Tyco required frequent travel that kept him from his family about eighty percent of the time.[39] Unfortunately, his marriage to Angie Suarez Kozlowski didn't survive. Kozlowski and his wife separated in 1995 and they divorced in 2000 after twenty-eight years of marriage. Corporate governance guru Robert A. G. Monks sat on the Tyco Board of Directors from 1984 until 1993, the years Dennis Kozlowski climbed the rungs of the corporate ladder until he reached the top. Monks said he's never known a CEO of a large corporation whose marriage wasn't negatively affected by the demands of the position. "Dennis was married to Tyco," he explained.[40]

Of Kozlowski's ascent in the company, Monks said, "For years, Dennis was the guy who ran around behind the elephant. He worked more and harder than anyone else. Dennis deserved to be CEO. He earned it."[41]

SIX

BECOMING CEO

Both Ralph Waldo Emerson and Theodore Roosevelt are attributed with saying "big jobs usually go to the men who prove their ability to outgrow small ones." Dennis Kozlowski personified the sentiment. During seventeen years with Tyco in positions of increasing responsibility, Kozlowski rose to each challenge. And he didn't just do what was expected of him. He worked more and harder and produced extraordinary results. By 1992, he had outgrown all of the jobs at Tyco but one.

L. Dennis Kozlowski was named CEO of Tyco International Ltd. in July of 1992. He was forty-five years old. He became Chairman of the Tyco Board of Directors six months later, in January of 1993.[1]

* * *

The day the Tyco Board of Directors named Kozlowski CEO, the Directors and then, and soon-to-be former, CEO John Fort were in the company's offices in Exeter, New Hampshire, as was Dennis Kozlowski. All were present to attend a scheduled Board meeting. A few weeks earlier while working in his Exeter office, Kozlowski received a telephone call from Philip Hampton, a member of Tyco's Board of Directors. Hampton asked Kozlowski to meet him to discuss the Board's plan to make a change in leadership. He wanted to talk to Kozlowski about becoming the next CEO. "I couldn't get to New York fast enough," Kozlowski recalled when years later he testified during his second criminal trial about how he became Tyco's CEO. "I met with Phil in his office [in New York,] and Phil said that John Fort has typically said he wanted to be the CEO for about ten years. The Board felt they were going to take him up on his ten year offer and it was time for a transition or change. I was his candidate and I was the person he would like to see become the Chairman and CEO of Tyco." The morning meeting stretched into lunch, so Kozlowski and Hampton continued their discussion over seafood at Oceana in Manhattan where Kozlowski shared with Hampton his vision for the company. As their meeting concluded, Hampton asked Kozlowski to contact Directors Joshua Berman and Robert A. G. Monks, both of whom wanted to have similar discussions with him. In the days soon after, Kozlowski met Josh Berman for Chinese food at Chin Chin in Manhattan and then he made a quick trip to Washington, DC to meet with Bob Monks. Near Monks's office in Georgetown, the two men ate Italian food as Kozlowski completed his third interview for the position of CEO.[2]

The three Directors shared with Kozlowski the Board's desire to make a change at the top and of plans to replace John Fort at the next Board meeting. Kozlowski said, "You may read that John Fort resigned. He didn't. He was fired."[3] In Fort's telling, he retired from the position of CEO.

John Franklin Fort III joined Tyco in 1974, the year before Kozlowski was hired by the company. Although their careers took the two men to the same position, Fort's background was significantly different than Kozlowski's.

* * *

568 SOUTH 10TH STREET

The Fifth Avenue apartment, the $6,000 shower curtain, living among Manhattan's elite—Dennis Kozlowski's lifestyle as an adult bore no resemblance to his childhood or to his parents' lives. Even though he had only modest material comforts when he was growing up, Kozlowski spoke fondly of his childhood. He said, "[W]e were poor. We just didn't know we were poor." The Kozlowski children had happy lives in Newark, New Jersey. Dennis Kozlowski and his younger sisters Joyce and Joan didn't know there were people with far more than they found in their cozy apartment in the three story building at 568 South 10th Street.

The Kozlowski family of five lived in the four narrow rooms of a railroad style apartment on the second floor of a six family apartment house. Even though both apartments had narrow rooms, the one on South 10th Street was nothing like the luxury Tyco duplex across the street from Central Park. The front room of the Newark apartment was a kitchen where the coal stove that heated the apartment was located. Coal was delivered to the basement of the apartment house and Kozlowski remembered that, to fuel the less-than-efficient stove, he and his father shoveled coal and brought it up to the kitchen during the cold months of the year. The back room of the string of four rooms in the apartment was the living room. A half century later, Kozlowski recalled that "the living room was closed off during the winter because the heat from the kitchen at the front of the apartment didn't reach the back room." The apartment didn't have a water heater, so for baths and dishes, water had to be heated on the stove.

In front of the living room was the bedroom in which the three children slept. Dennis Kozlowski had a cot and his two sisters shared a bed. This sleeping arrangement provided him little privacy. Perhaps because he had little alone time in his parents' home, Kozlowski came to value privacy as an adult—he craved it. He said he spent most of his waking hours as a child outside the apartment "because of the lack of space."

Robert "Bobby" Pastore, a lifelong friend of Kozlowski's, also grew up on South 10th Street in Newark. The Pastores lived across the street from the Kozlowski family. Even though he was four years Kozlowski's senior, Pastore remembered that he and Dennis Kozlowski, along with the other boys in the neighborhood, played stick ball, marbles, and hide-and-seek. Pastore described the neighborhood of Polish, Irish, and Italian families as a good place to grow up. "South 10th Street in Newark, New Jersey is now very rough," Pastore explained, "but it was not rough back when we were kids. It was a good place to grow up. We walked to grammar school and we played in the street." Pastore painted an idyllic picture of life on South 10th Street in the 1950s. "Dennis' parents and mine were good friends and like most people of their day, worked hard to make a better life for them as well as for us."[4]

The Kozlowski family had dinner together every evening at 5:00 pm. His mother Agnes Kozell Kozlowski cooked for the family seven days a week. "My mom was a good cook," Kozlowski said with conviction. She shopped at the many specialty shops in the neighborhood and each week, she went to the butcher shop and placed an order that was delivered to the apartment on Friday. She also shopped at the neighborhood bakery and fish shop. Kozlowski remembered his mother preparing short ribs, stew, and Polish food like pierogies. His favorite dinner was pot roast and Kozlowski said if his mother made something he didn't like, he gave it to the family dog. "Skippy was a mutt," he said. "We got him at a pet store around the corner." In the evening, the family gathered in the kitchen around an off-white Formica table, each taking his or her assigned seat. Over dinner, the family talked about the day. "Everything happened around the dinner table," Kozlowski recalled. "On Sunday, we had dinner right after church. Then Sunday night was sandwiches— mom didn't have to cook on Sunday evenings."

As a child, Kozlowski developed a lifelong love of baseball, no doubt encouraged by his father Leo Kozlowski, who played minor league ball as a young man. Both were die-hard Yankees fans. Kozlowski discovered another passion when he was a youngster. He fell in love with airplanes. "My parents used to take us to the Newark airport to watch the planes land," he said fondly. "When Uncle Mike flew in from Detroit on props planes, we could walk out as he was deplaning. I remember getting on the plane and thinking it was so cool." Kozlowski read everything about planes that he could find. "I read about the *Spirit of St. Louis* when I was in grammar school and I pictured myself in the cockpit with Charles Lindbergh as he fought off sleep over the Atlantic on his flight from New York to Paris. I read the history of planes that were built in WWI and WWII. I was fascinated with how they operated," he said. "Aviation was far more complex then," he explained. "There was nothing electronic. It took more intellect." Kozlowski flew for the first time at age eighteen when he traveled with a fraternity brother from Newark to Miami,

Florida on a Cessna 150. Kozlowski's love of flying endured. He piloted airplanes and helicopters throughout his adult life and estimated that he had over 10,000 hours in the air.

Dennis Kozlowski was a city boy and he enjoyed growing up in an ethnic urban neighborhood. However, Kozlowski was not a sophisticated or street smart kid. He described himself as an innocent Catholic boy who was naïve about the world. To illustrate, Kozlowski described his first date. "My seventh grade teacher was pretty nice," he said. "She tried to fix me up with a sixth grader named Lorraine. I didn't act on my teacher's suggestion very quickly, but I finally asked Lorraine to a dance when I was in the eighth grade and she was in seventh grade." Kozlowski walked with Lorraine to the dance where he spent the evening with his friends and she with her girl friends. "My first date was walking a girl three blocks to the school and not dancing with her," he laughed.

As a teenager, Kozlowski left behind the strict Felician nuns at his grammar school, Sacred Heart, and attended public high school. He went to West Side High School in Newark where his history teacher, Mr. Kresfeld, had a big impact on his life. "Mr. Kresfeld oversaw the debate team. I often sparred with him in class so he put me on the team," Kozlowski said. "In class, he asked questions that required an extra step of reasoning. I was the only one in class answering his questions." Kozlowski spent a lot of time practicing his debate skills until he could effectively argue either side of any issue. Eventually, Mr. Kresfeld made Kozlowski the head of the debate team. "He told me I was smart and capable," Kozlowski recalled. "He told me I was exceptionally smart. He was the first person to ever tell me that."

Kozlowski was often bored in school so he kept extra books under his desk. "I read as the other students caught up," he recalled. For as long as he could remember, reading was one of his greatest joys. "When I shared a bedroom with Joyce and Joan, after my sisters went to sleep, I used a pen light to read on my cot," he said. He liked to read biographies; he read about individuals who did great things with their lives and he read about inventors. "I liked to read about exceptional people," he explained. "Like Jackie Robinson, Dwight Eisenhower, and Charles Lindberg." Kozlowski's love of biographies grew in adulthood. During the years he was incarcerated, Kozlowski read hundreds of life stories about people who did anything from ending the Civil War to surviving weeks in a life raft in the Pacific Ocean during WWII to blowing a call in the ninth inning that ruined a pitcher's perfect game.

Even though he was a voracious reader and gifted student, college was not a certainty for Dennis Kozlowski. "My dad encouraged me to go," he said, "but my mom thought I should get a civil service job or join the military. She was more concerned about job security than education." Neither of Kozlowski's parents attended college and his dad didn't even graduate from high school. Kozlowski said both of his parents were intelligent, just not highly educated. As he recalled conversations he had with them, Kozlowski said, "[M]y parents pushed me to get a government job with security and a pension. They didn't encourage me to do big things or great things with my life."

Kozlowski said he parented differently and encouraged his daughters to pursue whatever they loved, but admitted that he didn't always know what those things were. "I pushed them toward business," he admitted, "because that was my thing."

"I grew up with nothing. I swore I would give my children a better education than I had," he said. "I thought with my hard working genes and a better education, they could do even more than I did."

As his high school graduation neared, Kozlowski interviewed with the Federal Bureau of Investigation (FBI) in a bureau location above the post office in Newark. Leo Kozlowski was a New Jersey public service transit system investigator. He also had a private detective business. Through his work, Leo had friends in the FBI, which is how his son got the interview. Dennis Kozlowski was offered a job as an office worker and was told that if he worked during the day and went to college at night, he could become an agent. For that reason, Kozlowski limited his college applications to universities in New Jersey. "I applied to night school and I also applied to go during the day," he explained. "When I was accepted, I thought it would be better to attend full time because of the draft." Kozlowski decided on Seton Hall, a Catholic university in South Orange, New Jersey. "I went to Seton Hall because it was only four or five miles from home," Kozlowski said of his choice. "I lived at home and usually rode my motorcycle to campus."[5]

Kozlowski worked between thirty and forty hours a week while he was a full-time college student. He paid his own tuition, which he remembered as approximately $700 a semester—$1,400 a year. More than forty years after he graduated from Seton Hall, Kozlowski's memory about his hard-earned tuition payments was surprisingly accurate. According to U.S. Department of Education statistics, the average tuition for private universities from 1964 to 1968, the years Kozlowski attended Seton Hall, was $1,414 per year.[6] Kozlowski also had to pay for the books required in his classes; he always bought used text books. On top of the funds needed for tuition and books, Kozlowski had to earn enough to pay his parents rent while he was in college. "It was important to my mother that I paid room and board while living at home," he explained.[7]

During his college years, Kozlowski had several jobs. He waited tables and he worked at a car wash. He also had a job working for pharmacist Frank Lewis at a drug store in Newark. Kozlowski considered Lewis a significant influence in his life. "He pushed me to do well academically," Kozlowski recalled. "He challenged my ideas about what I wanted to do and who I wanted to be." Kozlowski said Lewis brought discipline into his life. "He taught me to be proactive in the store," he recalled. "He taught me to sell, he taught me to think, he pushed me, and he became a valued mentor."

In addition to his jobs waiting tables, washing cars, and working at the pharmacy, Kozlowski played guitar in a band. He learned to play the guitar when he was twelve or thirteen years old, however the guitar was not the first musical instrument he mastered. Kozlowski first learned to play the accordion. There were many Polish-American families in his neighborhood and as a result, many children in his school played the accordion, which is why Kozlowski picked up the polka-band essential. "But I liked the Ventures," he explained, "so I switched to the guitar and it was a fairly easy transition. The music reads the same, the chords are the same, plus the guitar was much easier to carry around. And of course, the guitar is much cooler." Kozlowski's instinct about the coolness of the guitar was confirmed in 2013 by two independent studies conducted in France and Israel and published in *Psychology of Music* and *Letters on Evolutionary Behavioral Science,* respectively. The studies showed definitively that women are more attracted to a man when he is holding a guitar.

When the French and Israeli studies appeared in U.S. news outlets, late night television host Jimmy Fallon shared results of the research in his monologue and said, "a new study found that women think men holding a guitar are more attractive, even if they're not playing it." Fallon continued, "In a related story, guys with an accordion will die alone."[8]

Kozlowski organized a band when he was still in high school. His neighbor Stas Polakowski was a good drummer, his friend Walter Sumner was a good electric accordion player and keyboardist, and his friend Eddie Betz was a good woodwind player and according to Kozlowski, the most talented musician in the group. "We practiced at the Polish-American Falcons—a private club," he said. "They had a hall with a bar and a restaurant and we practiced on weekends when the hall wasn't booked. People heard us practice and hired us. We also played in the bar on Friday evenings—for tips."

Kozlowski played with the same band members through college. "I was the least talented musician," he said, "but the only one capable of getting bookings." The band played high school and college dances, weddings, at bar and bat mitzvahs, and in clubs. "We could play any kind of music—polka or rock 'n roll or Jewish music," Kozlowski said of *The Hi-Tones.* "We used fake books with all kinds of music. We practiced before events and learned how to play the music that had been requested."

During college Kozlowski met Gary Lewis, the son of his boss Frank Lewis, and the two became friends. "Gary was a very good saxophone player," Kozlowski said, "so I brought him to practice with the band." Kozlowski took some heat from the members of the Polish-American Falcons for bringing an African-American man into the club. "I didn't know how to handle it," Kozlowski said. "Gary was my friend and I looked up to Frank Lewis. He was smart and educated and he was African-American. I guess I didn't think it was a problem."

When Kozlowski started college in the fall of 1964, he decided to major in history because he loved the history classes he took in high school. However, as do many college students, Kozlowski changed his major at the end of his freshman year at Seton Hall. He tried out several majors until he eventually landed in the college of business where he decided to study accounting. "I started thinking about my future and I knew I was going to need a job," he said. "The hottest recruitment on campus was for accounting students." Of his pragmatic decision, Kozlowski explained, "I was living at home, working two jobs to pay for school, and I was living in the metropolitan New York area. I picked up the paper and there were hundreds and hundreds of entry level accounting jobs." During his junior year, Kozlowski got his first business experience when he worked for six weeks at Tungsall Electronics in Newark. It was the first in the string of positions that would ultimately lead him to that of Tyco's CEO.[9]

Dennis Kozlowski graduated from Seton Hall in 1968 with a Bachelor of Science degree in accounting. When Kozlowski attended Seton Hall, the university was an all male school and the young men were required to wear jackets and ties to classes. The university became co-ed in the fall of 1968, just after Kozlowski graduated. He admitted that during his four years of college, he didn't spend much time studying. "I studied as much as I could," Kozlowski said. "It was a very busy four years." Even though much of his time was spent working in the drug store and hustling gigs for the band, Kozlowski found time to join a fraternity at Seton Hall; he was a member of Delta Sigma Delta. "My social life revolved around the fraternity," he said. "We had a Saturday night party where we all brought our girlfriends. That was my only social life. The rest of my time was spent working and going to school."[10]

JOHN FRANKLIN FORT III

Kozlowski's predecessor at the head of Tyco grew up very differently than he did. John Fort's great-grandfather, John Franklin Fort, was the thirty-third Governor of New Jersey (1908–1911). Fort's gubernatorial term left a legacy of "moral rectitude, honesty and hard work . . . [d]uring a period in New Jersey history when corruption and an arrogant disregard for the commonwealt [sic] characterized government. . . ." Despite his honorable reputation and his work ethic, Governor Fort was criticized for both his policies and his performance. The criticism was not unlike that directed toward many leaders and seemed to center on Governor Fort's ineffectiveness and inability to be all things to all people. In his later years, Fort expressed disappointment in himself; he had hoped to accomplish great things as Governor and lamented because his achievements fell short. Former Governor Fort explained by telling the story of a little girl who asked her mother the difference between hope and expectation. "Well," said the mother, "I hope to see your father in Heaven, but I do not expect to."[11]

In addition to his lineage, the Governor's great-grandson came to Tyco with impressive credentials. He earned an undergraduate degree in aeronautical engineering from Princeton University and a Master's degree in industrial management from MIT, the alma mater of his predecessor Joe Gaziano. Fort began working for Simplex Wire and Cable Company in Cambridge, Massachusetts as a part-time production control clerk while he was a student at MIT and he continued with the company after completing his graduate degree. His initial assignment was at a factory in New Hampshire where the company produced underwater cable for the U.S. Navy. Fort quickly rose through the ranks at Simplex and eventually became Vice President and General Manager, positions he earned and held between 1966 and 1974. Under Fort's leadership, annual sales doubled to $12 million.[12]

When the company was sold to Tyco in 1974, Fort stayed on after the acquisition and for six years, he served as President of Simplex Wire and Cable, the company then operating as a Tyco subsidiary. In 1980, Fort was promoted to Tyco's Senior Vice President of Operations; with the new rank came a move to Tyco corporate headquarters. Two years later, Fort was named Chairman and CEO of Tyco after Joe Gaziano's sudden death in 1982. Fort served as CEO for ten years until Kozlowski succeeded him in 1992.[13]

*　*　*

Ten years seemed to be the unofficial term limit for Tyco CEOs. Gaziano served as CEO from 1972 until his death in 1982. John Fort was Tyco's CEO from 1982 until he was displaced by Dennis Kozlowski in 1992. And Kozlowski headed the company from 1992 until he was indicted by the Manhattan District Attorney on sales tax charges and fired by the Board of Directors in June of 2002. The Tyco Board named John Fort interim CEO during the summer of 2002, but he was quickly replaced by Edward Breen, who left his post as President and Chief Operating Officer (COO) of Motorola to take Tyco's top position in 2002. Breen had been Tyco's CEO for almost exactly ten years when he retired in September of 2012.

After his retirement, Breen was criticized when his $150 million golden parachute was disclosed in Tyco's proxy filed with the Securities and Exchange Commission in January of 2013.[14] Breen received ironically generous compensation and perks from Tyco during the decade he occupied the Chief Executive's Office. It was ironic because Breen played the role of redeemer who came to Tyco and righted the company after a very costly scandal, the heart of which was excessive executive compensation. In fiscal year 2012 alone, Breen's compensation was more than $23 million. In 2011, Breen pocketed more than $20 million. While the scandal was still ongoing, Breen was publicly criticized when the company disclosed payments of more than $420,000 for his and his special advisor's personal use of company aircraft in 2004. The proxy disclosing Breen's expensive executive perquisites was filed in January of 2005, just as the second trial of Tyco's former CEO and CFO was beginning in a courtroom in Manhattan—the two former executives were being tried for using unauthorized and excessive compensation and perks to support their lavish lifestyles.[15]

*   *   *

During the decade John Fort headed Tyco, he promoted Kozlowski multiple times. First, Fort named Kozlowski President of Ludlow Corporation and then placed him at the head of Grinnell. Fort clearly had confidence in Kozlowski's abilities as Ludlow and Grinnell were Tyco's two largest businesses at the time. During Fort's tenure as CEO, Kozlowski joined the Board of Directors in 1987, and he was named President and COO of Tyco in 1989. Years later, when testifying in Kozlowski's second criminal trial, John Fort said of his relationship with Kozlowski, "We worked very closely together. He was by far the best manager we had in the company, and had a lot to do with the success we had in the 10 years I was CEO." Fort praised Kozlowski's performance, testifying that "he was extremely competent. His financial skills was [sic] excellent. What was really excellent was his ability to look at the financial data and take very sound operating moves based on it. His analysis was excellent."[16]

Fort characterized his exit from the CEO's office quite differently than Kozlowski described it. Although Kozlowski stated unequivocally that Fort was fired by the Board of Directors, Fort said under oath, "I ran the company until I retired in 1992 as Chairman and Chief Executive Officer." However, multiple sources confirmed that, on the day the Board replaced him, Fort was taken by surprise, became irate, and demanded that the company buy back all of the Tyco stock he owned at the time, which Kozlowski, as the new CEO, agreed to do. After insisting that the company buy all of his Tyco shares, Fort remained on the Board—an olive branch extended by Kozlowski and the Board to sooth a very angry John Fort. Kozlowski said he didn't want to damage the company by allowing Fort's ouster to appear ugly. Kozlowski was strenuously advised that it was in Tyco's and his own best interests for Fort to sever all connections to Tyco and that Kozlowski should insist that he do so. But instead, Kozlowski acquiesced to Fort's desire to stay. He said, "I screwed that up." Kozlowski allowed Fort to hold a seat on the Board and to retain an office at Tyco. Kozlowski characterized his decision to allow Fort to remain on the Board and in his office at Tyco corporate headquarters as one of the worst decisions of his career. Kozlowski said, "John Fort, the former CEO who the board fired, wanted the job back after I grew the company for 10 years," something in retrospect he evaluated as a "BIG MISTAKE."[17]

In Kozlowski's telling, Fort was not privy to plans to replace him, but news of the Board's desire to make a change in the summer of 1992 reached Fort before the scheduled Board meeting. In the weeks preceding the meeting, Fort was reportedly away on vacation and thus absent from the corporate offices as changes were contemplated. Kozlowski recalled that Tyco Director Phil Hampton was also vacationing in the summer of 1992. By chance, Hampton found himself on the same cruise as Merrill Lynch analyst Carol Neves. "Phil probably had a couple of scotches and inadvertently talked to Carol about firing Fort," Kozlowski speculated. Upon learning that the Tyco Board intended to remove Fort, Neves called her professional contact and good friend Irving Gutin.

Irving Gutin was with Tyco for many years, and he held several high-level positions including head of mergers and acquisitions and head of investor relations; he was a Senior Vice President. Like Fort, Gutin became part of the Tyco conglomerate as part and parcel of an acquisition. Gaziano brought Gutin into the company during the $27 million Armin Corporation acquisition in September of 1979. Kozlowski said that Gutin, whom he described as loyal to John Fort, confronted him with the information he learned from Neves. As Kozlowski recalled the awkward conversation, he said, "I told Irving 'You heard something you shouldn't have heard. Sit on it.'"

Gutin disregarded Kozlowski's suggestion; he didn't sit on the information. Instead, he tracked down Fort, who had just returned from vacation, and shared the rumored news of the Board's plan to replace him. Not surprisingly, Fort questioned Kozlowski about the rumor he heard from Irving Gutin, who heard it from Carol Neves, who heard it from Phil Hampton. When Fort asked if he knew what the Board was planning, Kozlowski played dumb and told Fort he wasn't certain what was happening. A few days later at the board meeting, the rumor became reality; John Fort was out and Kozlowski was named his successor. Kozlowski said, "I remember the day of the meeting; John came out of the boardroom after speaking with the Directors and he asked me to go in."[18]

Once Kozlowski was in the room, the Directors presented him the opportunity to take the helm as Tyco's CEO. When they crafted their initial offer to Kozlowski, members of the Compensation Committee planned to cut by about $100,000 the salary Kozlowski was already making as President and COO. In lieu of a more lucrative salary, the Committee offered a package of performance-based compensation—incentives paid through the use of bonuses and grants of restricted shares that vested only if performance goals were met. Kozlowski's pay, specifically the pay-for-performance provisions of his compensation agreement with Tyco, became the basis of charges included in the Manhattan DA's 2002 indictment, and his compensation was the central issue of his criminal trials in 2003 and 2005.

In his trial testimony, Kozlowski explained his negotiations with the Board in July of 1992. He told the jury about the inclusion of bonuses and restricted shares in his compensation package, about his history of advocating and using incentive pay programs as he rose through the ranks at Tyco, and about the creation of a three-pronged compensation system:

The Board elected me the Chief Executive Officer of Tyco. . . . After that there became a question of compensation for me as the CEO. In the past John Fort's compensation was . . . his salary, bonus, but he also got restricted shares. . . . In John Fort's case, his restricted shares were vested over time. So he would be given a grant of shares [and] vesting would take place simply by being there. In our case, since I had come up with pay for performance throughout the operating divisions at Tyco and all the businesses I worked in, Ludlow or Grinnell, whatever the business was, we focused on pay for performance and I suggested to the Board that . . . I would like to have the upside of pay for performance and the downside, you know, if it doesn't work well, but I suggested to the Board that we institute a system where my restricted shares would vest based upon the formula on performance. That was worked out with the Compensation Committee at Tyco, and that gave rise to what developed as the three prong effort of our compensation system. An increase in earnings per share earned us stock, or in some cases share equivalents. An increase in our operating cash flow earned us cash bonuses and an increase in our earnings earned us a cash bonus. Initially that cash bonus was capped, but that was subsequently changed.

*   *   *

On the day Kozlowski was tapped to be CEO, he didn't immediately pocket the key to the Chief Executive's Office. Upon hearing that the proposed compensation package included a reduction in his salary, Kozlowski's cool reaction to the Board was "I need to think about it." As Kozlowski looked at the Directors after they proffered the Chief Executive's position, he thought, "what are my options if I decline the offer? Can I stay with the company or will I have to leave?" Unbeknownst to the Board, Kozlowski had other job opportunities available to him at the time. He was prepared to leave Tyco—and a reduction in his salary was not an enticement for him to stay. The Board had to come up with a more attractive offer before Kozlowski would agree to serve as CEO.

About an hour after Kozlowski hedged in response to the initial offer, the Board agreed to increase his salary and to further sweeten the deal, offered additional performance-based compensation. Kozlowski explained, "I was okay with the offer. I felt confident I could achieve the performance goals."[19]

Years later, Kozlowski pondered the discussions about compensation he had with the Directors on the day he became CEO. He said of the Board's lowball offer, "I don't know why they tried to cut my salary when making me CEO. The company was doing well, we were not struggling." With the wisdom of twenty years' hindsight, Kozlowski wondered if the initial offer he received in July of 1992 was an early indication of a dysfunctional Board.[20]

Robert A. G. Monks, one of the three Directors who interviewed Kozlowski for the CEO's slot, served on Tyco's Board from 1984 until 1993 and was connected to

Tyco from the company's inception—Tyco's incorporation documents were processed through the law firm where Monks practiced in 1962. Monks is a Harvard Law School alumnus and a respected expert and prolific author on a number of corporate governance issues. Long after both men's relationships with Tyco had ended and years since the two had been in contact, Dennis Kozlowski described Monks as a man on the leading edge of corporate governance reform and as someone who can be "a very harsh and fearless critic." When asked about his service as a Tyco Director, Monks said there came a time soon after Kozlowski was named CEO when he knew he had to leave the Board. More than twenty years after the fact, Monks used the exact same word that Kozlowski used to describe the Directors who sat on the Tyco Board in the 1990s. Like Kozlowski, Monks labeled the Board "dysfunctional."[21]

Monks remembered sitting through a meeting in 1993 when actions of the Directors became red flags to him—indicators of serious problems. Bob Monks, a stickler for doing things right, didn't want to be part of a Board that operated as the Tyco Board did at that time. As he considered his options, he spoke to a friend about his desire to disconnect from Tyco. Monks's friend shared an anecdote about being asked to leave a board of directors almost immediately after he suggested that board members participate in a self-evaluation process. Monks decided to replicate the scenario so in 1993, he asked Tyco Directors to participate in a self-evaluation process. In response to his suggestions, Monks was promptly asked to leave the Tyco Board. Monks said it was somewhat embarrassing to be removed, but after 2002, after the scandal and legal actions for which the Tyco Board was responsible, at least in part, his 1993 dismissal from the Tyco Board of Directors was viewed favorably. "At speaking engagements and events, among the qualifications and accomplishments identified when I'm introduced to an audience," Monks said, "is my timely departure from the Tyco Board."[22]

*   *   *

Once the Board and Kozlowski reached an agreement on compensation, Kozlowski succeeded Fort as CEO. However, Fort remained Chairman of Tyco's Board of Directors. That leadership structure was short-lived. Not long after Kozlowski was named CEO, the Board decided he should serve as Chairman as well.[23] Kozlowski explained during his trial that "[t]he Board noticed, for lack of a better word, some tension. . . . John Fort was a successful CEO for about ten years and he had a different style and different ideas than I did."[24] Kozlowski explained that after he became CEO, he and Fort addressed the same issues and opportunities in Board meetings and the two often expressed very different points of view.[25]

In Kozlowski's recollection, Phil Hampton broached the subject of Fort's chairmanship with him about six months after Kozlowski was named CEO.[26] Kozlowski said Hampton experienced a similar governance dilemma when he sat on the Board of Banker's Trust. Hampton saw the same type of tension between a CEO and a Chairman, and as a result of the difficulties he observed, he thought the Tyco Board would function more effectively with one person assuming both roles. Hampton said he planned to speak to the rest of the Board about Kozlowski assuming both positions.[27] His reasoning apparently persuaded the other Directors because shortly after Hampton's conversation with Kozlowski, the Board in January 1993 rejoined the roles of CEO and Chairman and vested both in Dennis Kozlowski.[28]

At the time, Kozlowski was no doubt happy to assume the chairmanship. Being both the CEO and Chairman of the Board gave him more clout, more control, and freed him from the tension and obstructions created by a Chairman whose management style and vision for Tyco were different than his own. In the short term, serving in both roles made Kozlowski's life easier. But in the long term, it may have been better both for Kozlowski and for Tyco if someone else had assumed the role of Chairman of the Board.

What's the old saying? Penny wise, pound foolish.

*   *   *

Leadership structure, specifically the question of whether the roles of CEO and Chairman should be held by a single person or split between two individuals, has been a hot topic among publicly traded corporations, their shareholders, activists, and regulators for the past several years. While the majority of Standard & Poor's (S&P) 500 companies continue to vest the roles of CEO and Chairman in a single individual, the past decade has seen an increasing number of companies splitting the roles.[29] According to the 2012 *Spencer Stuart US Board Index (SSBI)*, only 125 companies—twenty-five percent of the S&P 500—split the roles of CEO and Chairman in 2002. Reflecting the trend of the next decade, *SSBI* analysis of 2012 proxies revealed that 207 companies—forty-three percent of the S&P 500—split the roles of CEO and Chairman. The 2012 *SSBI* analysis also revealed that eighteen S&P 500 companies had formal policies requiring a split between board leadership and management control.[30]

Beginning in February of 2010, the SEC requires publicly traded corporations to disclose in annual proxy filings their board leadership structure including the rationale for either combining or splitting the roles of CEO and Chairman of the Board. Dodd-Frank also requires disclosure of leadership structure. There are many arguments advanced by proponents of splitting the roles and an equal number from advocates of combining board and management leadership. At the root of this dilemma is the inherent conflict of interest created by having the CEO, the individual responsible for management of the company, also serve as the leader of the board of directors, the body charged with overseeing, compensating, evaluating, and if necessary, terminating the CEO. The basic counterargument is that by vesting the roles of CEO and Chairman in the same individual, the company can operate more effectively, with a single vision, clear objectives, and unity of purpose. Research of this issue has produced inconclusive results. There is no clear answer as to whether one leadership structure is more effective than the other.[31]

The Tyco scandal seems a case study in the risks of vesting in one person the roles of both CEO and Chairman. If another individual had assumed the role of Chairman during Kozlowski's tenure as CEO, perhaps a second point of view would have counterbalanced Kozlowski's aggressive growth style. Perhaps the Board would have benefited from the combined strengths of different leaders— from the "tension" Kozlowski described in his trial testimony. By giving Kozlowski control over both management of the company and leadership of the Board, Tyco Directors arguably gave him too much freedom, too much control, and not enough direction. For the decade the company flourished under Kozlowski's leadership, the Board became increasingly hands off, investing ever less effort in oversight and paying minimal attention to corporate formalities—their primary duties as Directors of a publicly traded corporation. Had someone else been Chairman during the years Kozlowski was CEO, during the years his time and energy were consumed by travel, acquisitions, and concentrating on the "big picture," splitting the roles would have almost guaranteed more effective corporate governance. Kozlowski would no doubt have received more guidance, feedback, and oversight. At the very least, had there been a different Chairman when the waters got rough in early 2002, it would have been more difficult for the Board to blame Dennis Kozlowski for anything and everything.

Of Tyco during the years Kozlowski was both CEO and Chairman, Bob Monks described an environment that gave Kozlowski "no protection from his own worst instincts."[32]

PART TWO

TIMING IS EVERYTHING

The old adage "timing is everything" is true, which is probably why it has endured. Occasionally, an unlikely intersection of people, places, and circumstances conjures unexpected good fortune—the joy and magic of the human experience. It doesn't happen often, but on rare occasions, timing is perfect. With equal force and numinosity, the same kind of arbitrary temporal collision can end in tragedy when the fates align with exact synchronicity and, against all odds, produce a perfect storm. This doesn't happen often either, but on rare occasions, timing is perfect.

SEVEN

BIG TIME SCRUTINY

Dennis Kozlowski excelled as the CEO of Tyco International. There was rough water from time to time, but for the most part, his decentralized, efficient, acquisitive organization sailed for many years with the wind at its back. In the three decades before Kozlowski was named CEO, Tyco was a little known New Hampshire conglomerate. But even as the company grew substantially larger, it wasn't as widely recognized as companies of similar size and performance. Kozlowski and the Tyco Board thought the company's price/earnings ratio suffered—its stock was undervalued in part because of Tyco's relative anonymity. So, Dennis Kozlowski sought counsel from well-respected New York public relations guru Robert Dilenschneider with an eye to increasing Tyco's and by necessity his own visibility.[1] Of some of the first words of wisdom he received from Dilenschneider, Kozlowski recalled that "Bob said to me 'You know, the only whales that are harpooned are the ones that come to the surface.'"[2]

* * *

Due to efforts to boost exposure, and more significantly, because of the company's continued growth and strong performance, Tyco and its CEO gradually received more attention. The company appeared as one of "The Best Performers" on the list of the *Business Week-50* in March of 1997. Over the next several years, interest in the company escalated. Eventually, burgeoning interest in Tyco led to hundreds of articles in the *New York Times,* the *Wall Street Journal, USA Today, Fortune* magazine, *Money* magazine, and a plethora of other outlets. Kozlowski was featured on the cover of *Businessweek* in May of 2001 when the publication tagged him "The Most Aggressive CEO." Because of his seemingly fearless drive to grow the company through hundreds of mergers and acquisitions, Kozlowski was recognized as "perhaps the most aggressive dealmaker in Corporate America." He appeared on a *Businessweek* cover again in January 2002 after being named one of "The Top 25 Managers of the Year."

By the early 2000s, Kozlowski and Tyco were well known. The kid from Newark and the small New Hampshire company had made it to the big time.[3]

*   *   *

Once Tyco and Kozlowski were on the radar, every move the company and its CEO made seemed to be of interest to someone. Or to everyone. The larger the company grew, the more attention both Tyco and Kozlowski received—from journalists, analysts, investors, regulators, and others. Along with frequent public praise came occasional criticism and heightened scrutiny. Bob Dilenschneider's observation foreshadowed Tyco's newly found prominence; the whale became vulnerable to harpoons.

In October of 1999, Tyco had to address surprising allegations made by prominent short-seller David Tice. Short-sellers are traders who bet that the price of certain stock will fall. In order to short a stock, a short-seller borrows (for a fee) shares of a company's stock in an agreement with the owner of the shares that they will be returned on a certain date. The short-seller immediately sells the borrowed shares on the market at the current, and what the short-seller believes to be inflated price, wagering that the stock price will fall before the date the borrowed shares must be returned to the owner. If the stock price falls, the short-seller buys replacement shares for less than the borrowed shares were sold—and the short-seller makes a profit. However, if the price of the stock increases, the short-seller is forced to buy replacement shares at a higher price than the price for which the borrowed shares were sold—and the short-seller suffers a loss.

For example, if a short-seller believes ABC Inc.'s stock is overvalued, he or she borrows 100 shares of ABC Inc. with an agreement to return replacement shares to the owner in x number of days. On the day the short-seller borrows the shares, ABC Inc. is trading at $15 a share. The short-seller sells the shares on the market for $15 ($15 × 100 shares = $1,500) The short-seller has $1,500 in his or her pocket and an obligation to buy replacement shares to return to the owner from whom they were borrowed within the predetermined time frame. This is when the short-seller hopes the value of the company's stock will drop—he or she hopes the rest of the market will suddenly recognize the same overvaluation that the short-seller was smart enough to discern before everyone else. The short-seller hopes when ABC Inc. shareholders learn the stock has been shorted, they will believe they own overvalued stock and they'll rush to sell their shares. During the window of time after the short-seller sells the borrowed shares and before he or she must return replacement shares, the price of ABC Inc. drops to $10 a share. The short-seller buys 100 replacement shares for $1,000 (100 × $10 = $1,000), returns those shares to the owner from whom they were borrowed, and keeps the $500 profit. The short-seller wins because the stock of ABC Inc. dropped in value. If during the limited time frame the value of ABC Inc. doesn't fall but instead increases to $20 a share, the short-seller's cost of replacement shares would be $2,000, and he or she would suffer a loss of $500 on the transaction. If a short-seller predicts that the price of ABC Inc. will drop, the short-seller needs the price of the stock to fall. The short-seller has a financial interest in seeing ABC Inc.'s stock price drop.

According to some experts, short-sellers played a role in almost every financial crisis of the last 400 years. After the U.S. stock market crash in 1929, President Hoover condemned short selling, and short-sellers were called on the carpet again after the market crashed in October of 1987. David Tice, the short-seller who created public suspicions about Tyco, acknowledged that short-sellers, as a group, are not held in high esteem. In a 2008 *Reuters* article, Tice is quoted as saying "We've been the natural scapegoats for decades."

Short-sellers defend their role, say they're good for the market, and promote themselves as watchdogs who bring balance to the market by sniffing out stocks that are overvalued. For the *Reuters* article, written in the midst of the financial crisis of 2008, a self-reflective Tice said, "I feel like we are the good guys, but when the media attention is on us and the president and the treasury secretary are talking about it, it is kind of a lonely vocation."[4]

On Friday, October 8, 1999, David Tice publicly questioned Tyco's accounting methods and alleged that Tyco overestimated restructuring charges when it closed deals to buy or merge with other companies. Tice said of his allegations against Tyco, "We told people that Tyco was stretching the truth on reported performance, which didn't represent future growth prospects."[5] The market reacted immediately to Tice's claims. Within two trading days of his report, Tyco's stock price dropped sharply. Over the next two months, the value dropped by nearly fifty percent.[6]

Tice's opinion that Tyco stock was overvalued and should be shorted proved correct—the stock price fell just after he discovered and announced Tyco's questionable acquisition accounting. His timing was impeccable. But what was the *cause* and what the *effect*? Did the value of Tyco stock fall in October of 1999 because Tice was right about Tyco's acquisition accounting methods? Or did the value of Tyco shares drop because of damaging rumors floated by a prominent short-seller who was advancing his own interests—did Tyco stock plummet because of the allegations of someone who ran a business that profited when the value of stocks dropped?

Tyco International was exactly the kind of company David Tice featured at the time in his newsletter "Behind the Numbers." When asked in 2001 why he targeted Tyco, Tice told *MarketWatch* that "Tyco was a Wall Street darling with lots of buy recommendations and no sells from the analysts who followed the company." So Tice took a close look at Tyco's financial statements and concluded, contrary to the opinions of dozens of analysts, investors, investment bankers, and auditors, that the company should be shorted, that its organic performance was weak, and its growth was fueled primarily by an aggressive number of acquisitions. Tice made the serious allegation that Tyco purposefully overestimated restructuring charges so the company could make adjustments in future periods to enhance its earnings.[7]

Accounting rules at the time required that restructuring costs related to acquisitions be estimated and charged when deals closed. Of course, the *actual* costs of restructuring would not be known until after newly acquired companies were fully integrated—weeks or months later. Although estimates are by their very nature uncertain, acquirers were obligated to use professional judgment in forecasting costs, and restructuring charges had to be justifiable. Before taking charges, acquirers had to identify restructuring expenses that would be incurred by naming specifically any activities that would be discontinued, the method of disposition, the location of the named activities, and the expected dates of completion. The types of planned expenses included in restructuring charges (expenses for actions needed to implement strategic changes or to benefit from synergistic efficiencies) included consolidation or relocation of operations, the closing of plants and facilities, the termination of jobs, and impairment of the value of productive assets. For example, if integration included cutting 2,000 jobs, the acquirer had to identify and announce the 2,000 positions that would be eliminated. The costs of severance owed to the 2,000 identified employees could be included in restructuring charges.[8]

When acquisitions closed, restructuring charges had an immediate negative impact on earnings; the restructuring charges were expenses. However, after newly acquired companies were successfully integrated, weeks or months later, if the expenses the acquirers anticipated were more than the actual costs of restructuring, the companies had to make adjustments and write down the charges, sometimes called reserves or "cookie jars," which had a positive impact on pretax earnings in the quarters in which the adjustments were made.

For example, if an acquirer planned to close five facilities during the integration of an acquired company, the $10 million total cost of closing those facilities would have been included in the restructuring charge—and taken as an expense when the deal closed. But because of the efficient and orderly winding down of operations in three of the facilities, and effective revenue enhancements implemented during the first three quarters after the acquisition, two of the facilities slated to be closed remained in operation nine months later, and would continue to operate. As a result of the change of course, the actual costs of restructuring were only $8 million, less than the $10 million included in the restructuring charge. The acquirer had to make a $2 million adjustment—in essence reversing the expense booked earlier—which became a $2 million boost to pretax earnings in the quarter in which the adjustment was made. The adjustment directly affected operating income but was disclosed on a separate line—it was not buried in operating income.

This accounting method was vulnerable to abuse; an acquiring company could purposefully overstate restructuring charges and use the inflated amount in the "cookie jar" to manipulate earnings when needed in future periods. Arguably, this was not illegal or in violation of the accounting standards in place in 1999, when Tice accused Tyco of manipulating earnings, however, this method could create serious problems if resultant financial reporting was misleading to shareholders.

The market's reaction to David Tice's accusations was understandable and predictable. If Tyco had in fact intentionally overestimated restructuring charges, considering the number and size of acquisitions Tyco made during the late 1990s, the amount of reserves in its "cookie jar" could have been substantial, thus giving the company the ability to pump up earnings anytime it wanted to mask a bad quarter. For example, when Tyco completed the acquisition of AMP in April of 1999, the company announced that it expected to take a restructuring charge of at least $200 million.[9] If Tyco used an inflated number, if the company knew it wouldn't really incur costs of $200 million, it could have written down any excess in the future, in a quarter when earnings weren't as strong as expected. The fear was that investors would rely on numbers that reflected a quarter of strong performance when in reality, but for the adjustment of restructuring charges, performance for the quarter would have been lackluster. Kozlowski's aggressive goals for growth and propensity to acquire large companies with correspondingly large restructuring charges added fuel to Tice's fire.

In late 2007, the U.S. Financial Accounting Standards Board made changes to accounting standards for mergers and acquisitions, including the treatment of restructuring charges. For deals closed after December of 2008, material adjustments to restructuring charges had to be made to prior period financial statements—to the financial statements from the period in which the acquisition was completed— instead of reflecting adjustments in a later period.[10] The change in accounting standards prevented any further use of "cookie jars" or reserved charges that could be used to manipulate earnings.

During Kozlowski's second criminal trial, former Tyco Executive Vice President Brad McGee was asked to describe the company's reaction to Tice's allegations. McGee was the company's spokesperson in 1999 when Tice publicly questioned Tyco's accounting methods. As the company's spokesperson, McGee was unequivocally credible. He accepted a position at Tyco in 1991 and served in a number of high-level positions during the decade Dennis Kozlowski was CEO.[11] Kozlowski distinctly remembered how he came to hire McGee. He said, "During the years I was at Tyco, I received dozens of unsolicited resumes every day. My assistant put them into a folder and I would do a quick review before forwarding the folder to HR and they sent polite ding letters on my behalf. One day, I was flipping through the folder and I noticed Brad McGee's resume. He was local—in Exeter, New Hampshire. He had an MBA from Harvard, but what I really noticed was his Navy service. He worked on nuclear subs. When he sent his resume, he was working as a consultant. I thought we could use some internal consulting, so I asked him to come in and talk."[12] Kozlowski believed McGee was one of his best hires and said had things played out differently at Tyco, the leadership succession plan he envisioned would have seen Brad McGee as the company's sixth CEO.[13]

When he testified in court about the David Tice fiasco, McGee was asked if, when he was head of investor relations at Tyco, he observed short-sellers doing anything to drive down the company's stock price. "Yes, I did experience that," he responded. McGee said that short-sellers did " . . . everything from calling up our sell side analysts and . . . giving them information that was false about the company. They would call up reporters and try to feed stories with false information about the company. They might publish reports like Mr. Tice did or go on television and make comments about the company which were negative and which were false." McGee said that within a week of watching the market react negatively to what Tyco knew to be completely baseless accusations levied by Tice, Kozlowski wanted to speak directly with Tyco shareholders about the "malicious and unfounded rumors that were in the marketplace concerning Tyco." McGee recalled discussing ways to address the rumors and said, "Dennis's decision was that the quickest and best way for us to address what was going on in the market was talk to our shareholders directly and provide them with the company's view of, that the company fundamentally had not changed at all and there should be no concern with respect to Tyco stock or the company itself." So that's what Kozlowski did. He spoke to shareholders directly using scheduled conference calls during which he assured shareholders and other interested parties that the company's accounting methods were solid.[14]

Even though Tyco addressed them quickly and directly, Tice's allegations didn't die easily. Adding insult to injury, the Securities and Exchange Commission (SEC) launched an investigation into Tyco's acquisition accounting methods because of the market's costly reaction to Tice's report. On the day Tyco voluntarily announced the SEC investigation in December of 2001, the price of Tyco stock fell 23 percent. When the SEC decided to investigate Tice's claims, Kozlowski made the public statement that "[i]n light of the recent market activity in our stock, which is not justified by any development at the company, we welcome the opportunity to respond to this request. We remain confident of our accounting methodology, our public disclosures and the continuing strength of our business." The SEC wanted to review all supporting documents related to acquisition charges and reserves for the preceding six years. During that time period, Tyco had made more than 120 acquisitions.[15]

In December of 1999, Dennis Kozlowski must have been pleased that he hired Mark Belnick as Tyco's Chief Corporate Counsel in 1998, just a year before the company had to address the shit storm started by David Tice. Belnick, who oversaw the SEC investigation, had been with Tyco for less than sixteen months when the investigation began.

Belnick was exactly the kind of lawyer a company would want in its corner to deal with a serious regulatory investigation. Along with degrees from Cornell and Columbia, Belnick had an impressive background and an unblemished reputation.[16] Just prior to joining Tyco, he was a senior partner at Paul, Weiss, Rifkind, Wharton & Garrison, one of the most respected law firms in New York. In 1987, Belnick served as Deputy Chief Counsel to the U.S. Senate during the Iran-Contra Hearings. He served as Chief Counsel to the National Association of Securities Dealers (NASD) Select Committee in 1995 and played a role in reorganizing the NASD and Nasdaq.

Belnick's former colleagues at Paul Weiss held him in high esteem, both before and after he left the firm to join Tyco. They continued to hold Belnick in high esteem when he was indicted and tried for serious felonies by the Manhattan DA— charges related to his compensation at Tyco. On most days of Belnick's criminal trial in 2004, many Paul Weiss attorneys were in the courtroom in support of their former colleague. Just after he was acquitted by a Manhattan jury in the summer of 2004, a former colleague said of Belnick's character that he was a man who "wouldn't even go near the line." Mark Belnick indeed seemed to be a by-the-book straight shooter, a veritable Boy Scout; his sterling reputation was an asset to Tyco when the company addressed the SEC's concerns.[17]

At the front end of the investigation, Belnick went to Kozlowski and voiced the need to use outside counsel to assist in the probe. Belnick said Kozlowski's response was definitive: "Yes. Hire them." Belnick brought in William McLucas, the former head of SEC enforcement. If there was something shady buried in Tyco's acquisition accounting, McLucas would find it.[18]

With McLucas in tow, Tyco began producing documents to the SEC—tens of thousands of documents. Belnick said Kozlowski instructed him to cooperate fully with "no resistance. We need to give them everything. We need a clean bill of health." During Belnick's criminal trial in 2004, Mark Foley, former Tyco Senior Vice President of Finance, testified that when the investigation was announced, Belnick's instructions to the finance department were to be "open and honest" with those conducting the investigation. Foley said Tyco turned over more than 400 boxes of documents to the SEC.[19]

Early in the investigation, Belnick made an unexpected strategic decision: Tyco would offer up CFO Mark Swartz and head of finance Mark Foley and allow the SEC to question them directly. Tyco would allow the regulators to ask anything they wanted to know about the company's accounting methods. Kozlowski said it was actually Josh Berman who first suggested that Swartz and Foley open themselves up to SEC questioning. It was a high-risk plan to which the CEO agreed. But what if Swartz or Foley stumbled? What would happen if SEC investigators didn't hear what they wanted to hear? It was a gutsy decision, but Belnick, Kozlowski, Berman, Swartz, and Foley, on behalf of Tyco, had nothing to hide and they wanted SEC investigators to know they had access to anything they wanted—everything they needed to resolve questions about Tyco's acquisition accounting. William McLucas described the decision to offer up Swartz and Foley as "the right combination of street smarts, balls, integrity, judgment, and lunacy."[20]

During the months the company was under investigation and despite the blow to Tyco's stock price, the company continued to thrive. On March 20, 2000, Tyco was included on *Businessweek*'s list of the "50 Best Performers." On April 18, 2000, Tyco announced its second-quarter earnings—a 47 percent increase in earnings per share. The company announced on May 7, 2000 its agreement to acquire the Electronic OEM Business of Thomas & Betts for $750 million in cash, and on June 28, 2000, Tyco announced the planned $4.2 billion acquisition of global healthcare giant Mallinckrodt.[21]

Midsummer, the SEC officially closed its investigation of Tyco. On July 13, 2000, seven months after it began its probe, the SEC issued a "closing letter" and took no action against Tyco. Kozlowski recalled that there was a nonmaterial restatement of earnings the result of which bumped up earnings per share by one cent in a prior period. Beyond that, the SEC reported no problems after thoroughly combing through the books and records of Tyco International. It was very good news for Tyco, its shareholders, the trinity of Marks (Belnick, Swartz, and Foley), and a huge relief for CEO Dennis Kozlowski.[22]

In an interview after his acquittal in 2004, Belnick said he welcomed the pressure of the 1999–2000 SEC inquiry. "This is going to sound bizarre," Belnick said, "but during the SEC investigation, working night and day, I enjoyed working at Tyco." He explained, "I was working to save the company, and I hate to say that's enjoyable, but that's what I do." After the SEC probe ended favorably, Belnick and Foley each received a bonus for their work during the investigation. Kozlowski was consistent—the bonuses were pay for outstanding performance. Some of the charges for which Belnick was later indicted, tried, and acquitted involved the bonus he received for his contribution to the successful resolution of the SEC investigation. When asked during Belnick's trial about the bonuses he and Tyco's Chief Corporate Counsel received, Mark Foley testified that the bonuses were recorded in the company's books and records and "reflected as all other normal operating bonuses."[23]

* * *

Years after Tice's allegations and the SEC investigation had been laid to rest, another short-seller questioned and criticized as too aggressive Tyco's acquisition accounting methods. James Chanos of Kynikos Associates alleged that Tyco "spring-loaded" acquisitions. "Spring-loading" is a process used to make an acquired company appear less financially healthy at the time of acquisition—on the day the deal closes. In order to spring-load, the acquired company accelerates payment of expenses (at the instruction of the acquirer) during the weeks preceding the closing, writing off bad receivables, writing down inventories, and taking any other steps that will make the company appear less financially healthy at the time of closing. Spring-loading benefits the acquirer by making an acquired company's performance appear to improve immediately after the deal closes. Cash flow looks better, earnings improve, and because of the timing, the financial turnaround is attributed to the restructuring, cost-cutting measures, and revenue enhancements implemented by the acquirer. Like restructuring reserves, spring-loading techniques were not, in and of themselves, illegal or a violation of accounting standards in effect at the time, but could become a professional and legal concern if spring-loading resulted in misleading financial statements.

The spring-loading allegations were fueled by email messages provided to *Fortune* magazine by a few employees of Raychem, a Tyco acquisition that closed not long before Chanos raised concerns. The emails suggested that Tyco instructed Raychem to pay expenses early, before they were due, and before the acquisition was completed. Of note, Raychem employees wore black armbands to protest Tyco's acquisition of the company *before* the acquisition closed and *before* allegations of accounting improprieties were emailed to the magazine.

In response to *Fortune*'s questions about spring-loading, Brad McGee again staunchly defended Tyco's accounting methods, stating adamantly that "we do not manipulate earnings and cash flow at the business so we can get some kind of positive benefit after the acquisitions." McGee also referenced the SEC investigation and closing letter. How could there still be questions about whether Tyco's acquisition accounting was too aggressive or misleading? McGee explained that "there is a very rigorous set of checks that we have internally, where every adjustment must get Tyco corporate approval and approval by our auditors."[24]

During the entire decade Kozlowski was CEO, Tyco's independent auditor was PricewaterhouseCoopers (PwC), one of the "Big Four" accounting firms with the prestige, reputation, and hourly rates of top notch auditors. During Kozlowski's first criminal trial, his lead defense attorney Stephen Kaufman explained during opening statements how vital the opinions rendered by PwC were to his client. Kaufman asked the jury: "[Do] you know what outside auditors do for a company? They're giving you the Good Housekeeping Seal, they want to see if everything is kosher." Kozlowski said he and his top management team regularly sat down with the company's auditors and asked for details about Tyco's accounting methods. "Every quarter I asked them to rate Tyco on a scale from 1 to 5," Kozlowski recalled, "with 1 being the most conservative accounting methods they saw among the companies they audited and 5 being the most aggressive. They told me consistently that we were right in the middle—which is where you want to be. That's where I wanted us to be." Kozlowski said he placed great weight on the outcomes of audits and the opinions of PwC. "They were highly skilled auditors and a reputable firm and we paid them tens of millions of dollars to do their job," he said. "I believed they would find problems if they existed. I counted on it."[25]

*　*　*

A year and a half after David Tice's allegations were quashed by the SEC's lengthy and vindicative investigation, *Institutional Investor* magazine asked Dennis Kozlowski: "What do you think of when you hear David Tice's name?" Kozlowski's responded: "I think he's a short-seller who saw an opportunity to go after a company with a high multiple, who made up some stuff and made us into one of the more scrutinized companies in the world."[26]

EIGHT

THE GOOD OLD DAYS

"I wish there was a way to know you're in the good old days before you've actually left them."

Andy Bernard, *The Office*[1]

Not many people know how it feels to be on top of the world. For a while, Dennis Kozlowski knew what it was like.

THE RETENTION AGREEMENT

The company grew and prospered during the first few years of Kozlowski's leadership, but Dennis Kozlowski and Tyco International really hit their stride in the late 1990s. In 1996, Tyco was added to the Standard & Poor's (S&P) 500, a stock market index of the 500 largest U.S. companies based on market capitalization.[2] During his criminal trial, Kozlowski was questioned about Tyco and asked if it was a large company during the years he was the CEO. Kozlowski told the court and the jury that Tyco was large "by virtually any measure, sales or market capitalization, Tyco usually fell within the top 25 companies in the world in the last few years that I was running [the company]."[3] In 1998, Kozlowski was courted by Raytheon Company, a Massachusetts-based high tech company that, like Tyco, operated in four business segments: commercial and defense electronics, engineering and construction, aviation, and major appliances. The company's Board wanted Dennis Kozlowski to serve as its next CEO.

Kozlowski was elected to the Raytheon Board of Directors in June of 1995, so the Raytheon Directors knew him well and had no doubt watched and were impressed by Tyco's success and phenomenal growth over the three years Kozlowski sat with them in the Raytheon boardroom.[4] Kozlowski was tempted to take the reins of what was at the time one of the largest defense contractors in the world with annual revenue of nearly $20 billion; when the job was proffered in 1998, Raytheon was substantially larger than Tyco.[5] Kozlowski ultimately declined the offer, even though he could likely have negotiated compensation as CEO of Raytheon even more lucrative than the compensation opportunities he had with Tyco.

Raytheon was not the only company interested in luring Dennis Kozlowski away from Tyco in the late 1990s and early 2000s.[6] As his tenure at the head of the flourishing diversified conglomerate neared the ten year mark, Kozlowski was in demand. Despite occasional problems that ranged from serious to simply annoying, like the SEC investigation, David Tice, and a journalist Kozlowski thought had a grudge against Tyco, the company's performance under his leadership made Kozlowski a darling of executive headhunters. Even with frequent and serious external interest, Kozlowski was a Tyco loyalist. Over the years, he received many attractive offers to go elsewhere, but he always opted to stay with Tyco.

By the end of calendar year 2000, Kozlowski was weighing his options and he seriously considered embarking on a new endeavor; he planned to leave Tyco for the world of private equity.[7] He considered joining the Carlyle Group in Washington, DC, but was leaning more toward building his own private investment firm. Before 2001, Kozlowski had not signed an employment contract with Tyco. He and Mark Swartz were both at-will employees. Because of Tyco's strong performance and the enormous performance-based compensation Kozlowski received during the prior few years, there was concern on the Street that Kozlowski would pocket his earnings and move on to other pastures. The Board of Directors thought the time was right to secure an employment contract with their CEO; the Directors wanted an agreement that would offer investors and the Board assurance that Kozlowski would remain CEO of Tyco for many years into the future.

If the terms of a contract tell tales, the Retention Agreement the Tyco Board of Directors entered into with Dennis Kozlowski in January of 2001 shouted that the Board wanted very much for Kozlowski to remain Tyco's chief executive and was willing to pay whatever it took to keep him. Kozlowski said, "Mark [Swartz] worked with the Board to draft the agreement. I didn't work on the draft, but I believe it was derived from Jack Welch's compensation as disclosed in GE's proxy." The Board, on Tyco's behalf, entered into a Retention Agreement with Dennis Kozlowski the pecuniary value of which was so great that Kozlowski himself was shocked at the Compensation Committee's willingness to sign it.

Under the terms of the agreement, "in recognition of [Kozlowski's] significant contribution to the creation of shareholder value and leadership during his tenure as Chairman of the Board of Directors, President and Chief Executive Officer of the Company, [the Compensation Committee] wishes to obtain his commitment to serve as Chairman of the Board, President and Chief Executive Officer of the Company until his 62nd birthday on November 16, 2008 and his commitment to serve after his retirement as a consultant to the Company, at the direction of the then Chief Executive Officer of the Company."[8]

Upon his exit from the company, Kozlowski would receive "an amount equal to three times the sum of (x) [his] then current annual base salary (without giving effect to any reduction thereof following the Effective Date [of the agreement]) plus (y) the highest annual bonus (including cash, shares and other forms of consideration) earned by [Kozlowski] with respect to the eight fiscal years preceding the year in which the Date of Termination occurs (or an amount equal to the annual bonus including cash, shares and other forms of consideration earned by [Kozlowski] with respect to the Company's 2000 fiscal year, if higher)."[9]

(x) + (y) = $412,480,272, considering the floor of the agreement, which was Kozlowski's compensation in 2000. According to Tyco, Kozlowski's compensation during the years leading up to the Retention Agreement was as follows:

1997	$26,454,603
1998	$70,329,840
1999	$21,074,097
2000	$137,493,424[10]

In addition to the $412.5 million golden parachute, Kozlowski was granted 800,000 restricted shares of Tyco common stock on January 21, 2001, the day he signed the Retention Agreement. Each year for the following eight years on the anniversary date of the agreement, one-eighth (1/8) of the restricted shares would vest; if Kozlowski stayed with Tyco until his sixty-second birthday, all 800,000 shares would be fully vested.[11] On the day members of the Compensation Committee and Kozlowski signed the Retention Agreement, Tyco stock (TYC) closed at $84.85.[12] If the stock performed similarly over the next eight years, Kozlowski's 800,000 shares would be worth more than $67.9 million.

On top of the $412.5 million golden parachute and the 800,000 shares of TYC stock, Kozlowski would be paid one thirty-sixth (1/36) of the (x) + (y) amount each year for the rest of his life in exchange for thirty days of consulting services per year.[13] The Compensation Committee valued Dennis Kozlowski's consulting services to be worth at least $11,457,785 a year ($412,480,272 × 1/36). That's $381,926 per day of consulting work (($412,480,272 × 1/36) / 30). If a consulting day was eight hours long, Kozlowski's hourly rate would have been $47,740. Those numbers are based on Kozlowski's compensation in FY 2000. If Tyco performed better than in FY 2000 during any year before his birthday in 2008, the dollar amounts would have been even larger.

In addition, Kozlowski was to receive all fringe benefits available to him on the day he left the company or retired "including but not limited to relocation benefits [did the Tyco Board believe he would need to relocate in order to provide 30 days of consulting services per year?], security, sponsorships and events, grossed-up payments for New York state and city taxes, if applicable, health insurance coverage (including coverage for spouse (or domestic partner)), life insurance coverage and continued access to Company facilities and services, including access to Company aircraft, cars, office (with secretarial and administrative support), apartments and financial planning (tax, accounting and legal) services."[14]

Of course, the Compensation Committee had to draw the line somewhere. The generous and expensive benefits remained in effect only until Kozlowski's death.

In exchange for the $412.5 million, the 800,000 shares of stock, consulting fees, and what must be the most generous benefits ever offered to a former employee by a business organization, Dennis Kozlowski had to forego other opportunities available to him and agree to serve as CEO and Chairman of the Board of Tyco International Ltd. until November 16, 2008. At Phil Hampton's house in Naples, Florida on January 21, 2001, Compensation Committee members Phil Hampton, Stephen Foss, James Pasman, and Peter Slusser signed the Retention Agreement. As did Dennis Kozlowski.[15]

The Board of Directors and the members of the Compensation Committee must have felt absolute certainty and confidence in their CEO in order to offer such a rich contract. Even in the much-maligned world of executive compensation, Tyco's Retention Agreement with Dennis Kozlowski was extraordinary. Imagine how embarrassing it would be if, after entering the agreement, the company's performance faltered. Envision the extreme public scrutiny the Tyco Board would face: the criticism of shareholders, journalists, analysts—of everyone. The Directors would no doubt be sued, accused of breaching their duty to Tyco shareholders when they entered into the half-billion-dollar-plus employment contract. The agreement was so outrageous, the Directors may have been accused of criminal negligence. After the Compensation Committee signed the Retention Agreement on January 21, 2001, if Tyco did not continue on the same trajectory of growth and performance it experienced over the prior nine years under Kozlowski's leadership, the Tyco Board of Directors was screwed.

There was, however, one provision in the agreement that gave the Board a way out of performing everything promised in the contract. Under the terms of the Retention Agreement, if Kozlowski was terminated "with Cause," the company would have no further obligation to him.[16] "Cause" was defined as Dennis Kozlowski's "conviction of a felony that is material and demonstrably injurious to the Company or any of its subsidiaries or affiliates, monetarily or otherwise."

THE RECESSION OF 2001

Almost immediately after the Retention Agreement was signed, a recession hit the U.S. economy and ended the longest period of economic growth in history. Despite the downturn that began in the first quarter of 2001, Tyco continued to grow, perform, and acquire as had become expected. In February of 2001, the company announced a $400 million addition to its fire and securities services group with the acquisition of Scott Technologies, a designer and manufacturer of respiratory systems and other devices for the firefighting and aviation markets. Scott Technologies had projected annual revenue of around $250 million.[17]

On March 28, 2001, more good news came when *Businessweek* magazine named Tyco the number one performing company of 2000. The article noted that "[w]ith a bear market in full cry, uncertainty about the economy rampant, and much of Corporate America deep in hunker-down mode, Dennis Kozlowski might be expected to be a tad less ebullient. But the supremely self-assured chief executive at Tyco International Ltd. (TYC), who masterminded $9 billion worth of acquisitions last year and then stunned analysts in March by announcing he would spend another $9 billion to buy commercial-finance giant CIT Group (CIT), looks on the carnage as a call to action." The article quoted Kozlowski as saying: "This is a good environment for Tyco . . . [t]here will be more opportunities than there were when the economy was booming." Of Kozlowski's ability to lead Tyco through the recession, the article said that " . . . after helping build the conglomerate from a $20 million-a-year corporate also-ran into a $30 billion-a-year industrial giant, Kozlowski knows how to navigate rough waters." Tyco landed at the top of the list of best performing companies because of its stellar results. *Businessweek* noted that Tyco shareholders had benefited from Kozlowski's "go-get-'em" style and shared that "[i]n the past three years, the company's stock has returned 117%, including a 44% return in the past year alone, while Tyco's earnings on a latest-12-months basis have climbed 149%, to $4.8 billion, as sales rose 27%, to $30.3 billion."[18]

On April 27, 2001, Tyco was ranked number one in the "2001 *Reuters* Survey of U.S. Larger Companies;" the rankings were derived from data collected from analysts about the quality of information companies make available to them. Kozlowski said of the Reuters top spot, "Tyco is delighted to receive top marks in the prestigious 2001 *Reuters* Survey of U.S. Larger Companies. Having just reported that Tyco's second-quarter earnings per share rose 30%, it is especially gratifying to know that analysts have ranked Tyco first for plain talk." The 407 broker-analysts who responded to the survey ranked Tyco as the company with the best transparency, quality of reporting, and disclosure.[19]

THE WEDDING

Dennis Kozlowski's professional life had never been better. The company continued to perform despite the recession and both he and Tyco had become favorites of analysts and of the media. On May 28, 2001, Kozlowski appeared on the cover of *Businessweek,* tagged "The Most Aggressive CEO." The accompanying story lauded

Kozlowski for leading Tyco through the economic downturn; in the worst quarter for U.S. corporate profits in ten years, Tyco's earnings grew 33 percent and the company reported a 26 percent increase in sales. Kozlowski spoke of Tyco's recently announced plans to acquire The CIT Group, Inc., at the time the largest independent commercial finance company in the United States. It would be a $9.2 billion acquisition and seemed to break Kozlowski's rule against acquiring companies outside of Tyco's existing business divisions. Filled with his typical and seemingly unsinkable confidence, Kozlowski said, "I think CIT will be one of the best deals we've ever done."

The May 28, 2001 *Businessweek* feature article closed with personal information about "The Most Aggressive CEO." In addition to noting his place and date of birth (November 16, 1946), his education, employment history, and hobbies, the article revealed that Kozlowski's stake in Tyco at the time was 12.7 million shares worth $675 million. The article also shared family information, recognized Kozlowski's two daughters, and listed his marital status as divorced. With his combined marital status and net worth, Kozlowski may have been the most eligible bachelor in the U.S. in May of 2001. However, between the time William C. Symonds researched his article for *Businessweek* and its publication date, Kozlowski's status changed from divorced to married.[20]

On May 5, 2001, Dennis Kozlowski married his second wife in a small family ceremony on his prized historic 130-foot sailing yacht *Endeavour*. The couple exchanged vows just off the coast of Antigua.[21] Kozlowski met Karen Mayo in a restaurant in New Hampshire and the two dated for several years before they married.[22] Kozlowski did not speak of his second wife after the couple divorced in July of 2008 because of a confidentiality agreement. However, two years before the divorce was final, Kozlowski said in interviews that Karen visited him in prison only once—to tell him she wanted a divorce.[23]

It's easy to understand why Kozlowski and his second ex-wife agreed to confidentiality when they signed their divorce agreement. The second Mrs. Kozlowski and her then CEO husband became tabloid fodder after he was indicted in June of 2002, just a year after the two married. It must have been an incredibly stressful time for the bride and groom of a still new marriage. On top of serious legal woes, personal details of their lives were aired very publicly. Media interest in their private lives continued for several years. The reports were numerous, ugly, and usually mean-spirited.

Much of the media coverage stemmed from evidence presented during both of Kozlowski's criminal trials. Not much seemed to be off limits from the Manhattan DA's case. During the first of the two criminal trials, Tammy Cross, a former Tyco employee who handled Dennis Kozlowski's personal finances, was asked to reveal the price of a diamond ring Kozlowski bought in 2001.[24] The Assistant DA (ADA) asked Cross, "Do you recall how much money the diamond ring cost?" Her reply was, "Five million 38 thousand."[25] When the ADA asked Cross if she knew for whom her boss purchased the $5 million ring, she testified, "I believe it was for his wife."[26] The purchase of the ring was irrelevant to any of the charges in the indictment, as was much of the evidence presented to jurors in both trials. It's unclear why the court allowed the prosecution to admit the evidence.[27] Unfortunately for Dennis and Karen Kozlowski, the media reported almost all of the personal, intimate, easily sensationalized details revealed during the trials. After it was revealed in court, news of the price of Karen's ring appeared the following morning in the *New York Times*.[28]

After questioning Cross about the wedding ring, the ADA asked about the infamous fortieth birthday party Dennis Kozlowski threw for his wife a month after he married her.[29]

THE PARTY

Kozlowski spent a significant amount of time in Europe during the summer of 2001, focused on the company's electronics business. He visited all AMP facilities in Europe with then AMP President Juergen Gromer. "We were also putting the full-court press on Airbus," he said of his goals for the extended trip. "We wanted their business with us to grow to the size of our business with Boeing." Unlike much of Kozlowski's time and travel for Tyco, the summer of 2001 was about organic growth instead of buying companies. Kozlowski said he traveled during the week that summer, and on weekends he lived on *Endeavour*.

Every June for several years, Kozlowski hosted a birthday party for his former girlfriend, then wife Karen at their home in Nantucket. He knew months in advance there was a problem planning the 2001 event because he would be in Europe the entire month of June. Kozlowski also knew the European Air Show in Paris, which he had to attend on behalf of the company, was the week of June 16, 2001— the week immediately following Karen's birthday. He didn't want to break with tradition, so Kozlowski decided to host the perennial birthday bash in Europe. He brought the party to him.[30]

In testimony during Kozlowski's first criminal trial, former Tyco corporate event planner Barbara Jacques was asked about the birthday party for the CEO's wife.[31] As with Tammy Cross and several others, the prosecution questioned Jacques not only about her work at Tyco but also about the personal details of Dennis Kozlowski's life. With Jacques and another former Tyco employee, the prosecution solicited testimony about personal relationships the women had with Kozlowski. The ADA presented details of Kozlowski's personal life to the jury as evidence suggesting he used Tyco funds either to make his two so-called "mistresses" happy or to buy their silence about the wrongful acts of which he was accused. It would have taken an unreasonable stretch of the imagination to reach either conclusion.

Jacques told the jury she was involved in an intimate relationship with Kozlowski in 1986 and 1987. She said it ended mutually, on friendly terms, when Kozlowski "met somebody else" and that the two had no problem working together in the years after the personal relationship was over. Like the shower curtain, the wedding ring, and the Sardinia birthday party, the media loved the irrelevant yet juicy details revealed during Kozlowski's trials. After Jacques testified, she was thereafter referred to in stories with headlines such as "Mistresses on the Stand!"[32]

Jacques testified that Kozlowski first spoke to her about planning Karen's fortieth birthday party during the Tyco holiday party at the end of 2000. Jacques said after receiving the initial instructions from Kozlowski to schedule the June 2001 party, she had no further conversations with him about the types of events she was planning for Karen's birthday celebration. Kozlowski has long been credited with choosing the theme and activities. But in fact, Barbara Jacques planned the party.

If they chose to make the trip to Italy, the seventy-five party invitees had a list of events and activities available to them over the four or five days they spent at Hotel Cala di Volpe in Costa Smeralda on the island of Sardinia. Sardinia is an island in the Mediterranean about 150 miles off the west coast of Italy. Jacques said she planned for the guests "[a] welcome reception and buffet. During the day there were activities, bicycles available, they could go horseback riding, water skiing, sailing, golf. The next night we had a beach party for them. Following day there was a scavenger hunt and we took them to dinner at a restaurant—took over the restaurant and had the whole group at the restaurant and the final evening was the birthday party."

The party was legendary. On Thursday, June 14, 2001, the approximately seventy-five attendees who had flown to Italy to celebrate Mrs. Kozlowski's fortieth birthday were transported from the hotel to a country club that had been transformed into a Roman-themed fantasy land. The attendees, about half of whom were Tyco employees or Directors, were treated to an over-the-top extravaganza; it was an evening filled with excess, exuberance, and entertainment. When they arrived at the party, Jacques reported that the guests were greeted by "chariots and gladiators at the door with swords. As they went into the reception area, there were live male models, they had a reception, background music going, being played during the reception which was probably for an hour or so." During her testimony, the ADA interrupted Barbara Jacques and asked, "What did the live male models do?" to which Jacques responded, "Just looked good. . . ."[33]

In public displays that would haunt Dennis Kozlowski for the rest of his life, video of the birthday party was shown during his criminal trials. Over protests from defense counsel—all of whom feared Kozlowski and former Tyco CFO and co-defendant Mark Swartz would be unable to receive a fair trial because of the extreme prejudicial effect the video would have on the jury—the judge allowed thirty minutes of the four-hour video recorded during the party with an additional twenty minutes during which prosecutors showed still photographs of the festivities.[34] The jury saw images of the shirtless, buff male models outfitted in only flesh-colored briefs and cowboy boots as well as women in a similar state of undress who strolled around a sparkling pool occasionally posing with attendees for souvenir photos. There were video and photos of an ice sculpture of Michelangelo's *David* that urinated vodka, and a birthday cake in the shape of a woman with sparklers flickering from her breasts. The jurors saw video of party attendees dancing to the music of a band from Nantucket, E. Cliff and the Swing Dogs, before they enjoyed a second surprise musical performance. A guest who checked into the Hotel Cala di Volpe under the name "Elvis Smith" a day before the party was Kozlowski's special treat for his friends, family, colleagues, and his new wife. Jimmy Buffett and his band played for the birthday girl and her party guests for between forty-five minutes and an hour. The cost of bringing a little Margaritaville to Italy: $250,000.[35]

According to Jacques's testimony, an Executive Committee meeting and a Ty-Com (a Tyco subsidiary) Board of Directors meeting were scheduled on Sardinia the same week as the party.[36] In addition, the few days on Sardinia were offered as a retreat for several of the employees in attendance. "It was a mix of business and pleasure," Kozlowski said, "and something that happened over and over at Tyco. It was part of the culture, part of the pay-for-performance culture." He added that "those opportunities were how I connected the conglomerate; we got everyone together and made them feel like a part of a single organization. It was important."[37]

Kozlowski said because of the AMP visits, the focus on Airbus, and the European Air Show, he and other Tyco employees would have been in Europe in June of 2001, regardless of the events on Sardinia. "Those people had been working non-stop; they needed and earned a retreat," he explained.[38] Many of them, including Kozlowski, missed the Tyco Chairman's Council in Athens, Greece held a few weeks before the birthday party, because they were tied up with a deal.

Chairman's Council was a Tyco incentive program that recognized and rewarded top performers. Barbara Jacques explained that there were a few Tyco programs that rewarded employees with trips and retreats, all of which were a mix of business and pleasure. She said the Tyco retreats and incentive programs were similar to Sardinia—the same types of events and activities, the inclusion of spouses and significant others, liquor, food, and big-name bands. She noted that Chairman's Council and other Tyco events were held in desirable locations, such as New Zealand, Australia, Aspen, Colorado, and Athens, Greece. Jacques, who organized the events, said they had each cost as much as $2 million and she confirmed that Tyco paid for them in full—100 percent.[39]

The amount of trial time devoted to the party is inexplicable as none of the charges in the indictments of Kozlowski and Swartz had anything to do with the party. The evidence was irrelevant. However, the prosecution seemingly introduced evidence of the Sardinia party to suggest to the jury that Dennis Kozlowski used company money to pay for personal, extravagant expenses. The total cost of Tyco events and Mrs. Kozlowski's fortieth birthday party on Sardinia in June of 2001 was around $2 million.[40] Kozlowski was certain that his instructions to Jacques were to charge him for all personal expenses associated with Sardinia.[41] Jacques confirmed that Tyco was to pay for the business expenses and Kozlowski was to be billed for all personal expenses.[42] She also confirmed that all non-employees paid their own travel expenses to Sardinia. Jacques handled the division of costs between Tyco and Dennis Kozlowski—she determined what was business and what was personal. Kozlowski never saw the bills.[43] Jacques's division of expenses resulted in an almost 50/50 split, with Tyco footing about $1 million of the expenses.

It looked bad. Even though Tyco regularly threw extravagant, expensive events for its employees all over the world, the video and photographs of the excess on Sardinia were damning. It appeared that Kozlowski had a Roman orgy on the company's dime. Jacques confirmed that the Buffett performance was the only thing about the party of which Dennis Kozlowski was aware before he arrived on the evening of June 14. The theme, the nearly nude models, *David* pissing vodka, the togas, the gladiators, the laser show, the cake with sparkling breasts—they were all unexpected and unwelcome surprises to Dennis Kozlowski when he arrived at his wife's birthday party.[44] "It was not at all what I envisioned for that party," he claimed. "We had family present at that party. My wife's parents were there. My daughters were there. It was in bad taste and certainly nothing I would ever choose." Just like the $6,000 shower curtain.

Kozlowski's *modus operandi* during the years he was CEO included *absolute* delegation of decision-making and details, as he did with Barbara Jacques for his wife's birthday party. He was by choice focused completely on running the company and he had plenty of money. So he simply handed his checkbook along with his authority and responsibility to those around him who were paid generously to take care of the details of the CEO's personal life and financial affairs.

In the visitors' room at the Mid-State Correctional Facility more than nine years after the Roman orgy on Sardinia, Kozlowski and three former members of the *Endeavour* crew who were visiting him in prison talked about the night they attended the infamous birthday party. Kozlowski said, "It wasn't one of the better parties I've been at in my life."[45] Sparky, Lars, and Joe agreed that the party was not the wild event the media and the Manhattan DA portrayed it to be. All four said Kozlowski was only at the party for around three hours, maybe less, on the night of June 14, 2001.

It didn't matter that he found the party distasteful, and it didn't matter that he stayed only a few hours. It didn't matter that there were Tyco Directors and their spouses at the party. It didn't matter if many members of the top management team were there. It didn't matter that Kozlowski instructed Jacques to charge him for all personal expenses. It didn't matter that the theme was not his idea. Once the jury saw that video, once the media sensationalized juicy images of Kozlowski's Roman orgy, that birthday party was used to define him. The taint of Sardinia cost both Dennis Kozlowski and Tyco far more than the $2 million they spent on the birthday bash.

NINE

EXTRAORDINARY TIMES

Tyco and Dennis Kozlowski continued to prosper during fiscal year 2001, which ended on September 30th. In his letter to shareholders published in the 2001 Annual Report, the CEO described another year of outstanding performance with Tyco reporting double-digit percentage increases in revenue and earnings despite the 2001 recession. The accomplishments of FY 2001 included more than just the company's strong financial performance. The Tyco Board of Directors successfully negotiated and entered into Retention Agreements with both Kozlowski and Swartz; the wildly successful CEO and CFO would be leading Tyco and managing the company's growth for years to come. In more good news, Standard & Poor's upgraded Tyco's credit rating in the spring of 2001. The company was solid, growing, and the future looked bright.[1]

* * *

Tyco announced the completed acquisition of The CIT Group, Inc. (CIT) on June 1, 2001. It was an almost $10 billion deal—Tyco tendered both cash and stock for the commercial finance company. When the deal closed, Kozlowski said CIT was "an ideal fit for Tyco" and added great value including financing opportunities Tyco intended to offer its customers in several business units. He noted that CIT would be immediately accretive to earnings, as was expected of all acquisitions made by Kozlowski's Tyco, and stated that the addition of CIT would "result in enhanced levels of organic growth, recurring revenue, stable profitability and competitiveness across [all] Tyco divisions."

Albert R. Gamper, Jr. was President and CEO of CIT at the time of the acquisition. After Tyco acquired the company, he retained his titles and roles and Gamper joined the Tyco Board. At the time of the acquisition, he said the alliance would enhance CIT's "leadership position as an innovative global source of financing and capital leasing." Mike Snyder, who at the time was President of Tyco's ADT business, said that "our commercial customers have been asking for financing and leasing options for years and through our new relationship with CIT, we have the ability to quickly and knowledgably respond to our clients' financing needs effectively providing a higher level of customer satisfaction." Kozlowski envisioned CIT as a great benefit to customers—Tyco would manufacture and sell products, Tyco would provide installation and other services, and Tyco would benefit from the fees and interest customers paid to finance their purchases.[2]

The CIT deal seemed to break one of Kozlowski's hard and fast rules about the types of companies Tyco would and would not acquire. On numerous occasions, Kozlowski said "[a]cquire businesses that you know something about—no new platforms," and he emphasized that "[a] deal has to fit into one of our four areas of specialty and improve our preexisting business. There are no non-core businesses at Tyco and so no reason to acquire companies outside our areas of expertise." More than a decade after Tyco acquired CIT, Kozlowski insisted that the deal did not break his rules. "We had been considering the addition of a financing arm for quite some time," he explained. "CIT gave us the ability to offer financing to our customers. The acquisition was intended to enhance a number of our businesses by providing customers a one-stop solution." At the time of the acquisition, Kozlowski said he was open to adding other financial services firms—Tyco would use CIT as a platform to expand into finance the way the company used the Kendall acquisition to expand into healthcare.[3]

KENDALL INTERNATIONAL, INC.

Kozlowski believed the first significant acquisition Tyco made after he became CEO was Kendall International, Inc. He began thinking about expanding into healthcare businesses when Hillary Clinton spearheaded healthcare reform in 1993. With the market anxious about highly-politicized government healthcare initiatives, "everyone was selling," Kozlowski said, "but I wanted to buy." He thought the healthcare industry was a good place for Tyco.

Early in his tenure as CEO, Kozlowski looked for opportunities to make the company more recession-proof; he wanted to be less dependent on cyclical industries. "We were heavy in cyclical commercial building products companies," Kozlowski explained, "and we were already in the disposable medical products market. We were making transdermal patches for nitroglycerin and other heart medication, and we were also making portable electrodes—the old heavy electrodes used for EKGs were being phased out and we were making the small, portable electrodes that replaced them." Kozlowski said, "I liked the business. I liked the potential. I thought the healthcare business would give Tyco a more predictable earnings stream." Kozlowski was also attracted to the potential to dominate the market with the right products. He said, "[O]nce you received FDA approval, you had something of value that would last for a while. It made it more difficult for competitors to enter the market."

Tyco began looking at Kendall early in 1994. "The negotiations went on for a few months—the deal was on, and then it was off, and then on again," Kozlowski said. "Negotiations went on through the Memorial Day weekend and stretched into the summer." Finally, the companies agreed to a $1.8 billion stock purchase; the deal was announced on July 14, 1994. Kozlowski said he cancelled all of his plans for the summer of 1994. "Initially, our stock was hit pretty hard, so I had to go to investors, mostly sell-side analysts, and explain that Kendall really was a good deal and worked well for us," Kozlowski said. "I spent the summer trying to get their support. One big shareholder told me, 'Kendall is a bag of shit and somebody talked you into buying this bag of shit and it is going to ruin Tyco!'"

"Our investors were nervous about jumping into the healthcare industry," he said. "At the time, *everyone* was nervous about healthcare because of Hillary Clinton's initiatives. There was no good reason to stay out of healthcare—the patients were still going to be there, the demographics were the same, and I was a thousand percent convinced the government wasn't taking over healthcare. Not in my lifetime."

When the $1.8 billion Kendall acquisition was announced in July of 1994, Kozlowski told journalists that "[o]ur processes and equipment are virtually identical to those currently in use at Kendall, which should allow us to share manufacturing efficiencies and technology." Kozlowski also announced that "[t]he Kendall merger is a very important step in the strategy we developed several years ago to translate our manufacturing expertise in packaging into higher-margin products in the disposable medical products market." When the acquisition was announced, the company said the transaction would "create a $1.2-billion business segment that will serve as a platform for future growth." Kozlowski believed CIT, an acquisition met with similar skepticism as voiced during the Kendall deal, would provide Tyco the same type of opportunities in the financial services sector.[4]

THE CIT GROUP, INC.

In 2001, many people compared Tyco's pickup of CIT to General Electric (GE) and its finance unit GE Capital. Over the years, Tyco was often compared to GE, and Kozlowski seemed to use GE as a template for Tyco's long-term strategy. He considered CEO Jack Welch a "great business leader."[5] GE successfully operated GE Capital; Kozlowski was certain Tyco could do the same with CIT.

In contrast to Kozlowski's clear vision of CIT's place in a diversified manufacturing conglomerate, analysts questioned Tyco's acquisitive entrance into a new and unfamiliar platform—Tyco knew nothing of running a commercial finance business. However, analysts were soothed by Tyco's plan to leave Gamper and other top management in place at CIT.[6]

The CIT deal closed in June of 2001, and Kozlowski had great expectations that it would be yet another profitable multi-billion dollar addition. He had every reason to expect success. He and Tyco had traveled this route hundreds of times, and they had a nearly flawless record of spotting, analyzing, negotiating, buying, and integrating companies that created value for Tyco shareholders. Why would they have expected anything less of the CIT acquisition?

Dennis Kozlowski could not have predicted the devastating events that occurred during the six months after Tyco acquired CIT—events that shook the business and legal environments and changed the world as it existed in the summer of 2001.

THE 9/11 TERRORIST ATTACKS

September 11, 2001 was a picture-perfect fall morning in New York City; the air was crisp and the sky a true cerulean blue. The city sparkled . . . until 8:46 am EST, when American Airlines Flight 11 flew into the North Tower of the World Trade Center in lower Manhattan. The remains of the plane filled the gaping puncture wound in the side of the skyscraper and the impact resulted in a fireball of ignited jet fuel, the smoke from which could be seen on news reports across the country and around the world. The damage to the North Tower was severe, and it was obvious that many people inside the building were injured or killed. However, the magnitude and the meaning of the crash didn't become clear until seventeen minutes later when at 9:03 am EST, hijacked United Airlines Flight 175 flew into the South Tower of the World Trade Center. Millions who were viewing news reports of the first crash watched in stunned disbelief as the airliner crashed into the second skyscraper. *Terrorists.* The United States was under attack.

At 9:37 am, American Airlines Flight 77 crashed into the Pentagon in Washington, DC, and at 10:02 am United Airlines Flight 93 crashed into a field in Shanksville, Pennsylvania. At 9:45 am on September 11, 2001, U.S. airspace was shut down and did not reopen until September the 14th.

The world watched as the tragedy unfolded. At 9:58 am, the South Tower of the World Trade Center collapsed. In ten seconds, the building disintegrated into a plume of debris that coated lower Manhattan with the remains of 2 World Trade Center. The North Tower collapsed at 10:28 am. An hour earlier, the towers at 1 and 2 World Trade Center stood as symbols of American capitalism and embodied the strength of the U.S. economy. On a beautiful fall morning in September of 2001, they crumbled into ruins. In total, 2,973 people were killed during the 9/11 terrorist attacks—the deadliest ever on American soil.[7]

As a result of the attacks, the U.S. stock market was closed for four consecutive trading days—from the closing bell on Monday, September 10 until the opening bell on Monday, September 17. The New York Stock Exchange, located a few blocks from the World Trade Center, had not yet rung the opening bell on September 11 when the towers were attacked. It was the longest market shutdown since 1933, during the Great Depression. When the market reopened on September 17, it fell nearly 700 points, a 7.1 percent decline—the biggest single-day loss in history. By the end of the first week of trading after 9/11, the Dow Jones had dropped over 14 percent and the Standard & Poor's Index was down nearly 12 percent.

The loss of life was so great, it was difficult to bemoan the financial impact of the attacks. But the economic damages were profound; the losses reverberated through many industries and were felt around the world. The attacks exacerbated the 2001 recession in the United States and struck at the heart of American finance. Many individuals and organizations suffered tremendous financial losses as a result.

Dennis Kozlowski was in Midtown Manhattan on September 11, 2001. He and Mark Swartz were at the Essex House meeting with a group of investors and analysts, some of whom had left their offices in the North and South Towers of the World Trade Center to attend the Tyco meeting. In an interview with *CFO Magazine* in the fall of 2001, Mark Swartz said, "We were under way for about 20 minutes when we heard about a fire at the Trade Center." Once news of the tragedy reached the shaken New Yorkers, the meeting ended and never resumed. Immediately after the attacks, Swartz said he and his Tyco colleagues were "trying to figure out where we stood in the world." He said they focused on getting respirators and healthcare supplies to first responders. Tyco provided 400 portable respirators and 30 cases of wound-care supplies during the first days after the attacks. When the market reopened the following week, Tyco stock fell eighteen percent in the first ten days and Tyco's leaders, like those of thousands of other business organizations, were faced with managing the company through an unprecedented crisis. Kozlowski and Swartz fared better than many. Tyco bounced back quickly as Tyco stock returned to its pre-9/11 value in early October.[8]

* * *

Tyco's market cap peaked in December of 2001 when it reached $120 billion. When Kozlowski became CEO in 1992, Tyco's market cap was less than $2 billion. In January of 2002, Kozlowski was once again featured in a *Businessweek* cover story when he was named one of "The Top 25 Managers of the Year."[9] With the worst of the recession and the economic impact of the terrorist attacks behind them, Tyco and Dennis Kozlowski were poised to enter 2002 on strong footing.

ENRON

Corporate America was forever changed on December 2, 2001 when Enron declared bankruptcy. The Chapter 11 filing opened a Pandora's box of scandal the aftermath of which reordered U.S. business and legal environments. Many have dubbed December 2, 2001 as the marker of corporate existence B.E. (before-Enron) and P.E. (post-Enron).[10] The failure of the Houston-based energy giant cost thousands of employees and retirees their livelihoods and retirement savings. Shareholders were devastated as the value of Enron stock plummeted to mere pennies. Thousands of Enron's creditors also took a direct blow. But the ramifications spread far beyond those closest to Enron; its sins created an infectious atmosphere of suspicion and doubt, primarily targeted at other large, quickly growing corporations. Questions hung like ominous clouds over the market and darkened the boardrooms of many publicly traded corporations. How could this have happened? Where were the internal and external controls that should have prevented this type of scandal?

Regulators, prosecutors, and legislators reacted quickly and zealously. Some tried to capitalize on the scandal. In the post-Enron environment, there were rewards for those who spotted the next evil corporate empire. Many corporations, boards of directors, and executives found themselves vulnerable to heightened scrutiny and unwarranted attacks as Enron's long list of transgressions were projected onto them. The world forever changed on December 2, 2001. For Tyco and Dennis Kozlowski, the suspicions raised by David Tice two years earlier breathed new life, and scrutiny of the company ratcheted up as soon as Enron went down.

Of Enron's effect on Tyco, Kozlowski said, "We did hundreds of acquisitions and they all went according to plan for the most part. CIT failed because Enron failed. Moody's and S&P did what they said they would *not* do at the time of the acquisition. They dropped the credit rating and our cost of money went up. We knew that risk. We created a wall to keep CIT independent after we acquired it. Moody's and S&P messed up bad with Enron. They became extra cautious and it was a big problem for our cost of money. We had to spin off CIT. That was the beginning of the end."[11]

TEN

YOU SAY YOU WANT A RESOLUTION

During a Tyco Board of Directors meeting on May 12, 1999, Dennis Kozlowski presented a proposal through which shareholders requested a change in the company's governance policies. Shareholders wanted a majority of Tyco Directors to be independent—as "independence" was defined in the proposal.[1] They wanted assurance that there would be no conflicts of interest, no personal stakes or relationships that might taint the judgment of Directors when they made decisions on Tyco's behalf. The meeting minutes recorded that "it was the sense of the Board that it had in principle no objection to formally adopting a policy that a substantial majority of the Board should be independent directors and that indeed the Board had implemented such a policy. The Board noted, however, [the proposal] as submitted defined independence based on criteria that the Board felt were not appropriate for this purpose. Rather, the Board felt that the judgment regarding a director's independence should be made by the Board based upon his particular circumstances rather than through the application of rigid criteria."[2]

In response to the proposal, the Board reported to shareholders that a substantial majority of Tyco Directors would be independent—so long as the Directors themselves could subjectively determine the meaning of independent on a case-by-case basis. The Directors passed a resolution in which they codified their definition of "independence."[3]

WHEREAS it is important for the Board of Directors of the Company to have a substantial degree of independence from management

NOW, THEREFORE, BE IT RESOLVED that the following Statement of Policy be, and it hereby is, adopted:

A substantial majority of the directors of the Company should be outside (non-management) directors. The degree of independence of an outside director

may be affected by many factors, including the personal stature of the director
and any business relationship of the director with the Company or any business
or personal relationship of the director with management. A director, or firm in
which he has an interest, may sometimes be engaged to provide legal, consulting,
accounting or other services to the Company, or a director may have an interest
in a customer, supplier or business partner of the Company, or may at an earlier
point in his career have been an employee or officer of the Company. Depending
on their significance to the director and to the Company, such relationships may
affect a director's actual or perceived independence. Where such relationships exist, the Board of Directors should be mindful of them and make a judgment about
a director's independence based on his individual circumstances. This would
involve consideration of whether the relationships are sufficiently significant as
to interfere with the director's exercise of independent judgment. If a particular
director is not deemed sufficiently independent, the Board may nevertheless conclude that the individual's membership on the Board remains highly desirable
(as in the case of an inside director) in the context of the Board composed of a
majority of directors with the requisite independence. The overall result should be
a Board that, as a whole, represents the interests of shareholders with appropriate
independence.[4]

In other words, the Board's resolution allowed Directors to maintain a variety of
financially lucrative relationships with Tyco and still label themselves independent. It allowed continuation of many conflicts of interest that existed for decades
among the long-term members of the Tyco Board. Under the Board's definition
of "independence," for example, Tyco's legal work could continue to go to Director Josh Berman's law firm and at the same time, Berman would be considered an
independent Director. Berman, a former Tyco CEO, also maintained a full-time
office in Tyco's New York location, the company footed the costs of the office, and
yet under the Board's definition, Berman would still be considered independent.[5]

Then Director John Fort, who like Berman was also a former CEO, continued
to work out of his full-time office in Tyco's Exeter, New Hampshire location for
many years until he moved to Texas. Tyco paid the office expenses, and under the
definition of "independence" he and his fellow Board members adopted in 1999,
Fort could count himself an independent Director. When Fort was on the Board,
there were also questions about a buyout firm in which Fort was an investor. The
firm purchased $810 million worth of assets from Tyco in 1999, which raised con-
cerns about conflicts of interest.[6] However, under the newly adopted definition,
Fort could still be considered independent.

Director Stephen Foss leased his aircraft, helicopters, and pilot services to
Tyco, for which he received more than $750,000—on top of the Director's fees
he received from Tyco. In addition, Kozlowski said for years, Foss's wife was the

real estate broker Tyco employees were directed to use for any relocation property purchases.

Longtime Tyco Director Richard Bodman took $5 million from CEO Dennis Kozlowski to invest in a private stock fund he managed and yet could call himself an independent Director. Kozlowski said he lost the vast majority of the $5 million he invested in Bodman's fund. Director Frank Walsh held controlling interests in two firms that received more than $3.5 million for leasing aircraft and providing pilot services to Tyco between 1996 and 2000. There was a long list of Tyco Directors who benefited personally from selling services or leasing property to Tyco, and buying assets from or selling assets to the company. There were numerous real estate transactions in which Directors bought property from and sold property to Tyco. Directors solicited investments from officers and engaged in other business dealings between and among themselves—at the same time that they owed fiduciary duties to Tyco and its shareholders. Many financially beneficial relationships (beneficial to the Directors, not necessarily to Tyco) created clear and material conflicts of interest. There were too many blurred lines between personal matters and company business. But it was the way things had always been done at Tyco. The Tyco Directors' definition of "independent" was patently self-serving and did nothing to protect Tyco shareholders.[7]

Other definitions of "independent" are in stark contrast to the one adopted by the Tyco Board in 1999. Other definitions recognize that directors who receive personal benefits from selling to or buying from the company to which they owe a duty of loyalty are *not* independent. For example, Section 301 of the Sarbanes-Oxley Act of 2002, which establishes the requirement that audit committees be composed of independent directors, states that in order to be considered "independent," a director may *not* "(i) accept any consulting, advisory, or other compensatory fee from the [company]; or (ii) be an affiliated person of the [company] or any subsidiary thereof."[8]

Former Tyco director Stephen Foss testified as a witness for the prosecution during Kozlowski's criminal trials. When he was cross-examined by defense attorneys, Foss was asked about payments Tyco Directors received from the company in addition to the fees they were paid for their duties as Directors. Foss was also questioned about a meeting on February 20, 2002 during which the Board approved a change in "its policy with respect to whether or not directors could get paid for services provided to the company other than in their role as directors."[9] The meeting minutes recorded that "[t]he Board expressed its policy regarding the compensation of independent directors by unanimously adopting a resolution that no independent director shall receive any payment for services rendered to, for or at the request of the company, other than the Directors' fees received for his or her services as a director and the reimbursement of out of pocket expenses incurred in performing services as a director."[10] During his testimony, Foss confirmed that the Board changed the policy and redefined independence in February of 2002 so that "directors knew *from that time forward* they could not accept money from Tyco other than the money they would get as remuneration for being directors and for their out of pocket expenses as directors."[11]

The dramatic change to the long-protected policy was prompted by a payment made to Director Frank Walsh in 2001. That particular payment raised concerns among the Board members in January of 2002 and incited the rage of a handful of Directors. So why the change of policy? If it was wrong for a Director to accept a payment from the company in 2001, as some Directors insisted about the payment made to Walsh, if the payment to Walsh was a violation of company policy in 2001, why the need to change the policy in February of 2002? The actions and reactions of Directors related to an investment banking fee Walsh received were difficult to reconcile.

The root of the problem appeared to be perceived unfairness. A few members of the Tyco Board of Directors epitomized hypocrisy; they had for years received payments from Tyco in addition to their Directors' fees. Was the payment to Frank Walsh any different than dozens, or perhaps hundreds of other payments the company made to Directors? There was only one significant difference. The Walsh payment was *big*—$20 million. Walsh received more than the others. One among them had pocketed more from the company's coffers; one among them walked away with a greater personal financial benefit.

The reaction of the Tyco Board is perhaps best explained by the ultimatum game, an economic bargaining phenomenon first studied by economists Werner Güth, Rolf Schmittberger, and Bernd Schwarze in the early 1980s. Wharton Professor Adam Grant, in his 2013 book *Give and Take,* applied the ultimatum game to interpersonal relationships in a business organization. In the game, the "proposer" is given $100 and the authority to propose how to split the money between herself and a "responder." After the proposer offers a split of the money, the responder decides whether to accept or reject the proposed split. If the responder accepts, the split is implemented and both keep the amounts proposed. If the responder rejects the proposed split, both players receive nothing.[12]

If our proposer decides to keep $80 for herself and offers $20 to the responder, studies show the responder will very likely reject the split. Rationally, it seems he would accept any amount offered. Wouldn't it be better to have $20 than to walk away with nothing? But that's not what happens most of the time. Responders will hurt themselves in order to hurt others they perceive as being financially unfair to them. Studies show the vast majority of responders will reject a split that favors the proposer by 80 percent or more.[13] In our example, it costs the responder twenty bucks, but he is willing to forego the money to "punish" the proposer who tried to take more than she offered.

Some of the Directors on Tyco's Board in January of 2002 were so angry about the unfairness they perceived in the Frank Walsh payment, they were willing to destroy their friends, their colleagues, the company, and even themselves in their quest to get even. To punish Frank Walsh for taking more than they took. To punish Dennis Kozlowski and Mark Swartz for paying Frank Walsh more than they were paid. Those Tyco Directors rejected the payment and made sure everyone walked away with nothing. In the spirit of revenge, they killed the goose that laid the golden eggs.

ELEVEN

WHEN THE CIT
HIT THE FAN

Frank Walsh, Jr., an investment banker by profession, joined the Tyco Board in 1992 after he was recommended to the Governance and Nominating Committee by Dennis Kozlowski. The two men knew each other through their connections to Seton Hall University, where each had a seat on the Board of Regents. As a member of the Tyco Board, Walsh served as Chairman of the Compensation Committee for several years and he was lead director from 2001 until 2002.[1]

When he became CEO in 1992, Dennis Kozlowski established the position of lead director, then a relatively new practice in corporate governance. According to a 2011 Harvard Business School (HBS) case study, "Kozlowski had become one of the first CEOs/chairman to have a lead director." In the HBS case study, Kozlowski was quoted as saying, "I don't want mushrooms [in the boardroom]. I want these guys to be in the foxhole with me." The case study also shared Kozlowski's rationale for adding a lead director to Tyco's governance structure; he explained that the role would provide "a real good check and balance."[2] A federal judge who adjudicated the civil action Tyco filed against Frank Walsh years after Kozlowski appointed a lead director described the role more comprehensively when she opined that the lead director had "the responsibility for helping to coordinate the agenda of board meetings, the nomination of new directors, and the board's review of the performance of the Chairman."[3]

In addition to creating the position of lead director, Kozlowski insisted on having a management liaison to the Board. "Our governance under Joe Gaziano and John Fort wasn't as strong as it should have been," Kozlowski explained, "so when I was named CEO and Chairman, I created the roles of lead director and management liaison to the Board. I thought it would improve the flow of information to the Board. It gave the Directors access to people they could contact directly and speak with regularly."[4]

In recalling what he heard when former Tyco directors testified for the prosecution during both of his criminal trials, Kozlowski said, "For any of the Directors to say in court, under oath, that they didn't have access to information is total and complete bullshit!" He insisted that "the Board had access to anyone or anything in the company."[5] But that's not what the Directors said about the investment banking fee Frank Walsh received in 2001.

*   *   *

THE FRANK WALSH INVESTMENT BANKING FEE

Dennis Kozlowski, the Tyco management team, and the Board of Directors had considered for quite some time the possibility of creating or acquiring a finance unit.[6] When asked during Kozlowski's second criminal trial why Tyco was interested in The CIT Group, Frank Walsh explained:

> Tyco was being compared at the time favorably to General Electric Corporation. It was the configuration of the company, a group of industrial companies and so forth was viewed as very similar to G.E. and it was positive for the stock to have that view. A big part of General Electric's business was their unit called G.E. Capital which was among other things in the finance business. So for several reasons, including that it was viewed as a logical business for Tyco to get into, also a number of Tyco companies did business with commercial finance companies financing their machinery or whatever it might be, and there were a number of potential so-called synergies or fits in that area so that was in the very general discussions the Board would have as to what new ideas might be worth pursuing. That type of business was identified and I think universally agreed as something logical for us to look at if the opportunity came along."[7]

In mid-2000, Walsh told Tyco Directors during a brainstorming session in Bermuda that he had a connection to Al Gamper, then President and CEO of CIT. Walsh knew of the company and Gamper because "CIT was based in New Jersey not far from where I lived. Mr. Gamper lived nearby and over the years we had become friends from a variety of social church community activities, charitable things."[8]

Once Walsh pointed Tyco in the direction of CIT, the Board expressed interest in the company, after which Tyco's acquisition team spent a couple of months researching the commercial financing company. Kozlowski then called Walsh, told him CIT looked like an interesting target, and asked how best to proceed. In October of 2000, Walsh met with Gamper and pitched the idea of Tyco acquiring CIT. Immediately after the meeting, Walsh called Kozlowski to report what he learned. He recounted their conversation under oath during Kozlowski's second trial. Walsh said:

I told him that the meeting had gone very well, that Al was potentially interested. He had several major threshold issues that would be potential problems that would have to be dealt with, but on balance he was open to the idea. I had gone to great length to show him the reasons why I thought it made sense from his point of view and his people's, and he was—he indicated that—at that time their largest shareholder was a Japanese bank which owned about 20 percent of CIT and he indicated he wanted to run the thought by them. And he had a meeting coming up in Japan shortly thereafter, so that's where we left it and I reported to Dennis [what] were initial concerns to Al so that Dennis and his people could look into them and develop responses.[9]

Walsh connected with Gamper again after his return from Japan. He arranged and attended a meeting with Kozlowski and Gamper at a restaurant in Florham Park, New Jersey in December of 2000. Kozlowski said after the men exchanged pleasantries, they discussed the possibility of joining CIT with Tyco. During his trial testimony, Kozlowski recalled that "Al Gamper raised some concerns and those concerns involved rating agencies . . . the agencies that rate his credit which becomes a function of how much money he has to pay or CIT has to pay for money, and just wondered if the rating agencies would look negatively towards CIT being owned by an industrial company."[10] Kozlowski explained for the jury the significance of a corporation's credit ratings. "Rating agencies are companies like Standard and Poor's and Moody's. There are others. [They] assess the risks of a company's credit and they rate from triple A to double A, a whole rating system. The higher your rating, the cheaper you borrow [money]. The lower your rating, the [more] you have to pay because you are considered to be riskier and CIT had a fairly good rating; I think double A or someplace around there." Kozlowski continued by explaining that "[i]f you were to jeopardize that rating, your costs to run your business would go up substantially and could hurt your profits and hurt your ability to function as a business."[11] Gamper was right to raise concerns about the impact a combination with Tyco would have on CIT's ratings.

Walsh said, "[After the meeting] I drove Dennis back to the airport, we had a discussion before he left to go where ever he was going, and we agreed in our discussion that the conversation had gone very well, and that, you know, we were—it was a very interesting prospect. And Dennis volunteered at the time that should the transaction—should a transaction ultimately be accomplished that I should be entitled to an investment banking fee for the work I had done teeing it up, so to speak, getting it to that point."[12] Kozlowski's testimony was consistent with Walsh's recollection.

The acquisition team proceeded and a vote of the Tyco Board gave Kozlowski authority to move forward with the deal.[13] Walsh did not vote yea or nay—he was not present at the meeting when the Board approved the CIT acquisition. The minutes from that meeting did not indicate whether other Directors knew, or did not know, of the fee that Kozlowski and Walsh had tentatively discussed.

CIT and Tyco reached and announced a merger agreement in March of 2001, after which Walsh said he revisited with Kozlowski the possibility of receiving an investment banking fee for the role he played in bringing CIT to Tyco. Walsh said he and Kozlowski "had a brief discussion where I said I'd like to keep that fee discussion—keep that fee discussion we had had on the table and [Kozlowski] confirmed that it had never been off the table, I think were his words and that's where things stood at that time."[14]

During Kozlowski's criminal trial, Walsh confirmed that he reviewed the Form S-4 Registration Statement Tyco prepared in March of 2001. An S-4 is a form filed with the SEC—it is a public disclosure made as part of a plan of merger.[15] Walsh said the S-4 specifically disclosed investment banking fees that would be paid to Lehman Brothers and Goldman Sachs, but there was no indication that he would receive a fee. However, Walsh explained that when Tyco prepared the S-4, "there was no firm fee agreement. There had been that initial discussion and a subsequent discussion between Dennis and me that we had this fee discussion to deal with at some point, but there was no agreement." After he reviewed the SEC disclosures, Walsh spoke to Mark Swartz, who assured him that his fee had been properly disclosed in Tyco's financial statements. Swartz specifically referred to a *pro forma* balance sheet which reflected expenses Tyco would incur during the merger, including investment banking fees.[16] Years later in the civil action Tyco brought against Walsh, Swartz's assertion was confirmed when Federal Judge Denise L. Cote stated in her findings of fact that "Tyco recorded the entire $20 million payment on its books as a cost related to the acquisition of CIT."[17]

Tyco completed the CIT acquisition in June of 2001. Later that summer, Walsh reminded Kozlowski of the fee he was owed for his work in facilitating the deal. Kozlowski said Walsh wanted his investment banking fee calculated using the same scale used to calculate the fees paid to Goldman Sachs and Lehman Brothers; Walsh expected a fee of around $40 million.[18] When he testified during Kozlowski's trial, Walsh described the negotiation of his fee as " . . . a cordial civil discussion and the objective was to come up with something that was fair and market, the kind of thing that was conventional for a 10 billion dollar transaction."[19] Kozlowski researched the standard fee that would be paid for the services Walsh rendered to the company, after which he met with Walsh in July of 2001, at the same New Jersey restaurant where Walsh took him to meet Al Gamper several months earlier, and negotiated what both men believed to be a reasonable, arm's-length fee—considering what Tyco would have paid an investment bank to perform the same services in a $10 billion acquisition. Kozlowski authorized a $10 million payment to Frank Walsh and a $10 million charitable contribution to a charity of Walsh's choosing.[20] The $10 million payment to Walsh was one tenth of one percent (0.1%) of the $10 billion transaction.

On its face, a $10 million fee seems outrageous for the work Walsh did for Tyco to facilitate the CIT acquisition. But relative to the market rate investment bankers receive for referrals, or finder's fees, 0.1 percent is low. In 2012, an investment banker filed a civil action demanding a one percent finder's fee for initiating contact between Apple and Anobit that resulted in a $390 million acquisition. The investment banker expected between $3.9 million and $4.5 million, depending on applicable currency exchange rates. In a 2005 *Businessweek* article titled "The Facts on Finder's Fees," an investment banker said he would ask for one percent of the selling price but would be happy to settle for less.[21]

After Kozlowski and Walsh agreed on the 0.1 percent fee (0.2 percent, taking into account the $10 million charitable contribution), there were a series of faxes and communications between Walsh and Tyco—faxes addressed to then CFO Mark Swartz and faxes sent from Tyco to Walsh requesting an invoice for his services. Walsh provided an invoice on July 18, 2001. It read, "For investment banking services rendered in connection with the acquisition of The CIT Group Inc. . . . $10,000,000."[22] He also provided Tyco with information about the charity to which he designated the $10 million contribution.[23] After the charitable contribution was made, the organization provided Tyco a receipt reflecting the $10 million contribution and containing requisite tax information. The receipt was addressed and sent to Michael Robinson, then Treasurer of Tyco.[24]

Walsh testified that when he and Kozlowski met in July of 2001, Kozlowski "indicated he would prefer to keep the matter between the three of us; Mark, Dennis and myself." When Kozlowski testified, his recollection was somewhat different than Walsh's—but comparing the two men's versions of the conversation, it's easy to understand how there may have been some degree of miscommunication. When testifying in his own defense, Kozlowski was asked by his attorney Stephen Kaufman, "When you're having these discussions with him about the deal, did you ever say to him, Frank, don't tell anyone about the fee?" Kozlowski replied:

In July when I was having discussions with Frank and we were negotiating a fee, Frank suggested that he speak to other investment banks to get some guidance as to what an appropriate fee would be. I asked Frank that he keep our discussion on the fee during that time of the negotiations, *and the negotiations only,* I asked that he keep that between us. Now my concern there was if he were to go out and ask Goldman Sachs or Lehman Brothers or First Boston, their motivation is to drive up the fee. Because when an investment bank comes in to you to say we're going to do a nine, ten billion dollar—when an investment bank comes in and negotiates a fee, they show you what the last high fee was, what the high water mark was, so anybody Frank would be going to for advice would be very much motivated to get as much money as he possibly could.[25]

It seems Walsh left the meeting believing Kozlowski asked him to keep the payment a secret. If so, it may be another example of Kozlowski's failure to properly communicate and assess risk when dealing with someone he trusted—like when he hired his wife's friend to decorate the Fifth Avenue apartment and ended up with a $6,000 shower curtain. Former Tyco Director Robert Monks said, "Dennis wouldn't have said no to Frank Walsh. He respected Walsh, looked up to him—he trusted him."[26] According to both Walsh and Kozlowski, the payment was fair. And they didn't feel compelled to memorialize the agreement until Walsh was asked to supply an invoice for his services weeks after the deal closed.

Although the payment was legitimate, the degree of informality was inappropriate. Walsh and Kozlowski should have negotiated a fee up front if both believed Walsh was in a position to provide valuable services to Tyco. There should have been an express written agreement and the payment should have been disclosed to the rest of the Board. But as often happened in Tyco corporate headquarters, an informal agreement between two people who trusted each other was all that existed of the negotiation. When Walsh and Kozlowski needed evidence of what they discussed, there was little available. In their defense, neither Walsh nor Kozlowski imagined they would need documentation. It seemed neither man believed he was doing anything wrong at the time. However, doing business with someone he trusted once again came back to bite Dennis Kozlowski in the ass.

Even though Walsh believed Kozlowski asked him to keep the investment banking fee quiet, many people in the company were aware of and involved in processing the payment. Based on the number of open communications between Walsh and the company, the payment of the investment banking fee was not a closely held secret. Tyco requested and Walsh provided an invoice—not in a clandestine meeting in a dark alley where a top-secret document was passed between gloved hands, but via a company fax machine during a normal business day. Moreover, the receipt for the charitable contribution went to Michael Robinson, not to Kozlowski or Swartz.

Former Tyco Executive Vice President Brad McGee testified that he learned of the Walsh investment banking fee when documents arrived at CIT in 2001. McGee was working in the newly acquired finance unit at the time. In McGee's presence, then CIT Chief Executive Officer Al Gamper discussed with Mark Swartz the methods to be used to account for the fee. Would it be reflected on CIT's books or on Tyco's? At the time of this conversation, Gamper was slated to soon join the Tyco Board of Directors; it would have been unwise to forward documents to him and discuss accounting methods with him if Kozlowski and Swartz intended to keep the Walsh investment banking fee a secret. Gamper could have easily discussed the payment with other Directors.[27]

In addition to all of the other documents and communications, Walsh completed at the end of fiscal 2001 his annual Directors and Officers Questionnaire (DOQ), an instrument used to collect information needed to prepare the proxy and annual report. Walsh included the $10 million investment banking fee on his DOQ.[28] Both the fee and the charitable contribution were disclosed as related-party transactions in Tyco's fiscal year-end 2001 Proxy Statement, which was filed with the SEC and available for public viewing:

> Mr. Walsh, a director, was instrumental in bringing about the acquisition by a subsidiary of the Company of The CIT Group, Inc. (now Tyco Capital Corporation) of Livingston, New Jersey. For his services, Tyco paid Mr. Walsh a fee of $10 million. In addition, at Mr. Walsh's request, Tyco contributed $10 million to a charitable fund established under The Community Foundation of New Jersey. Mr. Walsh, as trustee of this fund, recommends the public charities to which contributions are made. At the time of the acquisition, Mr. Walsh owned 50,000 shares of common stock of The CIT Group, Inc., which were converted to 34,535 Tyco common shares at the exchange ratio applicable to all stockholders of CIT.[29]

Although the payment appeared to be processed in the regular course of business and was disclosed to the SEC as required, it became clear that most of the Directors on Tyco's Board were unaware until they read the 2001 fiscal year-end Proxy, after it was drafted in January of 2002, that Kozlowski authorized and Walsh received the $10 million payment.

The information was not well received.

During trial testimony, former Director John Fort said he received a phone call from Kozlowski before the regularly scheduled Board meeting in January of 2002 during which Kozlowski told him about the Walsh payment. Fort recalled that "[Kozlowski] told me that one of the matters we needed to take up [at the] upcoming meeting was to approve the payment to Mr. Walsh as a Board because it had to go in the proxy statement which was close to being ready to go to the printer. It was disclosed, something that had to be disclosed to the shareholders and we needed to approve it so that could go in the proxy that way."[30]

Fort then told the jury about the rest of that telephone conversation. He said, " . . . we talked about it and Dennis told me that at the time the acquisition was under consideration, Frank had told him that if this thing went through, you know, he probably should get a fee. It sounded like it was some sort of a joking fashion, but afterwards Frank asked for a fee. He asked for a 40 million dollar fee and Dennis had cut it back to 20 million and paid him." Fort said he spoke to two or three other Directors prior to the Board meeting but that he did not speak directly with Frank Walsh about the investment banking fee.[31]

THE HUDDLE

By all accounts, the Tyco Board's huddle in Boca Raton, Florida on January 16, 2002 did not go well. "Huddles" were informal gatherings of Directors for which no minutes were prepared to memorialize discussions and decisions.

By the end of 2001, a month before the huddle and just six months after the CIT deal closed, the acquisition had already proven to be a serious problem. As a result, Kozlowski spoke to Frank Walsh and asked him to return the fee he received. Kozlowski said, "We were going to have to very quickly spin off CIT, so I asked Frank to return the fee. I thought it seemed like the right thing to do. The acquisition wasn't working out. But at the time our investment bankers were telling us we could still sell CIT for around $12 billion, which would net somewhere between $2 and $3 billion for Tyco. Frank knew that and said there was no reason he should return the fee he earned. The company was still going to profit from the deal and there was no reason he should return the fee."[32] Walsh made a good point. Certainly Goldman Sachs and Lehman Brothers weren't going to return the fees they received as part of the CIT deal. By the time the Directors huddled in Boca Raton on January 16th, Kozlowski felt comfortable defending his decision to authorize the payment to Walsh, but from the reaction he received when he spoke to John Fort before Board members arrived in Florida, he suspected he and Walsh were going to face a few angry Directors.

The Walsh payment wasn't raised until near the end of the huddle, after the Directors wrapped up preliminary discussions about splitting Tyco into four separate companies. It was an intense day; the weight of the agenda items betrayed the informality implied by dubbing the meeting a huddle. And there were no minutes—the Directors did not document their discussions on January 16, 2002, even though the issues were clearly of great importance to Tyco shareholders.

Once the issue was broached, some of the Directors became very angry about the payment to Walsh and insisted that he immediately return the $10 million fee.[33] In the days before the huddle, Walsh learned that at least a few of his fellow Directors had questions about the payment, so he sought the advice of independent legal counsel who confirmed in writing that the investment banking fee was appropriate. During the huddle, Walsh presented a letter dated January 15, 2002 from James F. Tannenbaum of Stroock & Stroock & Lavin LLP opining that nothing in Tyco's bye-laws limited the company's ability to pay Walsh an investment banking fee and that "even a cursory review of our data base has identified a number of instances in which finder's fees have been paid to a director in connection with an acquisition."[34]

Despite the opinion of counsel, and even though the Directors should have had full access to and knowledge of the company's bye-laws, some of them questioned whether payment of the fee required Board approval. Several years later during the criminal trials, the same Directors still had no definitive answer to that question.[35] Notably, some of the Directors were supportive during the huddle and felt Walsh rightfully earned the fee.[36] But a few others levied ugly accusations at Walsh, and according to the findings of fact of Judge Cote in *Tyco. v. Walsh*, "the Board told Walsh to return the payment and advised him that if he refused, he would not be re-nominated to the Board."[37] At that point, Walsh reportedly picked up his things, told his fellow Board members "*adios*," and left the meeting. That was the last time Frank Walsh participated in activities of the Tyco Board of Directors.[38]

* * *

It was P.E., and the world had changed. In the highly charged post-Enron environment, the Tyco Board was subjected to unprecedented scrutiny and the Directors had serious issues to address in a very hostile environment. In addition to voicing concerns about the payment to Walsh during the January 16th huddle, they discussed and then officially decided a few days later during the January 20, 2002 Board meeting to break up the company. In addition to the stress induced by the Walsh controversy and the big decisions they made about the future of the company, the Directors had to deal with the rapidly declining price of Tyco stock (TYC). Just a few weeks earlier, TYC traded near $85 a share, and the company had a record-high market capitalization of $120 billion in December of 2001.[39] But by the end of January 2002, the stock had dropped below $50.[40] Tyco Directors were no doubt anxious about the state of the company. It was a difficult time for leaders of all large publicly traded corporations, but the leadership of Tyco seemed to suffer more than most.

Even so, it's difficult to reconcile the Tyco Directors' reaction to the payment Frank Walsh received. It was not unlike many other related-party transactions—other payments received by Directors over many years. Plus the Walsh payment was exactly like expenditures Dennis Kozlowski had approved hundreds of times.

During the criminal trials, John Fort was asked if Kozlowski had the authority to pay investment bankers in connection with acquisitions to which Fort testified under oath, "Yes, he did." Fort was asked if Kozlowski had a duty to disclose the Walsh payment to the Board of Directors. Fort testified under oath that "[t]he obligation was on Mr. Walsh, I don't know of any obligation on Mr. Kozlowski."

When asked if the Tyco bye-laws allowed a payment like the one Walsh received in connection to the CIT acquisition, Fort explained, "A director can act by himself in a professional capacity with the Board and receive a fee for it." Fort continued his explanation when he told the jury that he didn't know if the Board had any authority to approve or disapprove fees paid to Directors for services they sold to Tyco. It seemed such payments simply had to be disclosed.

Fort read in open court from the Tyco bye-laws: "Any director who, whether directly or indirectly, has an interest in a contract or proposed contract or arrangement with the company shall declare the nature of his interest at the meeting of directors during which the question of entering into the contract or arrangement is first taken into consideration."[41]

The same section of the bye-laws provided that "[a] Director shall not vote (nor be counted in the quorum) on any resolution of the Directors in respect of any contract or arrangement in which he is to his knowledge materially interested, and if he shall do so his vote shall not be counted. . . ."[42] For Frank Walsh, Dennis Kozlowski, and Mark Swartz, the penalty levied because Walsh failed to disclose the payment to the Board of Directors was far greater than having their votes disregarded.

Frank Walsh did not disclose to the Board, at least not in as timely a manner as they wanted, his interest in the CIT acquisition, as was required by the Tyco bye-laws. But he did not vote on the acquisition, which is compliant with the bye-laws. The Tyco Board approved the acquisition of The CIT Group at a special meeting held in Pembroke, Bermuda on March 12, 2001.[43] Frank Walsh was not present and he did not vote.

During that meeting, the Tyco Board empowered Kozlowski and Swartz to acquire CIT. The Board voted "that the officers of the Company be, and they hereby are, authorized and empowered to enter into all such agreements, to execute guarantees and to take all such other action necessary or desirable to implement each of the foregoing resolutions [to acquire The CIT Group]."[44] Relying on the express authority granted to him by that empowering resolution, Kozlowski authorized a payment of $10 million (plus an additional $10 million to charity) to Frank Walsh for services rendered in the CIT acquisition. By all accounts, and according to uncontroverted evidence presented during both trials, Dennis Kozlowski had the authority to approve investment banking fees. He had done so hundreds of times without a single problem.[45] Why was *this* time different?

TWELVE

"OH GOD, WHAT NOW?"

In addition to their collective perception of unfairness, anger about the size of the fee, and concern with the manner in which it was paid, the unexpected reactions of some Directors to the Frank Walsh payment had a lot to do with its timing. The dust from Enron's implosion was everywhere, and it polluted the air in the Tyco boardroom. Plus for the first time in more than a decade, things weren't going well. For ten years, it seemed everything fell in Tyco's favor. But the company's fortune had shifted, and the fates turned cold. As of January of 2002, everything went wrong.

* * *

On January 28, 2002, Global Crossing declared bankruptcy.[1] Like Tyco, Global Crossing was a Bermuda-based corporation. (In 1997, Tyco became a corporate citizen of Bermuda during a reverse merger with ADT Limited, an electronic security business then based in Bermuda. The ADT merger was one of the largest and most successful mergers and acquisitions during Kozlowski's tenure as CEO.) Global Crossing also operated in several of the same industries as Tyco. The two companies were intertwined; Global Crossing bought cable from Tyco, sold the circuits on the cable, after which Tyco installed the cable. Kozlowski explained, "When Global Crossing went bankrupt, Tyco investors got spooked. They were investors in Global Crossing as well as Tyco."[2]

When Global Crossing failed, the price of Tyco stock fell. The bankruptcy undoubtedly made Tyco shareholders anxious and played a part in the declining stock price. But the company was simultaneously and negatively affected by so many things during the first half of 2002, it's impossible to pinpoint the extent to which any single factor caused Tyco's stock price to suffer.

The first several months of 2002 became extraordinarily difficult for Tyco and Kozlowski. After the Walsh investment banking fee was disclosed, after the announcement of Global Crossing's bankruptcy, while dealing with the post-9/11

economy amid allegations of Enron-like accounting irregularities and other rumors floated by short-sellers and journalists, and with the company's announced
plans to split into four separate publicly traded corporations, the value of Tyco
stock continued to tumble. In his testimony during the trials, Brad McGee, who
was the head of investor relations and Tyco's spokesperson for several years, summarized the number and nature of rumors present in the immediate post-Enron
environment. McGee said, "There were rumors concerning whether or not there
was an SEC investigation of the company, rumors concerning whether there was
any type of off balance sheet financing vehicles. There were rumors concerning
how we accounted for dealer accounts. There were a whole host of rumors, mostly
issues that [had] been affecting other companies where people were trying to apply
them to us."

McGee explained that "we drew down on backup bank lines and there were
rumors in the market of whether Tyco was going to declare bankruptcy. Rumors in
the market that our auditors quit. Rumors in the market Dennis quit. Rumors in
the market Dennis fired [CFO] Mark [Swartz], and rumors Mark had quit. There
was a lot of anxiety concerning the stock and every hour there was a different rumor we had to face." Asked if any of the rumors were true, McGee said definitively,
"No they were not." McGee emphasized that he had a duty to Tyco shareholders to
address false information and rumors that surfaced because the faulty information
could have a devastating effect on shareholders. He explained that Tyco managers were responsible for providing complete and accurate information. "As part
of that," McGee said, "we have to make sure information in the market about the
company that is not accurate is corrected." McGee also made it clear to the jury that
market perception was the key driver of stock price.[3]

Mark Maremont was a reporter for the *Wall Street Journal* who wrote prolifically about Tyco for a number of years out of the newspaper's Boston bureau.
Kozlowski believed Maremont had a grudge against Tyco because so many of
Maremont's articles appeared to him to be unduly negative, and Kozlowski saw in
the articles what he knew to be sensationalized versions of the facts.[4]

McGee explained that "Mark Maremont always wrote with an investigative
bent. Before he was with the *Wall Street Journal*, Maremont was an investigator. His
mind-set was to look for a scandal." McGee recalled that "there were times when
Maremont had no choice but to write very positive news about Tyco and he did it,
but it seemed he reported good news about us begrudgingly." McGee had to deal
regularly with Maremont and his articles and said after a number of years, "when
anyone told me that Mark Maremont was on the phone for me, I'd think 'Oh God,
what now?'"

"I can still read an article from the *Wall Street Journal*," he said, "and know it
was written by Maremont without looking at the byline."[5]

Maremont authored an article that appeared in the *Wall Street Journal* in
early February of 2002 reporting that Tyco failed to fully disclose 700 acquisitions.

Kozlowski was shocked at the blatantly inaccurate information reported by what was once a reputable source of business news. Even David Tice, the short-seller who questioned Tyco's acquisition accounting methods for several years, said the information in Maremont's article was wrong. Tice, whose Prudent Bear fund was described as "a well-known short-seller of Tyco stock," was quoted in a *CNNMoney* article as saying "Tyco is really correct here. They did make the required disclosure in their cash flow statement as far as how much money they spend net of the cash they received of those companies, so I can see Tyco's point."[6]

Dennis Kozlowski said, "Mark Maremont seemed to want to make a career out of destroying Tyco. The kinds of expenditures he sensationalized in his article were very small—like when Tyco bought out ADT independent reps with 50 accounts. Those are the types of acquisitions that Maremont complained about. Yes, we disclosed them in our financial statements. No, we didn't issue a press release when we bought out a guy in Texas with a handful of home security accounts. If Tyco issued a press release every time the company spent small sums of money, Tyco press releases would have become meaningless and when the company needed to announce something material, something significant, it would've been overlooked due to the sheer volume."[7]

Even as he cast aspersions about Tyco on the pages of the *Wall Street Journal,* Maremont quoted in his article an accounting professor from Pennsylvania State University's Smeal College of Business who said that "Tyco's acquisition disclosures seem to be adequate under accounting rules, because investors were properly given the net cash spent on all its deals."[8]

The day Maremont's article was published—February 4, 2002—Tyco's CFO Mark Swartz and head of investor relations Michele E. Kearns wrote a "shame-on-you" letter to the editor of the *Wall Street Journal:*

To The Editor:

Today's story by Mark Maremont, "Tyco Made $8 Billion of Acquisitions Over 3 Years But Didn't Disclose Them," is blatantly false and malicious. The 240,000 employees of Tyco, to say nothing of your readers and the entire investment community, expect and deserve far better from *The Wall Street Journal.*

With regard to acquisitions made but not announced in 2001, the spending you call "undisclosed" was indeed disclosed by Tyco in its 2001 cash flow statement (page 46 of Tyco's 2001 Annual Report), in note 2 (page 54 of Tyco's 2001 Annual Report) and the MD&A section (page 31 of Tyco's Annual Report). Similar disclosures for 2001 and all prior years are contained in each appropriate Tyco Annual Report on Form 10-K and Quarterly Report on Form 10-Q.

With regard to the quality of Tyco's disclosures, we concur with Professor Ketz, who according to your story said, "Tyco's acquisition disclosures seem to be adequate under accounting rules, because investors were properly given the net cash spent on all its deals." But this isn't just about complying with the rules. In our extensive discussions with Mr. Maremont, we asked him to give us examples of other companies similar to Tyco that do a better job than Tyco on these types of disclosures. He was unable to provide a single example. Furthermore, at the end of our several hours of conversation with Mr. Maremont, he stated: "I understand exactly what the situation is. It's all right there in the cash flow." Bottom line: beyond the inflammatory headline, and given that the story itself concedes that everything that must be disclosed is disclosed, we fail to see the news value of the story you gave such prominence to in today's paper.

Perhaps it's a sign of the extraordinary times we're in that it seems necessary to remind *The Wall Street Journal* that there is a stark difference between issuing a press release and making disclosures. Tyco made over 350 acquisitions in 2001. Of these, over 90% were for less than $50 million. For a company with 2001 revenues of $36 billion, it makes no sense to issue press releases on transactions of this size. Many also involve private sales where, as is customary and common, we are bound from making public announcements by confidentiality agreements signed with the selling individuals or families. All of this was told to your reporter. Surely *The Wall Street Journal* is not suggesting that Tyco issue a press release each time it buys a small, privately held fire protection contractor or alarm company. And if indeed you are suggesting that, are you suggesting it to other companies as well, or just to Tyco?

In the current extraordinary market environment, more than ever, *The Wall Street Journal* has a responsibility to inform rather than sensationalize. In our view, and judging by the reactions to your story we have received this morning from many of our investors and analysts, today's article failed that test.[9]

In addition to having an immediate negative effect on the value of Tyco stock, the prolific amount of false information circulated in 2002 caused long-term problems. For example, the spin and inaccurate reporting found in sensationalized stories and the misstatement of facts included in dozens of articles eventually found their way into a multitude of lawsuits filed against Tyco, its Directors, its independent auditor, and against Kozlowski, Swartz, Belnick, and Walsh. The allegations included in complaints filed in many state and federal courts were lifted from articles like the one Mark Maremont wrote in February of 2002—sometimes the information appeared word for word in court documents.

For instance, these "facts" from Maremont's article appeared in the complaint for a class action securities action that ultimately settled for $3.2 billion:

2. The Tyco Defendants' Failure to Disclose Numerous Acquisitions During the Class Period

148. In addition to engaging in manipulative accounting, Tyco failed to disclose the sheer number of companies it was acquiring, and the amount it was

paying for each. According to a February 4, 2002 report in THE WALL STREET JOURNAL ("Tyco Made $8 Billion of Acquisitions Over 3 Years but Didn't Disclose Them"), defendant Swartz admitted that Tyco had spent about $8 billion over the three previous fiscal years on more than 700 acquisitions that were never announced to the public. . . . [10]

With the permanency of everything that appears on the Internet and the general assumption that if something was published, it must be true, what originated as clearly inaccurate, false, untrue, unfair, sensationalized, and sometimes malicious lies were over time transformed into "the truth." For example, if erroneous information that appeared in an outlet like the *Wall Street Journal* was copied by an attorney into a complaint filed with a court—the inaccurate information represented as a statement of fact (it was in the *Wall Street Journal,* so it must be true, right?)—others relied on the facts stated in a court document, the information then appeared in a dozen new articles, which led to its inclusion in textbooks used in the finest business schools in the United States, and what was in reality clearly inaccurate information over time transformed into the accepted truth. And that kind of "truth" lives forever in cyberspace.

Matt Lauer of NBC's *Today Show,* when interviewed for an October 2013 *Esquire* magazine article, shared his frustration with the same phenomenon—fiction transformed into accepted facts. Lauer was the target of rumors floated by the media when his co-anchor Ann Curry was fired from the morning show in 2012. Lauer said, "The way the media treated what happened with Ann Curry was a disappointing learning experience. I was disappointed by the laziness of the media, the willingness to read a rumor, repeat that rumor, and treat it as a fact.[11]

* * *

More difficulties befell Tyco in early 2002 when the company's formerly stellar credit rating was downgraded. Temporally related to Maremont's *Wall Street Journal* article, the rapid drop in the price of Tyco stock, and the company's use of its backup credit lines, Standard & Poor's lowered Tyco's rating and put the company on "credit watch" in February of 2002. Fitch and Moody's followed suit.[12] Kozlowski's Tyco found itself in unfamiliar territory. Just a year earlier, *Businessweek* ranked Tyco the number one performing company in the S&P 500.[13] But its newly downgraded rating made it impossible for Tyco to retain that coveted spot. In addition, the downgrade prevented CIT (by then renamed Tyco Finance) from upgrading its ratings, which increased the finance unit's cost of money.[14] Without access to cheap capital, CIT was not performing as it should. For its own sake and Tyco's, the finance company had to be sold soon after it was integrated into the Tyco conglomerate. Times were tougher than at any other point during Kozlowski's tenure as CEO. But the worst was yet to come.

THE TYCO BOARD OF DIRECTORS

Many of the troubles Tyco and Kozlowski faced in 2002 stemmed from the Board of Directors—how things were done, and had always been done in Tyco's boardroom. When he testified during Kozlowski's trials, Frank Walsh made it clear that in addition to the investment banking fee, he had other related-party transactions with Tyco—dealings that long predated the 2001 CIT acquisition. He spoke specifically of chartering two aircraft to the company for around seven years. When asked if others at Tyco knew of the arrangement under which a company Walsh owned benefited from Tyco's charter payments, Walsh said, "It was no secret, most everyone was aware of it, everyone on the Board were [sic]." When Assistant District Attorney Scholl asked him how the people on the Board were made aware of the arrangement, Walsh said, "Many of them were transported on this plane and when we came to Board meetings, the plane was usually there along with other private aircraft and everybody knew it was, knew what the arrangement was, knew it was indirectly my plane."[15] He did not mention in his testimony any formal disclosure of the charter payments to the Board. How could Walsh have known when the bye-laws were to be followed and when it was okay to disregard them? How would he have known the investment banking fee had to be disclosed when other related-party transactions did not? The expectations of Board members were wildly inconsistent.

That's how the Tyco directors functioned (or dysfunctioned). Before Enron, formalities were hit or miss. Maybe they followed procedures. Maybe they didn't. Maybe they expected the bye-laws to be followed. Maybe they didn't. Maybe they read company policies and SEC filings. Maybe they didn't. Maybe they recorded minutes of committee meetings. Maybe they didn't. Maybe they knew how the CEO and CFO were compensated. Maybe they didn't. Maybe they read the half-billion dollar retention agreement they entered into with Dennis Kozlowski in 2001. Maybe they didn't. As their former CEO and CFO were being tried for serious crimes, including theft of the investment banking fee paid to Frank Walsh, the Tyco Directors' testimony was telling:

> I don't know if, I don't know when, I don't know what the bye-laws require, I may
> have, I may not have, we may have, we may not have, I don't know what he said,
> I don't know when he said it, I didn't read that document—it was voluminous.

The shockingly frequent response of Tyco Directors on the stand, under oath, during the criminal trials of Kozlowski and Swartz was "I don't recall." It's difficult to understand how two men were stripped of a decade's worth of earnings and thrown into prison on the strength of "I don't recall."

Many of the Directors either didn't know or didn't care that their counterparts on the Board had extra-directorial relationships with Tyco; a number of Directors received money from Tyco for a variety of reasons over many years, and those relationships predated Kozlowski's tenure as CEO. During Kozlowski's first criminal trial, former Tyco Director Richard Bodman was asked if Joshua Berman disclosed to the Board all of the legal fees Tyco paid to Berman's law firm over many years—"[I]sn't it true that the board of directors never voted to make any of the payments that were made to board of director member Josh Berman, that you didn't know about until 2002, isn't that true?" Bodman replied under oath, "That may well be true. I really don't know the answer to that."[16] It's unfortunate that Bodman didn't see the announcements on Kramer Levin's website in which the firm touted its long-standing relationship with Tyco and publicized its representation of the company in multi-million and multi-billion dollar acquisitions—Tyco Director Joshua Berman was listed on the website among the Kramer Levin attorneys who sold their legal services to Tyco.

During the January 16, 2002 huddle, after a number of Directors made it known that the Frank Walsh payment was a serious problem for them, Dennis Kozlowski offered his resignation.[17] Kozlowski told the Directors if they thought his effectiveness had been seriously eroded by the Walsh transaction, he would leave the company. But the Board didn't want Kozlowski's resignation.[18] Clearly, the Directors didn't believe Kozlowski had done anything wrong, and certainly not anything criminal. If they did, they would have seriously violated their duties to Tyco shareholders by allowing him to remain in the most powerful position in the company. In her decision in *Tyco v. Walsh*, Judge Cote found that "[a]s of January 16, the board still had great confidence in Kozlowski's leadership of Tyco and therefore the board chose not to pursue the issue of the payment to Walsh any further."[19]

By the end of January of 2002, all appeared to be forgiven. The Directors didn't continue to chastise Kozlowski about the Walsh payment and the CEO's attention returned to running the company. Kozlowski put the Walsh controversy behind him and focused on breaking up Tyco and on selling CIT. Director Peter Slusser wrote a supportive letter to Kozlowski on January 28, 2002:

Dear Dennis:

This letter is to restate my hundred percent support for the split up of Tyco.

Your logic is very clear. The parts are worth more than the whole. The odds are very high that this result will be proven as these businesses operate on their own. The split up is a brilliant move, and your shareholders will be well rewarded.

If you need additional directors for the spin-off of companies, I would like to put my hat in the ring.

Your corporate move is bold and it will reward your shareholders.

All the best,
Peter Slusser[20]

On February 6, 2002, Slusser sent another letter to Kozlowski in which he wrote:

Dear Dennis:

The Annual Report for 2001 was outstanding.

- The spelling out of Tyco's management policies was clear and concise.
- The $4.7 billion of free cash flow speaks for itself.
- The amount of detail in the MD&A Section and Financial Statement should provide a diligent analyst with ample data.

You and your management continue to do a terrific job for your shareholders under difficult conditions.

Keep moving ahead.

All the best,
Peter Slusser[21]

On February 19, 2002, Slusser sent yet another letter, this one addressed to both Kozlowski and Mark Swartz, in which he wrote: "You two did a terrific job on your analyst telecast today. Stick with your program. Tyco and its shareholders will win in the end. All the best, Peter."[22]

Slusser was not the only supportive Director. On February 21, 2002, during a Special Meeting of the Board of Directors in Pembroke, Bermuda, the Tyco Board passed a resolution to formally designate Tyco's executive officers as required by the SEC.[23]

NOW, THEREFORE, be it

RESOLVED that the Company hereby designates the following persons as "executive officers" and as officers for purposes of Section 16 of the U.S. Securities Exchange Act of 1934:

L. Dennis Kozlowski	Chairman, President and Chief Executive Officer
Mark H. Swartz	Executive Vice President and Chief Financial Officer
Mark A. Belnick	Executive Vice President and Chief Corporate Counsel[24]

The Directors wouldn't have formally designated these men executive officers in fulfillment of federal securities law requirements if they had any suspicion that the payment to Frank Walsh was wrongful, would they? They wouldn't have reaffirmed Kozlowski and Swartz in the top two spots in the company if they didn't trust them.

In May of 2002, Director Peter Slusser once again gave Kozlowski a formal pat on the back. In a letter regarding an interview Kozlowski gave to Dow Jones on May 8th, Slusser wrote: "Dennis, Great job on your interview. $2.60 to $2.70 per share would be terrific for this fiscal year. In addition, your shareholders need your leadership for at least seven more years. Keep up the good work. Peter"[25] Seven more years—the length of time to which the company and Kozlowski agreed in the Retention Agreement signed a year earlier.

The Tyco Board of Directors met many times after the volatile January 2002 huddle. There were official meetings in February, March, April, and May of 2002. Over five months, and in all of those hours together, there were no suggestions that Kozlowski had done anything harmful, there were no discussions about ousting him, and the Board did not ask him to resign.[26] As Judge Cote observed in her opinion in *Tyco v. Walsh*, it was "hardly the kind of treatment that one would expect if the board were disavowing or even questioning the payment."[27]

But by the time Tyco Directors took the stand in Kozlowski's criminal trials (they were *former* Directors by the time the first trial began), they seemed to have revised history. During his sworn testimony, former Tyco Director Richard Bodman said that once he learned of the payment to Frank Walsh in January of 2002, he considered Dennis Kozlowski untrustworthy and knew him to be a thief. When he was asked why the Board didn't accept Kozlowski's resignation when offered, why they didn't ask for his resignation during the months following the January 2002 meeting, Bodman testified, "I was spending a great deal of time gathering facts along with other directors so that we knew exactly what difficulties we were facing."[28]

When asked if the $480 million Retention Agreement had anything to do with the delay in making decisions, Bodman testified that as of January 2002, he had never seen the agreement the Board had entered with Kozlowski a year earlier, and needed to read it before he made decisions about how to proceed. Bodman said under oath:

> If we let Mr. Kozlowski go in an improper fashion or a fashion that suited him in that retention agreement, we might have owed him a great deal more of the shareholders' money. And it didn't make sense to me, wasn't proper to me that a man should be paid more of the shareholders' money on top of the money that he had already stolen from the company. So I said, among the other directors, we all sat down to review that agreement to make sure we knew what the conditions were. These are not agreements that are a sentence or two. They're long. They're

substantial. And they have tricky words in them. And in the end we were successful in accepting Dennis' resignation without an obligation to spend more of the
shareholders' monies to get him out of there. It took awhile.[29]

The Retention Agreement contained one provision that gave the Directors a
way out of performing everything promised in the contract. Under the terms of the
contract, if Kozlowski was terminated "with Cause," the company would have no
further obligations to him. "Cause" was defined as Dennis Kozlowski's "conviction
of a felony that is material and demonstrably injurious to the Company or any of
its subsidiaries or affiliates, monetarily or otherwise."[30] Is that what Bodman suggested in his testimony? Did the Tyco Board read the terms of the Retention Agreement and discover there was just one way to get rid of Kozlowski?

Bodman was questioned about the rationale and wisdom of the Board's delayed plan to address the Walsh payment:

Q. And so you waited for four or five months, and worked with this thief during
   that period, correct, yes or no?
A. Yes.
Q. And you let the thief do other transactions in the name of Tyco during that
   period, yes or no?
A. Yes, we did.
Q. And you met with the thief three times in board meetings during that period
   and dealt with him, yes or no?
A. Yes, I did.[31]

After the first trial ended in a mistrial, the Manhattan DA opted not to call Richard
Bodman as a witness during the second trial.

*   *   *

In December of 2002, the SEC decided to bring a civil action against Frank Walsh
for violating federal securities laws when he signed a registration statement that
he knew contained material misrepresentations—i.e., the Form S-4 that disclosed
investment banking fees going to Goldman Sachs and Lehman Brothers during the
CIT acquisition with no mention of Walsh's fee. The case was settled before it was
filed. Walsh, without admitting or denying the allegations in the SEC's complaint,
consented to the entry of a final judgment that permanently barred him from acting as an officer or director of a publicly traded corporation and ordered him to
pay Tyco restitution of $20 million (with an offset for any restitution he might have
to pay as a result of a 2002 criminal action brought by the Manhattan DA—*People
v. Frank E. Walsh, Jr.*).[32]

On December 17, 2002, *People v. Frank E. Walsh, Jr.* ended when Walsh pleaded
guilty to a violation of New York General Business Law, agreed to pay $20 million

in restitution to Tyco, agreed to pay a $2.5 million criminal fine to the State and City of New York, and agreed to pay $250,000 to the Manhattan DA "in lieu of fines."[33] His plea agreement did not require prison time. Walsh reportedly gave his allocution to the court and then handed an envelope with $22.5 million to prosecutors in satisfaction of the criminal penalties assessed.[34] Walsh was the first and perhaps the only corporate director to be charged with a crime related to any of the Enron-era scandals.[35]

Walsh's legal woes did not end with the SEC action and the criminal charges levied by the Manhattan DA. On June 17, 2002, Tyco filed a civil action against Walsh in federal court seeking recovery of the investment banking fee. The case was filed more than five months after the huddle in Boca Raton. After Walsh was ordered in December of 2002 to repay the $20 million as part of his criminal sentence, Tyco didn't drop its lawsuit, even though the company received the relief they sought in the action. Instead, Tyco demanded interest on the $20 million (the $10 million he received and the $10 million that went to charity) from the date Walsh received payment, and the date Tyco made the contribution to the charitable organization, until Walsh pleaded guilty and paid restitution on December 17, 2002. (Tyco demanded interest from July 19, 2001 to December 17, 2002 at nine percent interest). In other words, Tyco demanded $4,286,084.81 in interest. The company also asked the court to order Walsh to pay Tyco's attorney's fees.[36]

In an opinion based on the clearest findings of fact and what is very likely the most legally sound reasoning found among the dozens of court decisions that emerged from the Tyco scandal, Judge Cote ruled for Frank Walsh in Tyco's civil action against him. The court described accurately that "[m]any board members were deeply distressed to learn that a payment of this magnitude had been made by Kozlowski to a director, but the board took no other steps at the meeting either to ratify the payment or to seek its return."[37]

The court found that "[a]s a fiduciary to Tyco, Walsh had a duty to disclose to Tyco's board that he stood to benefit personally from its approval of Tyco's acquisition of CIT. Indeed, § 64(7) of Tyco's Bye-Laws requires directors of the company to disclose potential conflicts of interest to the board," and Judge Cote held that "[a]lthough Walsh breached his fiduciary duty by failing to disclose his receipt of the $20 million payment, Tyco's board implicitly ratified his breach. It did so through its public filings and statements signaling approval of the payment, as well as its failure to seek return of the payment until months after learning of it."[38] In a succinct and accurate summary, the court opined:

> In 2001, when Tyco paid Walsh and his designated charity $20 million in connection with the acquisition of CIT, Tyco's Bye-Laws permitted its board "to grant special remuneration" to a director who "perform[s] any special or extra services" for Tyco. No later than the January 16, 2002 board huddle, Tyco's directors possessed "full knowledge" of the relevant facts—the circumstances of the payment to

Walsh and the amount of the payment. Fully informed as to the relevant facts, the board members presented Walsh with a choice: he could return the payment, or he could keep the money and leave the board. Walsh chose the latter course of action. For all he knew when he left the January 16 huddle, the board had allowed him to keep the money on the condition that he resign as director. Indeed, the board did not take any action after Walsh left the huddle other than refusing to permit Walsh to be re-nominated to serve on the board at the upcoming shareholders meeting. No mention whatsoever of the payment was made at the official board meeting held on January 20, just a few days after the board huddle at which the payment was discussed with both Walsh and Kozlowski. Further, Tyco's proxy statement disclosing the Walsh payment, filed promptly after the board learned of the payment at its January 16 huddle, contains no statement that the board disapproved of the payment or was seeking its return. Nor does it reveal that the payment was only reported to the board after it had already been made. Rather, the only reasonable reading of the disclosure is that both the company and the board found the payment to be appropriate under the circumstances; the proxy statement reports that Walsh was "instrumental in bringing about the acquisition" of CIT and that the $20 million payment was made in return "[f]or his services" in the transaction. If the board had any reservations about the legality or propriety of the payment, then it would have been expected to disclose those reservations in the proxy statement, for instance, by indicating that it had begun an investigation of the payment and the appropriate course of action to be taken to recover it.[39]

The court pointed to express statements made by then Director Josh Berman: "Berman's statements in February 2002 in defense of the wording of the proxy statement confirm that the board implicitly ratified the payment. Berman told Belnick that he was trying to 'steer a middle course' in which 'the Board just doesn't ratify, doesn't not ratify.' In other words, the board's press releases and SEC filings would suggest to the public that the board approved of the payment, but the board would not pass a resolution expressly confirming the payment. This is the very definition of implied ratification; the board's actions suggested its approval of the Walsh payment without expressly confirming it."[40]

The court was confident that the Board didn't do anything until May of 2002 and that its action in May was "best seen as a reaction to the firestorm of negative publicity that was descending on Tyco" at that time. The court identified the former Directors' revisionist history and stated that "[t]hese after-the-fact assertions are insufficient to overcome the historical record that in January 2002, with full knowledge of the payment, the directors decided not to pursue recovery. . . ."[41]

Following a bench trial (where the judge acts as both judge and jury) on October 12 and 13, 2010, all of Tyco's claims against Walsh were denied.[42]

Dennis Kozlowski with his mother Agnes when Kozlowski graduated from Seton Hall University in the spring of 1968.

Dennis Kozlowski in the boardroom in Exeter, New Hampshire where he became the CEO of Tyco International Ltd. in 1992. © William Taufic.

Kozlowski proudly showing off some of the valves manufactured by Tyco during the 1990s. ©
William Taufic.

Former Tyco CEO Dennis Kozlowski on the day he was sentenced, processed, and identified as inmate 05A4820 by the New York State prison system.

Former Tyco CFO Mark Swartz after being convicted and sentenced in 2005. Swartz was identified by the State of New York as inmate 05A4823.

PART THREE

RING AROUND THE WHITE-COLLAR OF CRIMINAL JUSTICE

Former Manhattan District Attorney Robert Morgenthau was long-known for his pursuit of white-collar criminals. Morgenthau said, "It's very important that the government doesn't go after only people who rob convenience stores. I made a point of going after people in positions of power and trust. The law applies to everyone. That's the message I wanted to send." More than a decade after he charged Tyco executives with serious crimes under New York State law, Morgenthau explained his decision to prosecute Dennis Kozlowski and Mark Swartz. He said, "It sent a message to a lot of people. You can't conceal information and get away with it."[1]

Robert Morgenthau was the inspiration for Manhattan District Attorney "Adam Schiff" on the long-running Dick Wolf television drama *Law & Order*. Morgenthau outlasted his fictional counterpart's tenure by decades. Morgenthau held the office from 1974 until he retired in 2009 at the age of 90. After leaving public service, Morgenthau along with his personal assistant of nearly 40 years, Ida Van Lindt, joined the New York law firm Wachtell, Lipton, Rosen & Katz on West 52nd Street in Manhattan.

THIRTEEN

"*POUR ENCOURAGER LES AUTRES*"

THE ART

Dennis Kozlowski's foray into the world of fine art proved to be one of his biggest mistakes. Kozlowski said he met art dealer Christina Berry on a Saturday afternoon in the summer of 2001 at the home of Bill Koch in Palm Beach, Florida. Berry worked for Fine Collections Management, a company that served as agent for wealthy clients interested in purchasing fine wine and expensive art. Kozlowski found out much later that Fine Collections Management was owned in part by Koch—something Koch didn't disclose when he invited Kozlowski to meet the art agent.[1]

Three Paintings for Tyco: $1.975 Million

In the summer of 2001, Berry helped Kozlowski and his wife select paintings for the Tyco apartment at 950 Fifth Avenue in New York. On behalf of the corporation, Kozlowski authorized the purchase of three paintings from the Richard Green Gallery in London in August of 2001 for a total price of $1.975 million (plus eight percent and an hourly fee for the services of Christina Berry). The paintings were hung in the apartment in September of 2001 and the invoice for the painting was sent to Tyco. As with real estate broker Dolly Lenz and the purchase of the 950 Fifth Avenue apartment, Berry testified in Kozlowski's criminal trial that she was unaware the paintings were purchased by Tyco; she considered Kozlowski and his wife her clients. Of note, Christina Berry was granted immunity from prosecution when sales tax on the purchase wasn't collected and remitted. Her testimony must be viewed in that light. Tyco employees confirmed during the criminal trials that the three paintings were recorded as assets on the books and records of the corporation, and the transaction was handled by individuals at Tyco other than

Kozlowski and CFO Mark Swartz—the purchase was not concealed. Evidence admitted during the trials proved the paintings hung in the Tyco-owned apartment and remained there after Kozlowski was ousted from Tyco in June of 2002.[2]

Four Paintings for Dennis Kozlowski: $8.8 Million

In December of 2001, Berry arranged for paintings from the Richard Green Gallery to be shipped to Kozlowski's home in Florida for his review. Kozlowski chose to purchase four of the paintings for a total of $8.8 million (plus, for Berry's services, an eight percent commission and an hourly fee). The invoice was sent to Tyco, but these paintings were for Kozlowski personally, not for the corporation. During his second criminal trial, Kozlowski produced a promissory note he signed on December 19, 2001 showing that he borrowed funds through Tyco's Key Employee Loan Program (KELP) to pay the entire $8.8 million bill. When asked on the stand if he repaid that loan, Kozlowski testified, "Yes, I paid that loan back to Tyco."[3]

A Monet for Kozlowski: $3.95 Million

In early December of 2001, Berry also arranged for Kozlowski to view a Monet painting that was at the Alexander Apsis Gallery at 930 Fifth Avenue in New York. Apsis brought the painting to the Tyco apartment for Kozlowski to view, whereupon Kozlowski agreed to pay $3.95 million (plus eight percent and an hourly fee for the services of Christina Berry) for the Monet. He made the purchase on January 3, 2002; Kozlowski signed another promissory note when he borrowed $3.95 million through KELP to pay the Alexander Apsis Gallery for the painting. When asked in court "Did you pay it back?" Kozlowski replied under oath, "Yes, I paid that back."[4]

Bragging Rights: Priceless

Kozlowski said he hosted a fundraising event for the Christopher Reeve Spinal Cord Injury and Paralysis Foundation in the 950 Fifth Avenue apartment soon after he made his first serious art purchases. "I bought the paintings and had them hung in the apartment before the event," he said. Kozlowski planned to move the pieces he owned personally to his home in Florida, or possibly to a home in another city after Tyco split up. Considering the company's plans at the time, Kozlowski believed he may be working out of another location and that Tyco would likely sell the Fifth Avenue apartment in the coming months. Kozlowski's pieces of fine art never made it to his home.[5]

During a 2008 interview he gave in the Mid-State Correctional Facility to Swiss reporter Peter Hossli, Kozlowski was asked why he wanted to buy a Monet and a

Renoir. Kozlowski replied, "It was more about bragging rights than anything else. I wanted to be an important art collector quickly. That was ridiculous. I know it and I regret it." Kozlowski admitted that the sole purpose for hanging the paintings in the Fifth Avenue apartment was to impress the rich and famous attendees of the charity event with his expensive collection of fine art. He learned the hard way that pride goeth before a fall.[6]

NEW YORK SALES TAX

In the State of New York, there is an 8.25 percent sales tax on the sale of tangible personal property in the state and in the alternative, a compensating use tax.[7] According to the New York State Department of Taxation and Finance, "New York State and local sales taxes are imposed on taxable property and services purchased or delivered to you in New York State. In most instances, when you purchase a taxable item or service in the state, or if it is delivered to you in the state, the seller will collect sales tax from you. The seller then pays the tax over to the Tax Department." Within the City of New York, vendors are obligated by law to collect the taxes or in the alternative, purchasers are to pay the taxes.[8]

New York sales tax or use tax is due when New York personal income tax returns are due. According to the Department of Taxation and Finance, "Failure to pay tax you owe by the due date may result in the imposition of penalties and interest, or both."[9]

THE WRONG SOLUTION

On April 25, 2002, Tyco announced that it was no longer going to split the company into four separate businesses—backpedaling from plans outlined three months earlier.[10] In a letter to Tyco shareholders, Dennis Kozlowski explained the about-face:

> Our rationale for the break-up plan was based on a simple premise. Despite superior growth in earnings and cash flow, Tyco was being valued at a significant discount to its peers. Among the reasons for the discount was the market's unease with highly complex companies that are in multiple business lines with few obvious synergies. By splitting up the company, we saw an opportunity to address these concerns and accelerate the creation of value for our shareholders. But we know now it was a mistake, and it is time for us to return our focus to what we do best.
>
> While our goal in changing the strategy was to do right by our shareholders, we came up with the wrong solution. In retrospect, it is now clear that we took the market by surprise with our announcement, and failed adequately to take into account the extraordinarily fragile market psychology and hostile environment

that has distracted and damaged our business in recent months. We compounded the problem by delivering some incremental bad news, especially lower earnings expectations tied to both the distraction as well as the continued downturn in the electronics and telecom industries. As your chief executive officer, I take full responsibility and am aware that Tyco's management has let you down.

Having said that, it's been upsetting to see inaccurate reporting and unsubstantiated rumors about Tyco given such a public platform. As stewards of a public company we know we are subject to scrutiny every day and the current climate is one in which all companies are under a microscope. We have always tried to be as transparent in our accounting as possible. Indeed, I consider our disclosure to be second to none among our peer companies. That some in the media would compare us to companies that may have intentionally misled investors through the use of financial chicanery is insulting and inaccurate. To be thrown into stories about "accounting scandals" damages our reputation and casts aspersions on our employees. Yes, critics have raised questions about our accounting, which is why we initiated weekly conference calls to address questions from analysts, investors, and even short-sellers who benefit from a stock's decline. We took all questions asked and didn't shy away from answering them. While we've tried to address the inaccurate reporting, of primary concern to me is how we communicate to you, our shareholders. That's one reason why I am writing to you today.

Right or wrong, one thing is certain: we pursued the break-up plan because we believed it was the best way to unlock value for our shareholders. As anyone who has invested in Tyco over the past decade knows, that is the principle that guides every decision we make. It guided our decision to break up the company. And now, as circumstances have changed, it is guiding our decision to keep it together and take the break up off the table—and to change the way we operate in certain fundamental ways.[11]

Kozlowski tried to reassure shareholders by reminding them of Tyco's long history of growth and solid performance. He wrote:

Let's not forget that we have one of the best track records of companies our size when it comes to delivering shareholder value. According to the *Wall Street Journal's* annual shareholder scoreboard, Tyco delivered average annualized returns of 30.5% for the 10 years ending December 31, 2001. That's the exact same figure the Journal cited for Microsoft's returns over the same time period. We can't lose sight of the enviable performance of this company over the years. Even including this year's decline in the share price, over 10 years the Company's total return is 535%, compared to the Standard & Poor's 500 stock index return of 225%. During my tenure as CEO, we have increased our cash flow per share by 29% annually and our earnings per share by 27%.

Kozlowski closed the letter with a personal note:

> The past few months have been difficult for Tyco's shareholders and employees. For me personally, they have been the most difficult of my career. But the issues are temporary and solvable. I am proud of our workforce. Despite the distractions, the men and women who have made Tyco a great company have proven to be resilient and remain committed to delivering quality services and products to our valued customers.
>
> We know we have some work to do if we are to regain your trust and confidence—and we are committed to returning Tyco to the track of superior performance and shareholder value creation that it delivered in the past decade. Our watchwords for the future are performance, communication and execution.[12]

* * *

The calendar changed from April to May and the difficulties of 2002 continued; life at Tyco did not improve. The company still needed to divest CIT and was dealing with the challenges presented by its recently downgraded credit ratings. While the decision to scrap plans to split up the company received mixed reviews in the market, there's no doubt that management's apparent indecision invited even greater scrutiny. According to Brad McGee, "It was an extraordinary time and Tyco was easy to attack because we were a large company with a lot of moving parts. Everyone had just watched other large companies skyrocket and then flame out." He explained, "Because of our size, our financial reporting was unavoidably complex and even though we were completely confident in our accounting and disclosures, and even though we communicated constantly with our shareholders, the attacks kept coming. With all of the uncertainty, a lot of shareholders got out and waited to see what happened."[13]

The company's stock (TYC) price reflected the struggles of the first four months of what had become the year from hell for Tyco and Dennis Kozlowski. On May 1, 2002, TYC closed at $28.21. A year earlier, it had closed at $74.18.[14]

THE INDICTMENT

Sometimes when it rains, it pours. On top of the business concerns that consumed his life twenty-four hours a day, seven days a week, Dennis Kozlowski learned in May of 2002 that he was somehow involved in a sales tax investigation being conducted by the Manhattan District Attorney. "I thought I was on the periphery of an investigation of one of the galleries that sold me art, or of a dealer who sold me art," Kozlowski explained. "I turned it over to my attorney and asked him to handle it. I had no idea *I* was being investigated."[15]

"At around 2 o'clock on Friday afternoon the weekend after Memorial Day, I received a call from my attorney Stephen Kaufman," Kozlowski recalled. That telephone conversation was one of the most shocking of his life. "He informed me that the Manhattan DA was going to indict me on sales tax evasion charges related to art that I purchased. He told me I was going to be indicted the following week." Kozlowski said, "But Stephen said 'Don't worry—don't worry about it. I'll never let it bring you down.'"[16]

Kozlowski was in his office in Boca Raton on Friday May 31, 2002 when he received Kaufman's call. "I didn't know when I left that evening," he said in a voice that after more than a decade was still heavy with shock and grief, "that I would never again return to a Tyco office."[17]

Even though the sales tax charges were a personal matter, Kozlowski was the CEO and Chairman of the Board of a huge publicly traded corporation. He was fully aware that he had to address his personal troubles with the Tyco Board. Because of his position, the company and its shareholders had an interest in any personal legal issues he faced. On Friday evening after he left his office, he spoke to Tyco Chief Corporate Counsel Mark Belnick, and over the weekend of June 1st and 2nd, Kozlowski called all of the Directors to inform them of the forthcoming indictment. Kozlowski recalled that Josh Berman told him he would have to step down because "there was too much mud on the windshield."[18]

Kozlowski said, "On Sunday I flew to New York. I spent the evening and well into the night on the phone with Stephen Kaufman. At around midnight," Kozlowski recalled, "I heard from Stephen Kaufman who heard from David Boies [the attorney the Board hired] who supposedly heard it from the Board—I was out. There was no Board meeting, there was no vote, they didn't speak with me, they didn't even give me a chance to explain or to gather additional information about the charges in the indictment. It was over. I was out."[19]

Dennis Kozlowski was indicted on Tuesday June 4, 2002 by Manhattan DA Robert Morgenthau on charges that he made an agreement with Christina Berry to evade the sales tax Berry was obligated to collect and submit for his art purchases.[20] It was clear the DA knew who Kozlowski was and what he did for a living. The sales tax indictment, which had nothing to do with Tyco, stated that "[t]hroughout the period of the conspiracy defendant Kozlowski was the Chairman of the Board, President, and Chief Executive Officer of Tyco International Ltd. ("Tyco") a publicly traded multinational corporation with reported sales of more than $36 billion in the fiscal year ending September 30, 2001."[21]

Kozlowski pleaded not guilty at a brief court hearing in New York on June 4, 2002; he was freed pending trial after posting a $3 million bond. The indictment included eleven felony counts, each punishable by up to four years in prison, and alleged that Kozlowski evaded around $1 million in sales tax on purchases of fine art. In an article published by *Tax-News* two days after the indictment, the writer observed that "[t]he authorities have decided to make a high-profile example of Mr. Kozlowski '*pour encourager les autres*. . . .'"[22] The reference is to Voltaire's *Candide*. "*Dans ce pays-ci il est bon de tuer de temps en temps un amiral pour encourager les autres*" translated means "in this country we find it pays to shoot an admiral from time to time to encourage the others."[23]

Considering the applicable New York State tax laws, it's clear Christina Berry and the galleries had the primary obligation to collect and submit sales tax on the art purchases. In fact, the Manhattan DA's indictment of Dennis Kozlowski was the first time a prosecutor in the State of New York ever charged a retail consumer with a crime for failing to pay sales tax. Berry seemed the obvious party to charge when sales taxes weren't collected and remitted. But instead of charging her, the Manhattan DA granted Berry immunity from prosecution.[24]

He didn't want Christina Berry. Morgenthau wanted the lion.

* * *

The Manhattan DA's office never interviewed Kozlowski—either before he was indicted or afterward. He wasn't asked about the art purchases or what he believed Christina Berry handled in her role as his agent.[25] In an interview in 2008, Kozlowski explained why the sales taxes were not paid at the time of purchase. He said, "I didn't know a whole lot about art when I was trying to collect some nice pieces of art. And I hired an agent to help me with the art. It was the agent's responsibility to negotiate the price of the painting, and to cover all the taxes and transportation. And then I just see the art hanging on the wall. That was my next step in this process. I wasn't consciously thinking about sales taxes." Kozlowski said that some of the evidence the DA used against him was found in email messages allegedly written by Christina Berry. He said, "I never used email. One would assume that this agent is the person messing up. However, nobody wants to prosecute an agent. Everyone wants to bring down a Chairman and CEO of a company."[26]

More than a decade after he charged Kozlowski with evading sales taxes, former Manhattan DA Robert Morgenthau explained why he indicted Kozlowski, the consumer, instead of charging the art agent who or the galleries that sold the paintings. "Kozlowski was too central to the case," he said. When asked how he was certain at the time that Kozlowski had any knowledge of whether the sales tax for the paintings had been paid, the former Manhattan DA said definitively, "Kozlowski knew those paintings were in New York, so he knew he was evading taxes. That's why I indicted him."[27]

Interestingly, one of the art purchases included in the indictment took place in January of 2002. Under New York law, sales tax on that purchase would not have been due from Kozlowski until April 15, 2003, ten and a half months *after* he was indicted.[28]

During Kozlowski's criminal trial (a trial on other charges) three years after the sales tax indictment, the Assistant DA solicited from Christina Berry sworn testimony that Kozlowski didn't negotiate the lowest price possible when he purchased pieces of art in 2001 and 2002. Berry said Kozlowski was always willing to buy without concern for the cost.[29] Berry's testimony is incongruent with the prosecution's theory that Kozlowski was trying to avoid $1 million in sales tax. Why would he be willing to pay top dollar for art, forego negotiating a lower price, and then try to evade the related sales tax?

Berry provided an example of Kozlowski's disregard for the amount of money he spent by telling the jury about pieces he viewed in a gallery in London. After Kozlowski and his wife decided on three paintings, Berry said, " . . . [W]e talked about it and Dennis said 'we should pay two million. I'll pay two million for these.' And I stopped and I said I think we can get it lower than two million. Let me try to get it lower for you." Berry said Kozlowski didn't want to wait for her to do comparison studies or to price shop at other galleries. She testified that "[h]e wanted to go forward with the purchase."[30] Kozlowski didn't haggle over the price of any of the pieces he purchased through Berry. It's difficult to understand why he'd willingly pay asking price for a painting and then try to save money by purposefully evading sales taxes.

After he was arraigned on the sales tax charges in New York, Kozlowski returned to Florida. At the time, Kozlowski lived in Boca Raton and worked primarily out of Tyco's offices there. Tyco moved many of the company's corporate functions to Florida after the ADT merger in 1997. When he arrived home after the arraignment, Kozlowski was unpleasantly surprised—Tyco had confiscated the company car he left parked at the airport. He was also prohibited from entering any Tyco facility; he was not allowed to retrieve personal items or personal records from company offices and he was prohibited from gathering his clothing, jewelry, or any other personal property from the Tyco apartment. On June 3, 2002, Tyco seized family photographs, artwork, and other valuable property that belonged to Kozlowski. The company also took possession of his personal financial records. More than a decade after that fateful summer weekend, Kozlowski still didn't know under whose authority personal property was taken from him. "I tried to get in touch with someone inside the company," he recalled. "But no one would talk to me. *No one.* I tried to call Mark [Swartz], Bodman, Fort, I tried to call everyone. But no one would talk to me. I didn't even have a personal checkbook. All of my personal financial records were in Tyco Executive Treasury. I didn't know where my money was and I had no way to find out. I couldn't pay for anything."[31]

Kozlowski never recovered any of his personal property. Not the multi-million-dollar paintings, not his personal income tax records, not his checkbooks, not his shirts that hung in the Tyco apartment, and not the pictures his daughters had drawn for him when they were little girls. As far as he knew, Tyco kept everything.[32]

* * *

The sales tax charges were ultimately dismissed and Kozlowski paid in full the sales tax due. When dismissing the sales tax charges in June of 2004—charges the Manhattan DA levied against Kozlowski two years earlier, charges that cost him the positions of CEO and Chairman of the Board and irreparably damaged his reputation—New York Supreme Court Justice Michael Obus ruled that in New York, the failure to *collect* sales tax is a crime but failure to *pay* sales tax is not a crime.[33]

An article about the decision that appeared in the *New York Law Journal* explained that Section 1817(c)(2)(a) of New York State Tax Law criminalizes "only a vendor's failure to collect sales tax. . . ." Justice Obus observed that the Manhattan DA's charges against Kozlowski involved a "unique application" of the statute and noted that the charges were not based on Kozlowski's actions as a principal, a charge that would clearly exceed the scope of the statute, but instead were based on the theory that Kozlowski acted in concert with the vendors in a plan that resulted in failure of the vendors to collect and submit sales tax.[34]

The media was merciless and prolific in its coverage of Kozlowski's indictment on sales tax charges in June of 2002 but showed little interest when those charges were dismissed in June of 2004. Numerous articles, books, textbooks, and case studies erroneously report or imply that Kozlowski was convicted on tax evasion charges. He wasn't.

* * *

The Tyco Board of Directors didn't wait for Kozlowski to be adjudicated on the sales tax charges. Upon receiving news from their longtime CEO and Chairman that he was facing personal legal issues, the Directors summarily and immediately ousted Kozlowski. Wendy Lane, the junior-most Tyco Director in June of 2002, explained the Board's actions in an interview she provided for a 2011 Harvard Business School case study. Lane said after Kozlowski called each of the Directors during the first weekend of June in 2002 and informed them of the sales tax indictment, "[t]he board met telephonically about the matter and how to reorganize management. Some of the directors suggested a leave of absence until ultimate guilt was established; others of us were firm that [Kozlowski] be asked in no uncertain terms to resign."[35]

Lane shared concerns the Board considered beyond the sales tax charges. She said, " . . . [T]he employment agreements were an impediment since substantial severance payments would have been triggered without an ultimate conviction of guilt."[36]

Late on the night of June 2, or early in the morning of June 3, 2002, the Tyco Board, over the phone through the Board's attorney David Boies, fired Dennis Kozlowski a day before he was indicted on sales tax charges.[37] The twenty-seven years

Kozlowski devoted to Tyco and the tremendous growth the company experienced under his leadership weren't enough for the Directors to give their CEO the benefit of the doubt or a scintilla of support, or to show him enough respect to meet with him in person or address him directly. They simply cut him loose.[38]

Interestingly, when former Tyco Director John Fort was on the stand during Kozlowski's second criminal trial, he was asked why, if the Directors knew it was wrong, they didn't fire Kozlowski immediately in January of 2002 when they learned of the investment banking fee Kozlowski approved for Frank Walsh in the CIT deal. Fort told the jury, "Well, here we had a situation where we have a CEO with a fantastic track record . . . [y]ou got to hope that your boss doesn't take action that fast if a situation like that comes up. It was—it was not immediate grounds for dismissal. We hadn't had a chance to really discuss it, but I don't think most boards react that way in any—I don't think any manager should act that way in an employee situation. We think first you should find out what is behind it, whether it was a genuine mistake. Find out what the consequences were to the company before they take action."[39] Apparently the Board's philosophy changed between January and June because by June, the Directors had more of a "shoot first, ask questions later" philosophy when it came to getting rid of their CEO.

Kozlowski said the Tyco Board of Directors was never "his board."[40] "The only director I brought to the Nominating Committee was Frank Walsh," he explained. "That's why allegations that I could do whatever I wanted without any oversight are ridiculous. Fort had a full-time office in the Exeter location while I was CEO. Josh Berman had a full-time office in New York. They all had access to anyone and anything they wanted." Kozlowski said, "Fort knew everyone and everyone knew him. He was CEO immediately before me. If Irving Gutin thought something wasn't right, he would have told Fort. There's no doubt about it. They weren't loyal to me and if I was doing anything even slightly questionable, they were right there and they could and would have called me on it. If there was anything they didn't know about, it was because they were willfully blind."[41] Kozlowski's assessment seemed to be accurate. When he faced personal legal issues for the first time in his life, not one Director was supportive or displayed even a hint of loyalty.

Perhaps the Board felt the only way to protect Tyco shareholders was to get rid of Kozlowski as soon as he told them he was going to be indicted. But what if the charges turned out to be erroneous? What if he was never convicted of the sales tax charges?

He wasn't.

If Tyco hadn't been struggling in 2002, if the Directors hadn't been angered by the Frank Walsh investment banking fee, if they hadn't recently been sued in a shareholder derivative action, if TYC price was up instead of down, it's interesting to consider whether the Tyco Board would have reacted in the same way.

* * *

Once he was charged by the Manhattan DA and ousted from Tyco, Kozlowski faced a number of humiliating and difficult tasks. To save them from any fallout related to his criminal charges, Kozlowski resigned from the boards on which he held seats. On June 3, 2002, Kozlowski resigned from Raytheon's Board of Directors, where he had served since 1995. Daniel P. Burnham, then Raytheon Chairman and CEO, said of the resignation, "Dennis Kozlowski has been an effective member of the board. We respect his decision and appreciate his many years of valuable service to Raytheon and its shareholders."[42] Eventually, Kozlowski stepped down from his seat on the Middlebury College Board of Trustees. Both of Kozlowski's daughters completed their undergraduate education at Middlebury, and he had been involved with the institution for many years.[43] He also left the Board of Regents at his alma mater, Seton Hall University, where Kozlowski Hall was renamed Jubilee Hall.

The year from hell continued. With every month that passed in 2002, Kozlowski's life had become more troubled. Shortly after the June 4th indictment, he retreated to his home in Nantucket. "I spent the summer thinking about what I was going to do next," he recalled. "I started putting together a private equity fund with a few other people. We met that summer at my house in Nantucket. I was going to do my own thing and keep a low profile. I was tired from all of the stress and negative publicity. I was planning a private, quiet life."[44] Unfortunately for Kozlowski, a private, quiet life was not in the cards.

FOURTEEN

INTERNAL INVESTIGATION

There's an ancient African proverb that considers the encounter between a hunter and his prey. In the Ewe-mina, Igbo, Togo, and other cultures, hunters were considered powerful and respected members of their communities and were even believed to possess supernatural powers. They were also known to tell great stories of their kills and were praised and admired for their conquests. But even as villagers celebrated the hunter, it was with awareness that they would never know all that happened during the hunt.[1]

> A young boy questioned his grandfather, "Is it true that the lion is the king of the jungle?"
>
> The old man looked at his grandson curiously and said, "Yes, my son, that is true, why do you ask?"
>
> "Well, Grandfather," said the boy, "if this is true, then why is it that in all the stories I read and all the ones I hear, the hunter defeats the lion. How can this be true?"
>
> The old man looked at his grandson and said, "And it will always be that way, my son, until the lion tells the story. Until then, tales of the hunt shall always glorify the hunter."[2]

* * *

The large majority of reports about Dennis Kozlowski's departure from Tyco state that Kozlowski resigned. But Kozlowski said he was fired over the phone at around midnight on the first Sunday in June of 2002.[3] In the end, the words spoken and heard that night through the chain of people who relayed information between the Tyco Board and Kozlowski don't really matter. Even if Kozlowski wasn't expressly fired, there's no doubt that he was constructively discharged—the Board made it impossible for him to continue as CEO and Chairman, which was the same as firing him.

If a severance agreement was negotiated between Tyco and Kozlowski over the phone that Sunday evening in June—and the Directors claimed there was a verbal agreement—it was very quickly breached because Tyco did not perform. The company where he worked for twenty-seven years didn't provide Dennis Kozlowski any severance or any of the benefits promised in his employment contract. In addition, the Directors did not comply with several provisions of that contract, the January 2001 Retention Agreement, which detailed the processes by which Kozlowski could resign and through which he could be fired.[4] Anything that occurred outside of the contractually defined process was presumably unenforceable or a breach of the agreement.

On June 3, 2002, Tyco issued a press release announcing " . . . that L. Dennis Kozlowski resigned as Chairman and Chief Executive Officer for personal reasons. Mr. Kozlowski also stepped down from the Board of Directors." In the same press release, the company announced that "[a]t the request of Tyco's Board, John F. Fort has agreed to assume primary executive responsibilities during an interim period while a search for a permanent replacement is completed." In his newly assumed role of interim CEO, Fort made his priorities known when he said, "We plan to complete the IPO [initial public offering] of CIT by the end of June." Fort also confirmed his support of a long-term operating strategy to focus more on organic growth. Of Kozlowski's sudden departure, Fort said that "[d]uring his tenure, Dennis Kozlowski grew Tyco to a $36 billion manufacturer and service provider operating in over 100 countries. We wish him well and thank him for his contributions."[5]

*   *   *

Tyco faced ongoing difficulties. Already dealing with a litany of serious challenges, the Directors' problems were compounded when legal actions were filed against them in April of 2002 over the Frank Walsh payment, breathing new life into an issue that appeared to have been put to rest. As external pressures intensified, tensions among Tyco insiders grew. In her interview for the Harvard Business School case study, former Director Wendy Lane said, "We didn't know what we didn't know, so we started to investigate a number of things." Lane explained that the Audit Committee, of which she was a member in 2002, asked for a review of accounting methods, which eventually were found to be compliant with Generally Accepted Accounting Principles (GAAP).[6]

Lane said when the Board learned that a senior manager was building a house that was "too expensive for his compensation level," the Compensation Committee asked for additional information on executive compensation and requested records of executives' use of company loan programs. She described an environment of suspicion and doubt, noted that prominent attorney David Boies had been retained by the Board, and said that as investigations unfolded, "certain inter-relationships were surfacing between various board members and management, such as investments and sales of houses." The case study quoted Lane as saying that she "did not know what to think or whom to trust." She also explained how the Audit Committee reviewed the details of corporate expenses, corporate expense accounts, and activity in the loan programs after which Lane interviewed both internal and external auditors who were fully aware of the payments and loans the committee questioned.[7]

In a similar description of the atmosphere and the mind-set of the Board in the late spring and early summer of 2002, John Fort testified that "the company was almost daily under siege in the press with rumors and accusations. The stock continued to fall. Then we reconsidered the break up, announced that we changed our mind on the break up. This was probably in April. The stock continued to fall. The press continued to be just very difficult on us." He recalled that "[i]n February, I believe, we changed the composition of the Nominating [and] Governance Committee and shortly after that I became lead director [to replace Frank Walsh]. I was already on [the Nominating and Governance Committee], Richard Bodman was on it, we added Michael Ashcroft and Joshua Berman, and we had four people on that, and one of the things was what to do—how should we pursue getting our money back [from Frank Walsh] and how we should do it." That's why the Board, through its Nominating and Governance Committee, initiated the 2002 internal investigation at Tyco.[8]

When the Board decided to launch the investigation, the scope was limited to the Frank Walsh investment banking fee. Interestingly, the Nominating and Governance Committee decided not to use the law firm Tyco's top lawyer Mark Belnick hired to conduct the investigation. Belnick had engaged Washington, DC-based Wilmer Cutler & Pickering, where William McLucas, the former head of enforcement at the SEC, practiced. McLucas was Tyco's outside counsel during the successfully concluded SEC investigation in 1999–2000. But instead of using Wilmer Cutler, the Committee decided to bring in David Boies.[9]

DAVID BOIES

In the findings of fact in *Tyco v. Walsh*, the U.S. District Court for the Southern District of New York detailed how Tyco came to hire David Boies to conduct the internal investigation into the Walsh payment. Three and a half months after the January 2002 Board of Directors' huddle, the four members of the Nominating and Governance Committee—Ashcroft, Berman, Bodman, and Fort—met via telephone on April 29, 2002 and decided to recommend to the full Board that action be taken to recover the investment banking fee paid to Frank Walsh. As part of that discussion, the four Committee members made it known to the full Board that they expected to supervise any legal action that was initiated, and the Committee promptly retained Boies, Schiller & Flexner. The Committee asked the law firm to complete the internal investigation in about six weeks.[10]

As a well-known and successful litigator, David Boies accumulated a long list of impressive accomplishments and awards—and a great deal of media attention. He is best known for his work in some very high-profile cases. In the late 1990s, Boies served as Special Trial Counsel for the U.S. Department of Justice during the Microsoft antitrust case. In perhaps his most high-profile performance, Boies argued before the U.S. Supreme Court on behalf of former Vice President Al Gore in the case that determined the outcome of the 2000 presidential election. In addition, Boies was instrumental in litigation that expanded marriage rights to same-sex couples.[11]

The Tyco Compensation Committee unexpectedly hired a 'big gun' when they brought in David Boies to handle the Walsh investigation. Former Tyco CEO and Director Josh Berman explained the choice: "We were determined to get the $20 million back from Frank Walsh. It was wrong, dead wrong of him to take that money, and it was our responsibility to get it back." Berman said, "I brought in Boies. By reason of his reputation, I believed our decision to hire him would convince Walsh that we were serious. Boies had credibility with the Board and with Walsh."[12]

It was also somewhat surprising that Boies took the job; it didn't seem the kind of work that was in the prominent litigator's wheelhouse. According to Boies biographer Karen Donovan, Boies and the members of his firm did not have the "depth of experience" to handle the Tyco matter compared to the ousted law firm Wilmer Cutler. Donovan wrote that despite the case being outside his *forte*, " . . . Boies could not pass up Tyco, or, for that matter, most cases in the spotlight." She also explained that "Boies's representation of Tyco spawned a new crop of Boies headlines, like the one that appeared in a profile of him in the Sunday edition of the *New York Times* in June 2002, under the headline 'Company in Trouble? Just Let Him Loose.'"[13] That's exactly what the Directors did after they hired David Boies.

In May of 2002, Tyco Chief Corporate Counsel Mark Belnick advised Boies that he didn't believe a lawsuit against Frank Walsh, which Boies had advised the Board to initiate, was in the company's best interest.[14] There seemed to be growing tension between Belnick and Boies, and by extension, between Belnick and the Board. Mark Belnick was fired on June 10, 2002, a few weeks after voicing his opinion to David Boies.[15] As it did with Kozlowski, the Board fired Belnick with no warning and no opportunity to discuss the rationale for the termination. Belnick recalled that a Tyco Director came to his office in New York and said, "You're fired, and you've got two minutes to get out," after which two large security guards physically removed Belnick by grabbing his shoulders and escorting him out; the company's top lawyer was paraded past his colleagues as he was led from the building.[16]

After he was acquitted in 2004 of charges brought by the Manhattan DA as a result of the Boies internal investigation, Belnick gave an interview to *New York Magazine.* "I was trying to do the right thing all the time at Tyco," he explained, "[t]hat's all I ever wanted to do. My end was to make Tyco a model of corporate governance."[17]

With Kozlowski and Belnick gone and David Boies advising them, the Directors seemed to become more engaged and significantly more aggressive. On June 17, 2002, a week after Belnick was fired, Tyco filed an action against Frank Walsh. The Board had waited more than five months to sue the former Director, and the timing of their delayed action appeared to be related to shareholder lawsuits filed against them. (Tyco's claims against Walsh were dismissed eight years later.)[18] In its new and more aggressive form, the Board also expanded the internal investigation that was originally focused on Walsh into a probe of Tyco's top management—two of whom (Kozlowski and Belnick) were no longer with the company.

Not long after the Board expanded the scope of the Boies investigation, and in the unavoidable spotlight focused on Tyco as a result of Kozlowski's sales tax indictment and sudden departure from the company, the Directors found themselves under attack. During the summer of 2002, information surfaced about many questionable financial transactions between individual Directors and Tyco—the conflicts of interest that were commonplace at the company for many years suddenly became serious problems. In addition to what was portrayed as self-dealing by some of the Directors, the media reported details of company loan programs and of the total compensation the Board paid and executive perquisites it provided to Tyco executives. There were implications that the Board failed to provide proper oversight and that the Directors might be civilly and even criminally liable for neglect of their duties. Multiple sources reported that the Manhattan DA might charge the Directors with securities fraud, racketeering, and other serious crimes.[19]

Years later during the executives' criminal trials, former Director Stephen Foss was asked about some of the tensions that affected the Board at that time.[20] Foss told the jury about a letter written by Patty Prue. Patricia "Patty" Prue was the head of human resources. In June of 2002, she wrote a letter to the Board of Directors that read: "As you know, I plan as always to assist you and the Board with whatever requests you have in conjunction with my role as head of Human Resources. However, as a result of the fact that I was recently pressured by Josh Berman to engage in conduct which I regarded as dishonest, and which I refused to do, I will decline to have any personal contact with him in the future. In addition, I ask that Josh not go to my staff with any requests for information or directions."[21]

According to a September 2002 article in the *New York Times,* Prue told a grand jury that the company's attorneys and Berman "put pressure on her, unsuccessfully, to get her to doctor the minutes of a compensation committee meeting." The article reported that those minutes proved that all three members of the

Compensation Committee knew about loans the company made to Kozlowski, Swartz, and Belnick, even though the Boies investigation had reported that the three executives concealed those loans. The Directors' knowledge of executive pay and perks was the key issue in the criminal trials of Kozlowski, Swartz, and Belnick. *New York Times* journalists Andrew Ross Sorkin and Jonathan Glater wrote, " . . . [T]he compensation committee minutes and the accusations from [Prue] may undermine the credibility of the board and the Boies report, which makes no mention of either."[22]

Former Director Foss told the jury that the Board took no formal action as a result of Prue's letter and request.[23] Josh Berman denied Prue's accusations and said she misunderstood his request.[24] Notably, Berman was not a member of the Compensation Committee, and he was not one of the Directors whose decisions and knowledge were included in the meeting minutes in question. In other words, if he asked that the minutes be altered, it would have been to cover up for others, but not for himself.

* * *

On July 25, 2002, about eight weeks after the company announced Kozlowski's departure, the Tyco Board appointed Edward D. Breen the company's next Chairman and Chief Executive Officer. Breen was the former President and Chief Operating Officer of Motorola, Inc.[25] Kozlowski was out, Breen was in, and yet Tyco shareholders were far from happy. Investors had good reason to be upset. The day Breen was hired, Tyco stock closed at $11.63. A year earlier, on July 25, 2001, the stock had closed at $72.55.[26] How quickly things had changed for Tyco shareholders.

On Breen's first day as CEO, angry representatives of the company's largest institutional shareholders confronted him in Tyco's New York offices and demanded that Kozlowski-era Directors be replaced.[27] Ralph Whitworth of Relational Investors LLC, then with ownership of seven million Tyco shares, threatened a proxy fight. Whitworth had the backing of other institutional shareholders. For example, Bill Miller of Legg Mason Funds Management told the *Wall Street Journal* that "[e]very one of those old board members should tender their resignations immediately." Miller stated, "I am perfectly prepared . . . to vote for a different slate if that's what it takes."[28] Whitworth was quoted in an article that appeared in the *New York Daily News* in August of 2002 saying "[e]ither they knew what was going on or they were asleep at the switch—both are terminal."[29]

In 2011, former Director Wendy Lane told business researchers, "If you are under attack as a director you do not want to resign." She explained further by stating that " . . . if you resign you lose control over not only the information flow but the information itself, the litigation process and settlement or adjudication proceedings. There is also an implication you were at fault."[30]

Dennis Kozlowski agreed completely with Lane's assessment of what happens to an individual who isn't present during a time of crisis. Once Kozlowski was out of the company, information about him seemed to procreate as quickly and prolifically as colonies of wild rabbits. After June 3, 2002, no one at Tyco would speak to the departed CEO. He had no access to the information that David Boies was accumulating and interpreting—all done without including Kozlowski in the investigation.[31]

Kozlowski said, "I knew David Boies was hired to investigate the Frank Walsh payment. That was going on while I was still there and I didn't object to the investigation."[32] Kozlowski never spoke to David Boies—not before he left the company, and not after. "I was supposed to meet with him a couple of different times when I was still at Tyco, but I had to reschedule. I was trying to sell CIT. That was my priority at that time, so when I had to be at a meeting with Dick Fuld of Lehman Brothers or on a call with Warren Buffett, I canceled everything else and I was at the CIT meetings." Kozlowski admitted that, at the time, he was consumed with selling CIT and had very little interest in the internal investigation. Kozlowski wondered over the years, as he sat in prison, if David Boies held those rescheduled meetings against him.[33]

Being outside the company during the internal investigation put Kozlowski at a huge disadvantage. He had no ability to provide input, he wasn't asked to explain anything—he had no idea what was happening at the company where he spent twenty-seven years of his life. And as Wendy Lane explained, "[T]here is also an implication you were at fault."[34] Kozlowski said, "I didn't know anything about the scope of the investigation being expanded—I didn't know that I was part of the internal investigation until sometime in August [of 2002]."[35]

LEAKS AND SPIN

Throughout the summer of 2002, someone involved with the investigation (it had to be someone at Tyco, or someone with the Boies firm, or someone in the DA's office) was feeding information from inside the company to the media. The $6,000 shower curtain, Kozlowski's art purchases, the locations and sizes of his personal homes, charitable contributions Kozlowski authorized (reported by the media as if Tyco was the only large corporation to ever make sizable charitable contributions), the Directors' questionable financial dealings with the company—many details allegedly found during the investigation were leaked to and reported by the media. At the time, the only criminal allegations against Kozlowski were for failing to pay sales taxes. Because he was the first consumer ever charged in New York, it seems the media could have given Kozlowski the benefit of the doubt until the charges were adjudicated. But the media isn't restricted by the constitutional right to due process. The media can make allegations, prosecute, and convict without an indict-ment, arraignment, or trial.

A scathing article appeared on the front page of the *Wall Street Journal* on August 7, 2002. In a sensational account of spending and looting, Tyco-phile re-porter Mark Maremont and his co-author Laurie Cohen reported and ridiculed Kozlowski's lavish lifestyle. Maremont and Cohen cited as their sources "people investigating the company" and "people familiar with the company."[36] There were no named sources.

The *Wall Street Journal*'s compelling headline—"Executive Privilege: How Tyco's CEO Enriched Himself—Mr. Kozlowski, Ex-Chief, Got Secret Loans, Spent Firm's Cash as His Own—A $6,000 Shower Curtain"—drew readers into a tale of Enron-era excess and extravagance. Maremont and Cohen claimed that Kozlowski "regularly reached into Tyco coffers to finance his extravagant lifestyle and polish his image." Interestingly, the unnamed sources cited in the August 2002 article— the "people investigating the company"—told Maremont and Cohen that "Tyco paid for the Fifth Avenue duplex," that Tyco "bought the Fifth Avenue duplex," and that 950 Fifth Avenue was what "Tyco considered a corporate apartment."[37] At some point, those "people" must have forgotten because repeated testimony during the criminal trials was that the Fifth Avenue apartment was a secret about which only Kozlowski and Swartz had knowledge.

Maremont and Cohen wrote that "[t]he allegations against Mr. Kozlowski fol-low a wave of disclosures of CEO hubris and greed. Like other top executives who have come under fire in recent weeks, Mr. Kozlowski allegedly took advantage of the 1990s boom to help himself to a smorgasbord of financial rewards."[38]

"The allegations? What allegations?" Kozlowski recalled thinking when he saw the *Wall Street Journal* article. "Whose allegations?" According to Kozlowski, he didn't know he was being investigated when the article appeared in the *Wall Street Journal* in August of 2002. Kozlowski had been in Nantucket all summer crafting plans for a private equity fund. He had no knowledge of anything going on at Tyco; he didn't know there were problems inside the company.[39] But accord-ing to the *Wall Street Journal*, and unbeknownst to Kozlowski, there were already "allegations" of serious wrongdoing. In fact, Maremont and Cohen stated that "Mr. Kozlowski's brazen use of a public company as his personal cash machine looms as a particularly egregious case [of CEO hubris and greed]."[40]

Maremont and Cohen's word choices appeared to unnecessarily and inaccu-rately imply wrongdoing—they transformed innocuous information into a scandal they seemingly uncovered through investigative reporting. For example, they wrote of Kozlowski that " . . . he *quietly* put *his* doctor and fitness trainer on the Tyco payroll . . ."[41] The Tyco employees in question weren't *his* doctor and *his* trainer. Ac-cording to a company spokesperson, the doctor and the fitness trainer to whom the article referred were hired as part of Tyco's corporate wellness program.[42]

In a 2013 article titled "Your Company Wants to Make You Healthy" written by *Wall Street Journal* reporter Jen Wieczner, the newspaper reported that "[n]early 90% of employers offer wellness incentives, or financial rewards or prizes to employees who work toward getting healthier, according to a recent survey from Fidelity Investments and the National Business Group on Health."[43] Wieczner wrote about corporate wellness programs at Caterpillar Inc., JetBlue Airways Corp., and Johnson & Johnson. All were cast in a positive light. None of the three were accused of *quietly* hiring individuals to run their wellness programs, as if it was scandalous or criminal to do so.

The Maremont and Cohen article mentioned that the U.S. Attorney in New Hampshire investigated the claims made about Kozlowski and Tyco. However, the U.S. Attorney did not pursue any criminal charges as a result of that investigation. Maremont and Cohen also disclosed Kozlowski's assertion that Tyco owed him "tens of millions" of dollars in deferred compensation—money Kozlowski had earned but that was held by Tyco at the time he was ousted in June of 2002.[44] However, the journalists didn't chastise Tyco for keeping Kozlowski's earnings and they didn't investigate Kozlowski's claims.

On the evening of August 7, 2002, the day Maremont and Cohen's article appeared on the front page of the *Wall Street Journal,* Maremont gave an interview that was broadcast by NPR's *All Things Considered* during which he talked on the air about Kozlowski's spending and his lavish lifestyle: birthday parties, mansions, and fine art. Maremont once again used words like "quietly" and "secretly" as he told listeners that Kozlowski wrongfully took more than $100 million from Tyco.[45]

More than ever before, his status as a public figure caused problems for Dennis Kozlowski in 2002. The magazine covers, press interviews, and newspaper articles that had been written about him over the prior several years came back to hurt him. The whale had surfaced, and the media threw many harpoons.

Just like the February 2002 *Wall Street Journal* article about hundreds of "undisclosed acquisitions"—a story Tyco and others quickly and vehemently refuted—Maremont and Cohen's August 7, 2002 article had an immediate negative effect on the value of Tyco stock. TYC dropped five percent and the volume of trading increased by around a million shares on the day the article ran.[46] The "people investigating the company" weren't acting in the best interest of Tyco shareholders when they leaked sensational information, some of which was untrue, some of which was unrelated to any criminal charges that were or would be alleged, most of which was spun by the media, and all of which was used to portray Dennis Kozlowski as a thief, a liar, a scoundrel, and a criminal.

Kozlowski was tried in the court of public opinion based on selective information leaked by nameless "people investigating the company" and then spun onto the front page long before he was afforded any type of due process. The leaks weren't good for Tyco, they weren't good for Tyco shareholders, and they hurt Dennis Kozlowski, which begs the question: Who benefited from the smear campaign?

* * *

After he was named CEO, Ed Breen began ridding Tyco of Kozlowski-era Directors and employees. One of the first to go was CFO Mark Swartz. By all accounts, Swartz played a significant role in assisting David Boies and his team with the internal investigation during the summer of 2002. However, on August 1st, he was presented with a severance package and a request for his resignation.[47]

When he took the stand in his own defense during his second criminal trial in 2005, the former CFO recounted the day he was asked to leave. Swartz said, "David Boies told [me and the other Directors] in the meeting on August first due to all the focus on the company and press attention, the most they could pay out at that point was 50 million dollars and his hope was that the balance of 25 million, once things quieted down in a few months would be paid to me."[48] That day, Swartz signed an agreement with Tyco in which he waived his right to enforce the 2001 Retention Agreement, and in which the company, among other things, agreed to give Swartz all amounts due him under the company's deferred compensation program, the value of his 401(k), the value of his executive life insurance policy, and amounts due under the senior executive retirement program. In total, the Directors, as advised by David Boies, agreed to pay Swartz $50 million in severance. Mark Swartz signed that agreement on August 1, 2002. Signing on behalf of Tyco: an attorney from Boies, Schiller & Flexner.[49]

The agreement included Swartz's resignation from the Board, but he continued in his role as CFO for another month and a half, until September 11, 2002. Over those weeks, he fulfilled all of his normal duties; he handled SEC filings, he worked on Sarbanes-Oxley requirements with the new CEO, he spoke with shareholders—he did everything he had done as CFO for many years. During his trials, Swartz told the juries that when he left work on his last day with Tyco, it was to fly "to New York . . . to be arrested the following day in connection with my job as CFO of Tyco." Swartz then told the juries that "Ed Breen and David Boies had offered a Tyco provided airplane for [my wife] Karen and me to fly home from New York." When asked if he took them up on their offer, Swartz said, "We did."[50] It was an interesting and pricey perk offered to a man the company and the Manhattan DA just accused of stealing from the company, in concert with Dennis Kozlowski, more than $170 million.

DAVID BOIES AND THE MANHATTAN DA

In an article that appeared in the *American Lawyer* in 2005, Andrew Longstreth explored the increasingly common arrangement in which an attorney who is hired to conduct a corporate internal investigation coordinates the investigation with a prosecutor. Longstreth described this type of private attorney as "a fact-finder with a badge—the newest (and highest paid) government agent." The article noted that corporations have been known to enter agreements with the government in which both sides share information related to their investigations. Prosecutors get what they want—access to the findings of the law firm that conducts the internal investigation—and the corporation is able to claim privilege for any evidence discovered during the investigation that the company doesn't want to reveal or that doesn't advance the prosecutor's case.[51] For the corporation and the prosecutor, it's like having your cake and eating it too. Unfortunately, it denies anyone charged with crimes as a result of the investigation access to evidence that would be available but for the arrangement between the prosecutor and the private attorney.

David Boies testified that from the first day his firm was engaged by Tyco's Nominating and Governance Committee, he cooperated fully with the Manhattan DA. Boies said he began sharing information with the DA on June 3, 2002 (the day Kozlowski was ousted from Tyco in anticipation of his imminent indictment on sales tax charges) and his cooperation continued up to and including the day Boies was on the stand, which was April 11, 2005. Of working with prosecutors during a corporate internal investigation, Boies said, "You want to work closely with them and you identify them early and you bring them into the investigation."[52]

Boies told the jury that over the nearly three year time period, he provided all documents the DA requested and he consulted with the DA's office regularly before, during, and after the Manhattan DA indicted former Tyco CEO Dennis Kozlowski, former CFO Mark Swartz, and former Chief Corporate Counsel Mark Belnick on September 12, 2002. Boies also confirmed that his law firm received from Tyco $45 million in legal fees in less than three years.[53] That's an average of more than $1.3 million per month.

The most serious problem created by the triangular corporation-private attorney-prosecutor cooperative relationship is that it creates an evidentiary loophole. Prosecutors are required to provide anyone accused of a crime any and all exculpatory evidence that the prosecutor possesses. However, when evidence of alleged wrongdoing is filtered through an investigating private attorney, any evidence that tends to incriminate the accused may be turned over to the prosecutor, and the corporation may withhold from the prosecutor and from the defendant any evidence that tends to disprove guilt. Prosecutors have no duty or ability to turn over to the defendant evidence they do not possess. And the private attorney who conducted the internal investigation along with the corporation may claim the evidence is privileged or work product, the work of an attorney prepared in anticipation of litigation; both are protected. The attorney may choose not to turn over the evidence, even if he or she knows it will prove the accused is not guilty.

In this scenario, exculpatory evidence exists, but the person accused of a serious crime has no opportunity to see it, or to present to a jury evidence that would prove he or she is not guilty.

THE INDICTMENT

Internal investigations like the one conducted at Tyco during the summer of 2002 generally take federal investigators and regulators many months or even years to complete. However, the Manhattan DA, with the full cooperation of David Boies and Tyco, put together a massive indictment in about three months. On September 12, 2002, Dennis Kozlowski and Mark Swartz were jointly indicted in ninety pages of dramatic allegations that read like a script from *Law & Order* or *The Sopranos*.

The first thirty-five felony counts included in *People v. Kozlowski and Swartz* were charges typically reserved for the prosecution of organized crime figures. The Manhattan DA charged the former CEO and CFO with enterprise corruption, the New York State equivalent of charges under the federal Racketeer Influenced and Corrupt Organizations Act (RICO). The DA accused Kozlowski and Swartz of running a criminal enterprise out of Tyco corporate offices. The indictment labeled it the "Top Executives Criminal Enterprise" or "TEXCE." According to the indictment, "Defendant Kozlowski was the boss of the criminal enterprise," and "Swartz was chief of operations of TEXCE." The indictment claimed TEXCE was created and operated for the purpose of obtaining money by theft, fraud in the sale of securities, and other frauds, and was operated from January 1, 1995 through, on, or about September 9, 2002. The DA named eighty separate acts of enterprise corruption that covered the first fifty-eight pages of the indictment.[54]

It is worth noting that the former executives were charged by a local district attorney. Considering the scope, seriousness, and nature of the allegations, this type of prosecution is far more common in federal court, not a state court. Professor Christo Lassiter of the University of Cincinnati College of Law, a criminal law scholar and expert on white-collar crime, said it was "very usual—even rare that Kozlowski was criminally prosecuted by a local DA but not by a U.S. Attorney."[55]

In an article that appeared in the journal of the American Bar Association in 2010, criminal defense attorney Roger L. Stavis, of the New York firm Gallet, Dreyer & Berkey, was quoted as saying "There have been many instances over his long tenure as DA where [Morgenthau] creatively applied our state criminal statutes to bring cases which the U.S. attorney could have and would have brought under the broader federal criminal statutes—if they fit."[56] Morgenthau was known throughout his career for aggressively prosecuting white-collar crime. If he could make charges fit against Kozlowski and Swartz in 2002, charging the high-profile, wealthy corporate executives was consistent with his *modus operandi*.

If there was evidence of the magnitude alleged in the Manhattan DA's indictment, federal prosecutors almost certainly would have charged the Tyco executives. They did not. But with Morgenthau's history of going after those in positions of power and trust, and considering the post-Enron environment where most every elected official, like the Manhattan DA, wanted to be seen as tough on white-collar crime, the aggressive prosecution of Kozlowski and Swartz in the State and City of New York was for Morgenthau the right time, the right defendants, and the right place.

All eighty enterprise corruption charges were thrown out before Kozlowski and Swartz went to trial. There was no evidence to support those charges. However the remaining felony counts were serious crimes for which the former executives would face a judge and jury. Twice.

FIFTEEN

PEOPLE V. KOZLOWSKI I

Sometime during August of 2002, Dennis Kozlowski learned that the Tyco Board of Directors had expanded the scope of the internal investigation beyond the Frank Walsh investment banking fee, and that David Boies and his legal team were looking into Kozlowski's activities as the head of the company. Kozlowski said, "I wasn't concerned. I hadn't done anything wrong or secretively—everything was done properly, as far as I knew, and everything was documented." He added, "I wasn't concerned because I had nothing to hide." He was aware that Mark Swartz was still at Tyco and that John Fort was the interim CEO. "I heard that everyone at Tyco was told not to talk to me," he said. "I hadn't spoken to anyone since the beginning of June. I tried to contact many people, but no one would speak to me. Not even Mark."[1]

On September 11, 2002, Mark Swartz wrapped up his final day as Tyco's CFO and boarded a plane to New York City. Dennis Kozlowski would soon be reunited with his former colleague.

THE INDICTMENT

"I was in Nantucket," Kozlowski recalled. "I had gone out to dinner on September the 11th and just after I got home, I received a call from my attorney Stephen Kaufman. He told me that I had to be in New York the next morning—I had to go to New York to turn myself in. I was being indicted." He said, "I was completely taken by surprise. I had no idea what the charges could be. The thought of grand larceny never crossed my mind."[2]

Kozlowski made the trip to Manhattan the following morning. He had only twelve hours to process the devastating news. "It was horrible," he recalled. According to reporters who were there, Kozlowski, Swartz, and former Tyco Chief Corporate Counsel Mark Belnick were led into the courtroom—in handcuffs. All three former Tyco executives pleaded not guilty to the extraordinary list of felony charges alleged in the Manhattan DA's indictments against them.[3]

Belnick was indicted separately. He was charged with several counts of falsifying business records—crimes that could send him to prison for up to four years. When the arraignment concluded on September 12, 2002, Belnick was released on a $1 million bond.[4]

The news for Belnick was bad, but Kozlowski and Swartz found themselves in far more dire straits. All of the felonies in the September 12th indictment in which they were jointly charged carried harsh penalties—several could send the former executives to prison for up to thirty years.

In addition to the criminal charges, the Manhattan DA requested and was granted a restraining order that froze both men's assets. Kozlowski said, "When I was at the arraignment, [Assistant Manhattan District Attorney John] Moscow handed me a court order freezing my assets. I couldn't spend any money and I no longer had control over any of my assets."[5] The DA ensured that the vast resources of the men remained intact until the case was decided. If either or both were found guilty, the sentences for the crimes charged would undoubtedly include restitution to Tyco as well as significant criminal fines. Even so, it seemed a harsh and punitive order—considering they were innocent until proven guilty. Or they were supposed to be.

Kozlowski explained of the unexpected restraining order, "My checks bounced. Anything that was outstanding, anything that had just been paid—the checks bounced."[6]

"After that," Kozlowski said, "any money I needed, to pay bills or to live on, had to be approved through a lengthy process. The request went from my attorneys to the judge for a stipulation and then to the DA's office, to [Assistant District Attorney] Amyjane Rettew who could agree or disagree to the stipulation. I spent $6 in legal fees to get approval for every dollar I needed to pay bills."[7]

"I could no longer make any changes to my investments," he complained. "I was stuck if any investment went bad." Kozlowski said there was only one expense that was easy to pay: "They allowed fast and easy expenditures of my money for legal fees."[8]

Kozlowski was in shock. He didn't once consider the internal investigation at Tyco would lead to a criminal indictment of anyone, least of all himself. And the restraining order triggered a sudden and extreme lifestyle change for the former CEO—a change that was not temporary. At this writing, eleven years after Assistant DA John Moscow handed him the court order in September of 2002, Kozlowski's assets remained frozen. Kozlowski had no access to or control over his finances for eleven years—and counting.[9]

During his arraignment, the judge set Kozlowski's bail at $100 million. With his assets frozen, he could not access his own money to post the required bond.

Surprisingly, it was Kozlowski's first wife Angie who posted the $10 million bond that allowed him to leave the courthouse that day. "My first wife of 27 years is the Mother Teresa of ex wives," he said. "She posted my bail when I was indicted in 2002."[10]

In the dozens of articles that appeared in the media on the day the three former Tyco executives were indicted, Tyco was already being compared to Enron, WorldCom, and Adelphia—all enveloped at the time in high-profile scandals. For example, *CNNMoney* reported that "Tyco is one of several large corporations whose books are being scrutinized by prosecutors and federal regulators; Enron Corp., WorldCom Inc. and Adelphia Communications also among them. The latter three firms have filed for Chapter 11 bankruptcy protection from creditors."[11]

Even though it would forever be classified as one of the large Enron-era corporate scandals, one very important difference set Tyco apart from the others: Enron, WorldCom, Adelphia, and Global Crossing declared bankruptcy. Tyco did not.

After Kozlowski and Swartz were ousted, there were rumors that Tyco might suffer the same end as Enron, *et al.* However, according to Kozlowski, Tyco was never in jeopardy. Others who were at Tyco during 2002 and 2003 confirmed his assessment of the company's soundness.[12] As a witness for the prosecution, Tyco's Treasurer Michael Robinson was asked under oath during the second criminal trial about Tyco's financial condition in 2002. He explained that the CIT acquisition was not well received by the market and that the price of Tyco stock was down. He also made clear that, as the company's Treasurer during and after the years Kozlowski headed the company, he had specific knowledge of the company's financial condition. Robinson confirmed that in 2002, Tyco was fundamentally sound. Robinson was asked:

Q. Was there any realistic chance [at] the end of May of 2002 that Tyco would go bankrupt?
[Assistant District Attorney] MR. SCHOLL: Objection.
THE COURT: If you can answer I'll permit it.
A. No, there were rumors to that affect, but we were a viable company.[13]

Robinson's assessment was accurate. Tyco did not become insolvent; the company bounced back and thrived as a large multinational conglomerate until 2011 when, under the leadership of CEO Edward Breen, the company was split into three separate publicly traded corporations.

* * *

When he was indicted, Kozlowski could not have imagined it would be years before the charges against him would be resolved. His first trial began on September 29, 2003, more than a year after the arraignment. He was convicted at the conclusion of a second trial that began in January of 2005, after which he was sentenced on September 19, 2005, more than three years after he was indicted.

Kozlowski's life as he knew it ended on September 12, 2002. After that, he was a criminal defendant living in legal limbo. He had no access to his assets and he was the target of frequent, often erroneous, and sometimes vicious media attention. Former CEO Dennis Kozlowski was a criminal defendant for 1,104 days. Of that time, he spent 432 days in two trials that consumed over eleven months of his life. His legal defense cost tens of millions of dollars of his money, which was closely guarded by the Manhattan DA.

September 12, 2002 was a watershed day for Dennis Kozlowski. After that, his life would never be the same.

PEOPLE V. KOZLOWSKI I

Supreme Court, New York County
Manhattan Criminal Courthouse, 13th Floor
100 Centre Street
New York City, New York
September 29, 2003

The first trial commenced on September 29, 2003. The high-profile case was assigned to the Honorable Michael J. Obus, Justice of the Supreme Court of New York. The proceedings were held on the thirteenth floor of 100 Centre Street in Manhattan—the Criminal Branch of the New York Supreme Court. It was just like an episode of *Law & Order*—except it wasn't a drama that would be resolved in sixty minutes.

At the table for the Manhattan DA were Assistant District Attorneys Marc Scholl, Kenneth Chalifoux, Ann Donnelly, Gerard Murphy, and Connie Fernandez.[14] Kozlowski's lead defense attorney was Steven Kaufman, whom Kozlowski hired when he learned of the sales tax investigation in the spring of 2002. Kaufman added to the defense team by bringing in Austin Campriello and Jim DeVita. Representing Mark Swartz was lead defense counsel Charles Stillman along with James Mitchell and Michael Grudberg. On trial were two highly paid former executives who would sit through months of the Manhattan DA's presentation of the evidence used against them.[15]

THE CHARGES

By the time the trial began, many of the charges alleged in the September 12, 2002 indictment had been dismissed because there wasn't enough evidence to support them. What remained were fourteen counts of grand larceny in the first degree, sixteen counts of falsifying business records, a charge of conspiracy to commit larceny and possession of stolen property, and one count of securities fraud.[16]

"Lying, Cheating and Stealing"

After days of jury selection were completed, the prosecution gave its opening statement on October 7, 2003. Assistant District Attorney (ADA) Chalifoux addressed the twelve newly seated jurors and laid out the prosecution's "lying, cheating and stealing"–themed case. ADA Chalifoux began by saying:

> This case is about lying, cheating and stealing. It's about two employees who were entrusted with the money and the assets of a company. And they abused that trust. They were entrusted with the assets that belonged to other people, to the shareholders and the owners of Tyco. It's about these two defendants, defendant Kozlowski and defendant Swartz, who shamelessly violated that trust by treating the company's bank accounts as if they were their own. They raided the company's assets, the assets again that belonged to the shareholders. And they used them on themselves. They used them on other employees. And they used them for things such as gifts to themselves, money that they took and gifts to other people. You will find that the defendants used the money of Tyco not for their own—not for Tyco's benefit, but for their own benefit and the detriment of Tyco. That's the stealing.
>
> Defendants had an obligation to tell the owners of the company what they were doing with those assets. They had an obligation to tell the board of directors and its committee and the public as well. They had an obligation to tell them that they were using it for themselves. But instead of revealing that information, defendants lied. They lied to the people whose interests they were hired to protect. They created false company documents. And they used those documents to help themselves commit and conceal their crimes. That's the lying.
>
> By stealing from the company and lying about it, they manipulated the price of the company's stock. They falsely represented that they were careful in the management of Tyco funds, when in fact they were spending millions of dollars on themselves for things like apartments, and yachts and art work. The lies and false impressions that they created kept the stock price higher than it would have been had investors known the truth. Defendants then sold shares of Tyco stock, hundreds of thousands of shares of stock at that inflated price. And they took the money for themselves. And they misrepresented the risks that the shareholders faced. By doing that, they lined their pockets with millions of dollars in proceeds from fraudulent stock sales. That's the cheating.
>
> This is a calculated scheme that lasted for years. It was designed by the defendants to steal money and to cover it up. And it was very successful. They stole a hundred and 70 million dollars. Think about that for a moment. Get an idea of

how much money that is when the power ball or the Lotto hits a hundred million. It makes primes. You will see it on TV. You will see it in the paper. People lining up to buy tickets. These two didn't win the jackpot. They stole it. And jackpot winners, sometimes they can hold press conferences. It's up to them. They can announce their winnings. But the defendants had an obligation to hold essentially what is the same thing as a press conference. They had an obligation to tell the owners of the company and the board of directors what they were doing with the money. It's mandatory, not optional. But they didn't do it. They hid it from the directors and from the [shareholders] (another one of their goals). And they successfully kept the shareholders and the public in the dark for years.

ADA Chalifoux also explained to jurors that, "[d]uring the course of their conduct, during the course of their crimes, these defendants were the gatekeepers of information. They had absolute power. If you remember when we talked in jury selection about power versus authority. They had the power to take this money. But they didn't have the authority."[17]

Criminals Act in Criminal Ways

After the jury heard the prosecution's theory of the crimes, the defense presented a summary of the other side of the story. Lead defense counsel Stephen Kaufman spoke to the jury on Kozlowski's behalf. Kaufman said, "I come before you and tell you that my client Dennis Kozlowski is neither a liar . . . a cheat nor a thief. What he has done is come to this courtroom to protect that which is the most important thing in his life, apart from his family, and that is his liberty."[18]

*   *   *

Kaufman mentioned something almost in passing during his opening statement. He told jurors that Kozlowski "was not a detail person. He was very much a concept individual and a very hard working person."[19] Kozlowski's work ethic was incontrovertible. Anyone in or around Dennis Kozlowski's life, even when he was a child, knew he was a workaholic.

But the observation that he was not a detail person was something about Kozlowski that people didn't notice, or if they recognized it in him, they didn't assign much importance to it. Kaufman's observation, although somewhat difficult to believe considering Kozlowski's background as an internal auditor, appeared to be accurate. There was ample evidence that Kozlowski did not pay attention to details. The nitty-gritty, nuts-and-bolts, annoying, time-consuming details that every adult must manage seemed to bore him or to elude him, and often he seemed unwilling to grasp, remember, deal with, or even consider details.

His younger sister Joyce described her brother precisely. She wrote of her brother: "For someone with a business/accounting educational background, a meteoric rise to power in the world of mergers and acquisitions, and a remarkable 'head for numbers,' Dennis never remembers birthdays, anniversaries, etc. It would be sad if it weren't so comical! I actually made a calendar for him when he was in prison so he could remember significant events in people's lives—you would think with all that time on his hands it wouldn't have been an issue to keep a few dates straight—but not our Dennis!"[20]

Perhaps this deficit explains why he wasn't an internal auditor for long. He gravitated to positions that required vision and the capacity to analyze the big picture, and in which the ability to deal with details was far less critical. Unfortunately for Kozlowski, his inattention to detail, his inability to appreciate the importance of details, and his pattern of delegating responsibility for many of the details in his life to others left him vulnerable—especially when he needed to prove how the details in his life had been handled. Because he had no idea. He had left the details to others.

Granted, he was in a demanding chief executive position and his time was at a premium, but perhaps he was too trusting when he allowed others to take care of things for which he would be held accountable. Perhaps he willingly and intentionally delegated responsibility for the details of his life because he didn't like those tasks. Maybe he felt his time was too valuable to spend any of it dealing with the mundane. Throughout his life, Kozlowski tended to participate in activities at which he excelled. Maybe he didn't want to deal with details because he wasn't good at it.

Kozlowski, an extremely high-functioning person, lacked some of the basic skills that are common in most adults. It seems implausible, but Dennis Kozlowski was naïve—even as he spent many years immersed in very sophisticated business transactions. During the same years he worked on hundreds of multi-million and multi-billion dollar acquisitions, he had very little knowledge of or concern for what was happening with his personal finances. A Tyco employee in the company's Executive Treasury department controlled his bank accounts, paid his bills, managed his investment accounts, handled the paperwork necessary when his restricted shares vested and taxes were due, she processed and signed his name on the promissory notes required when he used the company's loan programs, and she wired money from his accounts when he needed to pay for large purchases like jewelry, boats, and parties. Kozlowski said, "I didn't have time to keep up with those things. My electricity was turned off because I didn't take time to pay the bill. I needed someone to make sure that didn't happen again."

Kozlowski said to solve this problem, "Mark [Swartz] suggested the Executive Treasury department, and I just turned everything over to them."[21] It proved to be a costly decision. This arrangement made it appear as if Kozlowski used Tyco's money for himself.

* * *

During his opening statement, Kaufman explained to the jury how Kozlowski came to know, value, and promote Mark Swartz to the position of CFO. Kozlowski first became aware of Swartz while working on the Kendall acquisition in 1994. On nights when he was working at midnight trying to close the deal, he could always find Swartz still at work whenever he needed to speak with someone from finance. Mark Swartz had a work ethic much like Kozlowski's. He was also impressed with Swartz's focus, attention to detail, and the quality of his work. Kaufman told the jury that "[t]hey became a team, to put it simply. Dennis was the outside man and Mark Swartz was the inside man . . . they both had talents in all areas, but it gave Dennis what he needed, the comfort of knowing that there was a person who could look after the details certainly much better than Dennis could do because he was working so hard on the growth of the company." The Kozlowski-Swartz team did great things for Tyco for a long time. But after the 2002 indictment, what was seen for years as a successful combination of complementary talents was re-characterized as a criminal conspiracy.

In addition to telling the jury a little bit about Dennis Kozlowski during his opening statement, Kaufman countered the prosecution's "lying, cheating and stealing" contentions: "There [is] no second set of books. There's no insider that's going to come to that witness stand and talk in hush hush terms about secret conversations with my client about corrupt and criminal acts."

"Criminals act in criminal ways," Kaufman explained to the jury, "and [Kozlowski and Swartz] did not act in any way which was unlawful, which was corrupt, which was done with an intention to be willfully violating laws."[22]

Pay-for-Performance Compensation

Most of the charges against Kozlowski and Swartz centered on their compensation between the years 1995 and 2002. Basically, the prosecution alleged that bonuses Tyco paid to Kozlowski, Swartz, and to dozens of other people were unauthorized and therefore, the amounts of those bonuses were stolen. The crime: grand larceny in the first degree. The sentence if convicted: an indeterminate sentence of one to twenty-five years.

New York Penal Law Section 155.42. Grand larceny in the first degree.
    A person is guilty of grand larceny in the first degree when he steals property and when the value of the property exceeds one million dollars. Grand larceny in the first degree is a class B felony.

New York Penal Law Section 70.00. Sentence of imprisonment for felony.

(1) The sentence of imprisonment for a felony . . . shall be an indeterminate sentence.

(2)(b) For a class B felony, the term shall be fixed by the court, and shall not exceed twenty-five years;

(3)(b) The minimum period shall be fixed by the court and specified in the sentence and shall be not less than one year nor more than one-third of the maximum term imposed.

Related to the prosecution's claims that they stole their bonuses, Kozlowski and Swartz were charged with using company loan programs to further their larcenous activities. The CEO and CFO borrowed large sums of money through Tyco's KELP and relocation loan programs. Although they repaid most of those loans with what was indisputably their money, they paid down or paid off other loans with what the prosecution claimed and the defense refuted were unauthorized bonuses. The prosecution's theory was that the executives took multi-million dollar loans, signed promissory notes documenting their indebtedness to the company, and then a few months later, declared bonuses that were unknown to and unauthorized by the Board of Directors. Instead of receiving those bonuses in the form of cash, the amounts were used to pay off or pay down outstanding loan balances that were on the books and records of the company.

In simple terms, Kozlowski and Swartz were charged with grand larceny in the first degree for taking millions of dollars when they received four bonuses two of which were used to pay down or pay off balances of outstanding loans owed to Tyco.

*   *   *

Tyco's "Compensation Committee Benefit Plans" included several different plans and company policies.[23] Among the company-provided benefits were the 1994 Restricted Stock Plan, the Board of Directors' Deferred Compensation Plan, the Key Employee Loan Program, and the Incentive Compensation Plan, which was the company policy under which the questioned bonuses were paid to Kozlowski and Swartz.

Tyco International Ltd. Incentive Compensation Plan

The stated purpose of the Incentive Compensation Plan (the Plan) was "to attract and retain senior executives who will contribute to the long-term success and growth of Tyco, to reward the executives for increased profitability of Tyco with resulting increased stockholder value, to establish performance goals based on the growth of Tyco and to motivate executives to achieve company objectives." The policy required the Compensation Committee to annually " . . . determine and define the specific targets and goals ... within the first ninety days of each fiscal year for which the incentive compensation is being earned. Such determination shall be documented in the Committee minutes."[24]

The Plan provided the process through which earned compensation was to be paid: "Awards under the Incentive Plan shall be payable annually, after the completion of the Company's annual audit and acceptance of the final financial results by the Company's Board of Directors (generally within three months of the end of the fiscal year). Prior to any payments from the Incentive Plan, the Committee will certify that the performance goals have been satisfied."[25]

During his opening statement, Stephen Kaufman explained to the jury the process used to administer Tyco's pay-for-performance incentive compensation plan:

> So what is the system? Compensation Committee meets, they fix a target, everyone knows what the target is, you review it at the end of the year and you see how well you've done. And Dennis received, if they exceeded the target, a portion of the benefits which incur to the company and obviously to the shareholders. The price of the stock [increased tremendously] during the nine years he was running the company. And that's what I mean by pay for performance. There's no chance here. There's no luck here ... It's all according to [a] formula.[26]

Kaufman then informed the jury that Tyco's books and records were audited by PricewaterhouseCoopers (PwC). He explained how the auditors reviewed the results of the company's financial performance every year, including the numbers used to calculate incentive pay. Kaufman explained it like this:

> They go to their accountants [PwC], whose presence was not noted this morning [by the prosecution], but you know what outside auditors do for a company? They're giving you the Good Housekeeping Seal, they want to see if everything is kosher. They go to [PwC] and say, you know, the Compensation Committee met at the beginning of the year, the year is over now, we figured it out, and these are the targets and this is how much they exceeded the target. Would you please certify our report? And the accountants, the outside auditors did that. Open and visible.
>
> Let's not kid each other. If [Kozlowski and Swartz] wanted to cheat on making money, if they wanted to steal from the company that I've described to you, would they do it openly and visibly? Would they create records which anyone can come in and look at?[27]

Charles Stillman, head of the Swartz defense team, addressed jurors after they heard from the prosecution and from Kozlowski's attorney. Stillman began by referencing an analogy he had used earlier, during jury selection. He said:

I told you about pancakes. I told you about making pancakes. And I talked about how it's not a pancake until you turn it over. Well, you've heard the district attorney's version of what he thinks the evidence is going to show. And I suggest to you most respectfully that some of the things you will hear are going to surprise you. Why would you be surprised? Not because the evidence is going to show you that Mark Swartz took something he did not earn. Quite the opposite. The evidence is going to show you the completely open manner in which the supposedly criminal transactions there . . . on another [of the prosecution's] colorful chart[s] . . . [t]he evidence is going to show you the openness which Mark conducted himself as he did his job. Mark Swartz did not hide anything because he had nothing to hide."[28]

*   *   *

The first witness in the first trial took the stand on October 8, 2003. Over the next six months, the prosecution called nearly fifty witnesses. The testimony and evidence was inconceivably voluminous and covered a wide range of topics. Some witnesses were asked to explain, line by line, information and numbers contained in a variety of company documents; some witnesses were asked to tell the jury about accounting methods and mechanics, like how and why entries were made to the general ledger; there were lists of loan balances and payments, questions about whether PwC audited certain transactions, explanations of how company policies were administered, and lots of questions about who told whom to do what and why. There were scores of form names, policy provisions, contract clauses, and an alphabet soup of acronyms: KELP, SEC, PwC, CEO, CFO, W-2, SCM, S-1, TME, 10-K, MBA, GAAP, 8-K, CIT, IPO, HR, CPA, IRS, EBIT, LDK, MHS, S-K, TME, AMP, BOD, ADT, F-3, EDGAR, EPS, S-4, COO, KFT, TGN.

OMG!

The jury heard about annotations, adjustments, allocations, appendices, grossups, remuneration, commercial paper, vestings, loan forgiveness, short-sellers, spreadsheets, credits, footnotes, calculations, columns, derivative transactions, nonrecurring gains and losses, institutional investors, schedules, reconciliations, letters of credit, and the financial and procedural ins and outs of many fiscal years of the vast conglomerate. There were countless references to the Board and to the Directors and to the Board's Committees—all of the terms and references were used as if jurors had extensive backgrounds in business, corporate governance, securities and tax law, and an understanding of fiduciary duties.

Throughout five months of testimony, many witnesses were asked directly or indirectly about Tyco corporate culture: what was it like to work there? Tyco in-house counsel Brian Moroze testified a couple of weeks after the trial began. Moroze had an impressive background: Yale undergrad, law degree from the University of Virginia, and he served as an officer in the U.S. Army. After the Army, he worked in the Civil Rights Division of the U.S. Department of Health, Education, and Welfare. Moroze was an attorney for another publicly traded corporation before he joined Tyco in 1986, when John Fort was the CEO. When he testified at Kozlowski's trial, Moroze had been with Tyco for seventeen years and he was still Deputy General Counsel at the company.[29] Much like Brad McGee and Mark Belnick, Brian Moroze did not seem like the kind of person you would want around if you were trying to do anything questionable. Another Boy Scout.

Moroze was asked about Tyco corporate culture. Because he had experience inside other large corporations, he was able to testify with some perspective. He told the jury that Tyco was "not a company that was overly concerned with formalized decision-making protocols." Moroze joined the company several years before Kozlowski was named CEO, and he confirmed that the informal nature of decision-making was done the same way when John Fort was the CEO as it was when Kozlowski headed the company.[30]

Moroze also testified about legal documents he drafted and retained in the normal course of business at Tyco. Counter intuitively, the prosecution entered into evidence documents that showed indisputably that the transactions they described to the jury as concealed crimes were found on the books and records of the company. Moroze told jurors that many people, from secretaries to lawyers to heads of operating divisions, played a part in processing and recording transactions that the prosecution used as proof of Kozlowski's secreted criminal activity. Moroze said he regularly discussed those documents, policies, loans, and other records with outside law firms and with Tyco's auditor, PwC.[31]

It was an odd criminal case; both sides used the same evidence. There seemed to be few disputed facts because almost everything in question was recorded in Tyco company documents and records.

Many Tyco employees, whether current or former employees at the time of their testimony, were asked if they felt they did anything wrong while performing their duties at Tyco. They were questioned about whether they were asked to do anything wrong and if they were pressured to do anything wrong. The witnesses were also asked if they were told to hide information or keep any secrets. The answer to those questions, in every case but one, was no. The sole exception was head of human resources Patty Prue, who testified that she was asked by a Director to alter meeting minutes. However, not a single Tyco employee testified that he or she was asked by Kozlowski or Swartz to hide or conceal information. Despite all the bad press, with dozens of lawsuits pending against the company and its Directors, not a single employee testified that he or she hid, concealed, or was asked or pressured by the Defendants to hide or conceal anything from anyone.

Moroze, who was still employed as a Tyco attorney when he testified, said that he was never asked to conceal, hide, destroy, or do anything else that he believed was wrong. He also confirmed that if he had concerns about anything, if he believed anyone was doing something wrong, he could have gone to both Senior Vice President Irving Gutin and to former Tyco CEO John Fort to discuss any problems. However, Moroze didn't need to go to them because he had no concerns about anything he did or saw or was asked to do at Tyco.[32]

In addition to calling scores of witnesses to walk through the details behind hundreds of numbers and to explain the contents of dozens of documents, prosecutors spent an inordinate amount of time introducing evidence of Dennis Kozlowski's lifestyle. They showed video of the Roman orgy–themed birthday party in Sardinia. But Kozlowski was not charged with stealing the $1 million Tyco paid for the business expenses incurred in Sardinia. The prosecutors brought in a jewelry salesperson to tell the jury about the expensive items Kozlowski purchased from Harry Winston, including the wedding ring for his second wife (who was referred to as his "mistress" instead of his wife), even though the purchases had nothing to do with the charges in the indictment. Prosecutors introduced evidence about Kozlowski's yachts, his homes, and his spending habits—much of which was clearly irrelevant to the charges for which Kozlowski was on trial. The six-month trial could have been conducted in a fraction of the time if only evidence relevant to the charges was introduced to the jury. Even the jurors identified the prosecutors' thinly veiled efforts to bias them against the rich, greedy, overpaid executive who had big houses, bought pricey gifts, threw extravagant parties, and had expensive taste. In that courtroom, to those jurors, the prosecution likened being wealthy to being a criminal.[33]

After the jury heard four months of testimony from prosecution witnesses, the Manhattan DA rested. Dennis Kozlowski did not testify in his own defense and he called no witnesses. It was a risky strategy, but somewhat understandable because it appeared the prosecutors failed to prove their case. However, it seems the defense could have countered the damaging evidence of Kozlowski's vast compensation and generous executive perquisites with a parade of executives who lived the same way. The jurors could have used some perspective—no one on the jury had compensation and benefits anything like those Tyco provided to Kozlowski. The defense also could have called forensic accountants and fraud examiners to explain how the transactions in question were recorded in the normal course of business—and that there was nothing unusual or hidden. The defense could have called expert witnesses to explain corporate governance and the authority vested in executive officers. The same witnesses could have told the jury that the role of director of a publicly traded corporation is not a passive job; Tyco Directors had both legal and ethical duties. White-collar crime expert Christo Lassiter opined, "The defense should have called witnesses. They could and should have established that Kozlowski was acting within the accepted norm."[34]

There was only one witness for the defense. Mark Swartz opted to take the stand, which he did on February 9, 2004. Swartz testified for several days after

which the prosecution called one rebuttal witness: attorney David Boies. Boies testified briefly about a conversation he said he had with Mark Swartz regarding one
of the disputed loans.[35] After Boies stepped down from the witness stand on March
1, 2004, there was no more evidence to be presented. The attorneys discussed passionately with Justice Obus how the jury would be instructed on each of the felony counts. After those discussions concluded, Justice Obus addressed the jury on
March 18, 2004—almost six months after the trial began.

> The fundamental duty of the jury, as we told you at the outset, is to determine the
> facts. You are a fact-finding body and the law says you are the exclusive judges of
> the facts. On the other hand, and with equal emphasis, I charge you that you are
> bound to accept the law of the case as it is given to you by the Court. After you
> have determined the questions of fact, apply the law as charged and render your
> verdicts based upon the facts as you have decided them to be under the law as
> charged by the Court.
>
> Whatever your verdicts may be in this case, each verdict must be by unani-
> mous vote of the 12 members of the jury.
>
> ... [E]very defendant in every criminal case is presumed to be innocent until
> and unless his guilt is proven beyond a reasonable doubt. And the burden to proof
> a defendant guilty beyond a reasonable doubt always rests with the People.
>
> There is no burden upon either defendant to prove anything. The law accords
> each defendant the presumption of innocence and requires you give each one of
> them the benefit of that presumption throughout the trial until such time that you
> are convinced that the People have proven his guilt to your satisfaction beyond a
> reasonable doubt.
>
> Now, what does our law mean when it requires proof of guilt beyond a rea-
> sonable doubt. The law uses the term, proof beyond a reasonable doubt to tell
> you how convincing the evidence of guilt must be to permit a verdict of guilty.
> The law recognizes that in dealing with human affairs, there are very few things
> in this world that we know with absolute certainty. Therefore, the law does not
> require the People to prove a defendant's guilt beyond all possible or conceiv-
> able doubt. On the other hand, it is not sufficient to prove that the defendant is
> probably guilty. In a criminal case the proof of guilt must be stronger than that; it
> must be beyond a reasonable doubt. . . . Proof of guilt beyond a reasonable doubt
> is proof that leaves you so firmly convinced of the defendant's guilt that you have
> no reasonable doubt of the existence of any of the elements of the crime, or of the
> defendant's identity as a person who committed that crime.

Before the jury began deliberations, Justice Obus explained the charge of
grand larceny under New York Penal Law: "Under our law, a person is guilty of
grand larceny in the first degree when he steals property and when the value of the

property exceeds one million dollars. A person steals property and commits larceny when, with the intent to deprive another of property or to appropriate the same to himself or a third person, such person wrongfully takes, obtains or withholds such property from an owner of the property."

Justice Obus also instructed the jury that the defendants could not be found guilty if the prosecution failed to prove the requisite criminal intent: "I note further in this regard in order to establish that a defendant acted with the requisite larcenous state of mind, the People must prove that the defendant did not act under a claim of right made in good faith. That is that he did not believe that he had authority to take the property. The defendant does not have the burden of proof in taking the property he acted under a claim of right made in good faith. Rather, the prosecution must prove beyond a reasonable doubt that the defendant knew he did not have authority to take the property."[36]

Jury deliberations in *People v. Kozlowski and Swartz* began on March 19, 2004.

* * *

Two weeks before Kozlowski's case went to the jury, Martha Stewart was convicted in a federal courthouse only two blocks from the state courthouse where Kozlowski's case was being heard. In a verdict that ignited a media feeding frenzy, Stewart was convicted of four counts of conspiracy, obstruction of justice, and making false statements. The stories spawned by scores of media outlets reflected the highly charged, almost rabid environment. It was not a good time to be a wealthy corporate executive—especially not an executive accused of white-collar crimes. *USA Today* reported that " . . . for federal prosecutors here, the verdict was a huge victory. At a time when the Justice Department has gone after the architects of massive frauds at Enron, WorldCom and Global Crossing, Manhattan prosecutors were criticized for picking on Stewart over a profit of about $50,000."[37]

Of course, numerous articles reporting Stewart's conviction also mentioned the trial wrapping up just a couple of blocks away.[38]

"MISTRIAL BY MEDIA"

Twelve days after the case was given to the jury, Justice Obus suddenly ended the deliberations when one of the jurors received a threatening letter at her home. On April 2, 2004, after six months and four days of trial, Justice Obus informed the jury, the Defendants, and the prosecutors that "[t]he court has no choice but to declare a mistrial at this time."

Jury deliberations had become contentious over the nearly two weeks jurors spent reviewing evidence and determining guilt or reasonable doubt on multiple felony charges. Frustrated jurors informed Justice Obus that the atmosphere in the jury room was "poisonous" and many believed they would not be able to reach a verdict. Much of the tension seemed to center on Juror No. 4, a seventy-nine-year-old retired teacher who had a law degree from New York Law School. Juror No. 4 told the panel during deliberations that she would vote to acquit on all charges. But when the judge declared the mistrial, the jury was reportedly close to rendering a split verdict, finding the defendants guilty of some counts and not guilty of others.

Juror No. 4 was first identified publicly as Ruth Jordan when a reporter claimed to see what he described as Jordan signaling the defense table with an "OK" sign as she came into the courtroom during jury deliberations. Although that journalist reported that he saw the "OK" gesture, others said Jordan was simply brushing back her hair. Justice Obus was quoted by journalist Andrew Ross Sorkin in the *New York Times* as saying "There is no finding that this juror has done anything wrong."[39] After the trial, Jordan vehemently denied giving any kind of gesture to anyone in the courtroom.[40] Dennis Kozlowski said, "I didn't see the juror do anything. I didn't see an "OK" sign or any other gesture. I honestly had no idea what Maremont thought he saw."[41]

Mark Maremont of the *Wall Street Journal*—the same Mark Maremont who wrote dozens of articles about Tyco and Dennis Kozlowski—was the first to release Ruth Jordan's name to the public. And he identified her in a *Wall Street Journal* article *during* jury deliberations. David Carr of the *New York Times* wrote: "Last week, breaking journalistic convention, The Wall Street Journal's Web site and The New York Post published the juror's name." Carr quoted David Bookstaver, then the communications director for the New York State Office of Court Administrators. Bookstaver said, "It has been an unwritten rule in the news business that even though jurors' names are public information, you gather those facts, but then hold them. You now see what happens when those conventional rules fall apart."[42]

Professor Kathleen Brickey of the Washington University School of Law dedicated much of her career to the study of corporate and white-collar law. Brickey researched and published extensively about the media and its effect on corporate scandals and white-collar criminal prosecutions. In an article published by the *Iowa Journal of Corporate Law*, she wrote that "Enron and its progeny spawned an unprecedented amount of press coverage." Professor Brickey observed that "[w]hile it was a safe assumption that the sagas of Enron and—to a lesser extent—media icon Martha Stewart would receive sustained media attention, the sheer magnitude of the corporate governance scandals fueled extraordinary coverage of massive frauds at WorldCom, Tyco, HealthSouth, and Adelphia, to name but a few."[43]

Brickey declared Kozlowski's trial a "mistrial by media" as she described how the *Wall Street Journal* published the name of juror Ruth Jordan. Brickey noted that Maremont's article started a media frenzy as the *New York Post* followed his lead and labeled Jordan the "Holdout Granny" in a front-page story that included a caricature of the elderly juror. Other media outlets picked up Maremont's story—all of which were published and read as the jury was deliberating.[44]

Brickey opined, "So assuming *arguendo* the story was worth covering—but also acknowledging that the reporting was, of necessity, one-sided [because Maremont could not interview Jordan]—what did the personal details about Ruth Jordan add to the newsworthiness or importance of the report? Was it necessary to provide her name, picture, and background in order to convey what reporters saw (or thought they saw) in open court?" She observed that " . . . as can readily be seen, it is not always easy to discern the proper balance between competing goals of the media and the courts. But if the press is to effectively perform its watchdog role, it should be mindful of the occasional need to watch itself."[45]

As he declared the mistrial, Justice Obus apologized to jurors; he told them he was sorry the system was unable to protect them. After receiving the stunning news, Kozlowski left the courthouse without comment. He later spoke by phone with Andrew Ross Sorkin and said, "I'm really disappointed that a verdict was not reached, because I feel strongly about our innocence." Charlie Stillman told reporters, "I didn't spend six months of my life and put my client on the stand for two days of direct and six days of cross for a mistrial. We came to win."[46]

How much did the mistrial cost? What was the value of six months of time, effort, and the resources of all involved, including the cost to the taxpayers of New York? How much? Tens of millions of dollars? Probably more. Who should be indicted for grand larceny for wrongfully taking those millions?

SIXTEEN

PEOPLE V. KOZLOWSKI II

After Justice Obus declared the mistrial in April of 2004, Kozlowski retreated to his home in Florida, but traveled to New York regularly for trial preparation meetings with his legal team. The anticipation of yet another lengthy trial weighed on him. For more than two years, his energy, attention, time, and resources were by necessity focused solely on resolving his legal issues. Adding to his anxiety were financial concerns. Kozlowski's assets had been frozen since the day he was indicted in September of 2002. All of his expenditures continued to be overseen and subject to the approval of Manhattan Assistant District Attorney (ADA) Amyjane Rettew.[1]

A lot of time had passed since he was indicted, and even though he had already lived through one criminal trial, Kozlowski continued to find his circumstances surreal. It was inconceivable to him that he had to defend himself against serious felony charges. Again.

PEOPLE V. KOZLOWSKI II

Supreme Court, New York County
Manhattan Criminal Courthouse, 13th Floor
100 Centre Street
New York City, New York
January 18, 2005

The second trial began on January 18, 2005, nearly ten months after Justice Obus declared the first a mistrial. Kozlowski made the trip to New York on the Sunday evening before the start of the trial on Tuesday morning. He stayed in Midtown Manhattan and on Monday evening, the evening before the trial began, Kozlowski walked to a grocery store on Third Avenue where he by chance ran into Ruth Jordan, the "OK" juror from the first trial. Because of the part she played in the mistrial, Kozlowski knew her face. Jordan recognized him immediately. Dennis Kozlowski and Ruth Jordan were strangers who played significant roles in each other's lives. He said their interaction was short and friendly, and certainly an unexpected and bizarre encounter on the eve of his second trial. [2]

The next morning, Kozlowski awoke to a freezing cold January day. He rode to the courthouse with his daughter Sandy, as the two would do every morning for the duration of the trial. Unlike the first trial, Sandy was now one of her father's attorneys. Or at least she *tried* to be a member of his defense team. Sandy Kozlowski was a 2003 graduate of Columbia Law School and was admitted to the bars of both New York and Massachusetts. Kozlowski thought his daughter would bring passion and fire to the defense. "She didn't get paid. She moved to New York and participated in my defense full time," Kozlowski said. "She got along well with the other members of the legal team."[3] Stephen Kaufman continued to serve as lead counsel for Kozlowski, assisted by Jim DeVita, Austin Campriello, and Sandra Kozlowski.

Sixth Amendment Right to Counsel of Choice

The Manhattan DA strongly objected to Sandy's role as her father's attorney, fearing her presence would make Kozlowski sympathetic to jurors. In response to the DA's objection, Justice Obus prohibited Sandy from sitting at the defense table with the rest of the attorneys. Kozlowski recalled that " . . . Sandy couldn't sit in the well."[4] Was it unexpected that Kozlowski's daughter, an attorney licensed in the State of New York, would appear in court on her father's behalf? Why would the jury have felt sympathy? It seems her participation in the case would have been expected. As is true in most families, Dennis Kozlowski trusted his daughter's advice more than that of any other attorney. It would have been far more surprising if she had *not* been on her father's legal defense team.

Justice Obus's concession to the Manhattan DA's request on this issue is troubling. United States Supreme Court Justice Antonin Scalia, when penning the opinion of the Court in *U.S. v. Gonzalez-Lopez* in 2006, summarized the long-recognized right under the Sixth Amendment to the U.S. Constitution of the criminally accused to be represented by legal counsel of choice:

> The Sixth Amendment provides that "[i]n all criminal prosecutions, the accused shall enjoy the right . . . to have the Assistance of Counsel for his defence." We have previously held that an element of this right is the right of a defendant who does not require appointed counsel to choose who will represent him. See *Wheat v. United States,* 486 U. S. 153, 159 (1988) and *Powell v. Alabama,* 287 U. S. 45, 53 (1932) ("It is hardly necessary to say that, the right to counsel being conceded, a defendant should be afforded a fair opportunity to secure counsel of his own choice"). The Government here agrees, as it has previously, that "the Sixth Amendment guarantees the defendant the right to be represented by an otherwise qualified

attorney whom that defendant can afford to hire, or who is willing to represent the defendant even though he is without funds." *Caplin & Drysdale, Chartered v. United States,* 491 U. S. 617, 624–625 (1989).[5]

During jury selection at the beginning of the second trial, ADA Owen Heimer, who took the lead role for the prosecution during the second trial, expressed strong feelings about Kaufman identifying Sandy Kozlowski in the courtroom. He characterized her involvement with her father's defense as one of Kozlowski's "unwarranted appeals to sympathy."[6] In response to the prosecution's objections, Kaufman explained, " . . . I just want your Honor to know that Ms. Kozlowski, who uses that name, is a graduate of Columbia Law School, has been working in this matter for the last four, five months.[7] At the time of her father's second trial, Sandra Kozlowski was a qualified, licensed attorney in the State of New York.

In addition to objecting to her presence at the defense table, the ADA who approved and disapproved expenditures from Kozlowski's frozen assets refused to pay attorney Sandra Kozlowski legal fees for her services. Kozlowski's defense attorney Austin Campriello explained the situation to the court:

> I can simply advise the Court, when Ms. Kozlowski first indicated a willingness to work with us I discussed the matter with the prosecutor who was supervising Mr. Kozlowski's financial affairs, because frankly my initial thought was, that since she is a graduate of Columbia Law School, since she is a lawyer, that since she would be working that typically under those circumstances one gets paid and I discussed it with the prosecutor. The prosecutor has been using restrained assets to pay us. I was told that was an absolute non-starter. There was some shock expressed that I would even consider it and obviously in light of that Ms. Kozlowski is not being paid, has not been paid, will not be paid.[8]

An individual accused of crimes has a right under the Sixth Amendment to legal counsel of choice. Both the Manhattan DA and the New York Supreme Court seemed to cross that well-defined line. The DA refused to pay Sandra Kozlowski for her legal services, thereby constructively preventing Dennis Kozlowski from the representation of his counsel of choice. When the court prohibited Sandy Kozlowski from sitting at the defense table with her client, who also happened to be her father, his Sixth Amendment rights were once again violated. The U.S. Supreme Court has not limited the Sixth Amendment right to counsel of choice to attorneys who are *not* relatives.

* * *

People v. Kozlowski and Swartz II was conducted in the same courtroom as was the first trial. Kozlowski was far too familiar with the aging, austere room on the thirteenth floor of the Manhattan courthouse. It must have been difficult for every-one entering the courtroom that cold, gray January morning to begin again what promised to be another long, exhausting, complex trial. Justice Obus, the ADAs, defense attorneys, and Defendants could only hope that the second time around, there would be a resolution.

Between the two trials, Kozlowski suggested that his defense team consult with a public relations expert to help counter the information prosecutors would un-doubtedly provide to the media throughout the second trial, as they did during the first trial. Kozlowski explained, "Every day during the first trial, the DA held a press conference and would spin what happened in court that day. I would leave court feeling good that we had a positive day, but the next morning I would read articles that were completely inaccurate. The articles described nothing like what had actu-ally happened in the courtroom the day before."[9]

Kozlowski suggested Howard Rubenstein, who is known to New Yorkers as the "dean of damage control."[10] Kozlowski's attorneys, however, did not think it necessary to address the media campaign that very quickly transformed Kozlowski from an admired, successful CEO into a free-spending, *nouveau riche* white-collar criminal. Kozlowski said, "Stephen Kaufman thought we shouldn't talk to the press even though the DA talked to the press every day. It was a mistake," Kozlowski admitted.[11]

Professor Christo Lassiter has studied the media's impact on criminal justice, specifically, the power of the media during and after high-profile criminal trials. Lassiter observed that "[t]he failure of the press is the dwindling significance of hard-hitting factual analysis. Compounding this problem is that the trend towards news analysis and commentary in lieu of factual reporting is dominated by person-ality, not by intellect. The current devolution of news to trendy spinmeisters leaves the public spinning in a sea of loosely-based, agenda-driven rhetoric *where facts do not matter.*" Lassiter pointed out that journalists "wear their demographic bias on their sleeves" and noted that "[b]y appealing to the segment of the public to which they cater, members of the press *help to create the news they wish to report*—a form of journalistic activism not unlike judicial activism in pernicious effect."[12] Lassiter said of the decision made by Kozlowski's attorneys, "It is always a mistake not to talk to the press."[13]

Kozlowski also suggested to his legal team between the trials that they hire Dr. Phil McGraw as their jury consultant. Kozlowski's friend Richard Trutanic recom-mended McGraw, and Kozlowski believed it was a good idea "but Steve Kaufman said 'no,'" he explained. Instead, they used the jury consultants Mark Swartz's at-torneys recommended. "The consultants called registered voters in New York to get a statistical sample—they asked about preconceived notions about me and Mark. I thought it was a foolish waste of time," Kozlowski said. "And of money." Kozlowski wanted the smartest jurors they could possibly get. "Mark Belnick was acquitted a few months before our second trial," Kozlowski explained, "and he had a very smart jury."[14]

*   *   *

Like the first trial, the second began with a variety of housekeeping matters between defense counsel, prosecutors, and the court. There were arguments about the DA's delay in giving evidence to the defense teams. The delayed production prompted defense attorneys to question whether the DA's office was withholding other evidence to which the defendants were entitled.[15] The Defendants fought throughout the trial, usually unsuccessfully, for the right to access evidence that they believed contained both *Rosario* material and *Brady* material.

Rosario material is evidence that must be produced during discovery, the time period prior to trial during which both sides are required to share the evidence they possess. The *Rosario* rule was established in New York in a 1961 decision of the court of appeals in *People v. Rosario.* Under *Rosario,* each party is required to produce any written or recorded statements of their witnesses that relate to the testimony that will be given by those witnesses during the trial.[16] *Brady* material is evidence in the possession of prosecutors that is exculpatory, or would reduce punishment if the defendant is convicted. This evidentiary rule was established in 1963 by the U.S. Supreme Court in *Brady v. Maryland.*[17] Disagreements over evidence occur in nearly every criminal trial. But in both trials in which the People of the State of New York prosecuted Dennis Kozlowski, evidentiary issues were critical, and the rulings almost certainly impacted the outcomes of the trials.

In a *Law & Order* episode titled "Under the Influence," the fictional Manhattan DA's office hid and withheld exculpatory evidence in order to convict a defendant of an excessively harsh charge "to make an example of him."[18] In the television show, both the DA and the judge had political agendas and they used the defendant's case to further their causes, without regard for the rights of the accused.

Sometimes life imitates art. Both Kozlowski and Swartz argued throughout the trials, and after both, for access to critical evidence that would likely have exculpated them. They were repeatedly denied access to that evidence. As in the television drama, it was also evident that the Manhattan DA had a political agenda—the prosecutor known for his aggressive prosecution of white-collar criminals no doubt wanted his pound of flesh during the Enron fallout. Eight years after Kozlowski and Swartz were convicted, former Manhattan DA Robert Morgenthau said of the case: "It sent a message to a lot of people."[19]

Throughout his career, Morgenthau was both applauded and criticized for his aggressive pursuit of corporate criminals—he was even called the father of white-collar criminal prosecutions. Gary Naftalis, a former Assistant DA in Morgenthau's office, told the journal of the American Bar Association that Morgenthau "talked about crime in the suites being as important as crime in the streets."[20] The

Manhattan DA was a seasoned eighty-five-years-old when the second trial of Ko-zlowski and Swartz began.

Morgenthau was long known for stepping into investigations and prosecu-tions that were generally handled by federal prosecutors, and at times his office was criticized for its investigation techniques and for its choice of targets.[21] Individuals accused of white-collar crimes by Morgenthau's office often chose plea agreements rather than going to trial, persuaded by the DA's reputation, New York's harsh sen-tencing guidelines, and a very tough state prison system.

In addition to the DA's interest in seeing Kozlowski and Swartz convicted, Tyco and its former Directors also had a stake in the outcome of the trial. If the men were acquitted, the Directors faced far greater culpability in dozens of civil actions that were filed against them. Plus, the Directors had to be thinking about the outrageous Retention Agreement they had entered with Kozlowski. Former Tyco Director Robert Monks hypothesized that after Enron, with the stock price down and the enormity of Kozlowski's compensation in the spotlight, "there were only two stories that could be told. Either the Board was negligent, maybe even criminally negligent, or Dennis was a thief. If the Directors intended Dennis to have everything he received, they would be seen as reckless and careless and would be held responsible. But if he stole everything, well that was certainly a better sce-nario for them." Monks explained, "So, the Board hired David Boies and Boies told the Board's version of the story—Dennis stole everything." The Directors' after-the-fact denials, their claims of ignorance about Kozlowski's compensation, "they weren't credible," Monks said. "That Board would have paid him every penny he wanted."[22]

*   *   *

The mistrial provided the DA's office a rare second bite at the apple, and prosecu-tors took advantage of the opportunity. They significantly changed the presenta-tion of evidence based on feedback from jurors who sat through the first trial.[23] Kozlowski said he thought the DA's office hired one of the jurors from the first trial to serve as a consultant during the second trial.[24] Clearly, it was a case the DA wanted to win. Morgenthau's office zealously prosecuted Kozlowski and Swartz a second time, and vehemently opposed the defendants' critical evidence requests during the trial and throughout the appellate process.

After resolving the arguments about evidentiary matters, but prior to the be-ginning of *voir dire* (the questioning of potential jurors) and jury selection, the court addressed the DA's request that both sides be prohibited from speaking with the press during the course of the trial.[25] The DA's request was provoked by an ar-ticle that appeared on the front page of the Sunday *New York Times* just two days before the second trial began. Andrew Ross Sorkin interviewed Kozlowski and in his article, observed that Kozlowski "portrayed himself as a self-made entrepreneur who has become the victim of an overzealous prosecutor interested in sensational headlines and a board trying to protect itself from shareholder lawsuits."[26] The article appeared balanced and presented both prosecution and defense views of the charges for which Kozlowski was about to be retried.

However, much to the prosecution's chagrin, Sorkin observed that "unlike Enron, WorldCom, or Adelphia, which all suffered from huge accounting frauds and sought bankruptcy protection, Tyco never entered bankruptcy proceedings or even laid off employees *en masse*. Indeed, today, Tyco's stock price has rebounded and is even higher than when Mr. Kozlowski left the company, though it still remains lower than its peak." Although Sorkin's article appeared factually accurate, the DA felt it painted a sympathetic picture of Kozlowski and that the timing of the interview was calculated to influence the jury pool. For that reason, the DA wrote a letter to the court requesting a ban on contact with the press.[27]

Ironically, another article about the case appeared in the *New York Times* the morning the second trial began. This article included an interview of John Moscow, who was formerly of the Manhattan DA's office. Moscow headed the investigation of Kozlowski, Swartz, and Belnick in cooperation with David Boies and Tyco. The Moscow article was certainly untimely for ADA Heimer and weakened his argument about using the media. Regardless, Heimer said "we stand by our letter. We think given recent events, it would be appropriate for the lawyers in this case to be directed not to speak to the press."[28]

In response to the ADA's letter, defense attorney Austin Campriello said, "Let me begin by suggesting in as gentle a tone that I can, I'm startled with what I perceive to be the hypocrisy and approach being taken by the People. What is, to use the ancient anglosaxin [sic] phrase, chutzpah." Campriello agreed with Heimer that "there is no comparison between the two articles because the article that appeared today criticizes and holds up to ridicule a juror on the day we are about to pick jurors. The article today criticizes the Court. The article today contains an interview of the District Attorney who felt compelled to make a comment. The article today is replete with quotes from the person who Mr. Heimer suggests has bad judgment, who is the architect of the case that brings us here today."[29]

Campriello went on to argue that there had been no misconduct of defense attorneys during the first trial and that the DA's request was unnecessary. Justice Obus agreed that "we did get through the last trial without a great deal of difficulty along these lines in terms of comments being made in the press by people participating in the trial." Justice Obus didn't ban the attorneys from talking to the press, but cautioned them that it was going to be difficult to find an unbiased jury, and that well-timed articles would not make the task any easier.[30] It's surprising that Kozlowski's defense counsel didn't happily agree to ADA Heimer's request for the media ban. Kozlowski's attorneys advised him not to address the media during both the first and second trials, but the DA's office made good use of the press. It would have been helpful to the defense if the DA's office didn't pitch the prosecution's case to the media throughout the second trial.

After taking care of preliminary matters, the court began the process of selecting jurors for what would inevitably be a very lengthy trial. Justice Obus summarized the charges for the jury pool and explained that "[i]n case there is any confusion about the matter, the company in question is not the toy company, it is a large company known as Tyco International."[31]

Justice Obus then educated the jury pool about the presumption of innocence, and he made very clear that individuals in the pool were not precluded from serving as jurors in the trial just because they possessed knowledge about the Defendants. The judge stated:

> ... [E]ven if you have already made some impressions about the matter generally, you are nevertheless eligible to serve here as long as you recognize the verdicts to be entered in this case must be based solely on the evidence introduced here and you feel that you are able to put everything else aside, approach the matter with an open mind, listen to the testimony of witnesses, consider whatever the evidence may be, reserve your decision until the end of the trial and then after you have heard everything, including the arguments of counsel, the Court's legal instructions, the evidence itself, at that point during the deliberations at the very end of the trial make a determination as to whether or not the evidence meets the People's burden of proof.[32]

Naturally, the defendants were concerned about a tainted jury pool, considering the extensive and exceedingly negative media coverage of Kozlowski, Swartz, and Tyco during the first trial, and in the months preceding the second one. The judge was also cognizant of the environment and cautioned the jury that "[w]e are not here for any larger purpose. Certainly the jury is not here to be sending messages to anybody. We are not here to conduct some kind of sociological study. We are not making some general evaluation of corporate governance in the United States."[33]

Despite the negative media coverage in the post-Enron environment, Kozlowski was optimistic as the second trial began. After the Kozlowski and Swartz mistrial was declared on April 2, 2004, Mark Belnick was acquitted of all charges on July 15, 2004. This gave both Kozlowski and Swartz reasonable hope that they too would be acquitted. Their optimism was also fueled by the offer of a plea deal. During the first week of the second trial, the DA offered a deal that would result in a prison sentence of between two and six years for both Kozlowski and Swartz. The offer required both Defendants to accept the plea bargain.[34]

Kozlowski met with his attorney Stephen Kaufman the evening after the deal was offered. The two met at Kaufman's townhouse in downtown Manhattan and then went out for pizza. Ever the dealmaker, Kozlowski thought they should negotiate with the DA, and suggested a counteroffer of one to three years. He recalled that "Stephen Kaufman was inclined to accept the DA's offer because he didn't think I could get a fair trial in New York. But Steve also thought it was a very 'tri-able' case." The other members of Kozlowski's criminal defense team thought they could win. He recalled that Bob Shwartz of Debevoise & Plimpton, one of the attorneys handling a half-billion dollar civil action Tyco had filed against Kozlowski, thought a plea deal would be devastating to the civil case—meaning it would cost Kozlowski a lot of money.[35]

Kozlowski remembered that both he and Mark Swartz were on the fence about the deal. He discussed it with his daughter Sandy and said she had no strong feelings either way. Of course, Sandy was a young woman, only in her mid-twenties. It would have been difficult for her to disagree with the rest of his attorneys, especially when that decision would have sent her father to prison. As he considered the plea deal, Kozlowski sincerely believed he had committed no crimes, and he felt certain he would be acquitted of all the charges levied against him. Unlike the first trial, Kozlowski planned to testify during the second one. He felt that by addressing the jurors directly, he could convince them that he and Mark Swartz did not steal money from Tyco.[36]

Kozlowski and Swartz ultimately declined the deal, a decision that cost them years of their lives. Kozlowski explained that "[i]f we believed we had stolen anything, we would have taken the deal. We thought we could easily prove beyond a reasonable doubt that we didn't steal the money." Kozlowski revisited this decision often during the years he spent in prison, especially after the first two years, knowing he would have been a free man had he accepted the plea deal. With the regret and clarity of hindsight, he said, "I should have taken the deal and considered it a cost of doing business."[37]

Although optimistic because of Belnick's acquittal and the offer of a plea deal, Kozlowski was greatly concerned about jury selection. Justice Obus told the jury pool that "[t]he defendants here are entitled to a jury of their peers, to a jury that includes people from various walks of life and who represent the diversity of this city."[38] However, the jury seated for the Defendants' second trial was not filled with their vocational peers. There were no corporate executives, no bankers, not even a single juror with a business degree. In fact, only one of the jurors had a four-year college degree. The charges against Kozlowski and Swartz were directly related to and intertwined with their occupations. In reality, the Defendants did not have a jury of individuals who had the backgrounds necessary to comprehend the mountain of sophisticated business, financial, and accounting information that was presented during the trial.

Neither Kozlowski nor his daughter Sandy recalled much serious discussion about waiving his right to a jury trial, a strategy often considered when the subject matter of a trial is so complex that jurors may have difficulty understanding the evidence.[39] In addition, a bench trial, where the judge acts as both the judge and jury, is sometimes favorable when defendants are not sympathetic. It is safe to say that Kozlowski and Swartz were not sympathetic defendants. But the defense teams opted to try the case *again* in front of a Manhattan jury.

Justice Obus informed the pool of potential jurors of the anticipated time commitment required for the trial. Jurors would be required to be in court Monday through Thursday from 9:30 am until 5:00 pm. The judge estimated a four-month trial, which was a significant underestimate. He explained that potential jurors could be excused from serving if the demanding time commitment would pose a hardship. Financial hardship allowed individuals in the pool who may have been better equipped to comprehend the evidence to be dismissed. Professionals with the education and experience necessary to understand the complex issues of the case were unable to be away from their jobs for several months, leaving in the jury pool individuals without the professional and business experience that may have allowed them to more easily comprehend the evidence presented during the trial. Among the many professionals dismissed was a self-employed publicist, who in addition to claiming financial hardship expressed bias about the defendants based on what he had read. "I had a vice-president pursuing business with the Tyco Company and I stopped it and they're on the black list."[40]

The publicist was not alone in his preconceived notions. Many in the jury pool shared their negative feelings about Kozlowski and Swartz. As the Defendants feared, many potential jurors were undeniably and detrimentally biased. One prospective juror told that judge "if you have not heard about the Tyco case you have been living in a cave." Knowing the gentleman was right, the judge said, "We understand everybody heard about it. Do you feel you can put this aside and wait until you hear the evidence and judge it based on whatever the evidence in the court is?" The prospective juror replied, "I really don't think I can do that." The opposite bias also appeared among the prospective jurors, but only once, when a potential juror told the judge, "I followed the first trial very closely in the newspaper, there is no way in the world I would find Dennis Kozlowski guilty."[41]

Individuals who remained in the pool admittedly had knowledge of the case, had read newspaper articles published during the first trial, and stated that they were aware that the Defendants lived a "very high life." They had heard about Kozlowski and the criminal charges on television, on Fox News and *The Daily Show;* had read articles in newspapers; and they had heard about the case "on the train" and in "water cooler talk." The potential jurors referenced articles in the *New York Times* and the *Wall Street Journal* and had heard interviews on public radio. They were aware of articles, videos, and photos on the Internet and specifically recalled seeing video of the infamous birthday party on Sardinia. Many individuals mentioned Enron, WorldCom, Martha Stewart, and voiced feelings about pervasive corporate greed.

Kozlowski remembered his concern during both trials when he saw jurors arrive at the courthouse each morning "with newspapers tucked under their arms."[42] He knew those newspapers often contained articles about him and reports of the ongoing trial, and he feared jurors were influenced by biased and often inaccurate information found in the newspapers they carried into the courthouse. His fears were legitimate; there was no way to shield jurors from the media coverage of the case.

Isaac Rosenthal, who at the age of twenty-two served as the foreman of the jury during the second trial, said, "I was aware of the coverage, I saw the *New York Post* and people asked me about the trial, but I barely took notice." Rosenthal said he was aware during the trial that there was a lot of media coverage of the case, but insisted that it didn't influence him. "All I knew was what I saw between 9 am and 4 pm in the courtroom," he explained.[43]

Instruct, Deceive, Conceal

Opening statements of the second trial began on January 26, 2005. ADA Heimer addressed the jury for the prosecution. He began by introducing the other Assistant District Attorneys at the table, all of whom participated in the first trial: Ann Donnelly, Connie Fernandez, Ken Chalifoux, and Mark Scholl.[44]

Heimer provided jurors with an overview of basic corporate governance. "The defendants answered to the Board of Directors," he said. "The Board of Directors had the power to hire and fire these two executives. Most importantly for this case, the Board of Directors and only the Board of Directors, acting through its Compensation Committee, had the authority to decide the compensation, to decide the pay of these two executives." Heimer didn't mention to jurors that Tyco Directors had duties, were responsible for oversight, and had power over Kozlowski and Swartz, which was counter to the explanation provided to the jury.[45]

Some of the "facts" included in the prosecution's opening statement were patently untrue. For example, Heimer told jurors that, other than Kozlowski and Swartz, the members of the Tyco Board " . . . didn't work at Tyco. They didn't have offices at Tyco. They didn't have a staff that worked for them at Tyco. Not even one secretary. They didn't have any day to day access to the inner workings of Tyco."[46] But, Director John Fort maintained an office in Tyco's Exeter, New Hampshire, location for years—after he was replaced as CEO and when his only connection to Tyco was as a Director. Likewise, Director Josh Berman maintained a full-time office in Tyco's New York location and, according to testimony during the trial, Berman reviewed many of Tyco's public filings over the years, he participated in drafting SEC filings, and "he reviewed the proxy materials on a regular basis."[47]

Heimer also told the jury that Kozlowski and Swartz were actively engaged in running Tyco, "[b]ut apart from these defendants the members of the Board of

Directors of Tyco were strictly part-timers. In fact, they spent so little time on Tyco business, you could barely even call them part-timers."[48] According to the *Corporate Director's Guidebook* of the American Bar Association (ABA), the role of director of a publicly traded corporation is not the passive, "part-time," responsibility described during the prosecution's opening statement. According to the ABA, " . . . to be a 'director' is to 'direct'—which means to become informed, to participate, to ask questions, and to apply considered business judgment to matters considered by the board,"—responsibilities that are a far cry from those ADA Heimer's attributed to the barely part-time Tyco Directors.[49]

From the onset of the second trial, which in this respect was not dissimilar to the first trial, the prosecution portrayed Tyco Directors as an ardent yet vulnerable group of barely part-timers from whom information was actively concealed. However, the overwhelming weight of the evidence presented during the trials revealed a very different situation in Tyco's boardroom. When Kozlowski was CEO, some Directors had offices at Tyco, they made use of administrative support, many Directors and their business organizations and firms transacted business with Tyco, a Director's wife was a paid broker for the sales and purchases of real estate for Tyco and Tyco employees, a Director's law firm was paid for years to represent the company, businesses owned in whole or in part by Directors purchased assets from or sold services to Tyco, and there was no reasonable doubt that Directors had access to any information they wanted about the inner workings of the company. No employee was ever told to hide or conceal anything, and no one was instructed to withhold any information from Directors. The testimony in both trials was uncontroverted on these issues.

In fact, Kozlowski himself made sure Directors had access to any information they wanted or needed. After he became CEO, he established the position of management liaison to the Board of Directors. The management liaison was directed to keep the Board informed, and was the primary contact for the Board's Compensation Committee. Kozlowski was quite certain that "the Board knew they could ask Barbara Miller, the first management liaison, and her predecessor Patty Prue for any information at any time. Plus it was the liaison's job to get information to them."[50] Kozlowski also insisted on having a lead director—a non-employee member of the Board who acted as a leader separate and apart from the Chairman of the Board. Because of those two roles—management liaison and lead director—Kozlowski and Swartz would not have been able to screen information from or filter information to Tyco Directors. But the prosecution and some of the Directors who testified during the trials painted a very different picture.

In addition to having access to information, Tyco Directors had a fiduciary duty to stay informed about how the company operated, including how executives were compensated. Kozlowski said, "I don't know how they could get on the stand and testify under oath that they didn't know how much the chief executive was paid. When I sat on boards, I always knew how much the CEO was paid. I made a point of knowing. It was an important part of being a director."[51] Clearly, the DA's office wanted to bolster the credibility of former Tyco Directors, many of whom would be called as prosecution witnesses and whose testimony was critical to the prosecution's case. In his opening statement, ADA Heimer began telling the Directors' side of the story. They were barely part-timers who were misled, kept in the dark, and restricted from information. They were vigilant in performing their duties yet still somehow duped by the CEO, the CFO, Chief Corporate Counsel, PricewaterhouseCoopers (PwC), external law firms that provided written legal opinions, and a no-action letter the company received at the end of an SEC investigation. Heimer portrayed them as innocents who were at the mercy of the powerful executive officers of Tyco.[52]

Heimer told jurors, "This case is the story of how two men, these two defendants, stole a 150 million dollars from a corporation named Tyco and from that corporation's owners, its shareholders."[53] The ADA summarized for the jury the grand larceny charges against Kozlowski and Swartz:

In August of 1999 these two defendants stole 37 and a half million dollars from Tyco and they falsely called that a bonus. [August 1999 bonuses were tied to the Kendall acquisition]

In September of 2000 these two defendants stole more than 48 million dollars from Tyco and its shareholders and they falsely called that a bonus. [September 2000 bonuses were tied to the TyCom IPO]

A short time later, in November of 2000, they stole more than 24 million dollars from Tyco and its shareholders and they falsely called that a bonus. [November 2000 bonuses were tied to the sale of ADT Automotive]

In March of 2001 defendant Swartz stole 1.2 million dollars from Tyco to get himself out of a bad real estate deal.

In August 2001 these defendants stole 12 million dollars from Tyco and its shareholders and they called that a bonus. [August 2001 bonuses were tied to the FLAG transaction]

From August of 2001 until January of 2002 defendant Kozlowski individually, and assisted by defendant Swartz, stole 14 million dollars from Tyco so that defendant Kozlowski could buy paintings to put in his homes. [The paintings to which ADA Heimer referred were never in any of Kozlowski's homes, and the prosecution produced no evidence to even suggest the paintings were in his homes.] This was Tyco's money he used.

And in July of 2001 these two defendants stole 20 million dollars from Tyco and its shareholders so that they could secretly benefit another director that worked with them at Tyco, a man named Frank Walsh.[54]

ADA Heimer informed the jury that "[t]he evidence is going to show you that these defendants did not earn this 150 million dollars. The evidence will prove to you that they stole this 150 million dollars and that they knew exactly what they were doing when they did it." The prosecution's theory of the crimes was "instruct, conceal, deceive," a slight variation from the "lying, cheating and stealing" mantra used during the first trial.[55]

Patty Prue, Senior Vice President of Human Resources and Management Liaison to the Board

ADA Heimer said the thefts he described to the jury required the involvement of Patty Prue, Tyco's head of human resources (HR). However, Prue was not indicted by the Manhattan DA. Instead, she was granted immunity from prosecution.[56] When asked why some individuals were indicted and others were not, former Manhattan DA Morgenthau explained that "you need an insider." Of how he made the decision about who would receive immunity, Morgenthau said, "You look for people who are telling the truth. You ask 'is she trustworthy?'" Asked if he considered giving Kozlowski immunity and using his testimony to prosecute others, Morgenthau said with certainty, "No."[57]

When Prue was called as a witness for the prosecution, she explained to jurors her responsibilities as Senior Vice President (SVP) of HR. She told jurors that she worked with the Compensation Committee both in her role as the head of HR and as the management liaison. Prue stated that she, with the assistance of her staff, gathered financial and compensation information and provided it to the Committee, including performance targets, results, and payouts for the Incentive Compensation Plan. She said her duties included communicating with Committee members about executive pay as well as the compensation of operating division presidents.[58]

During his testimony, former Chair of the Compensation Committee Frank Walsh said the Committee relied on the compensation information received from Patty Prue and was dependent on the data she provided.[59]

Prue told jurors the Compensation Committee had four members who were non-employee Directors, and that the Committee usually met four times a year "a few minutes before Board meetings." However, during the four years she worked with the Committee, Prue admitted that it met as infrequently as once a year. In addition to the brief official meetings that Prue said lasted only a few minutes and were usually held in Bermuda, where Tyco Board meetings generally took place, the Committee had "discussion sessions" in Tyco's New York and Boca Raton offices where members reviewed packets of information Prue prepared and provided to them in advance of the official meetings. Prue spoke of working with a variety of

Directors who served on the Compensation Committee during the years she was management liaison. She mentioned specifically Frank Walsh, Phil Hampton, Peter Slusser, and Steve Foss, but indicated that there were others.[60]

Prue also revealed that Donna Sharpless, a member of her staff, drafted the minutes for Compensation Committee meetings *before* the actual meetings took place. Furthermore, Sharpless did not attend any of the meetings. Prue explained that even though Sharpless wrote the minutes without attending the meetings, the pre-prepared minutes were reviewed for accuracy by those who actually attended, but sometimes not for weeks or months after the meetings.[61]

When asked how much she was paid by Tyco for her work as head of HR, Prue said her compensation for 1999 was $2,664,971.97. For 2000, Prue told jurors she was paid $5,591,505.34, and in 2001, Tyco paid Prue $6,797,483.83.[62] To be compensated at those levels, Prue must have been considered a highly capable HR professional.

THE BONUSES

There were four bonuses in question. The prosecution called them unauthorized bonuses that Kozlowski and Swartz concealed from the Board of Directors and therefore, the two executives committed grand larceny. The Defendants called them earned bonuses paid pursuant to the company's written Incentive Compensation Plan. The bonuses, all of which were very large amounts, were paid in connection with four very profitable transactions—extraordinary, one-time, nonrecurring events. In each case, Swartz's bonus was exactly half of Kozlowski's. According to their respective incentive pay agreements with the company, bonus calculations for Swartz always resulted in exactly half of what was due to Kozlowski. In addition to Kozlowski and Swartz, up to fifty other Tyco corporate employees received bonuses as a result of the same four transactions.

August 1999: Kendall pooling adjustment
Kozlowski's bonus: $25 million; Swartz's bonus: $12.5 million

September 2000: TyCom IPO bonuses
Kozlowski's bonus: $32 million; Swartz's bonus: $16 million

November 2000: ADT Automotive bonuses
Kozlowski's bonus: $16 million; Swartz's bonus: $8 million

August 2001: FLAG telecom bonuses
Kozlowski's bonus: $8 million; Swartz's bonus: $4 million

All of the bonuses were administered in the same way—not paid at the end of a fiscal year but calculated, paid, and accounted for as part of the deals during which they were earned. There was some uncertainty about whether this was allowable under the company's Incentive Compensation Plan. For example, the largest bonuses of those in question were paid in September of 2000 to those involved with the TyCom IPO, a transaction that resulted in a nearly $2 billion nonrecurring gain for Tyco. The TyCom bonuses were paid at the conclusion of the transaction instead of being part of bonus calculations, approvals, and payments at the end of the fiscal year.

When he was called as a witness for the prosecution during the second criminal trial, former Tyco Director and longtime Chair of the Compensation Committee Frank Walsh testified that the Committee, under a shareholder-approved compensation plan and by the authority vested in it by the Board of Directors, had the discretion to set the length of a performance period and to pay lump-sum bonuses. Defense attorney Jim DeVita asked Walsh if under the Tyco Incentive Compensation Plan "the gain on the sale of [a] business" would be included in the "calculation of the cash bonus based on earnings before tax." Walsh responded under oath, "As written, yes." The defense asked for this clarification so jurors understood that bonuses could be earned and paid at any time, not just at the end of a fiscal year, and that even though they didn't occur regularly, the company's gains from IPOs and similar transactions were definitely part of Tyco's bonus plans.

> MR. DEVITA: [I]f, for example, a subsidiary of the company issues stock and sells the stock to the public, and the company [realizes] a gain and earnings on that sale of stock to the public in the initial public offering, that also would be included in earnings before tax under this definition, correct?
>
> [ASSISTANT DISTRICT ATTORNEY] MR. SCHOLL: Objection.
>
> THE COURT: I'll permit the witness to answer if you can.
>
> [MR. WALSH]: You talking with intent or literal interpretation—
>
> MR. DEVITA: What the plan says.
>
> [MR. WALSH]: As written I believe you would be correct.[63]

Calculations of Incentive Pay

According to the Incentive Compensation Plan (the Plan) that was approved by the Tyco Board of Directors, the Compensation Committee, and Tyco shareholders, both Kozlowski and Swartz were to receive pay-for-performance based on relatively simple mathematical calculations. One of the three prongs of the Plan provided that if the company's pretax earnings exceeded the target set by the Compensation Committee at the beginning of the relevant fiscal year, Kozlowski was to be paid 1 percent and Swartz was to be paid one-half of 1 percent of the amount by which performance exceeded the pre-established goal. For example, assume the Committee set a goal of 15 percent growth of pretax earnings, and the prior fiscal year's pretax earnings were $1,000,000. Before any bonuses were payable, the company's pretax earnings would have to exceed $1,150,000 (15 percent increase over the prior fiscal year). If the company's actual pretax earnings for the year were $2,150,000, Kozlowski received $10,000—1 percent of $1,000,000 (the amount by which the performance exceeded the goal). Swartz received $5,000—one-half of 1 percent of $1,000,000.

Another prong of the Plan worked the same way; if the company's operating cash flow exceeded the targets set by the Compensation Committee, 1 percent of the overage went to Kozlowski, one-half of 1 percent to Swartz. The third prong involved application of a similar mathematical formula based on whether the company's earnings per share (EPS) exceeded the target set by the Compensation Committee.[64]

The performance goals were the responsibility of the Directors who sat on the Compensation Committee; they set the goals for each of the years in question.

During his summation at the end of the second trial, Swartz's lead defense attorney Charles Stillman reminded the jury of evidence that was presented through witness testimony and with documents admitted throughout the trial. Stillman said, "The [Incentive Compensation] Plan also allowed the directors to make early payment of bonuses and to pay bonuses in forms other than cash and stock only with the consent of the employees receiving the bonuses." Stillman also reminded jurors that after the Plan came into effect, "the first change that the directors made was to remove the cap on what bonus amounts could be received by Dennis Kozlowski and Mark Swartz."[65] In other words, bonuses were payable at any time and there were no caps on the amounts Kozlowski and Swartz could earn under the Plan.

Testimony from witnesses during the trial confirmed that the provisions of the Plan applied to nonrecurring gains from transactions when Tyco sold a business or common stock—like the gains Tyco experienced with the TyCom IPO, the sale of ADT Automotive, and the FLAG transaction. Nonrecurring gains had been part of incentive pay calculations at Tyco for many years—from the first year the plan was adopted by the Tyco Board. Under oath, SVP of HR Patty Prue acknowledged that one-time gains were included in bonus calculations, as did two former Chairs of the Compensation Committee, Frank Walsh and Stephen Foss. For example, Tyco sold Futuro in 1996, when Richard Bodman was the Chair of the Compensation Committee, and bonuses were paid on that gain. The same was true in 1999 when Tyco sold two large companies and experienced nonrecurring gains. Bonuses were paid on those gains, as part of the transactions. Not at the end of a fiscal year.[66]

The issue, then, was not whether Kozlowski and Swartz had earned the bonuses or whether the company could or should pay the bonuses. Under the Plan, the bonuses were payable to Kozlowski and Swartz. The crux of the grand larceny charges related to the bonuses was whether the Board of Directors *authorized* payment of the bonuses—a step required by the Plan.

The TyCom IPO

TyCom was part of Tyco's undersea cable unit. In 2000, Tyco raised almost $2 billion by selling 11 percent of TyCom in an IPO. Tyco acquired TyCom for $750 million and as with hundreds of other companies, Tyco implemented cost reductions and revenue enhancements that transformed TyCom into a more valuable enterprise. After the IPO, Tyco still owned 89 percent of the subsidiary and in addition, realized a substantial nonrecurring gain.

When he took the stand in his own defense during the second trial, Kozlowski explained how and why the TyCom bonuses were paid in September of 2000. Kozlowski told the jury, "Tycom [*sic*] was an acquisition Tyco did a number of years before and we took the company public. That is we sold about 11 percent of Tycom for about one point nine billion dollars. Our investment in Tycom or what we paid for Tycom was about 750 million dollars and had some other investments in the company; but this resulted in a very, very large gain for Tyco. By taking it public we made a separate company out of it. Tyco owned 89 percent of the company but shareholders owned the other 11 percent and it traded on the New York Stock Exchange. Tyco booked the large gain and that became part of our performance under the bonus formula for that fiscal year."[67]

Kozlowski explained discussions about the TyCom deal he had with Phil Hampton, then the Chair of the Compensation Committee. Kozlowski said:

I believe it was August of the year 2000 that I informed Phil [Hampton] we were going to take a very sizeable gain in Tycom, and Phil was in the loop on this because he was following the Tycom sale all the way. He would call me almost on a daily basis and say what is the interest in Tycom or are people going to be buying this deal, and we responded in the affirmative that it looked very good for us over the two week period we were out, we would be telling management and employees of Tyco and Tycom to sell this deal; and as a result I explained to Phil that—well, first I went to Mark [Swartz] and asked Mark to calculate what kind of bonus does this big gain mean to us, and Mark gave a range of a phenomenal number, something of about 60 to 65 million dollars on my behalf. That meant Mark would be receiving about half of that because typically Mark's compensation the way it worked was 50 percent of mine and I had further discussions with Phil about my feelings on that size bonus. I suggested that as opposed to taking 65 million dollars in a cash bonus or deferring it or doing whatever we would be then doing with the bonus, we cut my bonus in half and Mark's bonus in half and we use the remainder of those, of the bonuses earned here to reward other people in Tyco who were instrumental in the Tycom deal; that is people who primarily—we were thanking people who moved from Exeter, New Hampshire to Boca Raton, Florida that we reward them in a very special way.[68]

After Tyco's acquisition of ADT in 1997, most of Tyco corporate headquarters was relocated to Boca Raton, Florida, where ADT was located at the time the two companies merged. Kozlowski wanted to reward the employees who were asked to relocate from New Hampshire to Florida, and who played crucial roles in the successful TyCom IPO.

Kozlowski told the jury: "You have to keep in mind 1999 and 2000 were spectacular years for us. Our stock was going up I believe some 50 percent a year. Tycom was considered to be a very successful acquisition, a very successful acquisition and resale within a short period of time, and my intention or my plan was that I told Mark, was that the 50 or so employees who relocated from Exeter, New Hampshire that we forgive their home mortgages as part of a special bonus for monies that they borrowed to come to Boca Raton, Florida. We would forego a portion of our bonuses in order to reward other people who were critical and very important members of our team."[69]

"Since I was asking Phil for half the amount due to me [under] the formula," Kozlowski said, "I suggested to Phil that he communicate with . . . whoever he had to communicate with. He said he would handle that and I also told him that we would have any information. . . . Patty Prue would have the details as we worked this out and Patty was the liaison to the Compensation Committee and he to Patty." Kozlowski explained that he consulted with both Prue and Swartz as they planned the TyCom bonus and testified, "I'm certain I had meetings with them to discuss the bonus. I certainly met with Mark because Mark went along with the program of reducing his bonus by 50 percent as I did."[70]

In explaining the decision to pay down employees' relocation loans instead of paying cash bonuses, Kozlowski said that "[w]e 'forgave' loans only in lieu of paying cash bonuses. If I or someone earned a bonus and had an outstanding loan, the loan would be paid (i.e., forgiven) rather than a check being issued."[71]

When asked how much he ultimately received as part of the TyCom bonuses, Kozlowski said, "I believe it was instead of the 64 million dollars, it was approximately 32 million dollars." Kozlowski explained that his bonus was not paid in cash but instead was used to reduce the outstanding balance of the loan he took when he relocated to Boca Raton, Florida. He had taken the loan through Tyco's relocation loan program, a generous benefit that was available to and used by many employees, not just those at the executive level. Kozlowski told jurors, "Well, 19 million dollars of the bonus was loan forgiveness and the remainder was taxes." When asked if the $19 million paid off his relocation loan in its entirety, Kozlowski said,

"At the point in time after I paid off the relocation loan with the formula bonus, I believe I still owed about five and a half million dollars on my Florida relocation loan."[72] It's surprising that Kozlowski, if he was intentionally stealing from the company, didn't steal enough to completely pay off his outstanding loan.

Kozlowski said that his bonuses from nonrecurring gains had been calculated and paid in the same way since he was a Tyco division president. He explained:

> If we sold a building or sold a business or sold an asset, the profits on that would become part of our bonus formula. It was the only reasonable way to give management the incentive to sell assets that should be sold, if not, we would keep the asset, allow them to continue to . . . generate income, and you would continue to get a bonus on the stream of income from those assets. If strategically or operationally or emotionally or for whatever reason selling off a business was the right thing to do, the gain between the book value of that business and the selling value of that business was, always has been, any incentive system I ever had at Tyco, part of my bonus calculation. There is precedence for that when we sold the Muller business, sold the Grinnell business at Tyco, sold Futuro, this was in years prior to the Tycom bonus, and gains were all part of our bonus calculation and formula, and always had been.[73]

When head of HR Patty Prue testified, she too was asked about the bonuses. Prue was one of the forty-two employees on the list of recipients of TyCom bonuses in September of 2002; she received $1,269,396.74. The bonuses ranged from a low of $318,636.28 to a high of $32,976,067.85. Nine of the bonus payments exceeded $1 million. Kozlowski's memo announcing the bonuses along with the list of recipients was circulated to a number of people in the company including Mark Foley, who at the time was Tyco's SVP of Finance. In addition to Kozlowski's memo, many other documents and entries were created to announce, process, and account for the bonuses. Kozlowski did not calculate the bonus amounts. He said, "I spent zero percent of my time calculating bonuses."[74]

Prue testified that when she, Kozlowski, and Swartz talked about the September 2000 bonuses, they discussed Phil Hampton's role of in the process. Prue said, "In the meeting I had with Mark [Swartz], Mark told me Dennis had a conversation with Phil Hampton about the loan forgiveness, and that Phil had approved it. In the meeting with Dennis and Mark, Dennis mentioned that Phil, Mr. Hampton in his conversation, at least it was my understanding the Board knew about [the bonuses]." Prue explained her understanding "[i]n the context of Dennis talking about the Board wanting to reward the employees and the contributions that everyone made." With the blessing of Mark Swartz, Prue requested and received the opinion of outside legal counsel regarding SEC disclosure requirements for the bonuses paid to Kozlowski and Swartz. Marian Tse of Goodwin, Procter & Hoar in Boston provided the legal advice at Prue's request.[75]

Everything about the TyCom bonuses seemed to have been done as per usual at Tyco. The amounts of the bonuses paid to Kozlowski and Swartz were calculated according to the terms of the Incentive Compensation Plan—except both men took only half of the amounts due them, allotting their other collective half to forty other Tyco employees. There were numerous discussions and a clear paper trail that was very easy to follow.

Mark Foley, SVP of Finance at the time of the TyCom IPO, testified at length about discussions he had with several people in Tyco corporate offices and with PwC auditors regarding accounting methods used for the bonuses, which affected the books and records of both Tyco and TyCom. He said he discussed the bonuses with Swartz before they were paid and also said under oath that all of the bonuses in question were discussed with Richard Scalzo, the PwC partner who oversaw Tyco audits. His testimony about the TyCom bonuses filled more than forty pages of the transcript of the second trial.[76] If Kozlowski and Swartz tried to conceal the bonuses, as the prosecution alleged, they failed miserably.

No Meetings, No Memos, . . . and No Minutes

Unfortunately for Kozlowski and Swartz, nothing in Compensation Committee minutes reflected the Committee's approval of the TyCom bonuses. The terms of the Incentive Compensation Plan required Committee approval of pay-for-performance bonuses *before* they were released to the CEO and CFO. According to Kozlowski, Hampton gave him approval and said he would take care of the rest. According to Prue, September of 2000 was Phil Hampton's first month of service as the Chair of the Compensation Committee. Sadly, Hampton died in April of 2001, before questions about the bonuses were raised.

It turned out that, over the years, the Tyco Board of Directors and the Board's three committees (Compensation, Audit, and Nominating and Governance) failed to record and maintain meeting minutes as meticulously as anyone needed them to be when Kozlowski and Swartz were indicted. Kozlowski had a well-known distaste for bureaucracy, and a strong "no meetings, no memos" management preference. He believed a minimal corporate staff was the best way to run the company, but the sparse corporate operations that he insisted on when he was CEO did not serve him well when he needed well-kept books and records, and documentation that corporate formalities had been observed, to save him when there were questions. In addition to the Compensation Committee minutes having been written in advance of meetings by someone who didn't attend the meetings, there were Board huddles and Committee information sessions for which no minutes were created.

Trial testimony revealed other gaps—missing and incomplete minutes that should have but didn't reflect important decisions of the Board and of its Committees. For example, no Board or Committee meeting minutes reflected the Board's decision to hire David Boies to conduct the internal investigations in 2002. Furthermore, Boies testified that he attended Tyco Board meetings during the summer of 2002, yet there were no meeting minutes between June 3, 2002 and August 14, 2002—the time frame during which Boies testified that he attended meetings.[77]

Just as there were no meeting minutes that reflected approval of some of the bonuses paid to Kozlowski and Swartz, and just as no information was found in minutes about the investment banking fee paid to Frank Walsh, there were no minutes reflecting the Board's approval of fees paid to Director Josh Berman's law firm. There was no record of Board discussion, disclosure, or approval of fees paid to Berman's firm.[78] Unlike Kozlowski, Swartz, and Walsh, the Manhattan DA did not indict Berman and he was not called as a witness during either of Kozlowski's criminal trials, even though, according to Kozlowski, Berman was without a doubt the most influential Tyco Director when Kozlowski was the CEO.[79] Berman was, however, called as a prosecution witness during Mark Belnick's trial, which resulted in Belnick's acquittal. For unknown reasons, the transcript from that trial is sealed. Shockingly, the Tyco Board of Directors' Audit Committee kept no minutes at all until 2002. Mark Foley, who attended the Audit Committee meetings as the SVP of Finance but was not a Director or a member of the Committee, said under oath that Audit Committee members John Fort, Wendy Lane, and Richard Bodman (the same Director who said under oath during the first trial that he didn't read the half-billion dollar Retention Agreement when the Board entered into the contract with Kozlowski) didn't record or retain minutes during the years when the four bonuses in question were paid. Foley testified that he suggested a change, via an email to Director John Fort, in March of 2002:

Q. This is an e-mail from you?

A. Yes.

Q. To John Fort?

A. Yes.

Q. He was at that time the Chairman of the Audit Committee?

A. I believe so, yes.

Q. It says John, in light of everything going on recently, I thought it made sense
    for us to start keeping minutes of our Audit Committee meetings. That is
    dated March 6, 2002?

A. Yes.

Q. So up until that time, the members of the committee kept no minutes?

A. Yeah.[80]

In May of 2001, the Board of Directors approved the sale of $2 billion of Tyco stock to Lehman Brothers. There was a press release to this effect but absolutely no reflection of the Board's approval in meeting minutes.[81] A two billion dollar sale of stock, and not a single mention in the Board's meeting minutes. It seems no decision was too big to be excluded.

There was no approval of the bonuses paid to Kozlowski and Swartz in the minutes of the Board or of its Committees. Looking at the overwhelming evidence of sloppy, haphazard, negligent record keeping and even the complete failure to record minutes by the Board and its Committees, how could the Manhattan DA, the court, or the jury place any weight on the fact that approval wasn't found in the minutes? Lots of things were missing from meeting minutes—and sometimes there were no minutes at all. They were clearly not a source of reliable information.

* * *

After the CIT acquisition went bad in December of 2001, after some of the Directors were angered in January of 2002 when they learned of the $20 million investment banking fee paid to Frank Walsh, after the price of Tyco dropped in the post-Enron, post-Global Crossing bankruptcy market, after Kozlowski and the Board announced they were breaking up the company and then backpedaled, causing yet another drop in the stock price, with rumors swirling about accounting irregularities and a spotlight suddenly cast on Kozlowski's personal spending habits, after the Directors were sued, after Kozlowski was indicted on sales tax evasion charges, and after the Board hired David Boies to conduct an internal investigation and to represent the company in dozens of shareholder lawsuits, the Directors either could not recall approving the TyCom bonuses, or they testified that they did not approve the TyCom bonuses or the other three bonuses paid on nonrecurring gains between 1999 and 2001. Without documentation of the Board's approval, and without Directors who could remember approving the bonuses, with Phil Hampton dead and unable to confirm the conversations he had with Kozlowski, the Manhattan DA determined that Kozlowski and Swartz stole the money, charged them, and asked a jury to convict them of grand larceny.

* * *

The prosecution asked Patty Prue if she had opportunity to speak with Phil Hampton after Kozlowski and Swartz discussed the TyCom bonuses with her, after they told her Hampton was in the loop and was taking care of Board approval. Prue said yes, she spoke with Hampton at the Compensation Committee discussion sessions and at the Committee's official meetings in September and October of 2000.[82]

The ADA asked Prue: "And on any of those occasions did Mr. Hampton indicate to you that he was aware of 32 million dollars in loan forgiveness and gross-ups being obtained by Mr. Kozlowski?" Prue testified, "I didn't have any conversations with Mr. Hampton about this benefit."

Prue was then asked, "And did he ever mention to you that he was aware that Mr. Swartz had obtained 16 million dollars in loan forgiveness and gross-ups in September of 2000?" Prue responded, "No."

Justice Obus then clarified: "So that I'm clear, you're telling us that he never raised the subject and you never discussed the subject of the loan forgiveness to either Mr. Kozlowski or Mr. Swartz." Prue responded, "To Mr. Hampton, that's correct."[83]

It seems the question that both the judge and the ADA should have asked of Prue was if *she* raised the issue of the bonuses with Hampton. She was the head of HR and the management liaison to the Board. She was the source of compensation information the Compensation Committee received. She was very generously compensated by Tyco to perform her duties—in 2000, the year of the TyCom bonuses, Prue was paid more than $5.5 million.

According to Prue, it was her responsibility to keep the Compensation Committee informed about executive pay. In addition to Kozlowski's face-to-face discussions with her, on September 11, 2000 he sent her a memo about the TyCom bonuses with the subject line "Compensation." Why didn't Prue provide that information to the Compensation Committee and request approval? She was the head of HR. More than anyone else in the company, she should have had the most comprehensive understanding of the terms of the Incentive Pay Plan and the procedures it required—she was paid to know and to administer it. She testified that she was never asked or told to hide or conceal any information. She testified that it was her job to inform the Committee. During cross-examination, Kozlowski's attorney asked Prue:

> Q. In terms of performing your professional function as the liaison . . . of the
>   Compensation Committee, did you feel free within the exercise of your own
>   judgment to provide whatever you thought was appropriate to the Chairs of
>   the Compensation Committee . . . ?
> A. Yes.
> Q. And in creating those packets did you use your best judgment in putting
>   together whatever you thought would be helpful and appropriate?
> A. Yes.
> Q. Did you personally, for any reason, ever try to hold any information back
>   without being told by anybody, from the Compensation Committee?
> A. Never. Never.[84]

But Compensation Committee members testified that they either didn't recall receiving information about the TyCom bonuses or that they definitely did not receive the information. The testimony of the former Tyco Directors was the same regarding all four unapproved nonrecurring gain bonuses—even though Kozlowski and Swartz provided Patty Prue with the requisite information. Why were Swartz and Kozlowski held responsible for Prue's failure to perform her duties? If what happened at Tyco with the bonuses was criminal, why were Kozlowski and Swartz indicted instead of Prue? Why was she granted immunity? It raises the same concerns and questions as when Kozlowski was indicted for sales tax evasion instead of the art dealer who was legally responsible for collecting and remitting the sales tax—the art dealer to whom the Manhattan DA granted immunity.

During her trial testimony, Prue admitted that she received a severance package from Tyco. In March of 2003, six months after Kozlowski, Swartz, and Belnick were indicted, she signed an agreement with Tyco in which she received a generous separation package in exchange for her cooperation with pending and threatened litigation, her agreement to provide information during investigations, and to testify at trial. Under the agreement, Prue's legal fees were paid by Tyco, and the company vested shares that even with the deflated price of Tyco stock at the time amounted to more than $2.2 million. She retained real estate in Florida that the company had purchased and she received stock options; the company reimbursed her for state and local taxes she paid for four years; and the company agreed to indemnify her against any losses she might experience as a result of legal actions related to her employment with Tyco. In exchange, Prue agreed not to make any disparaging, critical, or detrimental comments about Tyco or her employment at Tyco, or to talk about the company's business affairs or financial condition, and Tyco agreed not to give any negative employment references about her.[85] Considering her central and critical role in the actions that were considered grand larceny by the Manhattan DA, the SVP of HR walked away with a much sweeter deal, *sans* criminal prosecution and a civil action with Tyco, than did Kozlowski, Swartz, and Chief Corporate Counsel Mark Belnick.

Management Representation Letters

The crux of the charges against Kozlowski and Swartz was that they intentionally and knowingly concealed the bonuses they received; when the company incurred four large one-time gains, the co-conspirators arranged for bonuses to be paid to themselves (and to dozens of others, but the bonuses paid to other employees were not part of the criminal charges because Kozlowski had the authority to set compensation for everyone other than Swartz and himself). It's difficult to determine what the former executives should have done differently. Other highly paid professionals in the company calculated the amounts due under the incentive pay plan, and Kozlowski and Swartz discussed the bonuses, both in writing and verbally, with Patricia Prue, the head of HR and liaison to the Board. Mark Foley, SVP of Finance, handled the discussions about how Tyco would account for the bonuses. In addition, Kozlowski and Swartz disclosed the bonuses in a "Management Representation Letter" provided to Tyco's independent auditor, PwC. In a letter dated December 19, 2000, the executives disclosed that "In connection with the calculation of the $1.760 [billion] gain on the public offering of shares in TyCom Ltd., the Company has deducted incremental bonus expenses of $85.1 million from the net proceeds received. These expenses represent remuneration of key Tyco and TyCom employees, paid solely in connection with their contributions on behalf of Tyco to the operation of TyCom Ltd. in prior periods and to the offering process. The remuneration is incremental to the employee's customary bonuses and is a direct result of the public offering of TyCom Ltd. shares."[86] In addition to the signatures of Kozlowski and Swartz, the letter was signed by Mark D. Foley and Jeffrey D. Mattfolk, both SVPs. The management representation letter was also provided to the Board's Audit Committee.

Although not evidence that the bonuses were approved, the management representation letter certainly is evidence that Kozlowski and Swart *believed* the bonuses were approved. It is evidence that they weren't concealing the bonuses, as the prosecution alleged. The letter seems convincing evidence that Kozlowski and Swartz did not intend to take the money wrongfully—it is compelling evidence that they believed they had a right to receive the bonuses. It is also evidence that Kozlowski and Swartz believed Tyco employees did their jobs and processed the bonuses as required.

Philip Hampton

Unfortunately for all involved, longtime and well-respected Tyco Director Phil Hampton succumbed to illness in April of 2001. Kozlowski's lead defense attorney Stephen Kaufman described his client's relationship with Hampton. Kaufman said Hampton was Kozlowski's "advisor, his consultant, and he would talk to him frequently and he was a great source of wisdom and counsel and comfort to Dennis as Dennis' career flourished at Tyco."[87]

In his Letter to Shareholders in Tyco's 2001 Annual Report, then Tyco CEO Kozlowski closed his letter with a tribute to his friend and mentor. Kozlowski wrote, "Sadly, Philip Hampton, a person who greatly helped us prosper, passed away in April. Phil was a long-time board member and we are profoundly grateful for his service. We will all miss his wisdom, judgment, vision and insight. His contributions were extraordinary."[88]

From his prison cell a decade after Hampton's death, Kozlowski wrote, "Philip Hampton was our Lead Director and very capable. He kept the Tyco Board in check. His death was tragic in many ways. I would not be in jail if Phil lived."[89]

"Whether or Not He Got the Money Does Not Affect Any of the Issues in the Case . . ."

Before Patty Prue was cross-examined during the second trial, ADA Heimer pre-emptively argued to Justice Obus (outside the presence of the jury) that the defense should not be able to present evidence to the jury showing that Kozlowski did not receive his bonus payments—the bonus payments he was accused of stealing. Heimer did not want the jury to know that those payments were retained by Tyco as deferred compensation. During the first trial, Kozlowski's defense attorney Jim DeVita elicited testimony from Prue confirming that Kozlowski did not take his bonus money out of the company and that when he was ousted in June of 2002, Tyco retained all of Kozlowski's deferred compensation. During his argument to the judge, Heimer said, "Whether or not he got the money does not affect any of the issues in the case . . . [s]o I don't know what the relevance is of the fact Mr. Kozlowski did not get this money when he left Tyco."[90] It's truly unfortunate for Kozlowski that jurors did not hear the ADA say it didn't matter that Kozlowski never received the money he was accused and convicted of stealing.

Kozlowski's attorney Austin Campriello explained to Justice Obus that Kozlowski's decision to leave in the company, in deferred compensation, the bonus money he was accused of stealing was relevant evidence of his intent. Campriello argued, "This is a trial that in large measure turns on intent. Many of the facts the parties agree on. The question is whether or not Mr. Kozlowski acted with criminal intent, and in that setting it seems to me we have an absolute right to demonstrate to this jury that Tyco, at the time Mr. Kozlowski was allegedly stealing money, was holding somewhere between 82 and 83 million dollars of Mr. Kozlowski's money. We are not going to go into whether it is still being held today or not, although the truth is it still is being held hostage today, but it was being held when Mr. Kozlowski left the company and when these crimes allegedly were committed." Campriello said, "It seems to me that goes right to Mr. Kozlowski's intent."[91]

"Tyco, I think even Tyco would probably agree they have no right to hold money in the deferred compensation program and indeed would violate ERISA [Employee Retirement Income Security Act] if they were doing it because of the sales tax indictment which has absolutely nothing to do with Mr. Kozlowski's performance as the Chief Executive Officer of Tyco," Campriello argued. "If Tyco continues to hold the money, Tyco is continuing to hold the money because of the events in this trial."[92]

Kozlowski's attorney Jim DeVita joined the argument, saying, "There are two additional points of relevance for the fact the money was there and Mr. Kozlowski did not receive it. When Mr. Walsh testified, the prosecution brought out the concept of . . . deferred compensation [which] means that the employee gets it at a later date. Well, in fact, he did not get it at the later date, and the point, it is important to establish that . . . this money is at risk because it is held by Tyco and not in Mr. Kozlowski's possession."[93] In other words, if Kozlowski was intentionally stealing money from Tyco, why would he willingly leave it—more than $80 million—in the company? Outside of his control and possession? When he could have removed it at any time?

DeVita continued, "Secondly, the last trial, and I presume this trial, the prosecution . . . offered evidence that at the time of Mr. Kozlowski's departure, there was an 18 million dollar . . . [loan] balance in his Key Employee Loan Program and it suggests he somehow walked away from that. Our position is in fact the balance was in his favor because offsetting that 18 million was 83 million of Mr. Kozlowski's money that the company still held when he left."[94]

DeVita emphasized, "The point is—it is relevant Mr. Kozlowski was willing to forego the receipt of the cash which created an obvious uncertainty about whether he would receive it in the future, . . . [i]t is relevant to his intent to steal that he [didn't take the $83 million] and that he has not received it even today."

It seems Dennis Kozlowski was charged with and convicted of robbing a bank when the money was still in the vault.

SEVENTEEN

CUT FROM WHOLE CLOTH

The expression "cut from whole cloth" was originally used to describe clothing the material for which was cut from a run of fabric taken straight from the loom—it was whole and had never been used for another purpose. Clothing that was cut from whole cloth was special. It was not seamed or structurally weak, but was well made and with integrity that set it apart from less valuable garments that were pieced together from remnants or from the repurposing of tattered cloth.

During the 1800s, tailors began advertising clothing as cut from whole cloth even though the claims were untrue—the clothing in fact was made from old fabric that was cut and creatively pieced together so it appeared to be of high quality when in fact it was weak and lacked structural integrity. The tailors' deceptive claims were fictitious and misleading, and their goods lacked integrity. Thus the phrase "cut from whole cloth" came to mean a fiction, a falsehood—a deceptive story represented as true, but when examined closely, was found to have no integrity.

*   *   *

In an interview she provided for a 2011 Harvard Business School case study, former Tyco Director Wendy Lane, who was a member of the Board's Audit Committee in 2001 and 2002, spoke of the Board's and her own reliance on independent audits. Kozlowski said that he, like Lane and the Board, relied greatly on the Pricewater-houseCoopers (PwC) audits each year. "We employed highly-paid professionals—accountants and attorneys. The services cost us tens of millions of dollars every year. Of course I relied greatly on the results of the audits. I met with the PwC people every quarter. I believed they would inform us if anything was being done wrong. They didn't find anything—they never found anything wrong," Kozlowski recalled.[1]

During his testimony during the second criminal trial, former Tyco SVP Mark Foley confirmed that Tyco paid PwC more than $56 million in 2000 and more than $51 million in 2001—two of the years during which the questioned bonuses were paid.[2] In July of 2007, PwC settled a class action lawsuit brought by Tyco share-holders as a result of the scandal. PwC agreed to pay $225 million but admitted no wrongdoing or failures in performing Tyco audits. When the firm settled with shareholders, PwC spokesman David Nestor said that the firm had been "prepared to continue to defend all aspects of its work" but that the cost of doing so "made settlement the sensible choice."[3] PwC had to settle. The firm had little solid ground to stand on after Kozlowski and Swartz were convicted of a long list of felonies. Wendy Lane stated that "there was no indication that anything was wrong. We had 80% of what would later be required with Sarbanes-Oxley. The accountants and internal controllers said everything was in order." She also said, "There were not the red flags you would have expected."[4]

Perhaps there was nothing to see, nothing to catch. Maybe there were no red flags. It's possible, maybe even likely that there was nothing wrong. It seems the entire case was cut from whole cloth.

THE FOOLISH USE OF KELP

Very few facts in the case were in dispute, so why did the trials require a combined eleven months to present evidence? Throughout both trials, the juries were subjected to voluminous testimony and a mass of other evidence, much of which seemed un-necessary because it was either unrelated to the charged offenses or it was not in dispute. For example, there was lengthy and detailed testimony about how, when, and why Kozlowski authorized the purchase of the Tyco apartment at 950 Fifth Avenue. Why bring in witnesses to go through the accounting process? The journal entries? Why bring in the broker who sold the apartment? Why bring in the housekeeper who cleaned it? Why was there testimony about how often Kozlowski and his wife slept there? Kozlowski never once disputed that Tyco purchased the apartment. Not a single witness disputed it. He never claimed that he owned the apartment. More rel-evantly, he wasn't charged with stealing the money that paid for the apartment. None of the charges had anything to do with the purchase or use of the Tyco apartment. Yet the jury heard volumes of evidence about the place. Tyco, the DA, and hundreds of media outlets used the fixtures the decorator chose for the apartment to ridicule, chastise, and judge Kozlowski's lifestyle. But there were no criminal charges related to the apartment, the doggy umbrella stand, or the $6,000 shower curtain.

The same is true of the birthday party. The jury saw video and photos of the Roman orgy–themed event. They heard that Tyco paid for about half of the ex-penses related to Sardinia events. Yet Kozlowski wasn't charged with stealing that money.

The prosecution did a masterful job of muddying the waters with irrelevant and explosive evidence of the spending habits of a newly wealthy business executive. The sensational details definitely helped them paint an unflattering picture for the jury.

Unfortunately for Kozlowski, he had made it quite easy for prosecutors.

Kozlowski was not charged with any crimes related to his use of Tyco's Key Employee Loan Program (KELP) or the relocation loan program—other than paying down or paying off his loans with unapproved bonuses. But his KELP loans and other loans he received from the company probably caused him more harm than anything else presented during the criminal trials.

Kozlowski used KELP and relocation loans long before he was Tyco's CEO. The loan programs were in place under his predecessor. The primary purpose of KELP was to allow employees to borrow funds from the company to satisfy the tax liability related to the vesting of restricted shares of Tyco stock. The vesting of Tyco restricted shares was a taxable event—it was income. The program was established to encourage executives like Kozlowski to retain their ownership of Tyco stock instead of selling it to satisfy the tax liability that arose as a result of vesting. KELP allowed employees to borrow up to 50 percent of the amount of shares that vested. For example, if an employee's restricted shares were worth $10 million on the day they vested, that employee could borrow $5 million from KELP. The employee had to immediately give enough of those funds to Tyco to cover the related payroll withholding required, but the remainder went to the employee. The wisdom of such a policy is subject to the business judgment of the board that adopts the policy, and subsequent boards that allow it to continue.

Kozlowski made a serious misjudgment about how his KELP loans were handled. When he was CEO, all of his personal finances were managed in a department of Tyco corporate called Executive Treasury. The duties of the individuals who worked in Executive Treasury were to manage the personal finances of the CEO and CFO.

All of Kozlowski's personal bills and expenses were paid through Executive Treasury. He sent all purchases, payments, and investments through the department, and all of his personal financial information was housed in Tyco corporate offices—in the Executive Treasury department. Kozlowski's personal financial matters circulated throughout Tyco corporate offices as wire transfers and other transactions were processed by a number of corporate employees.

When Kozlowski had vesting events—dates on which his restricted shares vested, dates on which he was responsible for payroll withholding, and when he was eligible to take loans through KELP, he did not transfer the loan proceeds out of the company into a personal account and he didn't pay his tax liability with those funds. Instead, Kathy McRae of Tyco Executive Treasury added the amount Kozlowski was allowed to borrow to "his KELP account," which was used as a quasi revolving line of credit. If Kozlowski was permitted to borrow $50 million on a day his restricted shares vested, McRae simply added $50 million to the amount Kozlowski had available, and then used the money to pay his bills as needed. She kept a running balance and increased the amount available in his "KELP account" every time his shares vested. Money went out of his account when bills needed to be paid. If he bought a boat for $15 million, she processed it through his "KELP account." Kozlowski's payment for the boat was then sent from Tyco to the seller. If a bill arrived from the lawn service at his house in Florida, McRae used KELP to pay it. There were hundreds of entries, anything from $350 in petty cash for Kozlowski's housekeeper to the $3.95 million payment to the art gallery for the Monet. There were volumes of invoices and payments—every one of Kozlowski's personal expenditures was processed through the company, through his "KELP account."[5]

McRae also made decisions about what were personal expenses and what were business expenses on Kozlowski's credit card bills. She managed the expenses for his yacht. Kathy McRae even helped with Kozlowski's first divorce. She testified during the trial that "[t]hey were growing the company. They didn't have time to take care of this much work and they gave me more work and more responsibility." McRae testified that she never believed she, Kozlowski, or Swartz was doing anything wrong. She also told jurors that PwC knew about and saw the KELP records and that she was never asked to hide anything. Kathy McRae said after Kozlowski was fired, he called her because he didn't know where his bank accounts were. He didn't even know his Social Security Number.[6] The record keeping used by Executive Treasury created blurred lines between the personal finances of the CEO, the CFO, and the company. Although it was possible to sort out what was personal from what was not, the web of intermingled records and access to all of Kozlowski's personal spending habits gave David Boies and the Manhattan DA a treasure trove of damaging evidence that was sold to jurors throughout two criminal trials.

Kozlowski paid back all of the loans, except the balance outstanding when he was indicted in June of 2002 and ousted from the company.

LOGIC AND REASONING . . . AND RELEVANT EVIDENCE

In addition to the charges related to their bonuses, the former executives were charged with grand larceny in the first degree for authorizing and paying the $20 million investment banking fee to Frank Walsh during the CIT acquisition ($10 million to Walsh, $10 million to a charity). There seemed to be no genuine dispute of the facts. All of the evidence came from Tyco's books and records, and the testimony of witnesses was consistent. Removing the mass of evidence about

Kozlowski's lifestyle and personal expenditures that served only to muddy the waters, and looking *only* at the relevant evidence, the elements of grand larceny are impossible to prove.

- The Tyco Board of Directors expressly granted Kozlowski authority to pay investment banking fees related to the CIT acquisition—this clear and uncontroverted grant of authority appeared in an empowering resolution that was memorialized in the Board's meeting minutes in March of 2001.
- Dennis Kozlowski authorized an investment banking fee paid to Frank Walsh for the work he did during the CIT acquisition (an exercise of Kozlowski's Board-granted authority) in July of 2001.
- Kozlowski approved hundreds of investment banking fees during his tenure as CEO.
- The company paid Frank Walsh a $20 million investment banking fee (based on Kozlowski's authorization) in July of 2001.[7]
- The investment banking fee was disclosed in Tyco's 2001 proxy.
- Between the years of 1992 and 2002, the Board of Directors did not once approve investment banking fees, even though hundreds were paid during that time period.[8]

The facts do not indicate or even imply criminal intent or acts. The facts show that the Board granted Dennis Kozlowski the authority to spend up to $200 million without Board approval, then when the Directors were sued after the payment made to Frank Walsh was disclosed, they were displeased with how Kozlowski exercised the authority they granted him, so they allowed and participated in the process that transformed his business judgment into a charge of grand larceny.

Other than the four bonuses and the payment to Walsh, the three additional grand larceny charges were related to Dennis Kozlowski's art purchases. Kozlowski and Swartz were charged with taking $1.975 million for the paintings Kozlowski purchased with his Board-granted spending authority for the Tyco apartment at 950 Fifth Avenue. The paintings were purchased with Tyco funds and were reflected as Tyco assets on the audited books and records of the company.

Kozlowski and Swartz were charged with grand larceny in the first degree for the $8.8 million paintings Kozlowski purchased in Florida when art dealer Christina Berry had the London gallery ship pieces to Kozlowski's home for his review. Kozlowski borrowed money through the KELP to pay for the paintings. He signed a promissory note for $8.8 million and repaid the loan. The paintings were insured in Kozlowski's name.

The two former executives were also charged with grand larceny in the first degree related to Kozlowski's purchase of a Monet painting for $3.95 million.

Kozlowski borrowed money through KELP to pay for the painting. He signed a promissory note for $3.95 million and he repaid the loan. This painting was also insured in Kozlowski's name.

All of the artwork in question hung in the Tyco corporate apartment. Dennis Kozlowski did not move or take any of the paintings—not the ones the company purchased and not the ones he purchased personally. When Kozlowski was indicted on sales tax charges in June of 2002—charges that were ultimately dropped—Tyco seized possession of all of the artwork in question and took possession of other art Kozlowski owned as well as all of his other personal property that was in any Tyco office, apartment, or facility on the day before he was indicted.

Who should be charged with grand larceny for taking Kozlowski's personal property, including multi-million dollar paintings? Or is Dennis Kozlowski not entitled to protections of the law because he made and spent a lot of money?

If the painting purchases were grand larceny, why were there no charges for the literally hundreds of other purchases that were processed exactly the same way through Kozlowski's "KELP account"? If the payment to Frank Walsh was grand larceny, why weren't the years of payments to Josh Berman's law firm? Or the unapproved payments for pilot and chartering services paid to other Directors? If the four bonuses were grand larceny, why not the other bonuses paid as a result of nonrecurring gains? Why just those four? The logic is very difficult to follow.

SUMMATIONS

Good faith = no criminal intent. No criminal intent = no crime.

The most critical element the prosecution had to prove was criminal intent. When Justice Obus instructed the jury, he told them that "in order to establish that a defendant acted with the requisite larcenous state of mind, the People must prove that the defendant did not act under a claim of right made in good faith. That is that he did not believe that he had authority to take the property. The defendant does not have the burden of proof in taking the property he acted under a claim of right made in good faith. Rather, the prosecution must prove beyond a reasonable doubt that the defendant knew he did not have authority to take the property."[9]

In his summation, Mark Swartz's attorney Charles Stillman told the jury that when they looked at all that had been presented over the prior months, "[t]hat evidence will be—perhaps better said, the lack of evidence demonstrates that the District Attorney has failed entirely to meet its burden of proving beyond a reasonable doubt that [the defendants are] guilty of any crime."

Stillman said, "My shorthand way of saying that to you now is good faith equals no criminal intent. In other words, as I said when we first spoke back in January, no criminal intent means no crime."[10]

DELIBERATIONS

The jury was charged and deliberations began on Thursday, June 2, 2005. On Friday, June 17, 2005, the jurors sent a note to the judge stating that they had reached a verdict.

PART FOUR

INGLORIOUS ENDING

EIGHTEEN

O5A482O

The jury returned with guilty verdicts—lots of them. Dennis Kozlowski was found guilty of twenty-two of twenty-three felony counts. Mark Swartz was found guilty of the same, plus one additional count of grand larceny. It was Friday, June 17, 2005. It had been three years and two weeks since Kozlowski's life began its downward spiral—since the sales tax indictment and his ouster from Tyco.

The newly convicted former executives were allowed to leave the courthouse the day the verdicts were handed down. Justice Obus said, "Under all the circumstances I'm satisfied at least for the period of time that the defendants will not be a flight risk, and that it is appropriate to allow them at liberty on the bail that has been posted, at least for this adjournment."[1]

SENTENCING

Supreme Court, New York County
Manhattan Criminal Courthouse, 13th Floor
100 Centre Street
New York City, New York
September 19, 2005

Kozlowski and Swartz, by then the white-collar version of Butch Cassidy and the Sundance Kid, returned to court on September 19, 2005. In the courtroom where they spent much of the prior three years, the former CEO and CFO of Tyco International were sentenced for the crimes of which they were convicted.

Justice Obus addressed Kozlowski and Swartz in turn. He said, "L. Dennis Kozlowski, you are before the Court for sentencing following your conviction after trial to 12 counts of grand larceny in the first degree, one count of conspiracy in the fourth degree, one count of violation of general business law, and eight counts of falsifying business records in the first degree."

THE COURT: Does Mr. Kozlowski wish to make a statement?

DEFENDANT KOZLOWSKI: Yes, your Honor. I have a very brief statement to make. First of all, I want to thank your Honor and all of the Court personnel for the many courtesies that have been shown to my family, my friends and to me in these proceedings which have run a span of three years. I hope your Honor concludes from the 130 letters you have received from people from all walks of life have provided you with an accurate picture of who I really am as opposed to the person portrayed at times in this courtroom and in some parts of the media. I also hope that in deciding what sentence to impose your Honor not only considers the verdict, but also considers all the positive things I have done in my life. Your Honor, I recognize the sentence will include incarceration. I ask you to please be as lenient as possible. Thank you very much.

After Kozlowski addressed the court, Mark Swartz also made a brief statement:

DEFENDANT SWARTZ: Your Honor, I never thought I would be in the position I am today, nor did I ever fear, and the reason is I always hold myself to a high standard of integrity, honesty. Every day I tried to make my family and me proud of the man I am. The assistant District Attorney was correct on one matter, and that is you have heard directly from me in two trials as to my views on my actions and the reasons for my actions. And in this very courtroom every word I said was the complete and honest truth. I ask you in making your decision on my sentence to consider my actions, the reason for my actions, and I also ask you to return me to my family as soon as possible because I do consider it a relationship of vital importance. And I have been fortunate in the continued support I received from my wife, parents, in-laws, kids, family friends and attorneys, and it's that continued support that I'll be forever grateful for. Thank you.

The defense legal teams submitted briefs in which they requested imposition of the minimum sentences allowable under New York law. Minutes before Kozlowski and Swartz were sentenced, Assistant DA Heimer opposed those requests, specifically in regard to Kozlowski, and stated, "The People recommend that the Court impose on Dennis Kozlowski the maximum consecutive prison sentence authorized by law." The Manhattan DA's office, in effect, asked for a sentence of 300 years (a maximum sentence of twenty-five years for each of the twelve counts of grand larceny to be served consecutively). Assistant DA Donnelly addressed the court with regard to Swartz, saying "It is our recommendation that this Court sentence Mark Swartz to the maximum sentence permitted by law."

Justice Obus, after having presided twice over the prosecution of Kozlowski and Swartz, stated before imposing sentences:

The Court has sat in this room with defendants and their families and their supporters, of course with counsel during two trials for large portions of the last two years and is cognizant of the ordeal this process has been and the pain the sentences to be imposed will undoubtedly cause to defendants and to others. That is inevitable in a matter like this. And while again I do not necessarily view the defendants' conduct in quite as stark terms as do the People, it is the Court's responsibility to impose sentences that are commensurate with the magnitude of the offenses in question.

Justice Obus added, "I will note for whatever it is worth, I do not view the defendants as security risks . . ."

After the People and the court had spoken, Kozlowski and Swartz faced the moment that they had no doubt feared since being indicted three years earlier. The court explained that prison terms imposed on the grand larceny counts would be the controlling sentences, as they were the most severe: "I'm imposing indeterminate sentences on each of those counts involving the unauthorized compensation to the defendants of an indeterminate term of imprisonment of eight and one third to 25 years."

Justice Obus ordered that the prison sentences be served concurrently and stated that the Department of Corrections would decide where the men would serve their time. In addition to imposing the maximum indeterminate prison sentences, the court ordered Kozlowski and Swartz to pay restitution to Tyco in the amount of $134,351,397—the total amount they were convicted of stealing from the company. Of the total, $97 million was apportioned to Kozlowski and $37 million to Swartz, although they were jointly and severally liable for the full amount. In addition, Swartz was ordered to repay an additional $1.2 million on a separate count of grand larceny for which Kozlowski was not charged.

On top of the prison sentences and restitution, Kozlowski and Swartz were ordered to pay criminal fines in the amounts of $70 million and $35 million, respectively. The criminal fines may very likely have been the largest ever imposed on individuals by the State of New York.[2]

Kozlowski said that as quickly as possible, he paid the ordered restitution to Tyco in full, and that he also paid in full the criminal fines due to the Manhattan DA.[3]

The newly sentenced soon-to-be inmates requested bail during the pendency of their appeals, but those requests were denied.

INMATE O5A4820

Kozlowski and Swartz were taken into custody as soon as the sentences were imposed by the court. Kozlowski recalled that "we were immediately cuffed and remanded. I was taken out the back door of the courtroom and directly to The Tombs, [a New York State prison,] which is by the courthouse. I was processed at

The Tombs. The sentencing was at 11:00 [am] and I was processed until around 1:00 [pm]. They took my mug shot, I was fingerprinted—they used electronic fingerprinting. After I was processed, I was placed in a cell at The Tombs for a couple of days."[4]

From that day forward, Dennis Kozlowski would be known to the State of New York as inmate 05A4820.

After spending two days at The Tombs, Kozlowski was moved at around 4:00 am to Rikers. Kozlowski said, "I hung out at Rikers for a couple of hours and then I was put on a bus and taken to Downstate, where I had to be processed again."[5] Downstate Correctional Facility is a maximum security New York State prison in Fishkill, about seventy-five miles due north of New York City.[6] Kozlowski was at Downstate for eight and a half months.

"I was in a cell by myself. It was maximum security, so everyone was in a cell alone," he explained. "I was allowed out of my cell for one hour every day. I never went outside—not for eight and a half months. I was allowed to have books so I spent most of my days reading. I had no access to a telephone—not for eight and a half months."[7]

Kozlowski said, "I was allowed to have visitors seven days a week. I had a lot of visitors. [My daughter] Cheryl would write letters to me and let me know who was coming to see me." Kozlowski said inmates were permitted to request new underwear and socks every nine months, which he did. "That seemed to trigger the move from Downstate," he said.

Kozlowski recalled that he was given about thirty minutes notice before he was moved. "Two COs [corrections officers] told me at 8:00 am that I was being moved. It was easy to pack," he remembered. "I was shackled and chained, and handcuffed. They put a black box over the cuffs and locked the black box to the chain around my waist. It's a miserable way to travel," he said. "I was in a van with two COs—I was the only inmate in the van. I asked as soon as I was put into the van where I was going to go. The orders were in a sealed envelope that could only be opened after we left the prison. The COs opened the envelope but didn't tell me where I was going. I think it was about a three hour drive and we ended up at Mid-State."

After he was unloaded from the van, Kozlowski was processed again, just as he had been at The Tombs and Downstate.[8]

MID-STATE CORRECTIONAL FACILITY

When he arrived at Mid-State in late May of 2006, Kozlowski settled into the cell in the protective custody unit where he would sleep for the next six and a half years. "I could never have imagined I would be there that long," he said.[9] During his years at Mid-State, he was assigned the job of doing laundry for the inmates in his unit, and he became the self-appointed "laundry czar," for which he was paid about a dollar a day. Like all prisoners of the State of New York, he wasn't allowed to touch money; his earnings went into an account from which he could purchase items from the prison's commissary.

Kozlowski saw many inmates come and go from the protective custody unit. There was a transgendered inmate whose clothing made his laundry duties a little more interesting.[10] Rapper Ja Rule, aka Jeffrey Atkins, was in June of 2011 placed in the same unit where Kozlowski was housed. In an interview he gave to the *New York Daily News* in February of 2012, Ja Rule said, "I was studying for my GED and Koz came in and talked to me and said, if you need any help, let me know." Ja Rule told the journalist that Kozlowski encouraged him to go to college and to study business. The rapper also said that former New York State Comptroller Alan Hevesi was serving time in the same unit with him and Kozlowski. Hevesi, who was convicted in a pay-for-play scandal that involved the New York State Common Retirement Fund, was paroled after nineteen months. Ja Rule was released from Mid-State in February of 2013 after serving his sentence for weapons possession. He immediately served three additional months in another facility for federal tax charges and was released in May of 2013.[11]

While he served his time, there were two suicides in Kozlowski's unit at Mid-State. "I found one of the guys," he recalled, "when I delivered his lunch. I looked into his cell and saw the guy had cut his wrists. He used one of the plastic razors they let us use to shave. There was blood everywhere. It was one of the worst things I saw in prison."[12]

Kozlowski passed the years at Mid-State doing laundry, reading hundreds of books, tutoring other inmates, and taking advantage of every prison program available to him. He also taught himself to paint—an interesting choice of hobbies, considering the consequences he suffered as a result of his venture into the world of fine art. Kozlowski said he lived for visits and for mail call. "I wrote and received hundreds of letters," he said. "From my friends, from family, from students, and from strangers. Every time the *60 Minutes* or *American Greed* episodes ran, I received dozens, maybe even hundreds of letters from people I didn't know."[13]

During the years he was in prison, which had not yet ended at the time of this writing, Kozlowski was strip searched more than 1,200 times—and counting. He wrote of the practice: "Nothing you ever read prepares you for the experience of being stripped naked in front of strangers who then examine every crevice and orifice of your body. I've never heard of contraband (illegal substances and/or weapons) brought into a prison in so obvious a way. The essential purpose of the strip search is to humiliate someone fortunate enough to enjoy a visit from a family member or friend." Kozlowski opined that "[e]very judge who declared the strip search constitutional should, just once, be commanded to strip, spread, bend, and lift while naked."[14]

Kozlowski wrote of his time at Mid-State: "It's difficult to see violent criminals and child molesters come and go here (serving 2 to 3 years) while my life passes by."[15] In February of 2011, Kozlowski wrote, "My 65 1/2 months in a NY State prison suck. It's the toughest of all tough places I've ever found myself. I'm far from happy, but I constantly seek to be at peace."[16]

Kozlowski's second wife filed for divorce in July of 2006, a couple of months after he arrived at Mid-State. The divorce was finalized two years later.[17]

During his lengthy prison sentence, Kozlowski had a lot of time to reflect on his life and all that had happened since he was a boy growing up in Newark, New Jersey.

THE PUNISHMENT

"The length of the sentence was a complete surprise," Kozlowski said. "I was expecting, worst case, up to five years."[18]

"There was an article in one of the papers that day—maybe the *Wall Street Journal,* that said five years was probably the longest sentence we'd receive," Kozlowski recalled. "I knew there would be prison time. I knew after the guilty verdicts there'd be a prison sentence. I checked with my legal team and other attorneys. They thought the worst case scenario would be an eighteen-month sentence. We were offered a two-year plea deal at the beginning of the trial. I had absolutely no warning that the sentence would be as severe as it was." As he remembered the moment the judge pronounced the sentence, he said, "It was shocking."[19]

Kozlowski and Swartz were tried, convicted, and sentenced at the height of public outrage over the Enron-era scandals, amid concerns about outrageous executive compensation, and ongoing media coverage of widespread greed and malfeasance in corporate America. Had they been convicted three years earlier or three years later, their sentences may not have been as harsh. It's also likely that, had the trial taken place anywhere other than New York, their sentences (if they were convicted) would have been less severe. However, in speaking about the severity of Kozlowski's sentence, former DA Robert Morgenthau said he had "no reason to believe the sentence would have been different" if the timing had not connected Tyco to Enron, World-Com, Martha Stewart, and other massive corporate scandals in the early 2000s.[20]

When asked about the sentences imposed on the former Tyco CEO and CFO, Isaac Rosenthal, the foreman of the jury that convicted Kozlowski and Swartz of a combined forty-five felony counts, said, "They got good sentences. The judge minimized the sentences. He could have imposed much harsher sentences based on the number of felony convictions." Rosenthal said he thought the sentences were fair.[21] Rosenthal also said that once the jury reached the first guilty verdict during deliberations, the rest of the guilty verdicts fell like dominos.

Bureau of Justice Statistics

Kozlowski's shock at the length of his prison term is understandable when the 100-to 300-month sentence imposed by Justice Obus is compared to Bureau of Justice Statistics. A look at state prison sentences, including the length of maximum sentences imposed and of the time actually served, reveals the severity of the sentence Dennis Kozlowski was ordered to serve.

All offenses for which state prison sentences were imposed:

Maximum sentence for the most serious offense:

Median	36 months
Mean	60 months
Kozlowski's maximum sentence:	300 months

Time served in prison:

Median	16 months
Mean	28 months
Kozlowski will serve at least 100 months.	

All violent offenses for which state prison sentences were imposed:

Maximum sentence for the most serious offense:

Median	60 months
Mean	81 months
Kozlowski's maximum sentence for *nonviolent* crimes:	300 months

Time served in prison:

Median	28 months
Mean	50 months
Kozlowski will serve at least 100 months for *nonviolent* crimes.	

For the offense of rape:

Maximum sentence for the most serious offense:

Median	108 months
Mean	132 months
Kozlowski's maximum sentence for *nonviolent* crimes:	300 months

Time served in prison:

Median	74 months
Mean	92 months
Kozlowski will serve at least 100 months for *nonviolent* crimes.	

For the offense of larceny:

Maximum sentence for the most serious offense:

Median	32 months
Mean	43 months
Kozlowski's maximum sentence for larceny:	300 months

Time served in prison:

Median	11 months
Mean	17 months

Kozlowski will serve at least 100 months for larceny.

For all property offenses:

Maximum sentence for the most serious offense:

Median	36 months
Mean	51 months
Kozlowski's maximum sentence for property offenses:	300 months

Time served in prison:

Median	13 months
Mean	20 months

Kozlowski will serve at least 100 months for property offenses.

Kozlowski's maximum sentence of 300 months exceeded the state prison sentences for *all* of the crimes listed by the Bureau of Justice Statistics, including the most severely punished offense of murder, for which the median sentence is 240 months, and the mean is 232 months. Dennis Kozlowski's maximum was five years longer than the sentence for murder.

At this writing, Kozlowski had served eight years in prison, and his next opportunity for parole was months in the future, meaning his minimum time served would be 100 months, if he is paroled at his next appearance before the parole board. According to Bureau of Justice Statistics, Kozlowski had already served more time—more than the median and more than the mean sentences—than those convicted of the following offenses:

Kidnapping (median sentence 30 months, mean sentence 56 months)

Rape (median sentence 74 months, mean sentence 92 months)

Robbery (median sentence 35 months, mean sentence 53 months)

DUI (median sentence 11 months, mean sentence 15 months)

Weapons offenses (median sentence 8 months, mean sentence 24 months)

Possession of drugs (median sentence 11 months, mean sentence 16 months)

Trafficking drugs (median sentence 16 months, mean sentence 23 months)

Burglary (median sentence 15 months, mean sentence 25 months)

Larceny (median sentence 11 months, mean sentence 17 months)

Grand theft auto (median sentence 11 months, mean sentence 18 months)

Fraud (median sentence 12 months, mean sentence 17 months)

Stolen property (median sentence 12 months, mean sentence 18 months)

Negligent Manslaughter (median sentence 37 months, mean sentence 52 months)

Kozlowski had already served more time than those convicted in state courts and incarcerated in state prisons for homicide. The median sentence for homicide is ninety-four months.[22]

His dramatically long sentence is indicative of the uniqueness of Kozlowski's case in a state court and prison system. It is far more common for white-collar crimes like those for which the Tyco executives were charged to be prosecuted by federal prosecutors and sentenced in federal courts, with the sentences served in federal prisons. But federal prosecutors declined to bring charges against Kozlowski and Swartz. Despite that, the Manhattan DA found serious crimes in Tyco's C-suite and prosecuted them under the laws of the State of New York.

APPEALS

Not surprisingly, Kozlowski and Swartz appealed their convictions. The first level of review was in the First Department of the Appellate Division of the New York Supreme Court. This intermediate court of appeals found the lack of evidence that the four questioned bonuses were approved (there was no approval found in the Compensation Committee minutes and the testimony of Compensation Committee members, who swore under oath they had no knowledge of the bonuses) showed a "consistent pattern of documentary omission over a period of years [that] constituted powerful evidence of defendants' intentional hiding of these payments from the directors and led inexorably to the jury's conclusion that the defendants took these bonuses without permission."[23]

In its opinion, the court devoted significant attention to one of the art purchases. Count 10 of the indictment, a charge of grand larceny in the first degree, was related to the $1.975 million payment for three paintings purchased at the Richard Green Gallery in London. Kozlowski selected the paintings to hang in the Tyco corporate apartment at 950 Fifth Avenue. The then CEO exercised the $200 million spending authority that had been granted to him by the Board of Directors, authority that was documented in a resolution in the Board's meeting minutes and recognized by the court in its opinion. However, the court found that "[w]hile he had authority to make capital expenditures of up to $200 million without board approval, this authority was to make purchases for business purposes, not personal use." The court opined that "[t]here is no indication of a business purpose for the purchase of these paintings. . . ."[24]

Hundreds of corporations own thousands of pieces of art. The *International Directory of Corporate Art Collections* lists approximately 800 corporate art collections. According to the International Art Alliance, publisher of the directory, businesses and corporations around the world own several million pieces of art, nearly as many as are on display in art museums. The Art Alliance reported that the total value of the art is worth several billion dollars and that "corporations spend millions every year purchasing art."[25]

In 1992, the year Dennis Kozlowski was named CEO of Tyco, the *New York Times* published an article titled "ART; When Corporations Become Collectors." In the article, the author revealed that "[i]n the last decade, the number of companies acquiring art has gone from 300 to about 1,200, according to the Directory of Corporate Art Collections." Among the corporations and art collections listed in the article were Prudential Insurance Company with more than 11,000 items, Chemical Bank with 2,000 pieces, AT&T with more than 3,500 pieces of art, and Ciba-Geigy with about 600 works of art.[26]

In a 2012 article, *Forbes* magazine listed the "World's Best Corporate Art Collections." *Forbes* identified Deutsche Bank with 57,000 pieces of artwork, UBS with 35,000 pieces of art, JPMorgan Chase with a 30,000 piece collection, Progressive Insurance with 7,800 works of art, Bank of America with collections that are sometimes loaned to museums, and Microsoft with 5,000 pieces of art.[27] All of the named corporations owned pieces of art similar to and often far more costly than the $1.975 million Kozlowski authorized Tyco to spend on three paintings for a corporate apartment. The court's finding that purchases of fine art could not be for "business purposes" is difficult to understand, considering it was and is common practice for corporations to own and invest in artwork. Will all of the executives of corporations that have purchased works of art face felony charges for authorizing the purchase of those pieces?

The court noted that the three paintings and the apartment in which they hung, the apartment to which the paintings were shipped and from which they were not moved, were reflected as assets on Tyco's books and records. The court also stated that Tyco Directors "had no idea" the Tyco apartment existed. Yet Tyco Director Josh Berman wrote a letter to the co-op board at 950 Fifth Avenue when Kozlowski approved the purchase of the apartment, and many individuals from Tyco had frequented the apartment. The CIT acquisition, the AMP acquisition, and others were negotiated in the Tyco apartment at 950 Fifth Avenue. It was hardly a secret.

But the court decided that the evidence supported the finding that Kozlowski embezzled the $1.975 million spent on the art "for his personal use without any intention of ever repaying it."[28]

After the jury's verdict was upheld by the First Department of the Appellate Division of the Supreme Court, the case was reviewed by the New York Court of Appeals.[29] One of the critical issues addressed on appeal was Justice Obus's decision to quash a defense subpoena on January 14, 2005, before the second trial began. The subpoena requested the notes from interviews of Tyco Directors conducted by the Boies law firm as part of the internal investigation during June and August of 2002—after Kozlowski was gone but while Mark Swartz was still the CFO. Justice Obus did not require Tyco to turn over the interview notes because he found the subpoena was a "fishing expedition." The appellate division found that the documents requested were not material and exculpatory, and that any error in Justice Obus's decision was harmless.[30]

The defense, however, believed that the interview notes were critical. The most damning testimony during the trials was that of former Tyco Directors, some of whom claimed to have no recollection of approving the four questioned bonuses, while others swore definitively that they did not know about the bonuses. Kozlowski and Swartz believed the Directors were fully aware of the compensation in question and only "forgot" about the bonuses after Kozlowski and Swartz were indicted—the Directors feared their own indictments and the financial consequences of dozens of civil lawsuits that were filed as a result of the charges levied against Tyco's former CEO and CFO. The Directors also admittedly wanted to avoid paying the outrageously large dollar amount due to Kozlowski under his Retention Agreement. The Directors were interviewed during June and in mid-August of 2002. The Boies team had already reviewed all of the executives' compensation and loan information before those interviews, and in cooperation with the Manhattan DA, had turned over select records that were used to indict former Tyco executives.

Kozlowski and Swartz firmly believed the Directors knew about the bonuses before they were interviewed and that they were aware that two of the bonuses were used to pay down the executives' KELP and relocation loan balances. The Directors had seen the way Kozlowski and Swartz used the loan programs. If they believed the compensation was in error, that the bonuses were not approved, or more relevantly, if they believed the bonuses or anything else Kozlowski and Swartz did were criminal acts, why did they allow Mark Swartz to remain in the second most powerful position in the company for months after they knew about the bonuses? Why did the Directors offer and then give Swartz a $50 million separation package in August of 2002 if they believed he and Kozlowski conspired to steal money from Tyco?

What did the Directors say during those interviews in August of 2002? If they said they knew Swartz to be a thief, shareholders, regulators, and law enforcement officials would have been up in arms because the Directors had allowed the thief to remain CFO and they gave him $50 million. If the Directors said they knew about the bonuses, that they were aware of how much the CEO and CFO were paid, the prosecution's case would have been destroyed and the Directors would have committed perjury when they testified otherwise during the criminal trials. The Directors would not win in either case, no matter what the interview notes revealed, so Tyco and prosecutors fought hard to keep critically important evidence from the Defendants.

The court of appeals reached a different conclusion about the subpoena than did Justice Obus or the appellate division. The state's high court found that the Defendants met the burden of identifying specific evidence, in this case, the director-witness statements, and had presented facts to show that the interview notes were reasonably likely to contain evidence that could contradict the statements of key witness for the prosecution. However, the court upheld Justice Obus's decision to quash the subpoena based on an argument that had not yet been raised. The court of appeals held that the Defendants could not have access to what were likely exculpatory interview notes of key prosecution witnesses because the Defendants didn't try to interview the Directors themselves during the summer of 2002.[31]

In effect, the court of appeals said Kozlowski and Swartz should have interviewed the Directors before they were indicted, before they knew there were going to be indicted, at a time when no one in the company would even speak to Kozlowski, let alone grant him an interview, and when Mark Swartz was still the CFO. It's difficult to comprehend why either man would have thought about collecting evidence during the summer of 2002. What if they had no idea anything they did at Tyco would ever be labeled a crime? (They didn't.) How would they have known what type of evidence to collect *before* they were charged?

Using the reasoning of the court of appeals, Kozlowski and Swartz should have anticipated that someday they might be accused of some type of criminal activity and should have collected evidence to defend themselves against some unknown future charges. The reasoning seems to ignore completely the presumption of innocence. In this case, the court of appeals assumed that Kozlowski and Swartz were guilty and that they knew they were guilty months before they were charged. The court shifted to the Defendants the burden of performing pre-indictment interviews with Tyco Directors who, unbeknownst to Kozlowski and Swartz, would someday testify against them. The court had to assume that Kozlowski and Swartz knew what crimes the DA would accuse them of committing. The court of appeals did not review the issue through the lens of presumed innocence. If Kozlowski and Swartz were innocent, and they may very likely be innocent, how could they have collected anticipatory evidence to protect themselves against allegations of crimes they did not commit?

In an article that appeared in the *New York Times* on September 23, 2002, journalists Andrew Ross Sorkin and Jonathan D. Glater revealed that "[t]hough the board of Tyco International has said that it was unaware of the extravagant pay packages and loans given to the company's top executives, minutes of the board's compensation committee show that group knew of many of the payments for months before the board took steps to disclose them." The article also reported that Patricia Prue, the former SVP of human resources who received immunity from prosecution, told a state grand jury and Mr. Boies's investigative team that then Tyco Director Josh Berman, who was a member of the Nominating and Governance Committee that oversaw the internal investigation, pressured her to change Compensation Committee meetings minutes—to alter records that reflected the Board's knowledge of executive compensation. In response, Berman said that Prue misunderstood his instructions.[32] Either way, there was plenty of doubt and many questions about who knew what about the bonuses.

It would be interesting to read those well-protected interview notes.

On October 16, 2008, the New York Court of Appeals affirmed the appellate division's decision. Kozlowski and Swartz had exhausted their appeals in the State of New York.

THE RIPPLE EFFECT

As soon as the executives were indicted, and with sensational details of wealth and extravagant spending reported in hundreds of media outlets, along with the official disclosures the Board opted to include in its September 2002 Form 8-K, civil actions by the dozens were filed by the Securities and Exchange Commission and by shareholders against Kozlowski, Swartz, Belnick, PricewaterhouseCoopers, the Directors, and Tyco International Ltd. David Boies and his law firm represented Tyco and the Board in actions filed against the company—the proliferation of lawsuits meant years of legal work for Boies, Schiller & Flexner.

Criminal law expert Professor Christo Lassiter said, "With indictments like the ones in this case, the ripple effect is unbelievable and the magnitude of damage is incalculable. Prosecutors are given great power, and with that power comes great responsibility. A prosecutor must exercise good judgment and prudence. Sometimes, prosecution does more harm than good."[33]

On behalf of Tyco, Boies, Schiller & Flexner filed an action against Kozlowski under the State of New York's faithless servant doctrine. In the massive civil action, the company asked for damages that included all of the compensation Kozlowski earned from Tyco between 1997 and 2002, forfeiture and repayment of benefits, and other damages that amounted to about half a billion dollars. In addition to paying restitution of $100 million to Tyco, Kozlowski was stripped of his earnings by the company for which he worked for twenty-seven years.

NO ACCOUNTING FRAUD

In addition to representing Tyco in numerous civil actions, Boies, Schiller also conducted what was called "Phase 2" of the investigation at Tyco to which, according to David Boies's biographer, the law firm assigned about twenty-five lawyers who collectively billed more than 15,000 hours. In addition, the law firm used more than 50,000 accountant hours in the second phase of the investigation. In the Boies biography *v. Goliath,* author Karen Donovan revealed the results of the investigation, which was said to find a "pattern of aggressive accounting." However, the Boies report noted that "[a]ggressive accounting is not necessarily improper accounting." The report also stated that in the instances of "questionable" accounting, there was no credible evidence of fraud, and the report concluded there was "no significant or systematic fraud affecting the Company's prior financial statements." The Boies report opined that "[f]ew, if any, major companies have ever been subjected to the corporate governance and accounting review entailed in Phase 2."[34]

After all of the rumors, reports, questions, and allegations that the accounting methods and financial statements at Tyco were fraudulent, misleading, and that disclosures were improper, there was never any definitive finding of such—even after numerous reviews and investigations. It seems the results of the 1999–2000 SEC investigation were accurate. There were no problems with Tyco's accounting. Yet more than a decade after the scandal began, reports, rumors, innuendo, and irresponsible journalism continued to inaccurately portray Tyco as one of the large corporate scandals that happened because of accounting fraud. It is simply not true.

WRIT OF *HABEAS CORPUS*

Having exhausted their appeals in the courts of the State of New York, Kozlowski and Swartz asked a federal court to throw out their convictions because they were denied access to potentially exculpatory evidence when the judge quashed the subpoena issued for notes taken by Boies, Schiller attorneys during interviews of Tyco Directors in the summer of 2002. Kozlowski and Swartz filed a petition for a writ of *habeas corpus* arguing that they were denied the right to present a defense—a right guaranteed by the U.S. Constitution.

When the U.S. District Court for the Southern District of New York heard oral arguments in the *habeas* action in December of 2011, more than six years after Kozlowski and Swartz entered prison, the Manhattan DA's office continued its fight to keep the evidence from the Defendants, based on the argument that defense attorneys did not follow the correct procedures to preserve the Defendants' rights. The DA's office relied on procedural default. A technicality. The court, the defense attorneys, and even Assistant DA Amyjane Rettew, who for years approved and disapproved expenditures from Kozlowski's frozen assets, all agreed that the content of the documents in question (the interview notes) was material and potentially exculpatory.

In oral arguments before the district court, ADA Rettew didn't argue that the requested evidence was irrelevant, or that the interview notes wouldn't change the outcome of the trial, or that Kozlowski and Swartz were guilty and deserved to be in prison. She didn't even argue that the documents were protected by privilege. Instead, her argument was that defense attorneys didn't meet a technical standard when they argued about the subpoena before Justice Obus, and therefore the defendants forfeited their constitutional rights.[35]

Alan Lewis of Carter, Ledyard & Milburn appeared on behalf of Kozlowski. In opposing the court of appeals' finding that the Defendants should have collected interviews of the Directors during the summer of 2002, Lewis stated, "So, in other words, what the court of appeals is . . . saying is that defendants in a criminal case lost their right to get evidence that is reasonably likely to contradict the statements of key witnesses for the People on the key issue of the case because they didn't do something to investigate the charges against them before those charges existed. And in that fashion the court of appeals turned our criminal justice system upside down." Lewis said, "In the history of our jurisprudence I don't think there's ever been a case in which any court has said a defendant loses his right to get something that's really important to his defense because he didn't defend the case before there was a case."[36]

Nathaniel Marmur, who represented Swartz, reasoned with the court by sharing an analogous case. Marmur said:

> Your Honor may remember the *Grasso* case where Dick Grasso was accused, very similar in the civil context, of getting I think a hundred million or some crazy number in compensation for running the New York Stock Exchange. And the directors there, all very important people, all said essentially we didn't approve this, we didn't know about this. There was an internal investigation that encountered these comments. And unfortunately in the world we live in, sometimes civil discovery, for reasons I've never been able to understand, is broader than criminal discovery. And the underlying statements came out and of course what we saw the directors absolutely knew about and had endorsed it. But the pressures demanded that they say otherwise. And of course that was our theory at trial."

Marmur told the court that " . . . [I]t is beyond my comprehension that it takes three levels of courts, including the New York Court of Appeals, for someone to say you actually can issue a subpoena for these documents."[37]

Marmur got to the heart of the matter when he stated, " . . . [W]e have out there documents that we firmly believe will show that Dennis Kozlowski and Mark Swartz did not steal money from Tyco, that these directors were on board the entire time. We would love the opportunity to present them to a jury."[38]

On February 7, 2012, the U.S. District Court for the Southern District of New York denied the petitions for writs of *habeas corpus*. Almost exactly one year later,

the U.S. Court of Appeals for the Second Circuit upheld the district court's decision—denying the petitions for *habeas* because the trial attorneys of Kozlowski and
Swartz failed to raise a constitutional issue regarding the ruling on the subpoena
at the time of Justice Obus's decision—the attorneys did not use the word "constitutional" when they objected to the ruling.[39] In October of 2013, the U.S. Supreme
Court denied Kozlowski and Swartz a review by the highest court in the country;
their appeals were finally exhausted.

*   *   *

The *habeas* decisions were counter to the basic ideology of our criminal justice
system—that individuals accused of crimes should have access to exculpatory
evidence if it exists. There are many good reasons for the procedural rules used
in our court systems, but should a procedural technicality be the basis for keeping innocent men in prison? Why would prosecutors want to deprive individuals
of evidence that might prove their innocence? Why wouldn't Tyco willingly turn
over the notes taken during interviews with Directors? Why the secrecy? Surely
individuals in the DA's office and at Tyco would not watch two men condemned
to prison for many years if they knew there was evidence to prove they did not
commit the crimes for which they were convicted. So why not just turn over the
interview notes?

This case highlights the questionable process through which a private practice
attorney performing a corporate internal investigation can filter select evidence to
a prosecutor and thereby initiate criminal proceedings against corporate insiders.
The process allows prosecutors to skirt evidentiary requirements. A prosecutor is
required to provide to defendants evidence that is in the prosecutor's possession.
If a private practice attorney performing a corporate internal investigation withholds exculpatory evidence from prosecutors while supplying evidence that tends
to incriminate, the prosecutor can honestly argue that he or she is not in possession
of the exculpatory evidence and therefore not in violation of rules of evidence. And
the private practice attorney can be called as a witness for the prosecution, testify
about evidence that was allegedly found during the internal investigation, and yet
shield any evidence that the company, the prosecutor, or the attorney does not want
to disclose. It is a very dangerous loophole.

The Manhattan DA did not have possession of the evidence subpoenaed by
Kozlowski and Swartz. Although Tyco supplied voluminous evidence to the DA,
the company did not turn over everything. The documents withheld, which likely
contained evidence that could exonerate Kozlowski and Swartz, could not be obtained by subpoena, through two levels of appeal in the New York State court system, or in the U.S. District Court, the U.S. Court of Appeals, or the U.S. Supreme
Court. The evidence exists, but Kozlowski and Swartz were not permitted to use
it to defend themselves.

*   *   *

U.S. Supreme Court Justice Hugo Black said, "There can be no equal justice where the kind of trial a man gets depends on the amount of money he has."[40] Similarly, U.S. Supreme Court Justice Lewis Powell said, "Equal justice under law is not merely a caption on the facade of the Supreme Court building, it is perhaps the most inspiring ideal of our society. It is one of the ends for which our entire legal system exists . . . it is fundamental that justice should be the same, in substance and availability, without regard to economic status."[41] When these esteemed jurists opined about the importance of fair treatment by our legal system for every individual, without regard for economic status, do you think they meant Dennis Kozlowski?

Since the creation of our legal system, there has been an ongoing discussion about the fundamental right of every individual to a fair trial without regard for his or her financial status. Of course, the discussions always happen in the context of ensuring that those of lesser economic means are protected. It's difficult to muster concern for the fate of the wealthy. With money comes the ability to hire the most capable, well-educated attorneys. Financial resources often allow an individual to gain the upper hand in our justice system, with the economically advantaged party able to clear more easily the hurdles that arise in all legal proceedings.

Is it possible that Kozlowski and Swartz were treated differently because of their economic status?

There is an assumption that the wealthy have the best lawyers, and perhaps the benefit of the doubt is denied them. There is little concern for the constitutional rights of people with money. Their fancy legal teams should have presented the best defense money can buy; therefore, if a wealthy individual is in prison, he or she must be guilty. Granted, Dennis Kozlowski is not a sympathetic victim. His extraordinary financial success impedes our ability to feel sympathy for him. However, the most fundamental ideals of our justice system require that he be treated fairly—without regard for his economic status. If there is evidence that may prove Kozlowski and Swartz are innocent of the crimes for which they were convicted, and for which they are serving lengthy prison sentences, shouldn't we all want that evidence to be considered? Should they be denied that evidence because of a procedural technicality? Has our legal system devolved to the point where procedural rules trump the goal of finding the truth? Even the rich and successful are entitled to the truth.

PAROLE

Dennis Kozlowski first became eligible for parole in April of 2012. He was hopeful about his chances; under the state's criteria, he was an ideal candidate. He had been a model prisoner and had a spotless discipline record. Years earlier, he paid in full $97 million in court-ordered restitution to Tyco and a $70 million criminal fine to the Manhattan DA. He had no prior criminal record and after years in prison, he was clearly remorseful when he appeared before the parole board. In addition, Kozlowski had a strong support network of family members and friends—all available to him during his transition from prison to normal life.

But, the New York State Board of Parole denied parole soon after Kozlowski's hearing ended on April 4, 2012. In its written decision, the board cited two reasons for its decision not to release Kozlowski: "concern for the public safety and welfare," and parole would "tend to deprecate the seriousness" of Kozlowski's offenses. Kozlowski had no record of violent or dangerous behavior, and there was no chance he could repeat his crimes—he could never again work for a publicly traded corporation. It's difficult to understand how he could be perceived as a danger to the public. As for the second reason, state parole guidelines consider the seriousness of crimes and factor in the inmate's criminal history. New York State's guidelines suggested a sentence of six to thirty months for the offenses for which Kozlowski was convicted, if the inmate had no other criminal history (the crimes of which Kozlowski was convicted in 2005 were his first brush with the criminal justice system). At the time of the hearing, Kozlowski was in his eightieth month of imprisonment; he had served more than twice the recommended maximum. How could granting parole after twice the suggested sentence had been served tend to deprecate the seriousness of the crimes?

Among the many people who wrote to the parole board on Kozlowski's behalf was Justice Obus, who informed the board that, should they "conclude that Mr. Kozlowski is an appropriate candidate for parole supervision at this time, I would not find that to be inconsistent with the Court's intentions when the indeterminate sentence was imposed."[42]

New York regularly releases violent offenders. Murderers, rapists, and child molesters are paroled, and usually after less time behind bars than Kozlowski had served. At the time of his hearing in April of 2012, Kozlowski was a sixty-five-year-old first-time offender who had been convicted of nonviolent crimes. And yet he was denied parole.

Believing it was in error, Kozlowski appealed the decision of the parole board. On February 5, 2013, New York Supreme Court Justice Carol Huff overturned the board's decision. Justice Huff found that the board would have "extraordinary difficulty identifying a factual basis to support the decision to deny release." Upon receiving the court's ruling, Kozlowski's attorney Alan Lewis said in a statement to the media, "We are enormously gratified by the Court's decision. In our view, it is unlikely that there is a more deserving candidate for parole in New York than Dennis Kozlowski."[43]

In a segment on Neil Cavuto's Fox Business Network progam *Cavuto,* that aired on February 14, 2013, former New York parole board Chair Edward Hammock discussed Justice Huff's decision. Hammock, who reviewed the facts, who clearly knew the criteria for parole in New York, and who had no connection to Kozlowski, unequivocally concluded that Kozlowski should have been paroled. Hammock also noted that, based on the instrument for risk assessment mandated by the New York legislature, the results of which were part of the record in the April 4, 2012 parole hearing, Kozlowski's risk assessment "guaranteed he's a minimal risk to reoffend." There was no lower risk assessment rating. Hammock said, "My opinion, and what would be the opinion of any right-thinking person, is that he should have been released."[44]

Instead of providing Kozlowski with a new parole hearing, as ordered by the supreme court, the state opted to appeal the court order. On July 2, 2013, the appellate division in a very brief ruling overturned the decision of Justice Huff and summarily reasoned that the parole board acted properly when it denied parole to Kozlowski. When the appellate division released its opinion, Kozlowski's attorney Alan Lewis said, "We respectfully, but strongly, disagree with the appellate division's decision and instead think that the lower court was entirely correct about the flaws in the Parole Board's decision."[45]

At this writing, Kozlowski remained in prison and was participating in the state's temporary work release program. Kozlowski had been in prison for more than eight years . . . and counting.

NINETEEN

OBSERVATIONS

In his opening statements to the jury at the beginning of the first trial in September of 2003, Dennis Kozlowski's lead defense attorney Stephen Kaufman said, " . . . [Y]ou will not find proof that Dennis Kozlowski is a cheat, a liar or a thief," after which Kaufman asked, "Who then is this man? What is his background? What has he done in his life time? How can we better understand who this man is?"[1]

I spent two and a half years trying to answer the questions Kaufman posed to jurors. My objective was to understand Dennis Kozlowski and to figure out what happened at Tyco that sent him to prison. I immersed myself in the businesses of Tyco International Ltd. I studied how Kozlowski developed as a manager, rose through the ranks, and became CEO, and I learned how he ran the rapidly growing diversified conglomerate that made a lot of money making and selling anything from home security systems, to fire sprinklers, to undersea telecommunications cable, to medical devices. I reviewed thousands of documents and spoke to those who worked in Tyco corporate operations when Kozlowski headed the company. I examined the corporation's structure, culture, accounting, financial statements, compensation policies, and governance. I became well versed in all things Tyco.

Looking back with the advantage of ten years' perspective and access to a mass of information, I envisioned what it was like to be at Tyco as Kozlowski built his career, and when he was CEO. I became a fly on the wall in Tyco corporate offices in 2002—when Kozlowski's world imploded and the company became ensnared in a very public scandal.

After processing everything I found and learned and saw, I have some observations that may be helpful to individuals who don't want to find themselves in the same dire circumstances that befell Dennis Kozlowski. At the time of this writing, Kozlowski had spent more than eleven of his sixty-six years dealing with legal issues related to being the CEO of Tyco International, and he remained a prisoner of the State of New York. He paid nearly $100 million in restitution to the company and $70 million in criminal fines to the Manhattan DA, and had spent well over $60 million in legal fees since his first indictment in June of 2002.[2] (It's presumed that the wealthy have the ability to buy their way out of trouble. Kozlowski certainly disproved that notion.)

In addition to the lengthy prison sentence, the restitution, the fines, and the legal fees, Kozlowski had to repay Tyco for all compensation and benefits he received from the date of what was determined to be his first act of disloyalty—which in effect means he worked seventy hours a week or more for many years and found himself without anything to show for his labors.

Kozlowski's career is a cautionary tale—it shines a bright light on the risks inherent in the executive suites of publicly traded corporations. The Tyco scandal was unforeseen, unlikely, and unexpected; it resulted from the convergence of many factors, some of which were in Kozlowski's control, others of which were not.

The problems at Tyco have often been attributed almost entirely to Dennis Kozlowski; he has been characterized as a "pig" and "the greedy boss." People said and wrote and published that Kozlowski was "evil" and had a "lack of moral direction." Analysis of the Tyco scandal was simplified to attacks on Kozlowski's character. It seemed few spent the time and effort required to understand the complex transactions and the compound problems at Tyco as well as the legal and business environments at that time. If we simplify the Tyco scandal, if we reduce the explanation to the moral failings of a single individual, we leave the door open for the tragedy to happen again.[3]

Since the scandal, journalists and others seemed shocked when Kozlowski's former colleagues had favorable and complimentary things to say about the former CEO. Richard Meelia headed Tyco's healthcare division for six years while Kozlowski was CEO. In a 2010 *Forbes* article, writer Daniel Fisher noted that Meelia learned how to "run a company the Dennis Kozlowski way." Fisher wrote that "Meelia has surprisingly kind things to say about Kozlowski, who now languishes in a prison in New York"[4] After he was convicted, Kozlowski often heard from former Tyco colleagues; some of whom he knew, some of whom he didn't know personally. He continued to receive letters and visits from them, even after he had been in prison for several years. Many of Kozlowski's former colleagues remained supportive throughout his prosecution and imprisonment, as did his friends and family members. I had the opportunity to meet and speak with several of them.

Everyone else, it seems, forgot entirely the many years during which Kozlowski was admired for his business success, his work ethic, his charitable works, his many fine qualities, and for his ascent to the top of Tyco. Those who don't know him only remember his fall. In an interview from prison in 2008, Kozlowski was quoted as saying "I hate my legacy to be a Sardinia party and an umbrella stand and a shower curtain."[5]

WHAT WENT WRONG?

Many complex factors contributed to the Tyco scandal and the tragic end of Kozlowski's career. Following are some of the most significant:

1. It was an extraordinary time.

- Enron, WorldCom, and other scandals heightened scrutiny, suspicions, and fear of bankruptcies in the market.
- The economy was troubled after 9/11.
- The CIT acquisition quickly became a problem for Tyco.
- The price of Tyco stock declined quickly and significantly after a decade of sustained growth.
- The Manhattan DA, who was long known for his aggressive pursuit of white-collar criminals, was at the ready. Like many prosecutors in the post-Enron environment, Robert Morgenthau was ready to investigate and prosecute highly compensated, high-profile executives he believed were abusing their positions of power.
- Old rumors about Tyco's accounting methods that were quelled by the positive outcome of the1999–2000 Securities and Exchange Commission investigation were revived in the precarious post-Enron environment.
- Some Tyco Directors were angered by the payment of a $20 million investment banking fee to their fellow Board member Frank Walsh.
- Kozlowski and the Board announced a plan to split up the company, then backpedaled—and the market did not react favorably to the indecisiveness. The price of Tyco stock continued to drop.
- Tyco shareholders filed derivative actions because of the Frank Walsh investment banking fee—no doubt unhappy with the company's performance during the first few months of 2002, nervous because of rumors and comparisons to Enron, and alarmed by the heightened scrutiny of Tyco that appeared frequently in various media outlets.
- The sales tax indictment, charges that were ultimately dropped, removed Kozlowski from Tyco. He had no input during the internal investigation, was never interviewed by anyone from Boies, Schiller or the Manhattan DA's office, and as former Director Wendy Lane said in her interview for a Harvard Business School case study, once you leave the company, ". . . [Y]ou lose control over not only the information flow, but the information itself, the litigation process and settlement or adjudication proceedings. There is also an implication that you were at fault."[6]
- Exposure of poor record keeping, sloppy governance, and a pattern of inaccurate and incomplete meeting minutes, missing meeting minutes,

or failure to ever create minutes when Directors met became a serious problem when Kozlowski needed documentation of decisions that were made by Tyco Directors.

- Tyco grew very quickly into a large company, but Tyco corporate remained a mom-and-pop shop. Company loan programs had been loosely administered for decades. In addition, there was far too much informality and familiarity in Tyco corporate offices—they lived with an "it has always been done this way" mentality.

- The Board of Directors gave Kozlowski increasingly more spending authority—it had increased to $200 million by 2001. It was the imperfect combination of a Board that was willing to grant inappropriate levels of authority and a CEO who was happy to have almost unlimited authority.

- Directors had entered into, on behalf of Tyco, what was by my calculations a nearly half-billion dollar Retention Agreement with Kozlowski less than a year before all of the problems began. However, if Kozlowski was terminated for cause, the company would have had no financial obligation to him. "Cause" was defined as Kozlowski's " . . . conviction of a felony that is materially and demonstrably injurious to the Company."[7]

If any of the foregoing had not happened, it is likely that Tyco would never have been caught in a costly scandal and Dennis Kozlowski would not have been indicted and convicted. It was a perfect storm.

2. The Directors

In my assessment of what went wrong at Tyco, the weak, dysfunctional Board of Directors is at the top of the list. The problems are too numerous to name, but following are some of the most troubling:

- Why was the testimony of Directors who said they could not recall approving or did not approve bonuses meaningful, or at all credible? They didn't recall or record many of their decisions.

- A Director testified that he didn't even read the half-billion dollar Retention Agreement until he wanted to figure out how to get rid of Kozlowski.

- Directors had "huddles" where no minutes were recorded—it's impossible to know what was and wasn't decided or approved during many undocumented gatherings.

- The Directors gave Kozlowski $200 million spending authority and for years allowed him to run the company based on his business judgment, which they applauded, encouraged, and rewarded. Meeting minutes were filled with resolutions empowering Kozlowski to act based on his judgment.

Then when things got rough, when there were civil lawsuits and the Directors faced possible criminal charges, they attacked Kozlowski's judgment—the same judgment he had exercised for years. He was accused of concealing information that was recorded on the books and records of the company in the ordinary course of business, and audited by PricewaterhouseCoopers. I've seen volumes of records. They exist. I found no evidence that anything was concealed or that anyone even attempted to conceal any information about compensation, bonuses, loans, or anything else.

• There were many conflicts of interest and unreported related-party transactions that involved and financially benefited Directors.

Robert Morgenthau was asked by the *Wall Street Journal* at the end of his thirty-five-year tenure as Manhattan DA whether he should have indicted Tyco Directors along with Kozlowski and Swartz. Morgenthau responded "probably."[8]

Jury foreman Isaac Rosenthal said that over the years, he thought about the case and wondered why the Directors weren't charged along with Kozlowski and Swartz. It seemed to Rosenthal that the Directors may also be culpable, and it appeared to him that Kozlowski and Swartz were scapegoats—the Directors pointed the finger at them when things got rough. When considering why the executives were charged and not the Directors, Rosenthal assumed it was politically advantageous for the DA to prosecute the top dogs. "I saved Morgenthau's job," he said.[9]

Former Director Joshua Berman, who was a member of the Nominating and Governance Committee that spearheaded the investigation of executive compensation, disputed his own compensation from Tyco when he was no longer a member of the Board. *Reuters* reported in 2007 that Berman filed an action against Tyco in which he claimed that "the company owed him at least $870,000 for consulting work he did during a five-month period following Kozlowski's resignation." Berman asserted in the complaint that he "agreed to leave his job at Kramer Levin Naftalis & Frankel LLP in 2000 to work at Tyco full-time at Kozlowski's request." Between July and November of 2002, he worked on "legacy matters" that had taken place during Kozlowski's tenure as CEO and that were then under investigation, according to the complaint.[10] It's an interesting revelation because prosecutors very clearly told jurors that Tyco Directors were barely part-timers who had access to nothing other than what Kozlowski and Swartz filtered to them. The stories are incongruous.

Dennis Kozlowski said of the Board's issues with him in 2002: "It was a dispute over compensation. It should have been resolved through negotiations or a civil action, if necessary." He also shared, "My biggest mistake was not being more proactive and insistent about having a better Board. If I could go back and do anything differently, I would have worked with a different Board. I had no tolerance for managers who didn't perform, but I tolerated bad Directors for a lot of years."

Kozlowski said of the Tyco Directors with whom he worked for many years, "It was the ultimate betrayal." [11]

3. Kozlowski's Personal Failings

Kozlowski's weaknesses, his personal failings, and some bad decisions also contributed to the problems at Tyco.

- Kozlowski's unwillingness to pay attention to details, and the delegation of responsibility for the details in his life left him vulnerable.
- Kozlowski lost perspective. He was caught up in the amount of money Tyco was earning, in the size of his own compensation, and the possibilities of the bull market of the 1990s. In a 2009 *Fortune* magazine article, contributor David Kaplan opined that Kozlowski was " . . . the embodiment of an earlier epoch of corporate greed and personal profligacy, circa a decade ago. Yet . . . Kozlowski now looks like small fry in the sea of financial shenanigans."[12] Kaplan was referring to the many unindicted individuals involved in the financial crisis of 2008, where the dollar amounts were far greater than those involved in the Tyco scandal.
- We all normalize the things in our lives. For Dennis Kozlowski, it became normal to see lots of zeros at the end of every dollar amount.
- Kozlowski's ambition blinded him. He grew the company very quickly—he was named "The Most Aggressive CEO" by *Businessweek* in May of 2001.[13] His pace was unwise. He wanted to achieve too much too fast.

4. The Jury

After spending two and a half years reviewing and studying the evidence presented during both criminal trials, I do not believe jurors in either understood the vast majority of the evidence. The corporate finance, accounting methods, compensation plans, and employment contracts at issue in the case were as complex as those used by any business organization in the world. Between the volume, the detail, the complexity, the length of the trials, and the experience and background needed to understand the information presented, I don't believe jurors could have understood much of what was presented. Jury foreman Isaac Rosenthal confirmed that some jurors slept through parts of the trial.[14]

I asked former Tyco Executive Vice President Brad McGee, who testified during both trials, if he thought the jury understood his testimony. He said, "No."[15]

I asked Robert Morgenthau if our jury system is equipped to fairly adjudicate a complex case like *People v. Kozlowski*. Mr. Morgenthau, with a razor-sharp legal mind at the age of ninety-three, told me a story about a case he tried in the

1960s. He told me about a jury on which there were five businessmen who became a "clique"; they felt they were more qualified than the rest of the jurors to understand the evidence. Mr. Morgenthau said there were two African American women on the jury, which he described as very unusual in the 1960s. Morgenthau said he heard a conversation between jurors in which the five businessmen were opining about the complexity of the evidence when one of the African American women said to them, "Don't you know what this case is about?" Morgenthau's point was that if jurors get the gist, if they have "a general sense of what the case is about, that's sometimes more important than understanding the details."[16]

With all due respect to Mr. Morgenthau—if I was on trial, I would want the jury to understand the details. And I feel strongly that our legal system is not capable of fairly adjudicating complex cases like Kozlowski's. Our system just doesn't work in its current form and with the rules in place.

What Did the Jury Have to Believe in Order to Find Kozlowski Guilty of 22 Felony Charges?

The jury in Kozlowski's second trial, the one in which he was convicted, had to believe beyond a reasonable doubt some things that I don't find reasonable.

1. *The jury had to believe beyond a reasonable doubt that Kozlowski stole money during the same time period that he declined an offer of significant additional compensation from the Board of Directors. The jury had to believe beyond a reasonable doubt that Kozlowski stole money instead of accepting a grant of 1,500,000 options for Tyco stock.*

   When he was questioned during the second criminal trial, former Director Frank Walsh, who was also a former Chairman of the Compensation Committee, was asked if Dennis Kozlowski or Mark Swartz ever turned down offers of additional compensation, to which he responded, "[Y]es, they did."[17]

   Kozlowski turned down 1,500,000 stock options offered to him by the Board at the very time he was allegedly stealing money from the company. Mark Swartz turned down 750,000 options. At the suggestion of Towers Perrin, a consulting firm hired by the Compensation Committee, the Committee voted to grant large numbers of stock options to both men to provide additional motivation for them to increase the value of Tyco stock. At the time, Kozlowski and Swartz did not have employment contracts with the company, so the substantial stock options were also viewed as an inducement for them to remain at Tyco. In its October 13, 1999 meeting minutes, the Compensation Committee: "RESOLVED, that Messrs Kozlowski and Swartz are granted performance-based option grants of 1,500,000 and 750,000 options respectively as of October 18,

1999. However, Messrs. Kozlowski and Swartz decided to decline the grant at this time."[18]

Kozlowski and Swartz were accused and convicted of stealing bonuses in August of 1999 and September of 2000, both within a year of when they turned down a total of 2,250,000 options.

Why would Dennis Kozlowski and Mark Swartz conspire and steal from Tyco? The Compensation Committee and the Board—they opened the door to the company's vault and threw money at the CEO and CFO in order to get them to stay. It's obvious. All one has to do is read their Retention Agreements. They didn't have to steal anything.

2. *The jury had to believe beyond a reasonable doubt that the Board of Directors and the Compensation Committee would have had accurate minutes that documented the Directors' decisions to approve the questioned bonuses if the bonuses were approved. The jury had to believe beyond a reasonable doubt that because approvals for the four bonuses were not found in meeting minutes, the bonuses were not approved.*

The overwhelming weight of evidence showed that the recording and retention of minutes from Tyco Board and Committee meetings was completely unreliable. There were numerous instances when there were no minutes. Many events, approvals, and decisions weren't reflected in meeting minutes—yet those decisions and actions of the Board clearly happened, even though there was no record found in the Board's minutes. The Audit Committee didn't begin recording or retaining minutes until the spring of 2002. Compensation Committee minutes were drafted before meetings by someone who never attended the meetings. The jury had to believe that despite overwhelming evidence that Tyco meeting minutes were unreliable, and often nonexistent, that the absence of approval of the bonuses in meeting minutes meant the bonuses weren't approved.

3. *The jury had to believe beyond a reasonable doubt that Kozlowski intended to conceal the receipt of the four bonuses even though they were recorded on the books and records of the company, included in management representation letters provided to PwC, and handled by several Tyco corporate employees in a number of different departments.*

Although not evidence that the bonuses were approved, the management representation letter is certainly evidence that Kozlowski and Swart *believed* the bonuses were approved. Why else would they point them out to PwC? The act of providing the information to auditors is evidence that they weren't concealing the bonuses, as alleged by the prosecution. The management representation letter seems convincing evidence that Kozlowski and Swartz did not intend to take the money wrongfully; it is convincing evidence that they believed they had a right to receive the bonuses.

4. *The jury had to believe beyond a reasonable doubt that Kozlowski would steal amounts that were calculated according to the Incentive Compensation Plan formula. No more. No less. And Swartz always stole exactly half of what Kozlowski stole (also in amounts that would have been due him under the Plan—had the bonuses been approved).*

5. *The jury had to believe beyond a reasonable doubt that Dennis Kozlowski did not receive approval for the bonuses from Philip Hampton, then Chair of the Compensation Committee.*

    Kozlowski told Swartz and Patricia Prue that Hampton took care of approval for the bonuses—and he gave them that information when Phil Hampton was still alive, when Swartz, Prue, and all of the other Tyco employees who processed and/or received bonuses as part of the same transactions could have (and may have) discussed the bonuses with Hampton. No Tyco employees testified that they were instructed or pressured to hide, conceal, or withhold information of any kind. The jury had to believe beyond a reasonable doubt that Kozlowski lied to people in Tyco corporate offices when he told them that Phil Hampton gave him approval for the bonuses—and Kozlowski just hoped against hope that no one would spill the beans to Hampton.

6. *The jury had to believe beyond a reasonable doubt that Hampton did not have those conversations with Kozlowski and that Kozlowski lied under oath about his mentor, friend, and trusted colleague.*

7. *The jury had to believe beyond a reasonable doubt that former Tyco Directors who testified during the trial were telling the truth.*

    Jurors had to believe that the clause of the Retention Agreement (the one that defined firing Kozlowski "for cause" and released Directors from performing their obligations to Kozlowski under the terms of the agreement) didn't bias the Directors, and that their own possible criminal indictments and dozens of civil lawsuits didn't influence their testimony. Jurors had to believe the Directors who testified were completely honest and not protecting their own interests.

8. *The jury had to believe beyond a reasonable doubt that Dennis Kozlowski intended to steal three paintings that were purchased with Tyco funds, even though the invoice for the paintings was sent to Tyco, the paintings were shipped to a Tyco apartment (an apartment that was reflected as an asset on the company's books and records), the paintings hung in the Tyco apartment and were never moved by Kozlowski or anyone else, and the paintings were reflected as assets of Tyco on the company's audited books and records.*

    Because jurors believed Kozlowski stole those paintings, they would also by necessity, using the exact same reasoning, have to believe the following:

My supervisor told me I was authorized to make purchases for my office in an amount not to exceed $10,000. I ordered furniture that cost $500. The furniture was shipped to the office, the invoice was sent to my employer, and my employer paid for the furniture. The furniture was reflected as an asset on my employer's books and records. I was suddenly fired and not allowed to return to my office, not even to collect my personal belongings. Three months later, I was indicted for stealing $500 worth of furniture (which remained in what used to be my office).

The jury believed Kozlowski committed grand larceny with regard to the paintings, so the jury would also have to believe I committed larceny with regard to that office furniture.

5. The Media

Mandi Woodruff said it all in her *Business Insider* article entitled "This Is What Everyone's Afraid to Say about the Rich." She wrote, "Americans love a good rags-to-riches fairytale, but here's a story people are far more interested in reading: Riches-to-rags."[19]

Kozlowski was crucified by the media. The media turned Kozlowski into the CEO everyone loved to hate. However, not all of the coverage was biased and inaccurate. As I read hundreds of articles during my research, I found that Andrew Ross Sorkin of the *New York Times* and Dan Ackman of *Forbes* understood the facts and did a far better job than most of discounting the irrelevant, sensational hype. Other than Sorkin and Ackman, the media coverage was largely unreliable and the information reported had to be fact checked before it could be used.

Kozlowski was for years shocked and appalled by the media's coverage of his story. "I've read things about myself that were complete fiction," he said. "I've been called names, ridiculed, and blamed for things that simply never happened. Everything in my life has been exploited by people in the media."[20] He added, "Whoever orchestrated the spin was masterful."[21]

6. Blurred Lines

The compensation of key employees was complicated by the use of restricted shares of stock that had various vesting schedules. Vesting was a taxable event for employees, which triggered use of the Key Employee Loan Program—a loan program that was administered far too loosely. Because of the way KELP was administered, all of Kozlowski's personal purchases were reflected on records that were housed inside the company. It's this process that fueled allegations that Kozlowski used Tyco as his personal piggy bank.

It is my understanding from reviewing the plan documents, reading the testimony given during the trials, and going through the loans and expenditures (invoice by invoice) processed through KELP, that Kozlowski did not borrow more than permitted by company policy. What prosecutors and the media objected to was not that he borrowed more than allowable; it was how he spent the money that he borrowed.

The primary purpose of the loan program was to encourage key employees to retain ownership of Tyco stock—to give them an option other than selling shares to pay taxes due when restricted shares vested. Kozlowski used the proceeds of KELP loans to pay many different types of obligations, not just to pay taxes. Kozlowski did not find it necessary or even important that he used the proceeds of the loans to pay taxes because money is fungible. Kozlowski had to pay his taxes. What did it matter which dollars he sent to taxing authorities? In his mind, it didn't matter if he paid the taxes due with the money in his wallet, or in his bank account, or from an investment account, or from amounts available to him through KELP. Money is money. Kozlowski believed that so long as he didn't borrow more than was permitted under the terms of the loan program, he was using KELP appropriately and could spend the loan proceeds as he wanted.

There were two important problems with KELP. First, the price of Tyco stock grew so dramatically, the value of the restricted shares that vested became huge, with correspondingly huge tax bills, and correspondingly huge amounts available through KELP. What was once a plan that allowed key employees to borrow modest amounts of money became a vehicle for borrowing tens of millions of dollars from the company. So, the plan in and of itself became problematic. Was it still in the best interest of Tyco shareholders for key employees to borrow from the company instead of selling shares of Tyco stock to pay their tax bills? Or had the amounts available under the terms of the policy grown too large? The plan should have been amended or discontinued by the Board of Directors. This type of oversight and judgment is the duty of corporate directors. The Tyco Board failed in its direction and oversight of company loan programs.

The Sarbanes-Oxley Act usurped the Tyco Board's options regarding loan offerings available from the company when in 2002 the federal law prohibited publicly traded corporations from making loans to employees.

The second critical issue was how the loan program was administered. The use of KELP as a running balance of available funds, while not a clear violation of company policy, did not conform with the spirit of the loan program. I examined the records and the record keeping used by the Executive Treasury department. It's possible to separate Kozlowski's personal expenditures from Tyco's. But the record keeping blurred the lines—or at least created the appearance of blurred lines. When Boies, Schiller investigators reviewed Kozlowski's KELP records, I'm certain they were shocked at how the former CEO's personal financial affairs were handled on a payment-by-payment basis using loan proceeds from KELP. I was shocked.

On its face, it was foolish. Kozlowski's personal invoices and bills were routed to Executive Treasury with notations that they were to be paid through "KELP." I don't know whose idea it was to handle the executives' personal finances and KELP loans in this manner, but it was one of the worst decisions among the dozens of poor decisions made at Tyco.

Kozlowski repaid his KELP loans—other than the amount outstanding on June 3, 2002, when he was indicted on sales tax charges and ousted from Tyco. In addition, his loan balances were audited by PwC and his KELP loan balances were disclosed annually. The sticking point was that two of the payments he used to reduce his loan balances were the questioned bonuses. The prosecution's theory was that Kozlowski borrowed from Tyco and then later fabricated bonuses he used to pay off or pay down the loan balances. Executive Treasury employees used foolish record keeping and it made the executives vulnerable to criticism. Of course, the employees in Executive Treasury weren't to blame. The executives were ultimately responsible and should have been more conscientious and less foolish about how their financial affairs were handled. There should never have been blurred lines between personal and company money.

7. Smoke and Mirrors

Somehow, the focus of the trials and of the media became how Kozlowski spent the proceeds of KELP loans—something that was *not* a crime. It is analogous to prosecuting someone for robbing a bank by presenting voluminous evidence of how he spent money that he borrowed from the bank—money he paid back to the bank.

Isaac Rosenthal, the foreman of the jury that convicted Kozlowski, said the jury read the Tyco bye-laws and based on the bye-laws and company policies, the jury understood how the loan programs were supposed to be used and believed, based on the evidence presented, that Kozlowski and Swartz abused the programs.[22]

I agree. I also believe the loan programs were used excessively and that the record keeping was foolish. Kozlowski and Swartz were not good stewards of the company's assets—and they had a fiduciary duty to be good stewards. However, breach of fiduciary duty and the sloppy use of company loan programs are not crimes. The only connection of the loan programs to the crimes charged was that two of the questioned bonuses were used to pay off or pay down loan balances. Kozlowski and Swartz were charged with grand larceny—how the money was spent was irrelevant. The only relevant question was whether the bonuses received were earned, approved, and payable. However, the prosecution did a masterful job of making the case about how Kozlowski spent money to support his extravagant lifestyle. The months of evidence presented at trial about what Kozlowski bought, his expensive taste, how he spent money, and the grandness of his life redirected everyone's attention away from the relevant issues—away from the elements of the crimes of which he was accused and convicted. If Kozlowski had been more prudent about his personal financial matters and had kept them completely separate from the company's, the trials could not have been muddied with irrelevant evidence about his lifestyle. The trials would have taken days or weeks instead of months, and the court and the jury would not have been distracted from the real issues in the case. Did the prosecution present evidence to prove beyond a reasonable doubt that Kozlowski and Swartz intentionally took money when they knew they had no right to have the money? That was the issue. Everything else was smoke and mirrors.

There were two counts of grand larceny for paintings Kozlowski purchased personally, for which he took loans from KELP, and then repaid the loans. These two counts are a complete mystery to me, as is the grand larceny count for the paintings purchased by Tyco. After two and a half years, I cannot grasp why these charges were included in the indictment, why they weren't thrown out by the court, and how the jury came to a guilty verdict. I found no evidence to support the charges. I am equally baffled by the grand larceny charge and guilty verdict for the investment banking fee paid to Frank Walsh. The relevant facts were not in dispute. I found no basis in law to support the conviction on that charge.

I did not address a securities fraud charge, which was so vague in allegation and in evidence admitted (or omitted) at trial, I am unable to explain it in a rational way. There were also several charges that Kozlowski and Swartz falsified business documents—the documents were questionnaires used to collect information for annual reports. The executives followed the instructions on the forms. Again, there was absolutely no evidence of their intent to do anything wrong.

8. "The Law Is Not a Perfect Tool."

As he passionately discussed *People v. Kozlowski* with me, former Manhattan DA Robert Morgenthau shared the wisdom of many decades when he said, "The law is not a perfect tool."[23] I agree.

CRIMINAL INTENT

There was plenty of evidence of extravagant spending, of overpaying employees, and of company benefits and perks that were far more generous than most of us ever see, and that were probably not in the best interests of Tyco shareholders. However, there was no evidence of criminal intent.

This is where the prosecution's case fell apart for me. I found no evidence that Kozlowski and Swartz intended to take anything they did not believe they had a right to take. On the contrary, there seemed to be ample evidence to show there was no criminal intent.

The prosecution's theme during the second trial was "instruct, conceal, deceive." Instruct? I found no evidence that anyone was instructed to do anything wrong. Every Tyco employee who testified said they were never asked or ordered by the Defendents to do anything wrong or to hide anything. Conceal? If Kozlowski and Swartz intended to conceal anything, they failed miserably. Nearly all of the evidence introduced during the trials was found on the books and records of the company. I've seen the documents, the records, and the evidence. All of the transactions were there—processed in the ordinary course of business. Deceive? The Tyco Directors testified that they were deceived. I have considerable doubt about that.

Nearly a decade after being acquitted of all charges levied against him by the Manhattan DA, Mark Belnick could barely speak about the years of his life that were destroyed by false allegations and a criminal trial. It was a deeply painful time for him and for his family and he preferred to leave the memories unstirred. Despite his reticence, he shared an inside view of Tyco and of Dennis Kozlowski that looked nothing like the portrayal of the company and the CEO that the prosecution played for the jury. Belnick said, "I was never pressured to do anything wrong. Never! Dennis never once tried to get me to do anything wrong, illegal, unethical. Never! If he did, I would have quit."[24]

At the time of this writing, Belnick and Kozlowski had not seen each other or spoken since they were indicted in September of 2002.[25] Eleven years later, it would have been easy for Belnick to throw Kozlowski under the bus. It would be easy for him to say that Kozlowski and Swartz, behind his back and hidden from him and everyone else, did all of the illegal and unethical things of which they were accused and convicted. Why not jump on the bandwagon? He had no reason *not* to blame Kozlowski and Swartz for all of the horrible things he and his family endured as a result of his relationship with Tyco. But Mark Belnick was adamant—nothing illegal was happening in Tyco's C-suite. What's his motivation for sharing that information? It's the truth.

I find it very difficult to believe that for ten years, *everyone* was wrong about Dennis Kozlowski and Tyco. Investors, analysts, PwC, law firms, the SEC, Tyco employees, and the Board of Directors. In April of 2001, analysts voted Tyco the company with the most transparent disclosures. The company was highly scrutinized. There were regulators, analysts, short-sellers, and journalists digging through Tyco's financial reporting, disclosures, and accounting method—for years. None of those highly skilled agencies, firms, and individuals found anything wrong until David Boies and the Manhattan DA arrived on the scene. How did they find problems that no one else discovered?

I spoke with several fine, honorable, highly respected people who worked closely with Kozlowski day after day, year after year, and they all told me without reservation that nothing shady or illegal was happening in Tyco corporate operations during the years Kozlowski was the CEO. I believe them.

* * *

Like all people, Dennis Kozlowski is neither all good nor all bad. He is a complex, multidimensional person who since 2002 has been terribly mischaracterized. For two and a half years, I audited Dennis Kozlowski's life. I ran a fine-tooth comb through his business dealings and I examined all the years he spent with Tyco International Ltd. I conducted hundreds of hours of interviews with Kozlowski, his former Tyco colleagues, his friends, his family members, the District Attorney who prosecuted him, the foreman of the jury who convicted him, and I spoke with a number of experts who helped me digest all of the information available to me so I could understand what happened to Dennis Kozlowski and to Tyco.

I spent scores of hours speaking with the man who is the subject of this book. Because he is controversial, I didn't rely on Kozlowski's telling of the story. I checked every fact that I could using independent, objective sources. To his credit, not one of the hundreds of facts Kozlowski provided to me proved to be inaccurate when verified through objective and reliable sources. Kozlowski's memory proved to be accurate and I believe he was truthful. I found no evidence to the contrary. He did not ask me to include or to exclude anything when I was writing this book, and he had no control over or knowledge of the content. From my first contact with him, I expressed my desire to understand what happened, and he said "go for it, go through all of the evidence, and let the chips fall where they may."[26]

Dennis Kozlowski made some bad decisions, but he made more good decisions than bad. There's no question that he got caught up in the power and the outrageous sums of money, and he lost perspective. Another serious problem was that he too closely identified with Tyco; Kozlowski was Tyco and Tyco was Kozlowski. Kozlowski measured his success by Tyco's success (something frequently used as an incentive for executives), and he measured his success by the amount of money he earned. He too literally evaluated his performance *by his pay.* It's strange. It seemed Kozlowski didn't want the money so he could spend it, or so he could accumulate it. Of course he had nice things, expensive toys, luxury homes, and for a while, he lived like a wealthy man. But the money represented something else to him. The amount of his compensation was the physical proof of his success. It was his equivalent of an Olympic medal or a Pulitzer Prize or an Oscar. It proved he was exceptionally good at running a company. It proved he was the best CEO. He wouldn't have stolen money—it would have cheapened what he valued most. He didn't want to *have* the money; he wanted to *earn* the money. For Kozlowski, that was the whole point.

Oczywista

After spending countless hours with my head in this case, all I can say is *oczywista*. Translated from Polish, *oczywista* means it's obvious, unmistakable. The evidence in this case speaks for itself. I do not believe Dennis Kozlowski committed any crimes. I do not believe he ever intended to commit any crimes. I believe the same is true of Mark Swartz, although I focused on Kozlowski's decisions and actions, not those of Swartz. I asked Mark Swartz, through his attorneys, to talk to me as I researched this book, but he opted not to participate.

My research was meticulous and I am confident that I understand the facts and the law. I looked at the same evidence and laws as the Manhattan DA, the law firm of Boies, Schiller & Flexner, and the jury, and I respectfully but strongly disagree with their conclusions.

That being said, I have a difficult time assigning blame or attributing bad motives. After meeting with former Manhattan DA Robert Morgenthau, I think that he believed he was doing the right thing in 2002 when he indicted the Tyco executives. I assume the jurors did the best they could with the mountain of complex and often irrelevant evidence that was heaped on them over many months of trial. In retrospect, the defense attorneys could have put on a stronger case. However, at the time, I'm sure they believed the prosecution failed to prove anything beyond a reasonable doubt. I don't think there was anywhere near enough evidence to convict Kozlowski and Swartz. I am also giving the benefit of the doubt to the attorneys of Boies, Schiller & Flexner, assuming they conducted an ethical investigation and did not knowingly watch individuals indicted, tried, and convicted of crimes they did not commit. Boies, Schiller attorneys were hired to do a job, and they did it.

And then there are the individuals who sat on the Tyco Board of Directors in 2002. After having reviewed thousands of company documents, speaking to many individuals who knew the Directors, and to Directors who were on the Board at the time, talking with individuals who were part of Tyco corporate operations when Kozlowski was CEO, and after having studied two criminal trials and mountains of evidence—I know the truth. I am also certain that the individuals who were Tyco Directors in 2002 know the truth.

LESSONS WE CAN LEARN FROM THE TRAGIC END OF KOZLOWSKI'S CAREER

I began this project as a learning experience, and I end it with what I learned (and I learned a lot):

1. Cover your ass! CYA! Document everything, make sure everything is documented, and recognize the risk in counting on other people to take care of important responsibilities for you—because if they don't do their jobs, you are still responsible. Pay attention to the details in

your work and in your life. Be mindful that you can't delegate personal accountability.

2. Make sure everything that should be disclosed is disclosed.

3. As a business organization grows, ensure that adjustments are made to accommodate the growth. Make sure the proper people and policies are in place to operate a growing organization legally and ethically.

4. Be a responsible steward of company assets. Never mix personal and business finances.

5. Exercise good judgment. Remember that you are responsible for you. Do what you know to be right, despite pressure to do otherwise. Be proactive in doing what is right. Don't wait until there's trouble to evaluate your actions and decisions.

6. Protect your reputation. It is one of your greatest assets and once it is tainted, it is difficult to rehabilitate.

7. Never ever sign an employment contract that says your employer can be rid of you with no further financial obligation only if you're convicted of a felony that's materially injurious to the company.

8. Know the rules. Follow the rules, even when it's a pain and takes too much time. Respect corporate formalities. They exist for good reasons. Cross every "t." Dot every "i." Consistently. Meticulously.

9. If company policies are bad for the company and hurt shareholders, change them to better serve those to whom you owe a duty. Don't get caught in an "it's-always-been-done-that-way" mentality. Don't take advantage of loose company policies and lax governance.

10. Recognize that not everyone has a moral compass in their backpack; be sure that you always pack and use yours.

11. Be aware that prosecutors have perhaps the greatest power in our society, and when they exercise that power, the effects can be wide-reaching and may do as much harm as good.

12. Realize that media spin is everywhere. Believe little of what you read. Do real research, rely on reliable sources, and discover the truth. Remain aware that people in the media have their own biases and interests, none of which may have anything to do with reporting the truth.

13. Accept the fact that many people act only in their own self-interest. Be wise when deciding who to trust.

14. Respect the truth, because the truth matters.

15. And the most important lesson of all. Perspective. Remember that money is just money. It is far from the most important thing in life. It is unwise to measure success by the size of your earnings. The cost of going to prison, even for only a day, is far greater than any paycheck you could ever earn. Ask Dennis Kozlowski.

* * *

Mid-State Correctional Facility
Marcy, New York
May 24, 2011

Dear Cathy,

You asked what is the first thing I'll do once I'm out of prison. I often think of free-dom. I cannot wait to embrace my daughters and my two grandchildren. It will be great to be free of fences, razor wire, jingling keys, barked orders, strip searches, a 24/7 fluorescent light, and a metal rack next to a toilet as a bed.

I look forward to doing what free people do. Close a bathroom door, go to the store, drive a car, open a door, call on a telephone, touch a computer. No one will open my mail but me. No one will monitor my telephone calls. Eat something decent whenever, wherever I desire. Use a knife and a fork. See a dog. Walk a beach. See the moon and stars.

Simple pleasures and the freedom to enjoy them are more precious than you can imagine.

Best Regards,
Dennis[27]

NOTES

People v. Kozlowski I, New York State Supreme Court, New York County, Indictment #5259-02, September 29, 2003–April 2, 2004.
People v. Kozlowski II, New York State Supreme Court, New York County, Indictment #5259-02, January 18, 2005–September 19, 2005.
URLs for online sources found in the Bibliography.

CHAPTER ONE: SIX WOMEN AND SIX MEN

1. *People v. Kozlowski II,* transcript at 16338:7–25, 16339:2, 16339:4, and 16339:13–24, June 17, 2005.
2. Dennis Kozlowski, interview with the author, Marcy, New York, May 21, 2011.
3. 2001 Annual Report Tyco International Ltd., "Consolidated Financial Statements," December 3, 2001, 42.
4. *People v. Kozlowski II,* direct examination of Dennis Kozlowski, transcript at 12095:7–9, April 27, 2005.
5. International Monetary Fund, "World Economic Outlook: The Global Economy After September 11," December 2001. "The global slowdown that had started most prominently in the United States in 2000 had, by mid-2001, become a synchronized downturn across almost all major regions of the world." Ibid. at 14. "Confidence is a major channel through which the September 11 attacks feed through to the global economy. An unforeseen event of the magnitude of the September 11 terrorist attack can radically alter the view of the future (including the level of uncertainty) for both consumers and businessmen. This provides an incentive to postpone or cancel spending, which, through Keynesian multiplier and trade channels, can reduce aggregate demand and output at home and in other countries." Ibid. at 19.
6. 2001 Annual Report Tyco International Ltd., "L. Dennis Kozlowski, Chairman of the Board of Directors and Chief Executive Officer, Letter to Shareholders," December 3, 2001, 15.
7. Ibid.
8. Kevin L. Kliesen, "The 2001 Recession: How Was It Different and What Developments May Have Caused It?" *Federal Reserve Bank of St. Louis Review* (September/October 2003). "The U.S. business expansion that started in March 1991 and ended exactly a decade later lasted more than a year longer than the previous record-long 1961–69 expansion." Ibid. at 23. See also, "Economists Call It Recession," CNNMoney, November 26, 2001. "The world's largest economy sank into a recession in March [2001], ending 10 years of growth that was the longest expansion on record in the United States . . ." Ibid.
9. 2001 Annual Report Tyco International Ltd., "L. Dennis Kozlowski, Chairman of the Board of Directors and Chief Executive Officer, Letter to Shareholders," December 3, 2001, 19.
10. Dennis Kozlowski, interview with the author, Marcy, New York, May 21, 2011.
11. Liz Harper, "Enron: After the Collapse," *PBS Newshour with Jim Lehr* (June 2002); and Voluntary Petition, *In re Enron Corp.,* No. 01-16034, 2001 Extra LEXIS 159 (Bankr. S.D.N.Y. Dec. 2, 2001). See also, United States Bankruptcy Court, Southern District of New York, "Enron Corp. Bankruptcy Information," last updated on February 22, 2013; Bruce Mizrach, "The Enron Bankruptcy: When Did the Options Market in Enron Lose It's [sic] Smirk?" *Review of Quantitative Financial Accounting,* Vol. 27 (2006), 365; and David Stout and Sherrie Day, "Ex-Chief Says He Didn't Know About Enron's Accounting Woes," *New York Times,* February 7, 2002.
12. John C. Coffee, "Understanding Enron: It's About the Gatekeepers, Stupid," *Columbia Law & Economics Working Paper No. 207,* July 30, 2002.
13. Simon Romero and Riva D. Atlas, "WorldCom's Collapse: The Overview; WorldCom Files for Bankruptcy: Largest U.S. Case," *New York Timtes,* July 22, 2002.

14. "ImClone ex-CEO Nabbed," CNNMoney, June 13, 2002.
15. Ray J. Grzebielski, "Why Martha Stewart Did Not Violate Rule 10b-5: On Tipping, Piggybacking, Frontrunning and the Fiduciary Duties of Securities Brokers," *Akron Law Review*, Vol. 40, No. 55 (2007), fn 7 and 56.
16. Securities and Exchange Commission Press Release 2002-110, "SEC Charges Adelphia and Rigas Family with Massive Financial Fraud," July 24, 2002.
17. Dan Ackman, "House Committees to Investigate Global Crossing," *Forbes*, March 13, 2002. "Had it not been for Enron—the scandal that has it all—the Global Crossing demise would have garnered more attention already on Capitol Hill and elsewhere." Ibid.
18. "Graphic: A Long Line of Accounting Scandals," *New York Times*, November 20, 2012.
19. Ibid.
20. Subrata N. Chakravarty, "Deal-a-Month Dennis," *Forbes*, June 15, 1998. " . . . Tyco's performance with Kozlowski at the helm has been truly impressive . . ." Ibid. See also, William C. Symonds, "The Most Aggressive CEO," *Businessweek* (Cover Story), May 28, 2001; and "The Top 25 Managers to Watch," *Businessweek* (Cover Story), January 13, 2002.
21. See for example, Daniel Eisenberg, "Corporate Greed: Dennis the Menace," *Time*, June 17, 2002; and Laura Italiano and Dareh Gregorian, "Pig Due to the Pen as Jury Pounds Tyco Thief Kozlowski," *New York Post*, June 18, 2005.
22. Dennis Kozlowski, interview with the author, Marcy, New York, May 21, 2011.

CHAPTER TWO: BA 0.043

1. *People v. Kozlowski II*, transcript at 16339:25, 16340:2–25, 16341:2–25, 16342:2–25, 16343:2–25, and 16344:2–10, June 17, 2005.
2. Dennis Kozlowski, interview with the author, Marcy, New York, May 21, 2011.
3. Joel Stashenko, "Ex-Tyco Executives Contest Use of Findings From Internal Probe," *New York Law Journal*, September 3, 2008. "In 2005, Kozlowski and Swartz were each convicted by a jury of 22 of 23 counts, including grand larceny, falsification of business records, securities fraud and conspiracy. Prosecutors said the case was the largest larceny ever prosecuted in New York state." Ibid.
4. Andrew Ross Sorkin, "Ex-Chief and Aide Guilty of Looting Millions at Tyco," *New York Times*, June 18, 2005.
5. Dennis Kozlowski, letter to the author, March 17, 2011.

CHAPTER THREE: 950 FIFTH AVENUE

1. F. Scott Fitzgerald, *The Crack Up*, ed. Edmund Wilson (New York, NY: New Directions, 1945). "When Fitzgerald's friend Edmund Wilson came to put together 'The Crack-Up,' the volume of Fitzgerald miscellany that appeared in 1945, five years after Fitzgerald's death, he included this entry, explaining in a footnote that 'Fitzgerald had said, 'The rich are different from us.' Hemingway had replied, 'Yes, they have more money.''" Letter to the Editor, "The Rich Are Different," *New York Times*, November 13, 1988.
2. *Psycho*, directed by Alfred Hitchcock (Los Angeles, CA: Paramount Pictures, 1960).
3. Dennis Kozlowski, interview with Morley Safer, "Dennis Kozlowski: Prisoner 05A4820," *60 Minutes*, originally broadcast March 25, 2007; and "Party's Over: Tyco's Kozlowski," *American Greed*, originally broadcast March 19, 2008.
4. See for example, Joann S. Lublin, "Dennis Kozlowski Talks Jail, Pay," *Wall Street Journal*, October 21, 2012. "As convicted hedge-fund manager Raj Rajaratnam gets ready to enter the prison system, L. Dennis Kozlowski, a poster child for the last wave of corporate scandals, is hoping he'll soon get out." Ibid. See also, William G. Flanagan, *Dirty Rotten CEOs: How Business Leaders Are Fleecing America* (New York, NY: Citadel Press, 2004). "And what of the poster child for corporate greed, L. Dennis Kozlowski? Kozlowski got to be the first of the Dirty Rotten CEOs in the criminal docket mainly because he was so flamboyant." Ibid. at 271; and Scott Green, *Sarbanes-Oxley and the Board of Directors: Techniques and Best Practices for Corporate Governance* (Hoboken, NJ: John Wiley & Sons, 2005). "In Dennis Kozlowski, prosecutors believe they have found the perfect poster child for executive greed and unethical practices." Ibid. at 194.
5. Michael J. De La Merced, "Dennis Kozlowski's Homecoming, of Sorts," *New York Times*, March 16, 2012.
6. Temporary Release Programs, *New York State (NYS)* Department of Corrections and Community Supervision, "Temporary Release," New York State Department of Corrections and Community Supervision defines "work release" as a program "which allows an inmate to leave a facility for up to 14 hours in any day to work at a job in the community or gain on-the-job training." Ibid.
7. New York State Department of Corrections and Community Supervision defines "furlough" time as that "which allows an inmate to go home to stay with his/her family for up to seven days to maintain family ties, look for employment or to seek post-release housing." Ibid.

8. Dennis Kozlowski, letter to the author, July 14, 2011.

9. Ibid.

10. Dennis Kozlowski interview with the author, New York City, New York, June 23, 2012.

11. Ibid.

12. Ibid.

13. *People v. Kozlowski I,* direct examination of Mariola Tarnachowicz, transcript at 05266:16–23 and 05273:6–12, November 25, 2003.

14. Dennis Kozlowski, interview with the author, New York City, New York, June 23, 2012.

15. Ibid.

16. Dennis Kozlowski, interview with the author, New York City, New York, June 23, 2012; and *People v. Kozlowski II,* direct examination of Dolly Lenz, April 22, 2005.

17. Dennis Kozlowski, interview with the author, New York City, New York, June 23, 2012; and *People v. Kozlowski II,* direct examination of Dolly Lenz, April 22, 2005. See also, Gabrielle Sherman, "Tyco Slashes Co-op," *New York Observer,* March 8, 2004; and Michael J. de la Merced, "Inside Stephen Schwarzman's Birthday Bash," *New York Times,* February 14, 2007.

18. *People v. Kozlowski II,* direct examination of Dolly Lenz, April 22, 2005.

19. Ibid. at 11764:2.

20. Joshua M. Berman, letter to the Board of Directors, 950 Fifth Avenue Corporation, March 30, 2000.

21. *People v. Kozlowski II,* direct examination of Dolly Lenz, transcript at 11764:13, 11766:13–16, and 11764:20, April 22, 2005.

22. Dennis Kozlowski, interview with the author, New York City, New York, June 23, 2012.

23. *People v. Kozlowski II,* direct examination of Kathy McRae, transcript at 11386:23–25, April 20, 2005.

24. *People v. Kozlowski I,* direct examination of Brian Moroze, transcript at 02070:22–25, October 22, 2003.

25. *People v. Kozlowski II,* direct examination of Dennis Kozlowski, transcript at 12252:17–25, 12253:2–4, and 12253:5–8, April 27, 2005. See also, *People v. Kozlowski I,* direct examination of Brian Moroze, transcript at 02073:9, October 22, 2003.

26. *People v. Kozlowski II,* direct examination of Kathy McRae, transcript at 11385:23, April 20, 2005; and cross-examination of Dolly Lenz, transcript at 11886:13 and 11761:14–16, April 26, 2005.

27. Dennis Kozlowski, interview with the author, New York City, New York, June 23, 2012.

28. Ibid.

29. *People v. Kozlowski II,* direct examination of Mark Foley, transcript at 04783:10–18, February 24, 2005.

30. Dennis Kozlowski, interview with the author, New York City, New York, June 23, 2012.

31. Tyco International Ltd., "Minutes of a Special Meeting of the Board of Directors," Tuckers Town, Bermuda, May 12, 1999, 7; and "Minutes of a Regular Meeting of the Board of Directors," Pembroke, Bermuda, October 3, 2000, 12.

32. Dennis Kozlowski, interview with the author, New York City, New York, June 23, 2012.

33. Ibid.

34. New York Department of Finance, Automated City Register Information System, "Manhattan, Block 01391, Lot 0001," document number 2004120802167001, Units 10 and 11, 950 Fifth Avenue, December 14, 2004.

35. *People v. Kozlowski II,* direct examination of Linda Auger, transcript at 08058:12–13, March 23, 2005.

36. New York Department of Finance, Automated City Register Information System, "Manhattan, Block 01391, Lot 0001," document number 2004120802167001, Units 10 and 11, 950 Fifth Avenue, December 14, 2004.

CHAPTER FOUR: EXECUTIVE PERQUISITES

1. John Lennon and Paul McCartney, "Strawberry Fields Forever," *The Beatles,* Capitol Records, 1967.

2. David Sheff, "The Playboy Interviews," *Playboy* (January 1981).

3. Robert Palmer, "Lennon Known Both as an Author and Composer," *New York Times,* December 9, 1980.

4. Michel Marie Deza and Elena Deza, *Encyclopedia of Distances,* 2nd ed. (New York: Springer), 2010, 586.

5. Dennis Kozlowski, interview with the author, New York City, New York, June 23, 2012.

6. "Divorce Deal Reveals Welch's Perks," CNNMoney, September 6, 2002; Matt Murray, Rachel Emma Silverman, and Carol Himowitz, "GE's Jack Welch Meets Match in Divorce Court," *Wall Street Journal,* November 27, 2002; ibid. quoting Nell Minow, editor of *The Corporate Library;*

PBS NewsHour transcript, "Executive Perks," September 16, 2002; and Edwin A. Locke, "Jack Welch Earned His Perks," *Christian Science Monitor,* September 23, 2002.

7. Dennis Kozlowski, letter to the author, February 19, 2011.

8. Beth Healy, "Executive Perks Are Still Alive and Well," *Boston Globe,* April 12, 2013. See also, Daniel Fisher, "The Most Outrageous Executive Perks," *Forbes,* June 27, 2012; and Nelson D. Schwartz, "The Infinity Pool of Executive Pay," *New York Times,* April 6, 2013.

9. See New York Stock Exchange website, https://nyse.nyx.com/.

10. Regulation S-K Item 402(c)(2)(viii), 17 C.F.R. § 229.402(s) (2010). "All other compensation for the covered fiscal year that the registrant could not properly report in any other column of the Summary Compensation Table. Each compensation item that is not properly reportable in columns (c)–(h), regardless of the amount of the compensation item, must be included in column (i). Such compensation must include, but is not limited to: A. Perquisites and other personal benefits, or property, unless the aggregate amount of such compensation is less than $ 10,000; B. All "gross-ups" or other amounts reimbursed during the fiscal year for the payment of taxes. . . ." See also, U.S. Securities and Exchange Commission, "Executive Compensation," last updated September 2, 2011.

11. U.S. Securities and Exchange Commission, "Executive Compensation and Related Persons Disclosure," last updated September 2, 2011.

12. Ibid.

13. Ibid.

14. The value of perquisites and personal benefits received by named executive officers and directors must be disclosed in the "All Other Compensation" column of the Summary Compensation Table. Ibid.

15. See for example, "Executive Perquisites—What 2012 Proxy Statements Have Revealed," *The Ayco Compensation & Benefits Digest,* Vol. 20, Issue 6, June 15, 2012. See also, "The Wall Street Journal/ Hay Group Survey of CEO Compensation Study 2011," June 6, 2012.

16. See for example, Michael Brush, "10 outrageously lavish CEO Perks," MSN Money, November 27, 2012. See also, "Eight Outrageous CEO Perks," *24/7 Wall Street Wire,* December 13, 2013; and Gary Strauss, "Despite Huge Salaries, CEOs Cling to Their Perks," *USA Today,* April 13, 2011.

17. "Executive Perquisites—What 2012 Proxy Statements Have Revealed," *The Ayco Compensation & Benefits Digest.* "Perquisites remain part of the executive compensation program at an overwhelming majority of companies and may play a role in attracting and retaining key executives." Ibid. at 1.

18. Ibid. at 4.

19. Dodd-Frank Wall Street Reform and Consumer Protection Act, Pub. L. No. 111-203 (July 21, 2010), Section 953. There are numerous and ongoing attempts to repeal some of the disclosure requirements of Section 953 of Dodd-Frank because the provisions are arguably burdensome and compliance impracticable. See also, Section 951. Section 951 of Dodd-Frank amends Section 14A of the Securities Exchange Act of 1934. See, Securities Exchange Act of 1934, Section 14A(a) (2). See also, Jennifer Liberto, "CEO Pay: Shareholders Get a (Little) Say," CNNMoney, April 21, 2011. "As part of the Dodd-Frank law reforming Wall Street, all public companies must now hold shareholder up-or-down votes on CEO pay. While the so-called 'say-on-pay' votes are symbolic and nonbinding, they're powerful enough to prompt a corporate powerhouse such as GE to shake up Immelt's pay package." Ibid.

20. *People v. Kozlowski II,* direct examination of Kathy McRae, transcript at 11437:19–22, April 20, 2005.

21. Dennis Kozlowski, telephone interview with the author, June 7, 2012.

22. *People v. Kozlowski II,* direct examination of Dennis Kozlowski, transcript at 12251:5–6, April 27, 2005.

23. Dennis Kozlowski, interview with the author, New York City, New York, June 21, 2012.

24. David Ropelk, "Inside the Mind of Worry," *New York Times,* September 28, 2012.

25. Dennis Kozlowski, interview with the author, New York City, New York, June 21, 2012.

26. *People v. Kozlowski II,* direct examination of Dennis Kozlowski, transcript at 12251:23–25, April 27, 2005. See also, Dennis Kozlowski, interview with the author, New York City, New York, June 23, 2012.

27. Alex Kuczynski, "Lifestyles of the Rich and Red-Faced," *New York Times,* September 22, 2002. The author included this information because she was shocked by multi-million dollar interior decorator bills for a 6,000-square-foot apartment. Apparently, it is the norm.

28. U.S. Securities and Exchange Commission, "Tyco International Ltd. Form 8-K," September 10, 2002.

29. Dennis Kozlowski, telephone interview with the author, June 7, 2012.

30. Ibid.

31. *People v. Kozlowski II,* direct examination of Linda Auger, transcript at 08059:19–24, March 23, 2005.

32. Mark Maremont and Laurie P. Cohen, "Tyco Spent Millions for Benefit of Kozlowski, Its Former CEO," *Wall Street Journal*, August 7, 2002.
33. Securities and Exchange Commission, "Tyco International Ltd. Form 8-K," September 10, 2002.
34. Ibid.
35. Ibid.

CHAPTER FIVE: BEHIND THE ELEPHANT

1. Dennis Kozlowski, telephone interview with the author, May 11, 2012.
2. Ibid.
3. *People v. Kozlowski II*, direct examination of Dennis Kozlowski, transcript at 12063:9–18, April 27, 2005.
4. Dennis Kozlowski, telephone interview with the author, May 11, 2012.
5. Ibid.
6. *People v. Kozlowski II*, direct examination of Dennis Kozlowski, transcript at 12064:3–5, April 27, 2005.
7. Ibid. at, 12064:13–16.
8. Ibid. at 12064:21–23.
9. Tyco Fire and Integrated Solutions, "Our History," http://www.tycofis.co.uk/About-Tyco/our-history (accessed May 17, 2013).
10. Funding Universe, "Tyco International Ltd. History" citing *International Directory of Company Histories*, Vol. 63 (New York, NY: St. James Press, 2004).
11. Ibid.
12. Ibid.
13. MIT Alumni Association, "Deceased Classmates," MIT Class of 1956; Carlton Macomber, "'71 Face-off with Soviets Led U.S. to 200-Mile Limit," *South Coast Today*, November 4, 1998; and "Westport's World's Lecture by William Wyatt Provides an Entertaining Look at Town History," *Dartmouth-Westport* (CT) *Chronicle*, August 18, 2004.
14. Carlton Macomber, "'71 Face-off with Soviets Led U.S. to 200-Mile Limit," *South Coast Today*; and "Westport's World's Lecture by William Wyatt Provides an Entertaining Look at Town History," *Dartmouth-Westport* (CT) *Chronicle*.
15. Dennis Kozlowski, telephone interview with the author, May 11, 2012.
16. Funding Universe, "Tyco International Ltd. History" citing *International Directory of Company Histories*, Vol. 63 (New York: St. James Press, 2004).
17. Dennis Kozlowski, telephone interview with the author, May 11, 2012.
18. Ibid.
19. *People v. Kozlowski II*, direct examination of Dennis Kozlowski, transcript at 12065:3–25 and 12066:2, April 27, 2005.
20. Ibid. at 12066:11–18 and 12066:3–6.
21. Robert A. G. Monks, telephone interview with the author, May 7, 2013.
22. Ibid.
23. Dennis Kozlowski, interview with the author, New York City, New York June 22, 2012.
24. *People v. Kozlowski II*, direct examination of Dennis Kozlowski, transcript at 12069:2–4, April 27, 2005.
25. Funding Universe, "Tyco International Ltd. History" citing *International Directory of Company Histories*, Vol. 63. (New York: St. James Press, 2004; and *People v. Kozlowski II*, direct examination of Dennis Kozlowski, transcript at 12072:10–11, April 27, 2005.
26. MIT Alumni Association, "Deceased Classmates"; Dennis Kozlowski, interview with the author, New York City, New York, June 22, 2012; Funding Universe, "Tyco International Ltd. History" citing *International Directory of Company Histories*, Vol. 63 (New York: St. James Press, 2004); and *People v. Kozlowski II*, direct examination of John Fort III, transcript at 01734;21–25, January 31, 2005.
27. Funding Universe, "Tyco International Ltd. History" citing *International Directory of Company Histories*, Vol. 63. (New York: St. James Press, 2004).
28. Ibid.
29. Ibid.
30. "Vertical integration of the supply chain" is the author's phrasing. In my interviews with him, Dennis Kozlowski did not rely on technical management terminology and never used buzz words. His descriptions of his vision, strategies, and actions came in plain language and did not sound like they came from a textbook.
31. *People v. Kozlowski II,* direct examination of John Fort III, transcript at 01738:5–6, January 31, 2005.
32. *People v. Kozlowski II,* direct examination of Dennis Kozlowski, transcript at 12072:21–25 and 12073: 2–12, April 27, 2005.

33. Ibid. at 12078:15–19.
34. Dennis Kozlowski, letter to the author, March 10, 2011.
35. *People v. Kozlowski II,* direct examination of John Fort III, transcript at 01738:7–12, January 31, 2005.
36. Robert A. G. Monks, telephone interview with the author, May 7, 2013.
37. *People v. Kozlowski II,* direct examination of John Fort III, transcript at 01738:7–12, January 31, 2005.
38. Dennis Kozlowski, letter to the author, March 10, 2011.
39. Dennis Kozlowski, telephone interview with the author, May 25, 2012.
40. Robert A. G. Monks, telephone interview with the author, May 7, 2013.
41. Ibid.

CHAPTER SIX: BECOMING CEO

1. Dennis Kozlowski, interview with the author, Marcy, New York, May 21, 2011. See also, *People v. Kozlowski II,* direct examination of Dennis Kozlowski, transcript at 12085:10–13, April 27, 2005.
2. Dennis Kozlowski, interview with the author, New York City, New York, June 23, 2012; and *People v. Kozlowski II,* direct examination of Dennis Kozlowski, transcript at 12082–12083, 12053:20–25, and at 12054:2–5, April 27, 2005.
3. Dennis Kozlowski, telephone interview with the author, May 8, 2012.
4. Robert Pastore, telephone interview with the author, July 3, 2012; and Robert Pastore, Letter to Commissioner Brian Fischer, New York State Department of Corrections and Community Supervision, October 29, 2011.
5. Dennis Kozlowski, telephone interviews with the author: May 8, 2012; May 9, 2012; and May 25, 2012.
6. National Center for Education Statistics, Institute of Education Sciences, U.S. Department of Education.
7. Dennis Kozlowski, telephone interview with the author, May 25, 2012.
8. Dennis Kozlowski, telephone interview with the author, May 9, 2012; Damian Fannelli, "Two New Studies Suggest Women Are More Attracted to a Man Holding a Guitar," *Guitar World,* May 10, 2013, citing studies published in *Psychology of Music* and *Letters on Evolutionary Behavioral Science;* and "Late Night with Jimmy Fallon," *Newsmax,* The Best of Late Night Jokes, May 9, 2013.
9. Dennis Kozlowski, telephone interview with the author, May 9, 2012.
10. "The History of Seton Hall," *2012-13 Undergraduate Catalog, Seton Hall University,* University Overview, 9; and Dennis Kozlowski, telephone interview with the author, May 9, 2012.
11. Eugene M. Tobin, "John Franklin Fort," in *The Governors of New Jersey 1664–1974: Biographical Essays,* ed. Paul A. Stellhorn and Michael J. Birkner (New Jersey Historical Commission, 1982), 174 and 177.
12. *People v. Kozlowski II,* direct examination of John Fort III, transcript at 01732:18–20, 01733:5–8, 01733:24–25, and at 01743:1–3, January 31, 2005; and "Former Tyco CEO to Address Sul Ross Commencement on Saturday," *Alpine* (TX) *Daily Planet,* May 10, 2013.
13. *People v. Kozlowski II,* direct examination of John Fort III, transcript at 01733:24–25, 01743:1–21, 01734:21–25, and at 01735:5–8, January 31, 2005.
14. Gary Strauss, "Retired Tyco CEO Gets $150 Million Exit Package," *USA Today,* January 13, 2013. See also, Michelle Leder, "Openers: Suits; The Fine Print," *New York Times,* January 29, 2006.
15. Ibid.
16. *People v. Kozlowski II,* direct examination of John Fort III, transcript at 01738:5–11, 01738:22–25, and 01740:13–17, January 31, 2005; *People v. Kozlowski II,* direct examination of Dennis Kozlowski, transcript at 12079:19, April 27, 2005; and Dennis Kozlowski, letter to the author, February 19, 2011.
17. *People v. Kozlowski II,* direct examination of John Fort III, transcript at 01735:12–13, January 31, 2005; Robert A. G. Monks, telephone interview with the author, August 5, 2013. See also, Dennis Kozlowski, interview with the author, New York City, New York, June 23, 2012; and Joshua Berman, telephone interview with the author, August 8, 2013.
18. Dennis Kozlowski, interview with the author, New York City, New York, June 23, 2012; and Dennis Kozlowski, telephone interview with the author, May 30, 2012.
19. Dennis Kozlowski, telephone interview with the author, May 30, 2012; Dennis Kozlowski, interview with the author, New York City, New York, June 23, 2012; *People v. Kozlowski II,* direct examination of Dennis Kozlowski, transcript at 12053:14–25, 12054:2–5, 12082:24–25, and 12083:1–25, April 27, 2005; and *People v. Kozlowski II,* direct examination of John Fort III, transcript at 01735:12–13, January 31, 2005.
20. Dennis Kozlowski, telephone interview with the author, May 30, 2012.

21. Robert A. G. Monks, telephone interview with the author, May 7, 2013; and Dennis Kozlowski, telephone interview with the author, May 30, 2012. See, Robert A. G. Monks, *Citizens Disunited: Passive Investors, Drone CEOs, and the Corporate Capture of the American Dream* (McLean, VA: Miniver Press, 2013). See also, Robert A. G. Monks, *Corpocracy: How CEOs and the Business Roundtable Hijacked the World's Greatest Wealth Machine—And How to Get It Back* (Hoboken, NJ: John Wiley & Sons, 2008); and Robert A. G. Monks and Nell Minow, *Corporate Governance*, 5th ed. (Hoboken, NJ: John Wiley & Sons, 2011).

22. Robert A. G. Monks, telephone interview with the author, May 7, 2013.

23. *People v. Kozlowski II*, direct examination of Dennis Kozlowski, transcript at 12085:15–22 and 12086:1–11, April 27, 2005.

24. Ibid.

25. Ibid.

26. Dennis Kozlowski, telephone interview with the author, May 30, 2012.

27. Ibid.

28. Ibid.

29. *Spencer Stuart Board Index*, "Board Composition," 27th ed. (November 6, 2012), 23.

30. Ibid.

31. U.S. Securities and Exchange Commission, "Proxy Disclosure Enhancements," Final Rule, adopted December 16, 2009, effective February 28, 2010; and Dodd-Frank, Section 972. Dodd-Frank amended the Securities Exchange Act of 1934 (15 U.S. C. 78a et seq.) by inserting Section 14B: "Not later than 180 days after the date of enactment of this subsection, the Commission shall issue rules that require an issuer to disclose in the annual proxy sent to investors the reasons why the issuer has chosen: (1) the same person to serve as chairman of the board of directors and chief executive officer (or in equivalent positions); or (2) different individuals to serve as chairman of the board of directors and chief executive officer (or in equivalent positions of the issuer)." Ibid.

32. Robert A. G. Monks, telephone interview with the author, May 7, 2013.

CHAPTER SEVEN: BIG TIME SCRUTINY

1. Dennis Kozlowski, interview with the author, New York City, New York, June 23, 2012.

2. Ibid. Robert Dilenschneider's wisdom appears to be adapted from quotes attributed to Henry Hillman ("A whale is harpooned only when he spouts") and Charles A. Jaffe ("Whales only get harpooned when they come to the surface, and turtles can only move forward when they stick their neck out, but investors face risk no matter what they do.").

3. I. Jane Dugan, "The Best Performers: The Business Week Fifty," *Businessweek*, March 24, 1997. "The companies of the S&P 500 are the most closely watched in America. Now, for the first time, we are ranking them on how well they perform. At the top are the Business Week 50—the new corporate elite." Ibid.; William C. Symonds, "The Most Aggressive CEO," *Businessweek* (cover story), May 27, 2001; and "The Top 25 Managers of the Year," *Businessweek* (cover story), January 13, 2002.

4. Daniel Trotta, "Short Sellers Have Been the Villain for 400 Years," Reuters, September 26, 2008.

5. Alistair Barr, "Short Sellers: The Good, the Bad, and the Ugly," *MarketWatch*, December 19, 2001.

6. "Dennis Kozlowski of Tyco International: King Conglomerate," *Institutional Investor*, April 1, 2001.

7. Alistair Barr, "Short Sellers: The Good, the Bad, and the Ugly," *MarketWatch*, December 19, 2001.

8. Mark P. Baumann, "Restructuring Charges," ACC7500: Financial Statement Analysis, Babson College.

9. "Tyco Completes Acquisitions of AMP," *New York Times*, April 6, 1999.

10. Financial Accounting Standards Board, "Statement 141—Business Combinations" (rev. 2007, effective December 2008).

11. J. Bradford McGee, telephone interview with the author, May 30, 2013.

12. Dennis Kozlowski, interview with the author, New York City, New York, June 22, 2012.

13. Ibid.

14. *People v. Kozlowski II*, cross-examination of J. Bradford McGee, transcript at 10057:20–23, 10058: 5, and 10058:8–17, April 7, 2005; and *People v. Kozlowski II*, direct examination of J. Bradford McGee, transcript at 09763:18–21, and 9765:18–25, April 6, 2005.

15. Floyd Norris, "Tyco Shares Plunge After Company Discloses S.E.C. Inquiry," *New York Times*, December 10, 1999.

16. Tyco International Ltd. Press Release, "Mark Belnick to Join Tyco International," August 27, 1998.

17. Steve Fishman, "The Convert," *New York Magazine*, June 2004, 2 and 11.

18. Mark Belnick, telephone interview with the author, May 14, 2013; and Steve Fishman, "The Convert," *New York Magazine*, June 2004, 2. When he was hired as outside counsel by Tyco in 1999, McLucas was with the law firm of Wilmer, Cutler, Pickering, Hale & Doore. Ibid.

19. Mark Belnick, telephone interview with the author, May 14, 2013; and "Witness Says Tyco Workers Told to Assist the S.E.C.," *New York Times,* June 3, 2004.
20. Dennis Kozlowski, telephone interview with the author, May 17, 2012; and Steve Fishman, "The Convert," *New York Magazine,* June 2004, 12.
21. Tyco International Ltd. Press Releases: "Tyco International Is Named Among 50 Best Performers by Business Week, Business Week Ranks Tyco Among Top Companies in Sales, Profits and Shareholder Return Performance," March 20, 2000; "Tyco International Reports 47 Percent Increase In Second Quarter Earnings Per Share, Strong Organic Growth Drives Earnings per Share Rise to 50 Cents from 34 Cents," April 18, 2000; "Tyco International Agrees to Acquire Thomas & Betts Electronic OEM Business, Acquisition Provides Excellent Strategic Fit, Will Be Immediately Accretive to Earnings," May 7, 2000; and "Tyco International to Acquire Mallinckrodt, Acquisition Will Have Immediate Positive Impact on Earnings, Strengthens Tyco Healthcare's Leading Positions in Medical Devices," June 28, 2000.
22. Herb Greenburg, "Does Tyco Play Accounting Games?" *Fortune,* April 1, 2002; and Dennis Kozlowski, telephone interview with the author, May 17, 2012.
23. Steve Fishman, "The Convert," *New York Magazine,* June 2004, 12; and "Witness Says Tyco Workers Told to Assist The S.E.C.," *New York Times,* June 3, 2004.
24. Herb Greenburg, "Does Tyco Play Accounting Games?" *Fortune,* April 1, 2002.
25. *People v. Kozlowski I,* Kozlowski defense counsel Stephen Kaufman, opening statements, transcript at 00110:23–25 and 00111:1–2, October 7, 2003; and Dennis Kozlowski, telephone interview with the author, May 17, 2012.
26. "Dennis Kozlowski of Tyco International: King Conglomerate," *Institutional Investor,* April 1, 2001.

CHAPTER EIGHT: THE GOOD OLD DAYS

1. Andy Bernard, *The Office,* "Finale," Season 9: Episode 23 (NBC), originally aired May 16, 2013.
2. "Corporate Background," *Tyco International Ltd.*
3. *State v. Kozlowski II,* direct examination of Dennis Kozlowski, transcript at 12052:22–25 and 12053:2, April 27, 2005.
4. Raytheon Company Press Release, "Kozlowski Elected To Raytheon Board of Directors," June 28, 1995.
5. "Raytheon Company (RTN)," *Hoover Company Profiles.*
6. Dennis Kozlowski, interview with the author, New York City, New York, June 23, 2012.
7. Dennis Kozlowski, interview with the author, New York City, New York, June 22, 2012.
8. Retention Agreement between Tyco International Ltd. and L. Dennis Kozlowski, (January 21, 2001).
9. Ibid. at Section (b)(i) as amended on August 1, 2001.
10. *Tyco International Ltd. v. L. Dennis Kozlowski,* U.S. District Court for the Southern District of NY, No. 02-7317, Complaint ¶6(g), September 17, 2002.
11. Retention Agreement between Tyco International Ltd. and L. Dennis Kozlowski, (January 21, 2001), Section 2(b).
12. TYC-NYSE, "Tyco Historical Prices, January 22, 2001" *Yahoo Finance.* Close price adjusted for splits and dividends.
13. Retention Agreement between Tyco International Ltd. and L. Dennis Kozlowski, (January 21, 2001), Section 3.
14. Ibid.
15. Dennis Kozlowski, interview with the author, New York City, New York, June 22, 2012. See also, Retention Agreement between Tyco International Ltd. and L. Dennis Kozlowski (January 21, 2001).
16. Retention Agreement between Tyco International Ltd. and L. Dennis Kozlowski, Section 5(3) and Section 1(a). If Kozlowski were to be terminated for Cause, "the Company shall have no further obligation to Executive other than the Accrued Benefits." Ibid.
17. "Economists Call It a Recession," CNNMoney, November 26, 2001; and Tyco International Ltd. Press Release, "Tyco to Acquire Scott Technologies, Acquisition Will Have Immediate Positive Impact on Tyco's Earnings, Broadens Product Line of Tyco Fire & Security Services and Provides Recurring Revenue Stream," February 5, 2001.
18. Joseph Weber, "The *Businessweek* 50–The Best Performers," *Businessweek,* March 23, 2001.
19. Tyco International Ltd. Press Release, "Tyco Is Top Pick in Reuters Survey of Larger Companies," April 27, 2001. The survey was conducted by Tempest Consultants and data was collected from 407 broker-analysts. Ibid.
20. William C. Symonds, "The Most Aggressive CEO," *Businessweek* (cover story), May 28, 2001, 68–77.
21. Sandra Kozlowski, interview with the author, New York City, New York, October 5, 2012.

22. "Jury Views Big Bash in Italy by Tyco Ex-CEO," *Los Angeles Times*, October 29, 2003.

23. Steve Dunleavy, "On Her First Prison Visit My Wife Said 'I Want a Divorce': Koz," *New York Post*, October 30, 2006.

24. *People v. Kozlowski I*, direct testimony of Tammy Cross, transcript at 07659:14–23, January 5, 2004.

25. Ibid.

26. Ibid. at 07659:18.

27. Ibid. at 07659:25–07660:1–6.

28. "Tyco Jury Hears of Ex-Chief's Bills," *New York Times*, January 6, 2004.

29. *People v. Kozlowski I*, direct testimony of Tammy Cross, transcript at 07655, January 5, 2004.

30. Dennis Kozlowski, interview with the author, New York City, New York, June 22, 2012.

31. *People v. Kozlowski I*, direct testimony of Barbara Jacques, transcript at 02107:16–25 and 02108:1–11, October 23, 2003.

32. See for example, Jerry Useem, "The Biggest Show No One's Watching MISTRESSES ON THE STAND! CRIMINALS IN THE ELEVATOR! PILES AND PILES OF REALLY BORING DOCUMENTS! HERE'S WHAT THE TRIAL OF FORMER TYCO CEO DENNIS KOZLOWSKI—NOW AT ITS MIDPOINT—IS REALLY LIKE.," *Fortune*, December 8, 2003.

33. *People v. Kozlowski I*, direct testimony of Barbara Jacques, transcript at 02164:13–25, 02165:1–9, 02174:3–12, 02175:2, 02168:10, 02174:3–12, 022217:10, 0222:20–21, 02220:22–25, 02221:1, and 02221:8–10, October 23, 2003.

34. "Jurors See Tape of Kozlowski's Party," CNN, October 29, 2003.

35. *People v. Kozlowski I*, direct testimony of Barbara Jacques, transcript at 02189:22–24, 02222:16–25 and 02223:1–16, October 27, 2003.

36. *People v. Kozlowski I*, cross-examination of Barbara Jacques, transcript at 02322:14–22, October 28, 2003.

37. Dennis Kozlowski, interview with the author, New York City, New York, June 22, 2012.

38. Ibid.

39. *People v. Kozlowski I*, cross-examination of Barbara Jacques, transcript at 02299:3–10, 02303:1–25, 02397:1–23, and 02314:1–18, October 28, 2003.

40. *People v. Kozlowski I*, direct testimony of Barbara Jacques, transcript at 02271:1–2, October 27, 2003.

41. Dennis Kozlowski, interview with the author, Marcy, New York, May 21, 2011.

42. *People v. Kozlowski I*, direct testimony of Barbara Jacques, transcript at 02256:5–9, October 27, 2003.

43. Dennis Kozlowski, interview with the author, Marcy, New York, October 16, 2011.

44. Ibid.

45. Ibid.

CHAPTER NINE: EXTRAORDINARY TIMES

1. 2001 Annual Report Tyco International Ltd.,"L. Dennis Kozlowski, Chairman of the Board of Directors and Chief Executive Officer, Letter to Shareholders," December 3, 2001, 15; and Roy Harris, "After Math," *CFO Magazine*, November 1, 2001.

2. Tyco International Ltd. Press Release, "Tyco Purchases the CIT Group, Inc.," June 1, 2001.

3. Dennis Kozlowski, letter to the author, February 19, 2011; Dennis Kozlowski, "10 Commandments," speech given at the Premier CEO Forum, September 17, 1999; and Dennis Kozlowski, interview with the author, New York City, New York, June 22, 2012.

4. Dennis Kozlowski, interview with the author, New York City, New York, June 22, 2012; and Reuters, "Tyco in $1.4-Billion Deal for Kendall International," *Los Angeles Times*, July 15, 1994.

5. Dennis Kozlowski, letter to the author, February 18, 2011.

6. Robin M. Grugal and Marilyn Alva, "Breaking News: Tyco Makes Big Move with CIT Acquisition," *Investors' Business Daily*, March 14, 2001.

7. National Commission on Terrorist Attacks Upon the United States, "The 9/11 Commission Report," July 22, 2004.

8. Dennis Kozlowski, interview with the author, New York City, New York, June 22, 2012; and Roy Harris, "After Math," *CFO Magazine*, November 1, 2001.

9. Suraj Srinivasan and Aledo Sesia, "The Crisis at Tyco—A Director's Perspective," *Harvard Business School*, Case No. 9-111-035, June 2, 2011, 3; Dennis Kozlowski, letter to the author, March 10, 2011; and "The Top 25 Managers of the Year"(Cover Story), *Businessweek*, January 13, 2002.

10. See for example, Len Costa, "The Rise of Compliance Man," *Slate*, May 26, 2004. See also, Alton B. Harris and Andrea S. Kramer, "Corporate Governance: Pre-Enron, Post-Enron," in *Corporate Aftershock: The Public Policy Lessons from the Collapse of Enron and Other Major Corporations*, ed. Christopher L. Culp and William A. Niskanen (Hoboken, NJ: John Wiley & Sons, 2003).

11. Dennis Kozlowski, letter to the author, March 10, 2011.

CHAPTER TEN: YOU SAY YOU WANT A RESOLUTION

1. Tyco International Ltd., "Minutes of a Special Meeting of the Board of Directors," Tuckers Town, Bermuda, May 12, 1999, 8.
2. Ibid. at 9. Note that the minutes include only male pronouns when referring to Directors. The Tyco Board of Directors in the late 1990s could be accurately described as an old boys' club.
3. Ibid.
4. Ibid. at 9–10.
5. Dennis Kozlowski, interview with the author, New York City, New York, June 22, 2012. See also *People v. Kozlowski II,* cross-examination of Stephen Foss, transcript at 05310:13–15, March 2, 2005.
6. Associated Press, "Apparent Conflicts of Interest with Tyco Board Raise Eyebrows," July 7, 2002.
7. Rob Boostrom, "Tyco International—Leadership Crisis," Daniels Fund Ethics Initiative, University of New Mexico, 2011, 3; and Dennis Kozlowski, interview with the author, New York City, New York, June 22, 2012.
8. Sarbanes-Oxley Act, Section 301, Public Law 107-204, July 30, 2002. (Emphasis added.)
9. *People v. Kozlowski II,* cross-examination of Stephen Foss, transcript at 05334:24–25 and 05335:1–3, March 3, 2005.
10. Ibid. at 05335:9–17.
11. Ibid. at 05335:25 and 05336:1–5. (Emphasis added.)
12. Werner Güth, Rolf Schmittberger, and Bernd Schwarze, "An Experimental Analysis of Ultimatum Bargaining," *Journal of Economic Behavior and Organization,* Vol. 3, No. 4 (1984), 367. See also, Adam Grant, *Give and Take* (New York, NY: Viking, 2013). Professor Grant relied on research conducted by Princeton psychologist Daniel Kahneman. See, Daniel Kahneman, Jack L. Knetsch, and Richard H. Thaler, "Fairness and the Assumptions of Economics," *Journal of Business,* (1986), 59.
13. Ibid. at 33.

CHAPTER ELEVEN: WHEN THE CIT HIT THE FAN

1. *People v. Kozlowski II,* direct examination of Frank Walsh, transcript at 02399:3, 02401:25, and 02402:1, February 3, 2005.
2. Suraj Srinivasan and Aldo Sesia, "The Crisis at Tyco—A Director's Perspective," *Harvard Business School,* Case No. 9-111-035, June 2, 2011, 1.
3. *Tyco International Ltd. v. Frank E. Walsh, Jr.,* 751 F.Supp.2d 606 (S.D.N.Y 2010).
4. Dennis Kozlowski, interview with the author, New York City, New York, June 22, 2012. See also, Suraj Srinivasan and Aldo Sesia, "The Crisis at Tyco—A Director's Perspective," *Harvard Business School,* Case No. 9-111-035, June 2, 2011.
5. Dennis Kozlowski, interview with the author, New York City, New York, June 22, 2012.
6. Ibid.
7. *People v. Kozlowski II,* direct examination of Frank Walsh, transcript at 02519:23–25 and 02520:1–18, February 3, 2005.
8. Ibid. at 02519:2–10.
9. Ibid. at 02522:18–25, 02523:1–11, and 02524:1–21.
10. *People v. Kozlowski II,* direct examination of Dennis Kozlowski, transcript at 12175:20–25 and 12176:2–7, April 27, 2005.
11. Ibid. at 12176:16–25 and 12177:2.
12. *People v. Kozlowski II,* direct examination of Frank Walsh, transcript at 02528:14–25 and 02529:1–9, February 3, 2005.
13. Special Meeting of the Tyco International Ltd. Board of Directors, "Meeting Minutes," Pembroke, Bermuda, March 12, 2001.
14. *People v. Kozlowski II,* direct examination of Frank Walsh, transcript at 02547:15–21, February 3, 2005.
15. See, U.S Securities and Exchange Commission, "Form S-4."
16. *People v. Kozlowski II,* direct examination of Frank Walsh, transcript at 02543:9, 02546:21–15, 02547:1, 02549:10, and 02550:11–15, February 3, 2005.
17. *Tyco International Ltd. v. Frank E. Walsh, Jr.,* 751 F. Supp.2d 606, 616 (S.D.N.Y 2010).
18. Dennis Kozlowski, interview with the author, New York City, New York, June 22, 2012.
19. *People v. Kozlowski II,* direct examination of Frank Walsh, transcript at 02566:1–5, February 3, 2005.
20. Dennis Kozlowski, interview with the author, New York City, New York, June 22, 2012.

21. Matt Brian, "Investment Banker Demands 1% of Apple's $390m Anobit Acquisition in Finder's Fee Lawsuit," *TNW*, May 15, 2012. See also, "The Facts on Finder's Fees," *Businessweek*, September 25, 2005.
22. Frank Walsh Jr., Invoice to Tyco International Ltd., RE: The CIT Group Inc. Acquisition, July 18, 2001.
23. Frank E. Walsh, letter to Mark H. Swartz, Tyco International U.S.A., July 25, 2001.
24. Susan Soldivieri, Community Foundation of New Jersey, letter to Michael Robinson, Tyco International, July 31, 2001.
25. *People v. Kozlowski II*, direct examination of Frank Walsh, transcript at 02572:5–8, February 3, 2005; and *People v. Kozlowski II*, direct examination of Dennis Kozlowski, transcript at 12194:15–17, 12194:18–25, and 12195:2–11, April 27, 2005. (Emphasis added.)
26. Robert A. G. Monks, telephone interview with the author, May 7, 2013.
27. *People v. Kozlowski II*, direct examination of J. Bradford McGee, transcript at 10009:19–25, 10010:2–8, and 10010:9–24, April 7, 2005.
28. *People v. Kozlowski II*, direct examination of Frank Walsh, transcript at 02584:4–11, February 3, 2005.
29. Tyco International Ltd., Proxy Statement Fiscal Year End 2001, January 28, 2002, 19.
30. *People v. Kozlowski II*, direct examination of John Fort, transcript at 01857:8–17, January 31, 2005.
31. Ibid. at 01859:3–11 and 01860:24–25.
32. Dennis Kozlowski, interview with the author, New York City, New York, June 22, 2012.
33. Srinivasan and Aldo Sesia, "The Crisis at Tyco—A Director's Perspective," *Harvard Business School*, Case No. 9-111-035 (June 2, 2011), 4.
34. *People v. Kozlowski II*, cross-examination of Stephen Foss, transcript at 05295:15–17, March 2, 2005. See also, *Tyco International Ltd. v. Frank E. Walsh, Jr.*, 751 F.Supp.2d 606, fn 3 (S.D.N.Y 2010).
35. *People v. Kozlowski II*, direct examination of John Fort, transcript at 01852:18–25 and 01853:1–5, January 31, 2005.
36. Dennis Kozlowski, interview with the author, New York City, New York, June 22, 2012.
37. *Tyco International Ltd. v. Frank E. Walsh, Jr.*, 751 F.Supp.2d 606, 619.
38. Suraj Srinivasan and Aldo Sesia, "The Crisis at TycoA Director's Perspective," *Harvard Business School*, Case No. 9-111-035 (June 2, 2011), 4. See also, *People v. Kozlowski II*, cross-examination of Stephen Foss, transcript at 05330:9–11, March 2, 2005.
39. Suraj Srinivasan and Aldo Sesia, "The Crisis at Tyco—A Director's Perspective," *Harvard Business School*, Case No. 9-111-035 (June 2, 2011), 3.
40. TYC prices adjusted for splits and dividends
41. *People v. Kozlowski II*, direct examination of John Fort, transcript at 01850:24–25, 01851:1–2, 01855:8–9, 01852:18–25, and 01853:1–5. See also, People's Exhibit 29-C, Tyco International Ltd. Bye-laws, Sections 64(2) and 64(7), March 27, 2001.
42. Ibid. at Section 64(8).
43. Special Meeting of the Tyco International Ltd. Board of Directors, "Meeting Minutes," Pembroke, Bermuda, March 12, 2001.
44. Ibid.
45. Dennis Kozlowski, interview with the author, Marcy, New York, May 21, 2011.

CHAPTER 12: "OH GOD, WHAT NOW?"

1. "Global Files for Bankruptcy," CNNMoney, January 28, 2002.
2. Dennis Kozlowski, interview with the author, New York City, New York, June 23, 2012.
3. *People v. Kozlowski II*, cross-examination of J. Bradford McGee, transcript at 09717, 10059:14–24, 10060:18–25, 10061:2–3, 10061:5, and 10062:7–18, April 7, 2005.
4. Dennis Kozlowski, interview with the author, New York City, New York, June 22, 2012.
5. J. Bradford McGee, telephone interview with the author, July 12, 2013.
6. Mark Maremont, "Tyco Reveals $8 Billion in Deals Made Recently, but Not Disclosed," *Wall Street Journal*, February 4, 2002; Dennis Kozlowski, interview with the author, New York City, New York, June 22, 2012; and "Tyco Spent $8B in Deals," CNNMoney, February 4, 2002.
7. Dennis Kozlowski, interview with the author, New York City, New York, June 22, 2012.
8. Mark Maremont, "Tyco Reveals $8 Billion in Deals Made Recently, but Not Disclosed," *Wall Street Journal*, February 4, 2002.
9. Mark H. Swartz and Michele E. Kearns, letter to the editor of *Wall Street Journal*, February 4, 2002.
10. *In Re Tyco International Ltd. Securities Litigation*, No. 02-1335-B (D.N.H. 2002).
11. Cal Fussman, "Matt Lauer: What I've Learned," *Esquire*, October 2013.

12. "S&P Lowers Tyco Debt Rating," *Businessweek*, February 3, 2002; and Andrew Ross Sorkin and Alex Berenson, "Doubts Voiced on How Much a Tyco Spinoff Might Raise," *New York Times*, April 27, 2002.
13. Tyco International Ltd. Press Release, "Tyco is Ranked Number One Performing Company by BusinessWeek," March 28, 2001.
14. Andrew Ross Sorkin and Alex Berenson, "Doubts Voiced on How Much a Tyco Spinoff Might Raise," *New York Times*, April 27, 2002.
15. *People v. Kozlowski II*, direct examination of Frank Walsh, transcript at 02516:8–15, 02517:1–22, 02517:21–22, 02517:23–25 and 02518:1–7, February 3, 2005.
16. *People v. Kozlowski I*, cross-examination of Richard Bodman, transcript at 01284:25 and 012085:2, October 20, 2003.
17. Dennis Kozlowski, interview with the author, New York City, New York, June 22, 2012.
18. Dennis Kozlowski, interview with the author, June 22, 2012. Dennis Kozlowski remained CEO and Chairman for nearly five months after the Board refused to accept his resignation on January 16, 2002. See also *People v. Kozlowski I*, cross-examination of Richard Bodman, transcript at 01284:25 and 012085:2, October 20, 2003.
19. *Tyco International Ltd. v. Frank E. Walsh, Jr.*, 751 F.Supp.2d 606, 612 (S.D.N.Y 2010). See also, "Tyco Officer Tells of Board Reaction to Fee," *New York Times*, February 18, 2004. During his testimony in the criminal trials, Mark Swartz explained to the jury that Kozlowski told Directors at the meeting on January 16, 2002 that he would resign if they thought he had done wrong regarding Mr. Walsh. Swartz said all of the Directors expressed support for Kozlowski. Ibid.
20. Peter Slusser, letter to Dennis Kozlowski, January 28, 2002.
21. Peter Slusser, letter to Dennis Kozlowski, February 6, 2002.
22. Peter Slusser, letter to Dennis Kozlowski and Mark Swartz, February 19, 2002.
23. Special Meeting of the Board of Directors Tyco International Ltd., "Meeting Minutes," Pembroke, Bermuda, February 20–21, 2002.
24. Ibid.
25. Peter Slusser, letter to Dennis Kozlowski, May 8, 2002.
26. *People v. Kozlowski I*, cross-examination of Richard Bodman, transcript at 01284:24–25, 012085:1–25, and 01286:1–2, October 20, 2003.
27. *Tyco International Ltd. v. Frank E. Walsh, Jr.*, 751 F.Supp.2d 606 (S.D.N.Y 2010).
28. *People v. Kozlowski I*, cross-examination of Richard Bodman, transcript at 01287:7–9, 01291:13–18, 01292:14–25, and 01293:1–3, October 20, 2003.
29. Ibid.
30. Retention Agreement between Tyco International Ltd. and L. Dennis Kozlowski, January 21, 2001, Sections 1(a) and 5(3).
31. *People v. Kozlowski I*, cross-examination of Richard Bodman, transcript at 01293:4–14, October 20, 2003.
32. U.S. Securities and Exchange Commission Press Release 2002-177, "SEC Sues Former Tyco Director and Chairman of Compensation Committee Frank E. Walsh Jr. for Hiding $20 Million Payment from Shareholders," December 17, 2002.
33. *Tyco International Ltd. v. Frank E. Walsh, Jr.*, 751 F.Supp.2d 606, 616 (S.D.N.Y 2010).
34. Andrew Ross Sorkin, "Tyco Figure Pays $22.5 Million in Guilty Plea," *New York Times*, December 18, 2002.
35. Ibid.
36. *Tyco International Ltd. v. Frank E. Walsh, Jr.*, 751 F.Supp.2d 606 (S.D.N.Y 2010).
37. Ibid. at 612.
38. Ibid.
39. Ibid. at 622-623.
40. Ibid. at 623.
41. Ibid. at 624.
42. Ibid. at 627.

PART THREE: RING AROUND THE WHITE-COLLAR OF CRIMINAL JUSTICE

1. Robert Morgenthau, interview with the author, New York City, New York, May 22, 2013.

CHAPTER THIRTEEN: "*POUR ENCOURAGER LES AUTRES*"

1. Dennis Kozlowski, telephone interview with the author, June 7, 2012; *People v. Kozlowski II*, direct examination of Christina Berry, transcript at 11028:9–24, April 18, 2005; and Dennis Kozlowski, interview with the author, Marcy, New York. May 21, 2011. "Mr. Koch, a serious collector of mostly Impressionist and modern art, is a shareholder of Fine Collections Management."

Carol Vogel, "Novice Collectors Are Magnets for Eager Art Advisers," *New York Times*, June 20, 2002.

2. *People v. Kozlowski II*, direct examination of Christina Berry, transcript at 11043:11–15, 11050:10–14, 11033:1–10, 11057:20–25, and 11058:2, April 18, 2005; Carol Vogel, "Novice Collectors Are Magnets for Eager Art Advisers," *New York Times*, June 20, 2002; and *People v. Kozlowski II*, motion to dismiss, transcript at 11956:12–25, 11957:2–25, and 11958:2–10, April 27, 2005.

3. *People v. Kozlowski II*, direct examination of Dennis Kozlowski, transcript at 12270:20–25 and 12271:2–18, April 28, 2005.

4. Ibid. at 12271:19–25 and 12272:2–15.

5. Dennis Kozlowski, interview with the author, Marcy, New York, May 21, 2011.

6. Peter Hossli, "I Am Innocent," Hossli.com, May 22, 2009. "Pride goeth before a fall" is a common saying derived from verses found in the book of Proverbs in the Bible. "Pride goeth before destruction, and a haughty spirit before a fall. Better it is to be of an humble spirit with the lowly, than to divide the spoil with the proud." Proverbs 16:18–19, King James Version.

7. New York State Tax Law Section 1817(c)(2)(a).

8. New York State Department of Taxation and Finance, "Tax Bulletin ST-913 (TB-ST-913)—Use Tax for Individuals (including Estates and Trusts)," June 17, 2010.

9. New York State Tax Law, Section 1817(c)(2)(a).

10. Tyco International Ltd. Press Release, "Tyco Retains Industrial Businesses, Plans 100% Public Offering of CIT–Letter Sent to Shareholders Detailing Rationale," April 25, 2002.

11. Ibid.

12. Ibid.

13. Brad McGee, telephone interview with the author, July 12, 2013.

14. TYC close price adjusted for dividends and splits.

15. Dennis Kozlowski, interview with the author, New York City, New York, June 22, 2012.

16. Ibid.

17. Dennis Kozlowski, telephone interview with the author, June 7, 2012.

18. Dennis Kozlowski, interview with the author, New York City, New York, June 22, 2012.

19. Ibid.

20. *People v. Kozlowski*, New York State Supreme Court, New York County, Indictment #3485-02 (order entered June 14, 2004).

21. Ibid.

22. Mike Godfrey, "Dennis Kozlowski Indicted On Sales Tax Fraud Charges," Tax-News.com, June 6, 2002. "*Pour encourager les autres*" is from Voltaire's *Candide* and refers to the execution of Admiral the Honorable John Byng in Portsmouth, England, on March 3, 1757. Voltaire, *Candide*, ch. 23 (1759).

23. Voltaire, *Candide*, 111, trans. John Butt (New York, NY: Penguin 1947).

24. David Armstrong, "Former Tyco Executive Moves To Dismiss Tax-Evasion Charges," *Wall Street Journal*, August 29, 2002. See also, Carol Vogel, "Novice Collectors Are Magnets for Eager Art Advisers," *New York Times*, June 20, 2002.

25. Dennis Kozlowski, interview with the author, New York City, New York, June 22, 2012.

26. Peter Hossli, "I Am Innocent," Hossli.com, May 22, 2009.

27. Robert Morgenthau, interview with the author, May 22, 2013.

28. New York State Tax Law, Section 1817(c)(2)(a).

29. *People v. Kozlowski II*, direct examination of Christina Berry, transcript at 11051:11–15, 11051:25, and 11052:2, April 18, 2005.

30. Ibid.

31. Dennis Kozlowski, interview with the author, New York City, New York, June 22, 2012.

32. Ibid.

33. *People v. Kozlowski*, New York State Supreme Court, New York County, Indictment #3485-02 (order entered June 14, 2004).

34. John J. Tigue Jr. and Jeremy H. Temkin, "Limitations on State Tax Prosecutions," *New York Law Journal*, Vol. 232, No. 54 (September 16, 2004); and New York State Tax Law Section 1817(c)(2)(a).

35. Suraj Srinivasan and Aldo Sesia, "The Crisis at Tyco—A Director's Perspective," *Harvard Business School*, Case No. 9-111-035, June 2, 2011, 5.

36. Ibid.

37. Dennis Kozlowski, interview with the author, New York City, New York, June 22, 2012.

38. Ibid.

39. *People v. Kozlowski II*, direct examination of John Fort, transcript at 01867:10–25, January 31, 2005.

40. Dennis Kozlowski, interview with the author, New York City, New York, June 22, 2012.

41. Ibid.

242   TAKING DOWN THE LION
42. PRNewswire, "Dennis Kozlowski Resigns from Raytheon's Board," June 3, 2002.
43. Pierce Graham-Jones, "Trustee Resigns Kozlowski Credited for Tyco Donation to Middlebury," *Middlebury* (VT) *Campus*, September 25, 2002. Director of Public Affairs Phil Benoit said, "Dennis Kozlowski's association with Middlebury College as a parent, as a donor and as a trustee has benefited this institution in many ways. As he leaves the Board of Trustees, we are very grateful for his many positive contributions." Ibid.
44. Dennis Kozlowski, telephone interview with the author, June 7, 2012.

CHAPTER FOURTEEN: INTERNAL INVESTIGATION

1. Simeon Messan Adagba, "Until the lion has his or her own storyteller, the hunter will always have the best part of the story," African Proverb of the Month (April 2006).
2. Adapted from stories and proverbs common to a number of African cultures. See "Proverbs with Historians." See also "The Old Man and His Grandson," *Lion Stories & Folklore*.
3. Dennis Kozlowski, interview with the author, Marcy, New York, May 21, 2011.
4. Dennis Kozlowski, interview with the author, New York City, New York, June 23, 2012; and Retention Agreement, Tyco International Ltd. and L. Dennis Kozlowski, Sections 1(a), 5(a), 5(b), 5(c), (12), (13), (15), and (18), January 22, 2001.
5. Tyco International Ltd. Press Release, "John Fort Assumes Primary Executive Responsibility for Tyco," June 3, 2002.
6. Suraj Srinivasn and Aldo Sesia, "The Crisis at Tyco—A Director's Perspective," *Harvard Business School*, Case No. 9-111-035, June 2, 2011, 4.
7. Ibid.
8. *People v. Kozlowski II*, direct examination of John Fort, transcript at 01867:10–25, January 31, 2005.
9. Ibid. at 01867:10–25 and 01880:1–7.
10. *Tyco v. Walsh*, 751 F.Supp.2d 606, 629 (S.D.N.Y. 2010).
11. Boies, Schiller & Flexner, "David Boies."
12. Joshua Berman, telephone interview with the author, August 8, 2013.
13. Karen Donovan, *v. Goliath: The Trials of David Boies*, (New York, NY: Vintage, 2005), 336–337.
14. *Tyco v. Walsh*, 751 F.Supp.2d 606, 630. (S.D.N.Y. 2010).
15. Steve Fishman, "The Convert," *New York Magazine* June 2004, 15-16.
16. Ibid.
17. Ibid.
18. *Tyco v. Walsh*, 751 F.Supp.2d 606 (S.D.N.Y. 2010).
19. Joann S. Lublin, "Tyco Holders Plan Proxy Fight to Oust Its Current Directors," *Wall Street Journal*, August 21, 2002. See also, Nancy Dillon, "Tyco board may call it quits; Resignation talk gives stock big lift," *New York Daily News*, August 22, 2002.
20. *People v. Kozlowski II*, direct examination of Stephen Foss, transcript at 05281:19–22, March 2, 2005.
21. Ibid. at 05282:11–18. See also, ibid. at Defense Exhibit A430.
22. Andrew Ross Sorkin and Jonathan D. Glater, "Some Tyco Board Members Knew of Pay Packages," *New York Times*, September 23, 2002.
23. *People v. Kozlowski II*, direct examination of Stephen Foss, transcript at 05283:18, March 2, 2005.
24. Andrew Ross Sorkin and Jonathan D. Glater, "Some Tyco Board Members Knew of Pay Packages," *New York Times*, September 23, 2002.
25. Tyco International Ltd. Press Release, "Tyco Appoints Edward D. Breen Chairman and Chief Executive Officer," July 25, 2002.
26. TYC price adjusted for splits and dividends.
27. Joann S. Lublin, "Tyco Holders Plan Proxy Fight To Oust Its Current Directors," *Wall Street Journal*, August 21, 2002.
28. Ibid.
29. Nancy Dillon, "Tyco board may call it quits; Resignation talk gives stock big lift," *New York Daily News*, August 22, 2002.
30. Suraj Srinivasn and Aldo Sesia, "The Crisis at Tyco—A Director's Perspective," *Harvard Business School*, Case No. 9-111-035 (June 2, 2011), 7.
31. Dennis Kozlowski, interview with the author, New York City, New York, June 23, 2012.
32. Ibid.
33. Dennis Kozlowski, interview with the author, Marcy, New York, May 21, 2011.
34. Suraj Srinivasn and Aldo Sesia, "The Crisis at Tyco—A Director's Perspective," *Harvard Business School*, Case No. 9-111-035 (June 2, 2011), 7.
35. Dennis Kozlowski, interview with the author, New York City, New York, June 23, 2012.

36. Mark Maremont and Laurie P. Cohen, "Executive Privilege: How Tyco's CEO Enriched Himself—Mr. Kozlowski, Ex-Chief, Got Secret Loans, Spent Firm's Cash as His Own—A $6,000 Shower Curtain," *Wall Street Journal,* August 7, 2002.
37. Ibid.
38. Ibid.
39. Dennis Kozlowski, interview with the author, New York City, New York, June 23, 2012.
40. Mark Maremont and Laurie P. Cohen, "Executive Privilege: Tyco's CEO Enriched Himself—Mr. Kozlowski, Ex-Chief, Got Secret Loans, Spent Firm's Cash as His Own—A $6,000 Shower Curtain." *Wall Street Journal,* August 7, 2002.
41. Ibid. (Emphasis added.)
42. Ibid.
43. Jen Wieczner, "Your Company Wants to Make You Healthy," *Wall Street Journal,* April 8, 2013.
44. Mark Maremont and Laurie Cohen, "Executive Privilege: How Tyco's CEO Enriched Himself—Mr. Kozlowski, Ex-Chief, Got Secret Loans, Spent Firm's Cash as His Own—A $6,000 Shower Curtain." *Wall Street Journal,* August 7, 2002
45. Mark Maremont, interview with John Ydstie, "Former Tyco Chief," NPR, *All Things Considered,* August 7, 2002.
46. TYC volume and adjusted close on the dates before, of, and after the August 7, 2002, *WSJ* article:

Date	Volume	TYC adjusted close
August 6, 2002	4,660,700	17.98
August 7, 2002	5,402,000	17.21
August 8, 2002	4,483,400	17.05

47. *People v. Kozlowski II,* direct examination Mark H. Swartz, transcript at 13664:2–9, May 10, 2005.
48. Ibid. at 13666:9–14.
49. Agreement between Mark H. Swartz and Tyco International Ltd, August 1, 2002.
50. *People v. Kozlowski II,* direct examination Mark H. Swartz, transcript at 13667–13668, and at 13689:10–24, May 10, 2005.
51. Andrew Longstreth, "Whose Side Is He On," *The American Lawyer* (February 2005).
52. *People v. Kozlowski II,* cross-examination of David Boies, transcript at 10256:2–6 and 10192:4–6, April 11, 2005.
53. Ibid. at 10257:11.
54. *People v. Kozlowski and Swartz,* Indictment #5259-02, September 12, 2002.
55. Christo Lassiter, interview with the author, Cincinnati, Ohio, May 13, 2013.
56. Terry Carter, "The Boss," *ABA Journal,* June 1, 2010.

CHAPTER FIFTEEN: *PEOPLE V. KOZLOWSKI I*

1. Dennis Kozlowski, telephone interview with the author, June 7, 2012.
2. Ibid.
3. CNNMoney, "Three Tyco Execs Indicted for Fraud," September 12, 2002.
4. Ibid.
5. Dennis Kozlowski, telephone interview with the author, June 7, 2012. Kozlowski's assets were frozen under an order issued on September 10, 2002. *Robert M. Morgenthau v. L. Dennis Kozlowski and Mark H. Swartz,* New York State Supreme Court, New York County, #402698-02, September 10, 2002.
6. Dennis Kozlowski, telephone interview with the author, June 7, 2012.
7. Ibid.
8. Ibid.
9. Dennis Kozlowski, interview with the author, Marcy, New York, May 21, 2011.
10. Dennis Kozlowski, letter to the author, March 10, 2011.
11. CNNMoney, "Three Tyco Execs Indicted for Fraud."
12. Dennis Kozlowski, interview with the author, New York City, New York, June 23, 2012. See also, Brad McGee, telephone interview with the author, May 30, 2013.
13. *People v. Kozlowski II,* cross-examination of Michael Robinson, transcript at 07356:11–25, March 21, 2005.
14. *People v. Kozlowski I,* transcript at 00001, September 29, 2003.
15. Dennis Kozlowski, telephone interview with the author, May 10, 2012; and *People v. Kozlowski I,* transcript at 00001, October 7, 2003.
16. *People v. Kozlowski I,* Supreme Court Justice Obus charge to the jury, transcript at 14103:22–25–14104:1–7, March 18, 2004.
17. Ibid. at 00023:3–25, 00024:1–25, and 00025:1–25.
18. Ibid. at 00102:20–25.

19. Ibid. at 00108:8–10.
20. Dennis Kozlowski's younger sister Joyce, email to the author, April 30, 2013.
21. Dennis Kozlowski, telephone interview with the author, June 7, 2012.
22. *People v. Kozlowski I,* transcript at 00108:10–25 and 00109:1, October 7, 2003.
23. Tyco International Ltd., "Compensation Committee Benefit Plans" (March 1995).
24. Ibid. at Appendix 2.
25. Ibid.
26. *People v. Kozlowski I,* transcript at 00109:15–25, 00110:1–25, and 00111: 1–25, October 7, 2003.
27. Ibid.
28. Ibid. at 00131:10–25 and 00132:1–3.
29. *People v. Kozlowski I,* cross-examination of Brian Moroze, transcript at 018975:1–25, October 22, 2003.
30. Ibid. at 02037:8–25 and 02038:1–23.
31. Ibid. at 02053:9–25 and 02054:1–23.
32. Ibid. at 02069:9–11.
33. Walter Hamilton, "Ex-Tyco Chief's Lavish Lifestyle Is Defended," *Los Angeles Times,* March 16, 2004.
34. Christo Lassiter, interview with the author, Cincinnati, Ohio, May 13, 2013.
35. *People v. Kozlowski I,* direct examination of David Boies, transcript at 12799:20–25 and 12800:1–8, March 1, 2004.
36. *People v. Kozlowski I,* Supreme Court Justice Obus charge to the jury, transcript at 14096:20–24, 14097:2–9, 14098:1–25, 14099:1–7, 14103:22–25, and 14104:1–7, March 18, 2003. (Emphasis added.)
37. Greg Farrell, "Stewart Convicted of Four Felonies," *USA Today,* March 5, 2004.
38. Ibid.
39. Andrew Ross Sorkin, "The Tyco Mistrial: The Overview: Tyco Trial Ended as a Juror Cites Outside Pressure," *New York Times,* April 3, 2004.
40. Kathleen F. Brickey, "From Boardroom to Courtroom to Newsroom: The Media and the Corporate Governance Scandals," 22 *Iowa Journal of Corporate Law* 625 (Spring 2008).
41. Dennis Kozlowski, interview with the author, Marcy, New York, May 21, 2011.
42. Michael D. Sorkin, "Kathleen Brickey Dies; Pioneering Law School Professor," *St. Louis Post-Dispatch,* June 21, 2013; and David Carr, "The Tyco Mistrial: The Media; Some Critics Say Naming a Juror Went Too Far," *New York Times,* April 3, 2004.
43. Kathleen F. Brickey, "From Boardroom to Courtroom to Newsroom: The Media and the Corporate Governance Scandals," 22 *Iowa Journal Corporate Law* 625 (Spring 2008).
44. Ibid. at 625 and 626.
45. Ibid. at 631 and 652-653.
46. Andrew Ross Sorkin, "The Tyco Mistrial: The Overview: Tyco Trial Ended as a Juror Cites Outside Pressure," *New York Times,* April 3, 2004.

CHAPTER SIXTEEN: *PEOPLE V. KOZLOWSKI II*

1. Dennis Kozlowski, telephone interview with the author, June 9, 2012.
2. Ibid.
3. Ibid.
4. Ibid.
5. *U.S. v. Gonzales-Lopez,* 548 U.S. 140 (2006).
6. *People v. Kozlowski II,* jury selection, transcript at 01565:17–25 and 01566:1–4, January 26, 2005.
7. *People v. Kozlowski II,* jury selection, transcript at 01023:20–25, January 22, 2005.
8. Ibid. at 01024:2–17.
9. Dennis Kozlowski, telephone interview with the author, June 9, 2012.
10. Blaine Harden, "Image Spinner at the Center of a Web; Rubenstein, 'Dean of Damage Control' for New York's Powerful," *New York Times,* September 30, 1999.
11. Dennis Kozlowski, telephone interview with the author, June 9, 2012.
12. Christo Lassiter, "The O.J. Simpson Verdict: A Lesson in Black and White," 1 *Michigan Journal of Race & Law* 69 (Winter 1996), 74–75. (Emphasis added.)
13. Christo Lassiter, interview with the author, Cincinnati, Ohio, May 13, 2013.
14. Dennis Kozlowski, telephone interview with the author, June 9, 2012.
15. *People v. Kozlowski II,* transcript at 00010:11–22, January 18, 2005.
16. *People v. Rosario,* 9 N.Y.2d 286 (1961).
17. *Brady v. Maryland,* 373 U.S. 83 (U.S. 1963).
18. "Under the Influence," *Law & Order,* Episode 8.11, NBC, created by Dick Wolf, directed by Adam Davidson, written by Rene Balcer, first broadcast January 7, 1998.

NOTES   245

19. Robert Morgenthau, interview with the author, New York City, New York, May 22, 2013.
20. Terry Carter, "The Boss," *ABA Journal* (cover story), June 1, 2010.
21. Kevin McCoy, "Feared D.A. Relishes Taking Down Hotshots," *USA Today,* June 23, 2002.
22. Robert A. G. Monks, telephone interview with the author, May 7, 2013.
23. Timothy L. O'Brien, "The Tyco Mistrial: the Prosecutor; White-Collar Crime Crusader Gets Chance to Refine a Case," *New York Times,* April 3, 2004.
24. Dennis Kozlowski, telephone interview with the author, June 9, 2012.
25. *People v. Kozlowski II,* transcript at 00002:23–25, January 18, 2005.
26. Andrew Ross Sorkin, "Ex Tyco Chief Is Humbled, but Unbowed," *New York Times,* January 16, 2005.
27. *People v. Kozlowski II,* transcript at 00002:23–25, January 18, 2005.
28. Ibid. at 00003:3–25 and 00004:1–16.
29. Ibid. at 00004:20–25 and 00005:1–25.
30. Ibid. at 00006:8–25 and 00007:1–8.
31. Ibid. at 00018:12–15.
32. Ibid. at 00678:20–15 and 00679:1–8, January 20, 2005.
33. Ibid.
34. Dennis Kozlowski, telephone interview with the author, June 9, 2012.
35. Ibid.
36. Ibid.
37. Ibid.
38. *People v. Kozlowski II,* transcript at 00025:14–17, January 18, 2005.
39. Dennis Kozlowski, interview with the author, New York City, New York, June 22, 2012; and Sandra Kozlowski, interview with the author, New York City, New York, October 16, 2012.
40. *People v. Kozlowski II,* transcript at 00026:21–25, 00027:1–4, 00027:23–25, 00028:1–17, and 00096:6–9, January 18, 2005.
41. Ibid. at 00166:6–15 and 00257:16–19.
42. Dennis Kozlowski, telephone interview with the author, June 9, 2012.
43. Isaac Rosenthal, interview with the author, New York City, New York, May 23, 2013.
44. *People v. Kozlowski II,* prosecution opening statement, transcript at 01446:5–9, January 26, 2005.
45. Ibid. at 01451:9–18.
46. Ibid. at 01452:16–21.
47. *People v. Kozlowski II,* cross-examination of Patricia Prue, transcript at 03431:2–24, February 14, 2005.
48. *People v. Kozlowski II,* prosecution opening statement, transcript at 01452:7–11, January 26, 2005.
49. ABA Business Law Section Corporate Law Committee, "Section 2," *ABA Corporate Director's Guidebook,* 6th ed. (American Bar Association, 2012).
50. Dennis Kozlowski, interview with the author, New York City, New York, June 23, 2012.
51. Ibid.
52. *People v. Kozlowski II,* prosecution opening statement, transcript at 01452:7–11. January 26, 2005.
53. Ibid. at 01446:19–22.
54. Ibid. at 01227:17–25 and 01448:1–18.
55. Ibid. at 01449:1–9.
56. Andrew Ross Sorkin and Jonathan D. Glater, "Some Tyco Board Members Knew of Pay Packages, Records Show," *New York Times,* September 23, 2002.
57. Robert Morgenthau, interview with the author, New York City, New York, May 22, 2013.
58. *People v. Kozlowski II,* direct examination of Patricia Prue, transcript at 03003:16–19, 03008:20–25, and 03019:1–14, February 9, 2005.
59. *People v. Kozlowski II,* cross-examination of Frank Walsh, transcript at 02437:8–25 and 02935:4–14, February 7, 2005.
60. *People v. Kozlowski II,* direct examination of Patricia Prue, transcript at 03020:7–25, 03021:1–12, and 03022:3–11, February 9, 2005.
61. Ibid. at 03034:12–25 and 03035:1–13.
62. Ibid. at 03012:9–22.
63. *People v. Kozlowski II,* cross-examination of Frank Walsh, transcript at 02714:1–23, 02737:8–25, and 02738:1–6, February 7, 2005.
64. *People v. Kozlowski II,* summation of defense, transcript at 14724:10–25, 14725:1–13, 14726:7–25, 14727:1–25, 14728:1–25, and 14729:1–19, May 23, 2005.
65. Ibid.
66. Ibid. at 14726:7–25, 14727:1–25, 14728:1–25, and 14729:1–19.
67. *People v. Kozlowski II,* direct examination of Dennis Kozlowski, transcript at 12126:9–25 and 12127:1 –12, April 27, 2005.
68. Ibid. at 12127:13–25, 12128:1–25, and 12129:1–22.

69. Ibid.
70. Ibid. at 12129:8–17 and 12130:21–24.
71. Dennis Kozlowski, letter to the author, February 7, 2011.
72. *People v. Kozlowski II,* direct examination of Dennis Kozlowski, transcript at 12131:3–5 and 12131:6–19, April 27, 2005.
73. Ibid. at 12132:2–25 and 12133:1–3.
74. L. Dennis Kozlowski, "Compensation," memorandum to Mark Swartz and Patty Prue, September 11, 2000. *People v. Kozlowski II,* People's Exhibit No. 408. Also, direct examination of Patricia Prue, transcript at 03075:24, February 9, 2005; and Dennis Kozlowski, telephone interview with the author, June 7, 2012.
75. *People v. Kozlowski II,* direct examination of Patricia Prue, transcript at 03065:23–25, 03066:1–10, 03130:3–25, 03131:1–25, 03132:1–25, and 03133:1–9, February 9, 2005. See also, Marian A. Tse, fax transmission to Donna Sharpless, Tyco International Ltd. re: Regulation S-K, January 19, 2001.
76. *People v. Kozlowski II,* testimony of Mark Foley, transcript at 04080–04089, February 16, 2005; and 04119–04151 and 04406:18–21, February 17, 2005.
77. *People v. Kozlowski II,* direct examination of David Boies, transcript at 10343:22 and 10386:10–25, April 12, 2005.
78. *People v. Kozlowski II,* cross-examination of Frank Walsh, transcript at 02638:22–25, 02639:1–25, and 02640:1–2, February 7, 2005.
79. Dennis Kozlowski, telephone interview with the author, June 9, 2012.
80. *People v. Kozlowski II,* direct examination of Mark Foley, transcript at 04451:1–11 and 04452:1–15, February 22, 2005.
81. *People v. Kozlowski II,* summation of Charles Stillman, transcript at 15042:7–12, May 24, 2005.
82. *People v. Kozlowski II,* direct examination of Patricia Prue, transcript at 03109:18–25, 03110:1–25, and 03111:1–6, February 9, 2005.
83. Ibid. at 03111:1–6.
84. Ibid. at 03269:2–10.
85. *People v. Kozlowski II,* cross-examination of Patricia Prue, transcript at 03898:15–25, February 16, 2005. See also, Separation of Employment Agreement between Patricia A. Prue and Tyco International (US), March 18, 2003.
86. L. Dennis Kozlowski, Mark H. Swartz, Mark D. Foley, and Jeffrey D. Mattfolk, letter to Pricewater-houseCoopers, December 19, 2000, at Paragraph 46.
87. *People v. Kozlowski I,* transcript at 00108:9–12, October 7, 2003.
88. Tyco International Ltd. 2001 Annual Report, L. Dennis Kozlowski, Letter to Shareholders, December 3, 2001, 19.
89. Dennis Kozlowski, letter to the author, February 9, 2011.
90. *People v. Kozlowski II,* prosecution opening statement, transcript at 03430:11–25, January 26, 2005, referencing *People v. Kozlowski I,* transcript at 03360–03362. See also, *People v. Kozlowski II,* transcript at 03431:2–10.
91. *People v. Kozlowski II,* transcript at 03427:16–17, 03436:15–25, and 03437:1–12, January 26, 2005.
92. Ibid. at 03427:14–23.
93. Ibid. at 03438:21 –25 and 03439:1–8.
94. Ibid. at 03439:9–25 and 03443:1–3.

CHAPTER SEVENTEEN: CUT FROM WHOLE CLOTH

1. Dennis Kozlowski, interview with the author, Marcy, New York, May 21, 2011.
2. *People v. Kozlowski II,* direct examination of Mark Foley, transcript at 04363:3–9 and 04368:3–8, February 22, 2005.
3. "Auditor Settles Tyco Class Action," *Los Angeles Times,* July 7, 2007.
4. Suraj Srinivasan and Aldo Sesia, "The Crisis at Tyco—A Director's Perspective, *Harvard Business School,* Case No. 9-111-035, June 2, 2011, 9–10.
5. *People v. Kozlowski II,* direct examination of Kathy McRae, transcript at 11300:22–25 through 11304:1–20, April 20, 2005.
6. Ibid. at 11289:18–25, 11290:1–2, 11315:6–25, 11317:1–16, 11320:2–8, and 11464:8–19.
7. On a motion to dismiss the grand larceny charge related to the Frank Walsh investment banking fee, the Kozlowski and Swartz defense teams argued the same points advanced by the author:

    MR. DEVITA: The million dollar payment to Mr. Walsh. There is absolutely no proof in this record that Mr. Kozlowski did not have the authority to make that payment. His general authority as CEO gave him the power to make that payment. The specific resolution that was passed as part of the CIT empowering resolution, which said he had the power to do anything he deemed desirable, gave him the authority to make that payment. During the course of the trial Mr. Walsh testified that he believed that Mr. Kozlowski had the authority to make that payment. Obviously, by virtue of the fact that he made the payment Mr. Kozlowski believed he had the authority to make the payment. I believe that Mr. Swartz testified at the last trial that he believed Mr. Kozlowski had the authority to make the payment. And if you credit the People's evidence during this trial, by virtue of the role Mr. Swartz allegedly played in the payment, he obviously believed that Mr. Kozlowski had the authority to make the payment. Mr. Fort testified on page 2056 that he believed that Mr. Kozlowski had the authority to make the payment. Mr. Slusser testified on page 8627 that he believed that Mr. Kozlowski had the authority to make the payment. And we believe that a fair reading of Mr. Foss on pages 5295 and 5331, and Mr. Pasman on 7721 through 7723, also indicate that they believed that Mr. Kozlowski had the authority to make the payment. It is terribly prejudicial to let this count go to the jury in light of undoubtedly be confused between the failure to advise the Board ahead of time, which is not a crime, and the lack of authority to make the payment, which the People allege is the crime. There is basically no proof other than the fact that Mr. Kozlowski did not tell the Board—the other Board members in advance about the payment that it in any way sullies the payment. And even that proof is not sufficient to carry the day for the People. So we would ask you to dismiss the 20 million dollar Walsh count for those reasons as well.

MR. MITCHELL: Judge, just a little bit to add on the Walsh payment on behalf of Mr. Swartz. Again, this is a larceny count, requires a showing of criminal intent. There is no evidence in this record that Mr. Swartz had anything but a good faith belief that Dennis Kozlowski had the authority to make the payment he did to Frank Walsh. I'm not going to mention the director testimony that Mr. Campriello has just mentioned. I will mention the bylaws that have been in evidence, seen many times by your Honor, that do present such authority to Mr. Kozlowski, but I also, just on behalf of Mr. Swartz, want to point out what evidence there is in this record is completely inconsistent with anything but a good faith belief that Mr. Kozlowski had the authority to make the payment. For example, what does Mr. Swartz do when he is asked to process the fee for Mr. Walsh? He asked Mr. Walsh to send him written invoices evidencing the fee. We seen [sic] those in there as evidence in the case. He takes those invoices and gives them to Mr. Robinson, the company's Treasurer, and has Mr. Robinson handle the actual wiring out of the money and knowing that those records will be part of the books and records as Mr. Robinson testified. Mr. Swartz speaks to Mr. Gamper from CIT at one point when Mr. Gamper has a question as to how the transaction is going to be recorded and why it is on CIT's books. And again, Mr. Swartz is involved at the time when Rick Scalzo from PWC asked Mr. Foley, what's the story of the disclosure of this issue. It will it be in the 10-K you heard from testimony from Mr. Foley when he talks to Mr. Swartz and the information gotten back to Mr. Scalzo was it is going to be disclosed in the upcoming proxy. None of these witnesses, when we asked them[,] ever said Mr. Swartz asked them to conceal the fact when there was a payment made to Mr. Walsh in any way, shape. That is inconsistent with any criminal intent. Finally the D&O [Directors and Officers] Questionnaire that came from Mr. Walsh. That came to Mr. Swartz through the Legal Department. The only evidence was he was provided to asked for a copy of it, not the original, and he gave it to the people in Finance a couple of days after getting it from Mr. Walsh—from Fati Sadeghi, Legal. None of it is inconsistent with a belief that this is something Mr. Kozlowski had authority to do.

People v. Kozlowski II, defense motion to dismiss, transcript at 11951:3–25 through 11056:1–4, April 27, 2005.

8. *People v. Kozlowski II*, cross-examination of Frank Walsh, transcript at 02952:1–5, February 7, 2005.
9. *People v. Kozlowski II*, Justice Obus charge to the jury, transcript at 16030:20–25 and 16031:1–2, June 2, 2005.
10. *People v. Kozlowski II*, summations, transcript at 14702:2–7 and 14704:9–14, May 23, 2005.

CHAPTER EIGHTEEN: O5A4820

1. *People v. Kozlowski II*, Supreme Court Justice Obus, transcript at 16359:9–24, June 17, 2005.
2. *People v. Kozlowski II*, sentencing, transcript at 00006:4–16, 00007:13–16, 000030:4–6, 00081:4–25 and 00082:1–5, 00082:8–25, 00083:1–9, 000086:9–11, 00089:7–22, 00095:17–25, 00096:1–5, 00096:11–17, 00097:25, 00098:1–3, and 00098:9–14, September 19, 2005.
3. Dennis Kozlowski, interview with the author, New York City, New York, June 23, 2012.
4. Dennis Kozlowski, telephone interview with the author, May 18, 2012.

5. Ibid.
6. New York State Department of Corrections and Community Supervision, "Facility Listing."
7. Dennis Kozlowski, telephone interview with the author, May 18, 2012.
8. Ibid.
9. Ibid.
10. Dennis Kozlowski, interview with the author, Marcy, New York, May 21, 2011.
11. Hillary Canada, "'Ain't It Funny?' Ja Rule Bonding with Hevesi in Mid-State," *Wall Street Journal*, February 2, 2012; J. Molloy, "Rapper Ja Rule, Serving Two Years for Gun Possession, Finds New Posse behind Bars," *New York Daily News*, February 2, 2012; Chris Dolmetsch, "Ex-New York State Comptroller Alan Hevesi Granted Parole," Bloomberg.com, November 15, 2012; and Christie D'Zurilla, "Ja Rule Is Done with Prison for Gun Charge but Isn't a Free Man," *Los Angeles Times*, February 21, 2013.
12. Dennis Kozlowski, interview with the author, Marcy, New York, May 22, 2011.
13. Ibid.
14. Dennis Kozlowski, letter to the author, May 24, 2011,
15. Dennis Kozlowski, letter to the author, March 17, 2011.
16. Dennis Kozlowski, letter to the author, February 4, 2011.
17. "Imprisoned Ex-Tyco Chief's Divorce Finalized," *New York Post*, July 17, 2008.
18. Dennis Kozlowski, telephone interview with the author, May 18, 2012.
19. Ibid.
20. Robert Morgenthau, interview with the author, New York, New York, May 22, 2013.
21. Isaac Rosenthal, interview with the author, New York, New York, May 23, 2013.
22. Bureau of Justice Statistics, "First Releases from State Prison: Sentence Length, Time Served, and Percent of Sentence Served in Prison, by Offense," data source: National Corrections Reporting Program, 2009, version dated May 5, 2011.
23. *People v. Kozlowski*, 47 A.D.3d 111 (1st Dep't 2007).
24. Ibid. at 116.
25. International Art Alliance, "International Directory of Corporate Art Collections," (2013).
26. Vivien Raynor, "ART: When Corporations Become Collectors," *New York Times*, March 1, 1992.
27. Samantha Sharf, "The World's Best Corporate Art Collections," *Forbes*, August 2, 2012.
28. *People v. Kozlowski*, 47 A.D.3d 111 (1st Dep't 2007), 116–117.
29. 11 N.Y.3d 223 (2008).
30. *People v. Kozlowski*, 47 A.D.3d 111 (1st Dep't 2007), 120.
31. 11 N.Y.3d 223 (2008), 243.
32. Andrew Ross Sorkin and Jonathan D. Glater, "Some Tyco Board Members Knew of Pay Packages, Records Show," *New York Times*, September 23, 2002.
33. Christo Lassiter, interview with the author, Cincinnati, Ohio, May 13, 2013.
34. Karen Donovan, *v. Goliath: The Trials of David Boies* (New York, NY: Vintage, 2005), 335–336.
35. *Kozlowski v. Hulihan*, U.S. District Court, Southern District of NY, 09CV7583, Oral Arguments, December 22, 2011, 58.
36. Ibid. at 18–20.
37. Ibid. at 75–76.
38. Ibid. at 81.
39. *L. Dennis Kozlowski v. William Hulihan*, 12-0764, and *Mark H. Swartz v. Superintendent Paul Annetts*, 12-07776, U.S. Court of Appeals for the Second Circuit, February 4, 2013.
40. *Griffin v. Illinois*, 351 U.S. 12, 19 (1956).
41. Lewis Powell, Jr., U.S. Supreme Court Justice, address to the ABA Legal Services Program, ABA Annual Meeting, August 10, 1976.
42. New York State Supreme Court Justice Michael J. Obus, letter Re: *People v. Kozlowski*, March 16, 2002.
43. Dunstan Prial, "Former Tyco CEO Kozlowski Granted New Parole Hearing," Fox Business News, February 7, 2013.
44. "Former Tyco CEO Dennis Kozlowski to Get New Parole Hearing," *Caruto*, Fox Business News, originally aired February 14, 2013.
45. Chad Bray, "Court Denies Parole Bid by Former Tyco CEO Kozlowski," *Wall Street Journal*, July 2, 2013.

CHAPTER NINETEEN: OBSERVATIONS

1. *People v. Kozlowski I*, opening statements, transcript at 00103:10–14, October 7, 2003.
2. Dennis Kozlowski, interview with the author, New York City, New York, June 22, 2012.
3. Peter Hossli, "I Am Innocent," Hossli.com, May 22, 2009, 1; and Matthew McCabe, "Top Ten Evil Businessmen," Listverse, July 23, 2012.

4. Matthew McCabe, "Top Ten Evil Businessmen," Listverse, June 23, 2012; and Daniel Fisher, "The Anti Dennis Kozlowski," *Forbes,* March 11, 2010.
5. Peter Hossli, "I Am Innocent," Hossli.com, May 22, 2009, 6. Even though the article was published in May 2009, the content was based on an interview that took place in January of 2008. Ibid. at 10.
6. Suraj Srinivasan and Aldo Sesi, "The Crisis at Tyco—A Director's Perspective," *Harvard Business School,* Case No. 9-111-035, June 2, 2011.
7. Retention Agreement between Tyco and Dennis Kozlowski, January 21, 2001, at paragraph 1(a).
8. James Freeman, "The World's District Attorney," *Wall Street Journal,* December 26, 2009. See also, Terry Carter, "The Boss," *ABA Journal,* June 1, 2010.
9. Isaac Rosenthal, interview with the author, New York City, New York, May 23, 2013.
10. Edith Honan, "Ex-Tyco CEO Sues Company for Consulting Pay," Reuters, December 11, 2007.
11. Dennis Kozlowski, telephone interview with the author, May 22, 2012.
12. David A. Kaplan, "Why Kozlowski Should Get Clemency," *Fortune,* November 23, 2009.
13. William C. Symonds, "The Most Aggressive CEO," *Businessweek,* May 27, 2001.
14. Isaac Rosenthal, interview with the author, New York City, New York, May 23, 2013.
15. Brad McGee, telephone interview with the author, May 30, 2013.
16. Robert Morgenthau, interview with the author, New York City, New York, May 22, 2013.
17. *People v. Kozlowski II,* direct examination of Frank Walsh, transcript at 02500:9–25, February 3, 2005.
18. Tyco International Ltd. "Compensation Committee Meeting Minutes," October 18, 1999.
19. Mandi Woodruff, "This Is What Everyone's Afraid to Say about the Rich," *Business Insider,* May 4, 2012.
20. Dennis Kozlowski, interview with the author, New York City, New York, June 22, 2012.
21. Dennis Kozlowski, telephone interview with the author, May 10, 2012.
22. Isaac Rosenthal, interview with the author, New York City, New York, May 23, 2013.
23. Robert Morgenthau, interview with the author, New York City, New York, May 22, 2013.
24. Mark Belnick, telephone interview with the author, May 14, 2013
25. Ibid. Also, Dennis Kozlowski, interview with the author, Marcy, New York, May 21, 2011.
26. Dennis Kozlowski, interview with the author, Marcy, New York, May 21, 2011.
27. Dennis Kozlowski, letter to the author, May 24, 2011.

BIBLIOGRAPHY

ABA Business Law Section Corporate Law Committee. *ABA Corporate Director's Guidebook,* 6th ed. American Bar Association, 2012.

Ackman, Dan. "House Committees To Investigate Global Crossing," *Forbes,* March 13, 2002, http://www.forbes.com/2002/03/13/0313topnews.html (accessed May 2, 2013).

Adagba, Simeon Messan. "Until the lion has his or her own storyteller, the hunter will always have the best part of the story," African Proverb of the Month, April 2006, http://www.afriprov.org (accessed April 26, 2013).

Armstrong, David. "Former Tyco Executive Moves To Dismiss Tax-Evasion Charges," *Wall Street Journal,* August 29, 2002.

Associated Press. "Apparent Conflicts of Interest with Tyco Board Raise Eyebrows," July 7, 2002, http://lubbockonline.com/stories/070702/bus_070702031.shtml (accessed July 7, 2013).

Barr, Alistair. "Short Sellers: The Good, the Bad, and the Ugly," *MarketWatch,* December 19, 2001, http://www.marketwatch.com/story/short-sellers-some-expose-fraud-while-others-become-the-scandal (accessed June 28, 2013).

Baumann, Mark P. "Restructuring Charges," ACC7500: Financial Statement Analysis, Babson College, http://faculty.babson.edu/halsey/acc7500/Restructuring%20Charges%20Accounting.doc (accessed July 1, 2013).

Belnick, Mark. Telephone interview with the author, May 14, 2013.

Berman, Joshua M. Letter to the Board of Directors, 950 Fifth Avenue Corporation, March 30, 2000.

Berman, Joshua M. Telephone interview with the author, August 8, 2013.

Bernard, Andy. "Finale," *The Office.* Season 9: Episode 23, NBC. Originally aired May 16, 2013.

Boies, Schiller & Flexner. "David Boies," http://www.bsfllp.com/lawyers/data/0001 (accessed July 15, 2013).

Boostrom, Rob. "Tyco International—Leadership Crisis," Daniels Fund Ethics Initiative, University of New Mexico, (2011), http://danielsethics.mgt.unm.edu/pdf/Tyco%20Case.pdf (accessed July 7, 2013).

Brady v. Maryland, 373 U.S. 83 (U.S. 1963).

Bray, Chad. "Court Denies Parole Bid by Former Tyco CEO Kozlowski," *Wall Street Journal,* July 2, 2013.

Brush, Michael. "10 Outrageously Lavish CEO Perks," MSN Money, http://money.msn.com/investing/10-outrageously-lavish-ceo-perks (accessed May 5, 2013).

Brickey, Kathleen F. "From Boardroom to Courtroom to Newsroom: The Media and the Corporate Governance Scandals," 22 *Iowa Journal of Corporate Law* 625 (Spring 2008).

Bureau of Justice Statistics, National Corrections Reporting Program. "First Releases from State Prison: Sentence Length, Time Served, and Percent of Sentence Served in Prison, by Offense. Data source: 2009, version dated May 5, 2011.

Canada, Hillary. "'Ain't It Funny?' Ja Rule Bonding with Hevesi In Mid-State," *Wall Street Journal,* February 2, 2012.

Carr, David. "The Tyco Mistrial: The Media; Some Critics Say Naming a Juror Went Too Far," *New York Times,* April 3, 2004.

Carter, Terry. "The Boss," *ABA Journal,* June 1, 2010, http://www.abajournal.com/magazine/article/the_boss/ (accessed July 14, 2013)

Chakravarty, Subrata N. "Deal-a-Month Dennis," *Forbes,* June 15, 1998, http://www.forbes.com/forbes/1998/0615/6112066a_print.html%E2%80%8E (accessed May 1, 2013).

CNNMoney. "Economists Call It a Recession," November 26, 2001, http://money.cnn.com/2001/11/26/economy/recession/ (accessed July 2, 2013).

CNNMoney. "Global Files for Bankruptcy," January 28, 2002, http://money.cnn.com/2002/01/28/companies/globalcrossing/ (accessed July 12, 2013).

CNNMoney. "Tyco Spent $8B in Deals," February 4, 2002, http://www.money.cnn.com/2002/02/04/companies/tyco/index.htm (accessed July 11, 2013).

CNNMoney. "ImClone Ex-CEO Nabbed," June 13, 2002, http://money.cnn.com/2002/06/12/news/waksal/ (accessed May 2, 2013).

CNNMoney. "Divorce Deal Reveals Welch's Perks," September 6, 2002, http://money.cnn.com/2002/09/06/news/companies/welch_ge/ (accessed April 25, 2013).

CNNMoney. "Three Tyco Execs Indicted for Fraud," September 12, 2002, http://edition.cnn.com/2002/BUSINESS/asia/09/12/us.tyco/ (accessed July 16, 2013).

CNNMoney. "Jurors See Tape of Kozlowski's Party," October 29, 2003, http://money.cnn.com/2003/10/28/news/companies/tyco_party/index.htm (accessed July 3, 2013).

Coffee, John C. "Understanding Enron: It's About the Gatekeepers, Stupid," *Columbia Law & Economics Working Paper No. 207,* July 30, 2002, http://dx.doi.org/10.2139/ssrn.325240 (accessed May 2, 2013).

Costa, Len. "The Rise of Compliance Man," *Slate,* May 26, 2004, http://www.slate.com/articles/business/moneybox/2004/05/the_rise_of_compliance_man.html (accessed July 11, 2013).

Davidson, Adam (director), and Rene Balcer (writer). "Under the Influence," *Law & Order,* Episode 8.11, NBC, first broadcast January 7, 1998.

De La Merced, Michael J. "Inside Stephen Schwarzman's Birthday Bash," *New York Times,* February 14, 2007.

De La Merced, Michael J. "Dennis Kozlowski's Homecoming, of Sorts," *New York Times,* March 16, 2012.

"Dennis Kozlowski of Tyco International: King Conglomerate," *Institutional Investor,* April 1, 2001, http://www.institutionalinvestor.com/Popups/PrintArticle.aspx?ArticleID=1027999 (accessed June 28, 2013).

Deza, Michel Marie, and Elena Deza. *Encyclopedia of Distances,* 2nd ed. New York, NY: Springer, 2010.

Dillon, Nancy. "Tyco Board May Call It Quits: Resignation Talk Gives Stock Big Lift," *New York Daily News,* August 22, 2002.

Dodd-Frank Wall Street Reform and Consumer Protection Act. Public Law No. 111-203, July 21, 2010.

Dolmetsch, Chris. "Ex-New York State Comptroller Alan Hevesi Granted Parole," Bloomberg.com, November 15, 2012, http://www.bloomberg.com/news/2012-11-15/ex-new-york-state-comptroller-alan-hevesi-granted-parole.html (accessed July 22, 2013).

Donovan, Karen. *v. Goliath: The Trials of David Boies.* New York, NY: Vintage, 2005.

Dugan, I. Jane. "The Best Performers: The Business Week Fifty," *Businessweek,* March 24, 1997, http://www.businessweek.com/1997/12/b35191.htm, updated June 15, 1997 (accessed June 29, 2013).

Dunleavy, Steve. "On Her First Prison Visit My Wife Said 'I Want a Divorce': Koz," *New York Post,* October 30, 2006.

"Eight Outrageous CEO Perks," *24/7 Wall Street Wire,* December 13, 2013, http://247wallst.com/2012/12/13/eight-outrageous-ceo-perks/2/ (accessed May 5, 2013).

Eisenberg, Daniel. "Corporate Greed: Dennis the Menace," *TIME magazine,* June 17, 2002, http://www.time.com/time/magazine/article/0,9171,1002664,00.html (accessed December 12, 2012).

Equilar. "Executive Compensation Survey," http://www.equilar.com/survey/ (accessed May 5, 2013).

"Executive Perquisites—What 2012 Proxy Statements Have Revealed," *Ayco Compensation & Benefits Digest,* Vol. 20, Issue 6, June 15, 2012, http://www.aycofinancialnetwork.com/news/digest/digest_1206.pdf (accessed May 5, 2013).

Fannelli, Damian. "Two New Studies Suggest Women Are More Attracted to a Man Holding a Guitar," *Guitar World,* May 10, 2013, http://www.guitarworld.com/two-new-studies-suggest-women-are-more-attracted-man-holding-guitar (accessed May 11, 2013).

Farrell, Greg. "Stewart Convicted of Four Felonies," *USA Today,* March 5, 2004, http://usatoday30.usatoday.com/money/media/2004-03-05-stewart_x.htm?csp=24 (accessed July 18, 2013).

Financial Accounting Standards Board. "Statement 141–Business Combinations" (Rev. 2007, effective December 2008).

Fisher, Daniel. "The Anti Dennis Kozlowski," *Forbes,* March 11, 2010.

Fisher, Daniel. "The Most Outrageous Executive Perks," *Forbes,* June 27, 2012.

Fishman, Steve. "The Convert," *New York Magazine,* June 2004.

"Former Tyco CEO to Address Sul Ross Commencement on Saturday," *Alpine Daily Planet,* May 10, 2013, http://alpinedailyplanet.typepad.com/alpine-daily-planet/2013/05/former-tyco-ceo-to-address-sul-ross-commencement-on-saturday.html (accessed May 11, 2013).

"Former Tyco CEO Dennis Kozlowski to Get New Parole Hearing," Fox Business News, February 14, 2013, http://video.foxbusiness.com/v/2166075850001/former-tyco-ceo-dennis-kozlowski-to-get-new-parole-hearing/ (accessed July 22, 2013).

Funding Universe, Tyco Fire and Integrated Solutions. "Our History," http://www.tycofis.co.uk/About-Tyco/our-history (accessed May 17, 2013).

Fussman, Cal. "Matt Lauer: What I've Learned," *Esquire,* October 2013.

Godfrey, Mike. "Dennis Kozlowski Indicted on Sales Tax Fraud Charges," Tax-News.com, June 6, 2002, http://www.tax-news.com/news/Dennis_Kozlowski_Indicted_On_Sales_Tax_Fraud_Charges ____8410.html (accessed May 28, 2013).

"Graphic: A Long Line of Accounting Scandals," New York Times, November 20, 2012, http://dealbook .nytimes.com/2012/11/20/graphic-a-long-line-of-accounting-scandals/ (accessed May 2, 2013).

Graham-Jones, Pierce. "Trustee Resigns Kozlowski Credited for Tyco Donation to Middlebury," Middlebury (VT) Campus, September 25, 2002, http://middleburycampus.com/article/trustee-resigns -kozlowski-credited-for-tyco-donation-to-middlebury/ (accessed July 13, 2013).

Grant, Adam. Give and Take. New York, NY: Viking, 2013.

Greenburg, Herb. "Does Tyco Play Accounting Games?" Fortune, April 1, 2002, http://money.cnn.com /magazines/fortune/fortune_archive/2002/04/01/320643/index.htm (accessed June 2, 2013).

Griffin v. Illinois. 351 U.S. 12, 19 (1956).

Grugal, Robin M., and Marilyn Alva. "Breaking News: Tyco Makes Big Move With CIT Acquisition," Investors' Business Daily, March 14, 2001, http://news.investors.com/business-the-new-america /031401-344758-breaking-news-tyco-makes-big-move-with-cit-acquisition.htm (accessed July 6, 2013).

Grzebielski, Ray J. "Why Martha Stewart Did Not Violate Rule 10b-5: On Tipping, Piggybacking, Front-running and the Fiduciary Duties of Securities Brokers," Akron Law Review, Vol. 40, No. 55, 2007.

Hamilton, Walter. "Ex-Tyco Chief's Lavish Lifestyle Is Defended," Los Angeles Times, March 16, 2004.

Harden, Blaine. "Image Spinner at the Center of a Web; Rubenstein, 'Dean of Damage Control' for New York's Powerful," New York Times, September 30, 1999.

Harper, Liz. "Enron: After the Collapse," The PBS Newshour with Jim Lehrer, June 2002, http://www.pbs .org/newshour/bb/business/enron/bankruptcy.html (accessed May 2, 2013).

Harris, Alton B., and Andrea S. Kramer. "Corporate Governance: Pre-Enron, Post-Enron," in Corporate Aftershock: The Public Policy Lessons from the Collapse of Enron and Other Major Corporations, ed. Christopher L. Culp and William A. Niskanen. Hoboken, NJ: John Wiley & Sons, 2003, http:// www.uhlaw.com/publications-corporate_governance_pre_post_enron.html (accessed October 11, 2013).

Harris, Roy. "After Math," CFO Magazine, November 1, 2001, http://www.cfo.com/article.cfm/30017 86/2/c_3046511 (accessed July 6, 2013).

Healy, Beth. "Executive Perks Are Still Alive and Well," Boston Globe, April 12, 2013.

Honan, Edith. "Ex-Tyco CEO Sues Company for Consulting Pay," Reuters, December 11, 2007, http:// www.reuters.com/article/2007/12/11/tyco-suit-idUSN1155610420071211 (accessed July 2, 2013).

Hossli, Peter. "I Am Innocent," Hossli.com, May 22, 2009, http://www.hossli.com/articles/2009/05/22/i -am-innocent/ (accessed April 7, 2011).

"Imprisoned Ex-Tyco Chief's Divorce Finalized," New York Post, July 17, 2008.

In re Enron Corp., No. 01-16034, 2001 Extra LEXIS 159, Voluntary Petition (Bankr. S.D.N.Y. December 2, 2001).

In Re Tyco International Ltd Securities Litigation. No. 02-1335-B (D.N.H 2002).

International Art Alliance. International Directory of Corporate Art Collections (2013), http://www.inter nationalartalliance.org/directory-of-corporate-art.html (accessed July 22, 2013).

International Directory of Company Histories, Vol. 63. New York, NY: St. James Press, 2004.

International Monetary Fund. "World Economic Outlook: The Global Economy After September 11" (December 2001), http://www.imf.org/external/pubs/ft/weo/2001/03/ (accessed April 30, 2013).

"Investment Banker Demands 1% of Apple's $390m Anobit Acquisition in Finder's Fee Lawsuit," TNW, May 15, 2012, http://thenextweb.com/apple/2012/05/15/investment-banker-demands-1-of -apples-390m-anobit-acquisition-fee-in-finders-fee-lawsuit/ (accessed July 13, 2013).

Italiano, Laura, and Darah Gregorian. "Pig Due to the Pen as Jury Pounds Tyco Thief Kozlowski," New York Post, June 18, 2005, www.nypost.com/p/news/item_gwBx5O9y0atn6kkyBkprUN+&cd=3 &hl=en&ct=clnk&gl=us (accessed May 1, 2013).

"Jury Views Big Bash in Italy by Tyco Ex-CEO," Los Angeles Times, October 29, 2003.

Kahneman, Daniel, Jack L. Knetsch, and Richard H. Thaler. "Fairness and the Assumptions of Economics," Journal of Business, Vol. 59, No. 4, 285- 300 (1986).

Kaplan, David A. "Why Kozlowski Should Get Clemency," Fortune, November 23, 2009, http:// money.cnn.com/2009/11/20/news/companies/tyco_kozlowski.fortune/index.htm (accessed July 24, 2013).

Kliesen, Kevin L. "The 2001 Recession: How Was It Different and What Developments May Have Caused It?" Federal Reserve Bank of St. Louis Review (September/October 2003), http://research.stlouisfed .org/publications/review/03/09/Kliesen.pdf (accessed May 1, 2013).

Kozlowski, Dennis. Interviews with the author, Marcy, NewYork: May 21, 2011–October 16, 2011.

Kozlowski, Dennis. Interviews with the author, New York City, New York: June 21–23, 2012.

Kozlowski, Dennis. Letters to the author: February 4, February 7, February 19, March 10, March 17, May 24, and July 14, 2011.

Kozlowski, Dennis. "10 Commandments." Speech given at the Premier CEO Forum, September 17, 1999.

Kozlowski, Dennis. Telephone interviews with the author: May 8, May 9, May 10, May 11, May 17, May 18, May 25, May 30, June 7, and June 9, 2012.

Kozlowski, Joyce (younger sister). Email to the author, April 30, 2013.

Kozlowski, L. Dennis. Letter to Shareholders, 2001 Annual Report Tyco International Ltd., December 3, 2001.

Kozlowski, L. Dennis. "Compensation," Memorandum to Mark Swartz and Patty Prue, September 11, 2000.

Kozlowski, L. Dennis, Mark H. Swartz, Mark D. Foley, and Jeffrey D. Mattfolk. Letter to Pricewater houseCoopers, December 19, 2000.

Kozlowski, Sandra. Interview with the author, New York City, New York: October 5, 2012.

Kozlowski v. Hulihan. U.S. District Court, Southern District of New York, 09CV7583, 2011.

Kuczynski, Alex. "Lifestyles Of the Rich And Red-Faced," New York Times, September 22, 2002.

Lassiter, Christo. Interview with the author, Cincinnati, Ohio: May 13, 2013.

Lassiter, Christo. "The O.J. Simpson Verdict: A Lesson in Black and White," Michigan Journal of Race & Law Vol. 1, 69-117. (Winter 1996).

Late Night with Jimmy Fallon, Newsmax, "The Best of Late Night Jokes," May 9, 2013, http://www.news max.com/jokes (accessed May 11, 2013).

L. Dennis Kozlowski v. William Hulihan, 12-0764, and Mark H. Swartz v. Superintendent Paul Annetts, 12-07776. U.S. Court of Appeals for the Second Circuit, February 4, 2013.

Leder, Michelle. "Openers: Suits; The Fine Print," New York Times, January 29, 2006.

Lennon, John and Paul McCartney. "Strawberry Fields Forever," The Beatles, Capitol Records, 1967.

Liberto, Jennifer. "CEO Pay: Shareholders Get a (Little) Say," CNNMoney, April 21, 2011, http://money .cnn.com/2011/04/21/news/companies/ceo_pay_packages/index.htm (accessed May 5, 2013).

Locke, Edwin A. "Jack Welch Earned His Perks," Christian Science Monitor, September 23, 2002.

Longstreth, Andrew. "Whose Side Is He On," The American Lawyer (February 2005).

Lublin, Joann S. "Tyco Holders Plan Proxy Fight To Oust Its Current Directors," Wall Street Journal, August 21, 2002.

Macomber, Carlton. "71 Face-off with Soviets led U.S. to 200-Mile Limit," South Coast Today, Massachus-sets. November 4, 1998, http://www.southcoasttoday.com/apps/pbcs.dll/article?AID=/19981104 /NEWS/311049917 (accessed May 17, 2013).

Maremont, Mark. "Tyco Reveals $8 Billion in Deals Made Recently, but Not Disclosed," Wall Street Journal, February 4, 2002.

Maremont, Mark, and Laurie P. Cohen. "Executive Privilege: How Tyco's CEO Enriched Himself," Wall Street Journal, August 7, 2002.

Maremont, Mark, and Laurie P. Cohen. "Tyco Spent Millions for Benefit of Kozlowski, Its Former CEO," Wall Street Journal, August 7, 2002.

McCabe, Matthew. "Top Ten Evil Businessmen," Listverse, July 23, 2012, http://www.listverse.com/20 12/07/23/top-10-evil-businessmen/ (accessed July 24, 2013).

McCoy, Kevin. "Feared D.A. Relishes Taking Down Hotshots," USA Today, June 23, 2002, http://www .usatoday.com/money/covers/2002-06-24-morgenthau.htm (accessed November 14, 2012).

McGee, J. Bradford. Telephone interviews with the author: May 30 and July 12, 2013.

MIT Alumni Association. "Deceased Classmates," MIT Class of 1956, http://1956.alumclass.mit.edu/ s/1314/clubs-classes-interior.aspx?sid=1314&gid=48&pgid=2480 (accessed May 19, 2013).

Mizrach, Bruce. "The Enron Bankruptcy: When Did the Options Market in Enron Lose It's [sic] Smirk?" Review of Quantitative Financial Accounting, Vol. 27 365-382 (2006).

Molloy, J. "Rapper Ja Rule, Serving Two Years for Gun Possession, Finds New Posse behind Bars," New York Daily News, February 2, 2012.

Monks, Robert A. G. Corpocracy: How CEOs and the Business Roundtable Hijacked the World's Greatest Wealth Machine—And How to Get It Back. Hoboken, NJ: John Wiley & Sons, 2008.

Monks, Robert A. G. Citizens Disunited: Passive Investors, Drone CEOs, and the Corporate Capture of the American Dream. McLean, VA: Miniver Press, 2013.

Monks, Robert A. G., and Nell Minow. Corporate Governance, 5th ed. Hoboken, NJ: John Wiley & Sons, 2011.

Monks, Robert A. G. Telephone interviews with the author: May 7, August 5, 2013.

Morgenthau, Robert. Interview with the author, New York City, New York: May 22, 2013.

Murray, Matt, Rachel Emma Silverman, and Carol Himowitz. "GE's Jack Welch Meets Match in Divorce Court," Wall Street Journal, November 27, 2002.

Nashua Corporation. http://www.nashua.com/ (accessed May 16, 2013).

National Center for Education Statistics, Institute of Education Sciences, U.S. Department of Educa-tion, "Tuition: Private not-for-profit and for-profit institutions," http://nces.ed.gov/programs /digest/d11/tables/dt11_349.asp (accessed May 8, 2013).

National Commission on Terrorist Attacks Upon the United States. "The 9/11 Commission Report," July 22, 2004.

New York City Department of Finance, Automated City Register Information System (ACRIS). "Manhattan, Block 01391, Lot 0001," Document number 2004120802167001, Units 10 and 11, 950 Fifth Avenue, December 14, 2004, http://a836-acris.nyc.gov/DS/DocumentSearch/Docu mentDetail?SearchType=DocID (accessed October 11, 2013).

New York Penal Law. Sections 70.00 and 155.42.

New York State Department of Corrections and Community Supervision. "Facility Listing," http://www .doccs.ny.gov/faclist.html#D (accessed July 22, 2013).

New York State Department of Corrections and Community Supervision. "Temporary Release: Programs," www.doccs.ny.gov/ProgramServices/temprelease.html (accessed April 20, 2013).

New York State Department of Taxation and Finance. Tax Bulletin ST-913 (TB-ST-913)—Use Tax for Individuals (including Estates and Trusts)," June 17, 2010, http://www.tax.ny.gov/pubs_and_bulls /tg_bulletins/st/use_tax_for_individuals.htm (accessed July 12, 2013).

New York State Tax Law. Section 1817(c)(2)(a).

New York Stock Exchange. https://nyse.nyx.com/ (accessed May 15, 2013).

Norris, Floyd. "Tyco Shares Plunge After Company Discloses S.E.C. Inquiry," *New York Times,* December 10, 1999.

O'Brien, Timothy L. "The Tyco Mistrial: The Prosecutor; White-Collar Crime Crusader Gets Chance to Refine a Case," *New York Times,* April 3, 2004, http://www.nytimes.com/2004/04/03/busi ness/tyco-mistrial-prosecutor-white-collar-crime-crusader-gets-chance-refine-case.html ?pagewanted=all&src=pm (accessed October 11, 2013).

Obus, Michael J. New York State Supreme Court Justice. Letter to Alan Lewis, Esq. re: *People v. Kozlowski,* March 16, 2002.

Palmer, Robert. "Lennon Known Both as an Author and Composer; Never Lost Sight of Dream Influenced by U.S. Rockers Songs of Conflict and Confusion Married Miss Ono in 1969," *New York Times,* December 9, 1980.

Pastore, Robert. Telephone interview with the author: July 3, 2012,

Pastore, Robert. Letter to Commissioner Brian Fischer, New York State Department of Corrections and Community Supervision, October 29, 2011.

PBS NewsHour transcript. "Executive Perks," September 16, 2002. http://www.pbs.org/newshour/bb /business/july-dec02/perks_09-16.html (accessed April 25, 2013).

People v. Kozlowski I. New York State Supreme Court, New York County, Indictment #5259-02, transcript, September 29, 2003–April 2, 2004.

People v. Kozlowski II. New York State Supreme Court, New York County, Indictment #5259-02, transcript, January 18, 2005–September 19, 2005.

People v. Kozlowski. 47 A.D.3d 111 (1st Dep't 2007).

People v. Kozlowski. 11 N.Y.3d 223 (2008).

People v. Rosario. 9 N.Y.2d 286 (1961).

Powell, Lewis, Jr. Address to the ABA Legal Services Program, ABA Annual Meeting, August 10, 1976.

Prial, Dunstan. "Former Tyco CEO Kozlowski Granted New Parole Hearing," Fox Business News, February 7, 2013, https://secure.fox.com/proxy/www.foxbusiness.com/business-leaders/2013/02/07 /former-tyco-ceo-kozlowski-granted-new-parole-hearing/#ixzz2bCyKLBBm (accessed August 6, 2013).

PRNewswire. "Dennis Kozlowski Resigns from Raytheon's Board," June 3, 2002, http://www.prnews wire.com/news-releases/dennis-kozlowski-resigns-from-raytheons-board-77724612.html (accessed July 13, 2013).

Raynor, Vivien. "ART: When Corporations Become Collectors," *New York Times,* March 1, 1992.

Retention Agreement between Tyco International Ltd. and L. Dennis Kozlowski. January 21, 2001.

Reuters, "Tyco in $1.4-Billion Deal for Kendall International," *Los Angeles Times,* July 15, 1994, http://ar ticles.latimes.com/1994-07-15/business/fi-16026_1_tyco-international-ltd (accessed June 1, 2013).

Robert M. Morgenthau v. L. Dennis Kozlowski and Mark H. Swartz. New York State Supreme Court, New York County, #402698-02, September 10, 2002.

Romero, Simon and Riva D. Atlas. "WorldCom's Collapse: The Overview; WorldCom Files for Bankruptcy: Largest U.S. Case," *New York Times,* July 22, 2002.

Ropelk, David. "Inside the Mind of Worry," *New York Times,* September 28, 2012.

Rosenthal, Isaac. Interview with the author, New York City, New York, May 23, 2013.

Sarbanes-Oxley Act. Public Law 107-204, July 30, 2002.

Schwartz, Nelson D. "The Infinity Pool of Executive Pay," *New York Times,* April 6, 2013.

Separation of Employment Agreement between Patricia A. Prue and Tyco International (US). March 18, 2003.

Sharf, Samantha. "The World's Best Corporate Art Collections," *Forbes,* August 2, 2012, http://www .forbes.com/pictures/ffgh45feh/ubs-art-collection-4/#gallerycontent (accessed July 22, 2013).

Sheff, David. "The Playboy Interviews," *Playboy magazine* (January 1981), http://www.john-lennon .com/playboyinterviewwithjohnlennonandyokoono.htm (accessed May 10, 2013).

Sherman, Gabrielle. "Tyco Slashes Co-op," *New York Observer,* March 8, 2004, http://www.highbeam .com/doc/1G1-116493637.html/print (accessed November 14, 2012).

Slusser, Peter. Letters to Dennis Kozlowski, January 28, February 6, and May 8, 2002.

Slusser, Peter. Letter to Dennis Kozlowski and Mark Swartz, February 19, 2002.

Soldivieri, Susan, Community Foundation of New Jersey. Letter to Michael Robinson, Tyco International, July 31, 2001.

Sorkin, Andrew Ross. "Tyco Figure Pays $22.5 Million in Guilty Plea," *New York Times,* December 18, 2002.

Sorkin, Andrew Ross. "The Tyco Mistrial: The Overview: Tyco Trial Ended as a Juror Cites Outside Pressure," *New York Times,* April 3, 2004.

Sorkin, Andrew Ross. "Ex Tyco Chief Is Humbled, but Unbowed," *New York Times,* January 16, 2005.

Sorkin, Andrew Ross, "Ex-Chief and Aide Guilty of Looting Millions at Tyco," *New York Times,* June 18, 2005.

Sorkin, Andrew Ross, and Alex Berenson. "Doubts Voiced on How Much a Tyco Spinoff Might Raise," *New York Times,* April 27, 2002.

Sorkin, Andrew Ross, and Jonathan D. Glater. "Some Tyco Board Members Knew of Pay Packages," *New York Times,* September 23, 2002.

Sorkin, Michael D. "Kathleen Brickey Dies; Pioneering Law School Professor," *St. Louis Post-Dispatch,* June 21, 2013.

"S&P Lowers Tyco Debt Rating," *Businessweek,* February 3, 2002.

Spencer Stuart Board Index, "Board Composition," 27th ed., November 6, 2012, http://content.spenc erstuart.com/sswebsite/pdf/lib/Spencer-Stuart-US-Board-Index-2012_06Nov2012.pdf (accessed October 11, 2013).

Srinivasan, Suraj, and Aledo Sesia. "The Crisis at Tyco—A Director's Perspective," Harvard Business School, Case No. 9-111-035, June 2, 2011.

Stashenko, Josh. "Ex-Tyco Executives Contest Use of Findings From Internal Probe," *New York Law Journal,* September 3, 2008, http://www.law.com/jsp/article.jsp?id=1202424231155&ExTyco_Exe cutives_Contest_Use_of_Findings_From_Internal_Probe

Stout, David, and Sherrie Day. "Ex-Chief Says He Didn't Know About Enron's Accounting Woes," *New York Times,* February 7, 2002.

Strauss, Gary. "Despite Huge Salaries, CEOs Cling to Their Perks," *USA Today,* April 13, 2011, http:// usatoday30.usatoday.com/money/companies/management/2011-04-11-CEO-perks.htm (accessed May 5, 2013).

Strauss, Gary. "Retired Tyco CEO Gets $150 Million Exit Package," *USA Today,* January 13, 2013, www .usatoday.com/story/money/business/2013/01/16/breen-tyco-pay/1840883/+&cd=1&hl=en&ct =clnk&gl=us (accessed May 19, 2013).

Swartz, Mark H., and Michele E. Kearns. Letter to the editor of *Wall Street Journal,* February 4, 2002.

Swartz, Mark H. and Tyco International Ltd. Agreement, August 1, 2002.

Symonds, William C. "The Most Aggressive CEO," *Businessweek* (Cover Story), May 28, 2001, http://www .businessweek.com/stories/2001-05-27/the-most-aggressive-ceo (accessed December 12, 2012).

"The Facts on Finder's Fees," *Businessweek,* September 25, 2005, http://www.businessweek.com/stories /2005-09-25/the-facts-on-finders-fees (accessed July 13, 2013).

"The History of Seton Hall," *2012-13 Undergraduate Catalog, Seton Hall University,* University Overview, 9, http://www.shu.edu/academics/upload/SETON_HALL_201213_UNDERGRADUATE_C ATALOGUE.pdf#page=8 (accessed May 8, 2013).

"The Top 25 Managers to Watch," *Businessweek* (Cover Story), January 13, 2002, http://www.business week.com/2001/01_02/b3714009.htm (accessed December 12, 2012).

"The Wall Street Journal/Hay Group Survey of CEO Compensation Study 2011," June 6, 2012, http:// www.haygroup.com/ww/downloads/details.aspx?id=33830 (accessed October 11, 2013).

Tigue, John J. Jr., and Jeremy H. Temkin. "Limitations on State Tax Prosecutions," *New York Law Journal,* Vol. 232, No. 54, September 16, 2004 http://www.maglaw.com/publications/articles/00059/_res /id=Attachments/index=0/07009040015Morvillo.pdf (accessed October 11, 2013).

Times Wire Service, "Auditor Settles Tyco Class Action," *Los Angeles Times,* July 7, 2005.

Tobin, Eugene M. "John Franklin Fort," in *The Governors of New Jersey 1664–1974: Biographical Essays,* ed. Paul A. Stellhorn and Michael J. Birkner (New Jersey Historical Commission, 1982), last updated April 11, 2011, http://slic.njstatelib.org/slic_files/imported/NJ_Information/Digital _Collections/Governors_of_New_Jersey/GFORJ.pdf (accessed April 14, 2013).

Trotta, Daniel. "Short Sellers Have Been the Villain for 400 Years," Reuters, September 26, 2008, http://www.reuters.com/article/2008/09/26/us-financial-shortselling-villainspics-idUS TRE48P7CS20080926 (accessed June 28, 2013).

Tse, Marian A. Fax transmission to Donna Sharpless, Tyco International Ltd. re: Regulation S-K, January 19, 2001.

"Tyco Completes Acquisitions of AMP," *New York Times,* April 6, 1999.

Tyco International Ltd. Bye-laws, March 27, 2001.

Tyco International Ltd. "Compensation Committee Benefit, Plans," March 1995.

"Tyco International Ltd. History," http://www.fundinguniverse.com/company-histories/tyco-interna
    tional-ltd-history/ (accessed May 17, 2013).

Tyco International Ltd. "Minutes of a Special Meeting of the Board of Directors," Tuckers Town, Ber-
    muda, May 12, 1999.

Tyco International Ltd. "Minutes of a Regular Meeting of the Board of Directors," Pembroke, Bermuda,
    October 3, 2000.

Tyco International Ltd. Press Release. "Mark Belnick to Join Tyco International," August 27, 1998.

Tyco International Ltd. Press Release. "Tyco International Is Named Among 50 Best Performers by Busi-
    ness Week, Business Week Ranks Tyco Among Top Companies in Sales, Profits and Shareholder
    Return Performance," March 20, 2000.

Tyco International Ltd. Press Release. "Tyco International Reports 47 Percent Increase in Second Quar-
    ter Earnings per Share, Strong Organic Growth Drives Earnings per Share Rise to 50 Cents from
    34 Cents," April 18, 2000.

Tyco International Ltd. Press Release. "Tyco International Agrees to Acquire Thomas & Betts Electronic
    OEM Business, Acquisition Provides Excellent Strategic Fit, Will Be Immediately Accretive to
    Earnings," May 7, 2000.

Tyco International Ltd. Press Release. "Tyco International to Acquire Mallinckrodt, Acquisition Will
    Have Immediate Positive Impact on Earnings, Strengthens Tyco Healthcare's Leading Positions in
    Medical Devices," June 28, 2000.

Tyco International Ltd. Press Release. "Tyco to Acquire Scott Technologies, Acquisition Will Have Im-
    mediate Positive Impact on Tyco's Earnings, Broadens Product Line of Tyco Fire & Security Ser-
    vices and Provides Recurring Revenue Stream," February 5, 2001.

Tyco International Ltd. Press Release. "Tyco Is Ranked Number One Performing Company by Business-
    Week," March 28, 2001.

Tyco International Ltd. Press Release. "Tyco Is Top Pick in Reuters Survey of Larger Companies," April
    27, 2001.

Tyco International Ltd. Press Release. "Tyco Purchases the CIT Group, Inc.," June 1, 2001.

Tyco International Ltd. Press Release. "Tyco Retains Industrial Businesses, Plans 100% Public Offering
    of CIT—Letter Sent to Shareholders Detailing Rationale," April 25, 2002.

Tyco International Ltd. Press Release. "John Fort Assumes Primary Executive Responsibility for Tyco,"
    June 3, 2002.

Tyco International Ltd. Press Release. "Tyco Appoints Edward D. Breen Chairman and Chief Executive
    Officer," July 25, 2002.

Tyco International Ltd., Proxy Statement Fiscal Year-End 2001, January 28, 2002.

Tyco International Ltd. Special Meeting of the Board of Directors. "Meeting Minutes," Pembroke, Ber-
    muda, February 20–21, 2002.

Tyco International Ltd. v. Frank E. Walsh, Jr. 751 F.Supp.2d 606 (S.D.N.Y 2010).

Tyco International Ltd. v. L. Dennis Kozlowski. U.S. District Court for the Southern District of New York,
    No. 02-7317, Complaint, September 17, 2002.

Tyco International Ltd. (TYC)—NYSE. "Tyco Historical Prices, January 22, 2001," Yahoo Finance,
    http://finance.yahoo.com/q/hp?s=TYC&a=11&b=22&c=2000&d=00&e=22&f=2001&g=d
    (accessed July 2, 2013).

"Tyco Jury Hears of Ex-Chief's Bills," *New York Times,* January 6, 2004.

"Tyco Officer Tells of Board Reaction to Fee," *New York Times,* February 18, 2004.

U.S. Bankruptcy Court, Southern District of New York. "Enron Corp. Bankruptcy Information," last
    updated February 22, 2013, http://www.nysb.uscourts.gov/enron.html (accessed May 2, 2013)

U.S. Securities and Exchange Commission. "Executive Compensation and Related Persons Disclosure,"
    http://www.sec.gov/rules/final/2006/33-8732a.pdf (accessed May 5, 2013).

U.S. Securities and Exchange Commission. Form 8-K, Tyco International Ltd., September 10, 2002,
    http://www.sec.gov/Archives/edgar/data/833444/000091205702035700/a2089398z8-k.txt (acces-
    sed November 12, 2012).

U.S. Securities and Exchange Commission. Form S-4, Registration Statement, http://www.sec.gov
    /about/forms/forms-4.pdf (accessed July 7, 2013).

U.S. Securities and Exchange Commission Press Release. "SEC Sues Former Tyco Director and Chair-
    man of Compensation Committee Frank E. Walsh Jr. for Hiding $20 Million Payment From
    Shareholders; Walsh Had Secret Agreement with L. Dennis Kozlowski to Receive Payment for
    'Finder's Fee' in Tyco's Acquisition of The CIT Group Inc.," 2002-177, December 17, 2002, http://
    www.sec.gov/news/press/2002-177.htm (accessed July 1, 2013).

U.S. Securities and Exchange Commission, Proxy Disclosure Enhancements, Final Rule, adopted De-
    cember 16, 2009, effective February 28, 2010.

U.S. Securities and Exchange Commission Press Release, "SEC Charges Adelphia and Rigas Family with Massive Financial Fraud," 2002-110, July 24, 2002, http://www.sec.gov/news/press/2002-110.htm (accessed May 2, 2013).

U.S. Securities and Exchange Commission. Regulation S-K Item 402(c)(2)(viii), 17 C.F.R. Section 229.402(s), 2010, last updated September 2, 2011, http://www.sec.gov/answers/execomp.htm, (accessed May 5, 2013).

Useem, Jerry. "The Biggest Show No One's Watching," *Fortune,* December 8, 2003, http://money.cnn .com/magazines/fortune/fortune_archive/2003/12/08/355135/ (accessed July 3, 2013).

U.S. v. Gonzales-Lopez. 548 U.S. 140 (2006).

Vogel, Carol. "Novice Collectors Are Magnets for Eager Art Advisers," *New York Times,* June 20, 2002.

Walsh, Frank Jr. Invoice to Tyco International Ltd., RE: The CIT Group Inc. Acquisition, July 18, 2001.

Walsh, Frank E. Letter to Mark H. Swartz, Tyco International U.S.A., July 25, 2001.

Weber, Joseph. "The Best Performers," *Businessweek,* March 23, 2001, http://www.businessweek.com /bw50/content/mar2001/bf20010323_620.htm (accessed July 2, 2013).

Werner, Guth, Rolf Schmittberger, and Bernd Schwarze. "An Experimental Analysis of Ultimatum Bargaining," *Journal of Economic Behavior and Organization,* Vol. 3, No. 4 (1984), 367.

"Westport's World's Lecture by William Wyatt Provides an Entertaining Look at Town History," *Dartmouth-Westport* (CT) *Chronicle,* August 18, 2004, http://www.ptatlarge.typepad.com/ptat large/2004/08/westport_world.html (accessed May 17, 2013).

Wieczner, Jen. "Your Company Wants to Make You Healthy," *Wall Street Journal,* April 8, 2013.

"Witness Says Tyco Workers Told to Assist the S.E.C.," *New York Times,* June 3, 2004.

Woodruff, Mandi. "This Is What Everyone's Afraid to Say about the Rich," *Business Insider,* May 4, 2012, http://www.businessinsider.com/why-we-all-secretly-love-to-hate-the-nouveau-riche-2012-5 (accessed July 24, 2013).

Ydstie, John. Interview with Mark Maremont, "Former Tyco Chief," *NPR All Things Considered,* August 7, 2002.

2001 Annual Report Tyco International Ltd., "Consolidated Financial Statements," December 3, 2001.

INDEX